EVANGELIZATION
IN
AMERICA

EVANGELIZATION IN AMERICA

Proclamation, Way of Life
and
The Catholic Church in the United States

David Bohr

PAULIST PRESS
New York, N.Y./Ramsey, N.J./Toronto

Library of Congress
Catalog Card Number: 77-80806

ISBN: 0-8091-2039-9

Published by Paulist Press
Editorial Office: 1865 Broadway, New York, N.Y. 10023
Business Office: 545 Island Road, Ramsey, N.J. 07446

Printed and bound in the
United States of America

Contents

Abbreviations

AA   *Apostolicam Actuositatem*, Second Vatican Council's Decree on the Apostolate of the Laity, November 18, 1965

AACC   G. Dyer, *et al., An American Catholic Catechism*, New York, 1975 (Originally published as an "American Catechism" in *Chicago Studies*. Vol. 12 No. 3 and Vol. 13 No. 3)

Abbott   W.M. Abbott, ed., *The Documents of Vatican II*, New York, 1967

ACW   J. Quasten and J.C. Plumpe, *Ancient Christian Writers*, Westminster, Md., 1961 ff.

AER   *American Ecclesiastical Review*

AG   *Ad Gentes*, Second Vatican Council's Decree on the Church's Missionary Activity, December 7, 1965

CD   *Christus Dominus*, Second Vatican Council's Decree on the Bishops' Pastoral Office in the Church, October 28, 1965

CTSA   *Proceedings* of the annual convention of the Catholic Theological Society of America

D (also, Denz.)   H. Denzinger, *Enchiridion Symbolorum, Definitionum et Declarationum de Rebus Fidei et Morum*, 31st or earlier edition, Freiburg, 1957. Cf. DS

DB   J.L. McKenzie, *Dictionary of the Bible*, London, 1965

DBT   X. Leon-Dufour, ed., *Dictionary of Biblical Theology*

DH   *Dignitatis Humanae*, Second Vatican Council's Declaration on Religious Freedom, December, 1965

DS   H. Denzinger and A. Schönmetzer, *Enchiridion Symbolorum, Definitionum de Rebus Fidei et Morum*, 32nd or later edition, Freiburg, 1963

DV   *Dei Verbum*, Second Vatican Council's Dogmatic Constitution on Divine Revelation, November 18, 1965

EN   *Evangelii Nuntiandi*, Apostolic Exhortation of Pope Paul

VI on Evangelization in the Modern World, December 8, 1975

GN&W L. Legrand, J. Pathrapankal, and M. Vellanickal, *Good News & Witness*, Bangalore 1973

GS *Gaudium et Spes*, Second Vatican Council's Pastoral Constitution on the Church in the Modern World, December 7, 1965

JBC R.E. Brown, J.A. Fitzmyer, and R.E. Murphy, eds., *The Jerome Biblical Commentary*, London, 1968

LG *Lumen Gentium*, Second Vatican Council's Dogmatic Constitution on the Church, November 21, 1964

L'OR *L'Osservatore Romano*

L'OR(E) *L'Osservatore Romano*, weekly English edition

NCE *The New Catholic Encyclopedia*, 16 vols., New York, 1967

NEB *The New English Bible*, Oxford and Cambridge, 1970

OT *Optatum Totius*, Second Vatican Council's Decree on Priestly Formation, October 28, 1965

PG J.-P. Migne, ed., *Patrologia Graeca*, 161 vols., 1857ff.

PL J.-P. Migne, ed., *Patrologia Latina*, 217 vols. + 4 index vols., 1844ff.

PO *Presbyterorum Ordinis*, Second Vatican Council's Decree on the Ministry and Life of Priests, December 7, 1965

RSV *Revised Standard Version* of the Bible

SAS J. Pathrapankal, ed., *Service and Salvation*, Nagpur Theological Conference on Evangelization, Bangalore, 1973

SC *Sacrosanctum Concilium*, Second Vatican Council's Constitution on the Sacred Liturgy, December 4, 1963

SE *Synodus Episcoporum—Assemblea Generale 1974*, English bulletins from the Comitato per l'Informazione

SM K. Rahner, *et al.*, eds., *Sacramentum Mundi*, 6 vols., New York, 1968

TDNT G. Kittel, ed., *Theological Dictionary of the New Testament*, Grand Rapids, 1964ff. English version of TWNT.

TPS *The Pope Speaks*

TS   *Theological Studies*

TWNT   G. Kittel, ed., *Theologisches Wörterbuch zum Neuen Testament*, 8 vols., Stuttgart, 1933ff. German version of TDNT

UR   *Unitatis Redintegratio*, Second Vatican Council's Decree on Ecumenism, November 21, 1964

Vorgrimler   H. Vorgrimler, ed., *Commentary on the Documents of Vatican II*, 5 vols., New York, 1966

Note: All biblical quotations, unless otherwise indicated, are taken from *The Jerusalem Bible* (New York, 1966).

Acknowledgments

The author wishes to express a special word of gratitude to The Most Reverend J. Carroll McCormick, D.D., Bishop of Scranton, for the time and opportunity to pursue a course of studies in moral theology, of which this work is but one of many fruits. Special thanks, too, must be conveyed to the Reverend Bernard Häring, C.Ss.R., the moderator of this work, and to all the professors of the *Accademia Alfonsiana* for their dedicated efforts to communicate and inculcate a knowledge and love of the gospel mystery with its implications for practical Christian living. A word of thanks must also be expressed to Monsignor John Tracy Ellis for his generous help and support in the initial planning stages of this work and to the Reverend Bernard Quinn of the Glenmary Research Center, Washington, D.C., for his interest and encouragement during this undertaking.

To the Reverends Timothy K. Johnson, S.S., Donn P. Raabe, and Gerald J. Washko, the author must express his very special gratitude for their deeply treasured friendship and support during the writing of this work, for their attentive listening in its planning stages and for their ideas, suggestions, and comments. The Reverend Joseph A. Hart gave generously of himself and his time in proofreading the text before it went to a very patient typist, Mrs. Mina Mariani. Furthermore, without the companionship and fraternal support of my fellow priests at the Casa Santa Maria—especially the Reverends Walter H. Cuenin, Robert J. Thelen, Kevin W. Irwin, John C. Nienstedt, and Walter J. Woods—and of the seminarians of the Scranton Diocese studying at the North American College, the author's life during the two years it took him to complete this study would have remained in a great measure impoverished and unfulfilled.

Rome, Italy
October 30, 1976

To Mom, Dad, and Grace—
My First Evangelizers.

Preface

It is my great pleasure to introduce this very fine and excellent dissertation by David Bohr, one of my doctoral students here at the Academia Alfonsiana. His study, which relates the Church's "essential and primary mission" of evangelization to the American context, is indeed both timely and providential. It is one of my firm convictions that the direction undertaken by the Catholic Church in the United States during the next few years will greatly influence the direction and posture assumed by the Universal Church during the last quarter of this century. The United States today is the recognized leader of the western world in technological progress and political affairs. Highly pluralistic and secular, American society travels a road which others will follow towards the year 2000. The Catholic Church in the United States during this most important and critical time is being called upon to provide the spiritual and moral leaven for this journey. The number of young, competent and dedicated theologians I have observed recently appearing in the American church fills me with hope that the United States will have the moral and spiritual leadership she will so surely need in the coming years.

David Bohr, in this unprecedented and long needed study of the American Catholic Church's evangelizing mission, brings to bear a thorough knowledge of the many aspects that comprise this apostolate. I greatly appreciate his clear exposition of the material as well as the balanced judgment and discernment he displays in his critique. There is never a rosy critique. It is most important, however, for evangelization always to predicate first the good of the culture it seeks to evangelize, and only after having discovered its goodness can we then face its weaknesses and needs.

This present work was first submitted as a dissertation leading to the conferral of a doctorate in moral theology. To study evangelization from the perspective of Christian morality sheds new light on the purpose and structure of both these fields. Evangelization, first of all, provides the context for the reintegration of dogmatic theology and moral theology. The meticulous casuistry of the recent past, alienated from the life of faith and everyday realities, is replaced by "the life-giving law of the Spirit in Christ Jesus" (Rom 8:2). Living "in Christ," the community of the faithful (the Church) makes visible once again his peace and

1

reconciliation as it applies the dynamics of the gospel mystery to the concrete situations and problems of contemporary living in our highly pluralistic and secular world. From this perspective, too, it becomes evident that evangelization is much more than just a verbal communication. Proclaiming the Good News necessarily involves incarnating it in lives of Christian witness. All these aspects of evangelization David Bohr brings out well in his development of what he refers to as the "*two moments*" of the evangelization process and in his presentation of the relationship between "orthodoxy" and Christian orthopraxis.

It has often been my experience that a person's choice of a topic for his doctoral dissertation greatly shapes and influences his future life's work. This I found to be true with my own dissertation, *Das Heilige und das Gute* (*The Holy and the Good*), close to thirty years ago. The integral relationship of religion and morality has influenced in some ways all my further research and teaching. It is my hope that this will also prove true with David Bohr. I would very much like to see him study and explore further the questions and directions he began to pursue in the last part of this work but which neither time nor space allowed him to do fully. In the two short years it took him to write this he has made a most impressive start.

Bernard Häring, C.Ss.R.
Academia Alfonsiana, Rome
November 25, 1976

Introduction

When Pope Paul VI in the beginning of 1973 chose "Evangelization of the Modern World" as the theme of the fourth Synod of Bishops, it was his utmost desire to focus the bishops' and the entire Church's attention on what he saw to be traditionally "the essential and primary mission of the Church."[1] Pope Paul's selection of this topic at this particular time—nearly a decade after the close of the Second Vatican Council—shows his deep and continuing concern for the implementation of the reform and renewal of the Roman Catholic Church that was begun at that Council. As Cardinal Lorscheider of Fortaleza (Brazil) pointed out in the "Panorama" presented at the opening session of the 1974 Synod:

> Real progress in pastoral work can be noted today in the Church; nevertheless, it appears that the Council has not yet had full effectiveness in the life of the Church with regard to its *interior renewal.* The Council is being applied rather more in its exterior form than in keeping with its spirit.[2]

In thus requesting the bishops to concentrate their reflections and theological efforts upon the Church's primary mission of evangelization,[3] Pope Paul VI evidently had foremost on his mind the necessity of giving a new impetus to the spiritual renewal of the Church envisioned by his predecessor John XXIII when he convoked Vatican II on Christmas Day, 1961. For Pope John at that time stated: "The beneficial influence of the Council deliberations must, as we sincerely hope, succeed to the extent of imbuing with Christian light and penetrating with fervent spiritual energy not only the intimacy of the soul but the whole collection of human activities."[4] Recapturing the echo of these words in 1975, Paul VI in *Evangelii Nuntiandi* described the evangelizing mission of the Church as "bringing the Good News into all the strata of humanity and through its influence transforming humanity from within and making it new."[5]

The Church today has gone beyond the pre-conciliar, simplistic concept of evangelization, which commonly attributed to this term the more limited meaning of missionary preaching in "pagan" lands, where

3

the Gospel is proclaimed for the first time to non-Christians.[6] This neces-sary, constitutive mission to proclaim Christ is now "considered not so much as an outgoing process of preaching but as a process of incarna-tion of the Word of God in a particular place and people in the context of the local Church witnessing to the Gospel in her life and thereby ful-filling the mission received from the risen Lord."[7] The Declaration of the International Theological Conference on Evangelization and Dia-logue in India elaborates further on this wider and more comprehensive understanding of the term when it states:

> By evangelisation we mean the imparting of the good news of salvation in Jesus Christ, through which men are ena-bled to share in the spirit of Christ, who renews and reconciles them to God. This the Church accomplishes not only through proclamation (Mk 16:15ff) but also through a life of Christian witnessing (Lk 24:47-48; Acts 1:8) by which it tries to show that the communication of the message of Christ is not simply verbal, but the witness of the whole life lived in the spirit and radiating the divine agape in the fellowship of a community.[8]

In its widest sense evangelization refers to the total process and en-tire context within which God chooses to reveal and communicate him-self to us in Word and Spirit. The Good News, the revelation of this lov-ing plan, is of its very nature incarnational. In the Old Testament God's self-revelation and self-communication become evident through human words, and he reveals his presence in the concrete events of salvation history, which culminates in the Incarnation of his Word in the New Testament. Jesus Christ is Love Incarnate (1 Jn 4:8 and Jn 1:14, also *GS* 22)—the "agape-kenosis" (Phil 2:5-11). "By this revelation then, the deepest truth about God and the salvation of man is made clear to us in Christ, who is the Mediator and at the same time the fullness of all reve-lation" (*DV* 2). Evangelization thus ultimately becomes the proclama-tion of the gospel mystery of the new and eternal life that God seeks to share with us in and through Jesus Christ. For in the words of St. John:

> That life was made visible:
> we saw it and we are giving our testimony,
> telling you of the eternal life
> which was with the Father and has been made visible to us.
> What we have seen and heard
> we are telling to you
> so that you may be in union with us,
> as we are in union

with the Father
and with his Son Jesus Christ. (1 Jn 1:2-3)

And in the gospel attributed to the same author, we hear Jesus say: "I have come so that they may have life and have it to the full" (Jn 10:10).

The Church, which the Lord Jesus inaugurated by preaching the Good News of the coming of God's Kingdom (cf. *LG* 5) has as its essential mission and primary apostolate the bringing of all men and women into full union with Christ (cf. *LG* 1). In the teaching of the Council Fathers at Vatican II: "The pilgrim Church is missionary by her very nature. For it is from the mission of the Son and the mission of the Holy Spirit that she takes her origin, in accordance with the decree of God the Father" (*AG* 2). The Church's initial undertaking of this divinely bestowed mission to proclaim the Gospel began with the first Pentecost recounted in Acts 2:1-41. The mission was given to her by Christ himself: "Go, therefore, and make disciples of all the nations; baptize them in the name of the Father and of the Son and of the Holy Spirit, and teach them to observe all the commands I gave you. And know that I am with you always; yes, to the end of time" (Mt 28:19-20). It is a continuation of Christ's mission given to him by his Father (Jn 20:21), when, after his baptism by John in the Jordan and after John's subsequent arrest, Jesus goes into Galilee and begins to proclaim the gospel mystery: "The time has come and the Kingdom of God is close at hand. Repent, and believe the Good News" (Mk 1:15).

The *one* divine economy of salvation is thus executed by the mission of the Son and the mission of the Holy Spirit. These missions constitute a dynamic, on-going process of evangelization as through grace and revelation they draw us into a communion of new life with the Father, Son, and Holy Spirit. This evangelical economy is the Mystery hidden through the ages and now revealed in Christ. It is the Good News of God's Kingdom already present in our midst. It is, furthermore, the "mystery of simplicity," a unitive whole comprising the entire context within which all theological reflection must occur.

One of the purposes of this study is to demonstrate this unitive whole, or gospel-worldview. Our aim is to show the interrelationships and necessary interdependence of the major present-day theological disciplines—scripture, dogma, moral and spiritual theology—as they seek to explicate this one divine evangelical economy. Overspecialization in each of these theological fields, and in the parts thereof, has clouded the Gospel's simplicity amid the myriad complexities of numerous treatises and apologetic tracts. Specializations are necessary and, indeed, justified, but they should never lose sight of their own place and contribution to the whole lest the forest be overlooked because of all the trees. The communication of the Gospel requires a unitive view so that the purity of its message with all the power of its impact may not be lost.

When viewed within the context of the evangelization process, the disciplinary interdependence of doctrine and moral once more comes into clear focus. They form two sides of one coin, as it were, as the Christian's spiritual-moral life is constituted by his living faith-response to the Good News. Thus, the process of evangelization itself is divided into *two moments*. First, there is "the explicit proclamation of the mystery of Christ and a direct invitation to adhere to his gospel."9 Herein the Mystery is communicated in all its objectivity. The Good News takes on flesh as Christ reveals the extent of his Father's love for us through the Paschal Mystery. Indeed, the objectivity of the gospel message lies not in precise words and sayings as much as in the revelation of Eternal Life in Christ. New Life is given us through the Church in the Spirit, and we are challenged to live according to this New Life by trying to love others as Christ has loved us. This *first moment* of the evangelization process constitutes a radical call to conversion, as well as a call for a continual conversion, for a dynamic, on-going and loving dialogue with the risen Lord who never ceases to summon us every minute of our lives through the Church, our neighbor, our historical, cultural and social milieu, and the "signs of the times."

The *second moment* of this evangelization process is our actual adherence to the Gospel, i.e., a lived faith-response which finds its expression in our spiritual-moral life. Living the Good News in faith-hope-love, we become signs and witnesses of Christ's Spirit present with us yet. Faith and morality, thus, cannot be separated (cf. Mt 7:24-27). We must do the truth in love (cf. Eph 4:15). Christian moral witness in turn becomes evangelization as others are led to seek an explanation for the hope that is in us (cf. 1 Pet 3:15). This ability to witness to Christ, however, comes only from the power of the Holy Spirit. Intimately associated with the Pentecost event, evangelization of its nature is Spirit-filled. This *second moment* provides the basis for a renewed moral theology or, even more appropriately, for a "theology of Christian living." Christian life based on the Gospel is a spiritual-moral life. Already redeemed and reconciled "in Christ," Christians are called in the Spirit to "mature" in Christ (Eph 4:13-16) and to become ever more and more transformed into his image. Indeed, Christian morality was originally viewed as a byproduct of this spiritual growth or maturing process.

In order to arrive at the ultimate objective of this study—namely, the promotion of the Catholic Church's continuing mission of evangelization in the United States of America—numerous elements comprising the gospel mystery and its effective proclamation must be treated herein. Parts I and II of this work will concern themselves with an analysis of the elements involved in the *two moments* of the evangelization process. Part I, entitled "Evangelization: Proclaiming the Good News," will treat the *first moment* in its biblical, historical and theological perspectives. The aim here will be to bring together from each of these three areas a comprehensive synthesis, or gospel-worldview, which will aid us in understanding our necessary and contemporary mission of explicitly proclaiming the mystery of Christ in a modern, secular and pluralistic age. Part II, entitled "Evangelization: Living the Good News," will treat of the *second moment* of the evangelization process, constituted by our lived faith-response to the proclaimed Word. Responding to the Good News in faith-hope-love, we incarnate it in a "way of life" which itself becomes a genuine proclamation. In this part we shall analyze the principal elements that comprised the early Christian "Way." From this study, then, we shall be able to discern and delineate the fundamental evangelical categories for contemporary Christian living, and likewise for a renewed moral theology. One of the arguments to be presented herein is that, when viewed in the entire context of evangelization, or the *one* divine economy of salvation, the contemporary theological disciplines of dogma and moral are integrally related. In addition, the fundamental and necessary interdependence of moral and spiritual theology will also come to the fore.

Finally in Part III, entitled "Evangelization and the Catholic Church in the United States Yesterday and Today," we shall arrive at the ultimate objective of our presentation. In order to promote the Catholic Church's continuing mission of evangelization within the contemporary American context, we shall first evaluate the historical efforts of the American church in this regard. The wider and more comprehensive understanding of evangelization presented in Parts I and II of this work will provide the criteria for this historical overview. With this background, then, we will analyze the contemporary situation to ascertain the questions and directions the Catholic Church in the United States must explore and pursue today in order to carry on effectively its continuing apostolate of evangelization.

NOTES

1. Paul VI, "Evangelization of the World: essential mission of the Church," (address during the general audience of October 30, 1974), quoted in

L'Osservatore Romano, English ed., 45 (November 7, 1974) 1. (Hereafter cited as *L'OR(E)*.)

2. Cardinal Lorscheider, "Panorama: A General Look at the Life of the Church since the Last Synod of Bishops," in *L'OR(E)*, 41 (October 10, 1974) 10. Italics in the original.

3. Cf. *Lumen Gentium* 23, where it is maintained that this task belongs primarily to the Episcopal College. (Hereafter cited as *LG*.)

4. John XXII, "Humanae Salutis," (December 25, 1961) in W.M. Abbott, ed., *The Documents of Vatican II* (New York, 1967) 707. (Hereafter cited as *Abbott*.)

5. Paul VI, *Evangelii Nuntiandi* (hereafter cited as *EN*), *L'Osservatore Romano* (December 19, 1975), par. 18 (hereafter cited as *L'OR*); Eng. trans., Vatican Polyglot Press, 1975.

6. For the various uses of the term "evangelization" cf. "Synod of Bishops —The Evangelization of the Modern World," publication for the use of the Episcopal Conference by the USCC (Washington, D.C., 1973) 1:

"The word 'evangelization' is commonly understood in several different senses today. In the first place, the term can mean every activity whereby the world is in any way transformed in accordance with the will of God the Creator and Redeemer. Secondly, the word is used to mean the priestly, prophetic and royal activity whereby the Church is built up according to Christ's intention. A third and more common meaning is the activity whereby the Gospel is proclaimed and explained, and whereby living faith is awakened in non-Christians and fostered in Christians (missionary preaching, catechetics, homilectics, etc.).

"Finally, the word 'evangelization' is restricted to meaning the first proclamation of the Gospel to non-Christians, whereby faith is awakened (missionary preaching: kerygma)."

7. L. Legrand, J. Pathrapankal, and M. Vellanickal, *Good News and Witness* (Bangalore, India, 1973) vii. (Hereafter cited as *GN&W*.)

8. "Declaration of the Nagpur Theological Conference on Evangelization" (October 6-12, 1971), in J. Pathrapankal, ed., *Service and Salvation* (Bangalore, 1973) 6. (Hereafter cited as *SAS*.)

Part I
Evangelization: Proclaiming
The Good News

"Go out to the whole world; proclaim the Good News to all
creation."   Mk 16:15

Announcing the message of salvation realized in the Christ Mystery
is the Church's primary imperative. The Good News must be spread
abroad. The Mystery hidden for ages and now revealed in Jesus Christ
(cf. Col 1:26-27) of its very nature is to be proclaimed and made known
to all the world for "they will not believe in him unless they have heard
of him" (Rom 10:14). The *first moment* of the evangelization process
concerns itself with this explicit proclamation of the Good News in all
its forms.

The first part of this work, then, examines what it means "to proclaim the Good News." Proclamation in its widest sense includes more
than just preaching or verbal communication. From the biblical, historical and theological evidence we shall see that "proclaiming the Good
News" also involves the witness value of living faith that shines forth
from the fellowship of New Life shared in the Christian community.
Proclaiming the Gospel, thus, has to do with all that promotes one's
conscious awareness of the Christ Mystery present in our midst and
that, likewise, invites and challenges us to believe it and appropriate it to
our own lives.

Under "Biblical Perspectives" (Chapter I) we examine the Old
and New Testament concepts of "good news" and "to preach" and their
equivalents with all that they implied at the time they were written. Our
main concern, of course, is to ascertain the content of the Good News,
the core of the gospel message, as proclaimed by Jesus and understood
by the primitive Church. We further explore Jesus' manner and mode of
proclaiming it as interpreted by the four evangelists. We also want to
determine the apostolic Church's understanding of the evangelizing mission entrusted to it by the risen Lord.

We will, then, trace this understanding as it evolves in the post-
apostolic and patristic periods. Chapter II, entitled "Historical

Notes," pursues this aspect as well as marks the various shifts in the Church's outlook on evangelization as influenced by the changing historical, cultural and social situations of the passing centuries. A large portion of this chapter is devoted to the rediscovery of the Church's mission precipitated by rapidly moving events of the past century. Our historical overview ends with the concepts pertaining to evangelization proposed in the documents and decrees of Vatican II, and in the work of the 1974 Rome Synod of Bishops on "Evangelization of the Modern World" (including Paul VI's apostolic exhortation *Evangelii Nuntiandi* of December 1975).

In Chapter III we have gathered together the latest "Theological Reflections" concerning this essential and constitutive mission of the Church. Starting with the Trinitarian Godhead's utterly free choice to reveal and communicate himself *ad extra* in *one* evangelical economy, the task unfolds with the mission of the Son and the mission of the Holy Spirit. Consequently, we must take into consideration the major doctrinal tracts of revelation, grace, and ecclesiology to demonstrate how the various theological areas categorically explicate and develop essential elements of this one divine plan. Finally then, we can reflect upon the overall process of evangelization that was inaugurated by this *one* plan, or "mystery of simplicity." Paralleling the divine missions, the evangelizing process is carried out in truth and love, in word and deed. Genuine orthodoxy is seen as necessarily including "orthopraxis" as well as adhering to "right teaching." Only in this manner can our lives proclaim the Good News we profess with our lips. Only in this way do we appropriate the Christ Mystery as our own and thereby integrate ourselves with the one divine evangelical economy of salvation. Sharing life and fellowship with the Father, Son, and Holy Spirit in the church community, we continue in Christ's Spirit the process of evangelization by bearing witness to the gospel mystery through our lives lived in genuine Christian faith-hope-love.

I
Biblical Perspectives

The faith experience of the apostolic Church remains forever the primary source of Christian theological reflection upon the Good News of God the Father's loving design for humankind. Therefore, the written account of the gradual unveiling of his all-benevolent plan, which begins with the books of the Old Testament, culminates in the writings of the New Testament where the four gospels are given a special preeminence. Our systematic study of this evangelization process starts here with a biblical analysis. After a brief look at the concept of evangelization in the Old Testament, we shall move quickly to the New Testament era and begin there with a content summary of Jesus' proclamation of the Good News. Next, we shall consider the Evangelists' presentation of the gospel-event, which in its turn will lead us into the apostolic Church's understanding of the fundamental meaning of Christ's resurrection and its missionary implications. Finally, we will review the contents and structure of this evangelizing mission and process as they come to us in the theological reflections of the Pauline Letters and the Johannine Corpus.

A. EVANGELIZATION IN THE OLD TESTAMENT

Gospel is good news. In the Septuagint translation of the Old Testament one can find the noun "gospel" ("evangelion") three times and the verb "euangelize" ("euangelizesthai") some twenty-three times. The verb is found in the historical, prophetical and sapiential books, but the noun appears only in 2 Kings; they are translations of "bissar" and "besorah" respectively.[1]

The word "gospel" in its common usage can mean any good news, such as the prophet describes when recounting the fall of Nineveh, the capital of Assyria, in 612: "See on the mountains the feet of the herald who brings good news" (Nah 1:15—NEB). But twenty-five years later Jerusalem herself would lie in ruins and her people be carried off into exile. Yet amid the universal gloom of her captivity, "the prophet of consolation" will ring out this thrilling message of hope:

> Comfort, comfort my people
> says your God;

11

> speak tenderly to Jerusalem and cry to her
> that her time of bondage is over
> that her penalty is paid. . . . (Is 40:1-2)

Jerusalem is now asked to relay the good news to the other neighbouring cities:

> Get you up to a high mountain,
> O Sion, herald of good tidings;
> lift up your voice with strength;
> O Jerusalem, *herald of good tidings*,
> say to the cities of Judah:
> Behold your God!
> Behold the Lord God comes with might
> and his arm rules for him! (Is 40:9-10)

Soon the vision becomes clearer. The prophet of consolation can already hear the steps of the messenger bringing from beyond the desert the news of the return of the Exiles:

> How beautiful upon the mountains
> are the feet of him who brings glad tidings,
> who heralds *peace,*
> who brings good things of *happiness,*
> who proclaims *salvation,*
> who says to Sion: Your God reigns.
> Hark, your watchmen lift up their voice;
> together they sing for joy,
> for they see face to face
> the return of the Lord to Sion. (Is 52:7-8)

Peace, happiness, salvation: such is the content of the good news.[2]

These three elements continued to appear together in Jewish tradition. According to a midrash on Isaiah 52, the prophet Elijah will appear three days before the coming of the Messiah, and his voice will ring out throughout all the earth proclaiming one of these three elements on each of the three successive days. Thus, by the time of Jesus, the announcement of the Good News had assumed a definite technical meaning in Israel's messianic expectation of the rule of God.[3]

A fundamental factor underlying the concept of evangelization in the Old Testament is the universalist understanding of God. Yahweh is Lord over all the nations and he uses them as his instruments (cf. Ps 110), and Yahweh's promise to Abraham applies to all the nations, who will subsequently, then, be blessed through Abraham and the chosen people (cf. Gen 12:3, 26:4). Thus, Israel has a particular role to fulfill. She must become a "light to the nations" (Is 42:6), so that they may all come to acknowledge Yahweh as God. She must be a living sign and witness of the holiness of God (cf. Lev 11:44-45). To this end the prophets are "sent" or "commissioned" by God in Israel. They receive their prophetic mission through a personal call of God (cf. Ex 3:10; Jer 1:7; Ez 2:3f, 3:4f) and are sent to Israel whose very existence itself is missionary in view of the salvation of all the nations. So we see here in the Old Testament the beginnings of an evangelization process and mission that will find its full development in the New Testament.

Elsewhere at this time, in the Greco-Roman world, the words "euangelion" and "euangelizesthai" also held technical meanings. They could refer to the good news of victory, such as in the case of Philippides, the soldier of Marathon, who ran to Athens in 490 B.C. bringing the good news of victory over Darius and collapsed dead on the Agora as he shouted: "Rejoice, Athenians! Victory is ours." On other occasions, "euangelia" denotes the thanksgiving sacrifices offered in the Temple. It also finds a place in Emperor worship, such as in the proposal from the famous inscription of Priene in the year 9 B.C., to start henceforth the beginning of the year on the birthday of the Emperor, giving as a reason that "the birthday of the god was for the world the beginning of good tidings ('euangelia') on his account."[4] A few short years later in Bethlehem of Judea another birth would be announced in a similar fashion with the words: "Do not be afraid. Listen, I bring you news of great joy, a joy to be shared by the whole people. Today in the town of David a savior has been born to you; he is Christ the Lord" (Lk 2:10-11).

B. JESUS PROCLAIMS THE GOOD NEWS

Scripture scholars tend to doubt that Jesus himself ever used the word "gospel," even though the synoptic accounts attribute its use to him.[5] Mark uses the noun "gospel" eight times but never the verb; Matthew uses "gospel" four times in passages dependent on Mark. Luke, on the other hand, never employs the noun, but only the verb "to evangelize," which appears ten times in his account. Thus it seems that "gospel" in Mark is basically redactional, a term he inherited—probably from Paul. Yet can its use attributed to Jesus, particularly in Mk 1:14-15, be considered strictly redactional? C. H. Dodd in this instance favors the opinion that Mark found it in an already existing tradition.[6] Stronger arguments seem to favor Jesus' use of the verb "to evangelize," especially in Mt 11:5 (=Lk 7:22) where Is 61:1 is quoted. Bultmann believes that it is very possible that Jesus would have quoted the prophet to describe his own work and ministry.[7]

Aside from the question of whether or not Jesus ever uttered the Aramaic equivalent of "gospel" and "to evangelize," what Jesus proclaimed certainly had the ring of Good News. In the words of Legrand: "Whoever may have composed it, the summary of Jesus' preaching given in Mk 1:15 is a masterpiece:

> The time is fulfilled
> The Kingdom of God is at hand
> Repent
> and believe the Good News."[8]

Accepting, then, this summary in Mk 1:15 as our starting point, we shall use it for an analysis and interpretation of Jesus' message.

1. *"The time is fulfilled."*

The promises of the prophets find their fulfillment here and now (cf. Is 52:9). God's promised intervention has arrived. This is not the announcement of a new philosophy, but the direct intervention of God promised in the eschatological times. God "has now committed himself fully, regardless of all human failure, to the advent of a new man in the person of His Son" (cf. Col 1:15-20; Mt 11:27-30).[9]

2. *"The Kingdom of God . . ."*

Here is the main concept of Jesus' preaching. "The Kingdom of God" or its alternate "the Kingdom of Heaven" appears seventy-eight times in the Synoptics. The Greek word for "kingdom" ("baseleia," or its Aramaic equivalent "malekutha") is basically nonterritorial and eschatological in its connotation. More appropriate English renderings of the phrase would be "the rule of God" or "reign of God." The word "kingdom" in modern parlance has further unhappy connotations. It usually suggests a return to monarchies, royalists and "the old order," notions that the twentieth century wishes to consign to the pages of history. But as Legrand observes: "In the concrete context of the intertestamental period, the notion of God's Kingship had revolutionary overtones. It condemned the existing state of affairs and looked forward to the future. One of the best renderings of the old phrase in modern language would be: God's Revolution."[10]

What, exactly, was expected to change with this Revolution? Surely it would usher in a period of peace, happiness and salvation—the triad of messianic expectations found in Isaiah 52. What images would this phrase summon to the minds of Christ's hearers? By the time of Jesus, Legrand explains:

> We can only say that in his ultimate intervention God was expected to rectify completely whatever had gone wrong:
>
> in politics: avenging the people of Israel enslaved by the Nations (cf. Dan 4, 7, 8, 10-11, etc.)
>
> in society: putting down the mighty and exalting the lowly, filling the starving with good things and sending the rich away empty, in the words of the Magnificat which are an apt summary of a theme frequently found in the literature of those days (Ps Sol 5:1, 2, 7, 10f; Qumran Hymns II 20-30, 32-36; III 5-7, 27-28 . . .)
>
> in the cosmos: by the creation of a new heaven and a new earth where "death shall be swallowed for ever and tears wiped away from all eyes." (Is 25:8, 65:17; II Bar 53)[11]

3. ". . . is at hand."

The Kingdom of God is imminent, "just around the corner." It is a present reality that one now has to face without delay. In a certain sense, "the last days" are here and one must decide *now*.

> This shift of perspective appears in the very style of Jesus. In Jesus' teaching, the Kingdom figures in the midst of a cluster of images borrowed from daily life and no longer from mytho-poetic phantasy. The Kingdom is like a seed, a farmer, a shepherd, a fisherman casting a net, a housewife preparing dough, a steward in trouble. . . . This is highly significant. It means that the notion of Kingdom is to some extent de-eschatologized. It does not belong any longer to escapist dreams but to earthly-bound realities. There was a danger in the thorough-going eschatologism and the supernaturalism of apocalyptic literature. The deep commitment to history of the early prophets of the Old Testament was replaced by a flight from reality. Evangelist of the Kingdom that is "at hand," Jesus returns spontaneously to the concrete style of the prophets and again brings faith in God to bear on the features of the history of man.[12]

Yet Jesus does not allow for historical integralism. The parables of the Kingdom portray an utter unpredictability on God's behalf. God's sovereignty is characterized by the undreamt-of superabundance of his Love, which to us appears as almost too good to be true. God does not act as we would act. He is the shepherd who leaves a flock of ninety-nine sheep to search out one stray (Mt 18:12-14). The "prodigal son" is welcomed back with fanfare (Lk 15:22-24); the workers hired in the last hour get priority over those who have toiled all day (Mt 20:1-16). The newness of God's rule and Kingdom can never be contained within the confines of time and history.

The Kingdom must continue to remain "already, but not yet" here. This is brought out in Jesus' language concerning the Kingdom. As Guillet comments:

> It is noticeable that, when speaking of the Kingdom, Jesus has freely recourse to two very different and yet converging types of language: the language of geneses, germinations and fruits, and the language of apocalypses, of the secrets which are revealed, of the mysteries which are unveiled. (Mk 4:11, 22; Mt 11:25)[13]

The Good News of the Kingdom contains a certain inbuilt paradoxical tension. For it is "basic to the message that the world and its situation are understood in the light of God's kingship, while the kingship is not a projection of anything of this world."[14] In Jesus, the Kingdom is the dynamism of God's love. It is grace! It is the power of God erupting in time, accompanied by words and deeds, parables and miracles. As Jesus tells the messengers sent to him by John the Baptist who is in prison: "Go back and tell John what you hear and see; the blind see again, and the lame walk, lepers are cleansed, and the deaf hear, and the dead are raised to life and the Good News is proclaimed to the poor" (Mt 11:4-5).

4. *"Repent."*

This one word takes us to the heart of the matter. It is the key to the Kingdom. It contains Jesus' first and most important challenge since "ultimately God's Revolution is everybody's concern and has to take place in everyone's heart and life."[15] Humanity's refusal to hear and accept this challenge becomes the root of evil: sin. "Through sin death entered the world" (Rom 5:12). Evil in the world cannot be attributed to superhuman powers beyond our control. Jesus here goes beyond the apocalyptic descriptions of evil by returning to the prophetical interpretation—the same interpretation found in the priestly author of Genesis whose theology of sin is but the reverse side of a theology of human dignity and freedom. Jesus' gospel proclamation announces God's power now at work removing from men and women their hearts of stone and putting in them a "new heart" (Ezk 11:18f). The Good News of God's Word is thus a "two-edged sword, piercing as far as the place where life and spirit, joints and marrow divide" (Heb 4:12—*NEB*). God's Revolution, as a radical upheaval in one's life, demands on our part the acceptance of this gift and power of God.

The Greek word used here, "metanoieite," means more than "repent." It literally means to change one's mind. But even more so, considering that it translates the Hebrew "shub", (noun, "teshuba"), it implies an about-face, a coming home to the love of God and his Covenant after having violated and forsaken this covenantal relationship. In the mind of Jesus, metanoia is a grace and a gift (cf. Acts 5:31, 11:18), which implies "a complete reversal in man's aspirations, judgements, scales of value, attitudes and actions."[16] This radical reversal in the way one looks at life is more concretely spelled out by Jesus in his calling to question the basic standards of his contemporaries:

> In the Kingdom the lowly are exalted and the mighty brought down (Lk 1:52): the poor and the children are those who matter; the first are last and the last first (Mk 10:31); the greatest becomes last and the servant of all (Mk 10:43-44); dignity is in serving and not in being served; anxiety for self realization is death and gift of self is life (Mk 8:35); and all this is summarized and fulfilled on the Cross, the sign of the radical *teshubah* in which he who was in the form of God humbled himself, and died the death of a slave, turning death into life and shame into glory. (Phil 2:6-9; Jn 17:5)[17]

This call of Jesus to conversion is universal in its scope: it addresses itself to Jew and Gentile alike. It is not a call to change religious affiliation as much as it is a challenge to a change of heart. From the Jew it demanded more than a legalistic observance of the Mosaic Law (Mt 5:28-40). Thus sinners, to the consternation of the Jews, often found themselves closer to God than those who believed themselves righteous.

5. *"Believe the Good News."*

Faith constitutes the only valid response one can give to Jesus' challenge. Faith is what Jesus sought to elicit from his hearers. He requires faith before working any miracles. In Nazareth, "he did not work many miracles there because of their lack of faith" (Mt 13:58), and to the woman with a hemorrhage he said: "Courage, my daughter, your faith has restored you to health" (Mt 9:22).

What is this faith that Jesus sought from his listeners? It can neither be faith in a hope for a miracle, nor an explicit intellectual assent to Christ's divinity, which at this point still remains only implicit. The faith Jesus wanted to elicit was faith in God's rule and sovereignty— faith in the Kingdom—as a living and concrete follow-up to metanoia. Thus faith in this instance means to trust in God's word and promise— to believe and to allow oneself to be transformed by the renewing power of God's Spirit at work in the world here and now.

> To put it in a language closer to the Gospels, faith consists in following the Lord and embracing his unpredictable and paradoxical attitudes, orientations, options and standards, accepting with him to give up stifling human securities to rely on the Father alone.
>
> This is what is meant particularly by the central section of Mk's Gospel (8:27-9:1) where the profession of faith of Peter (vv. 27-30) is followed by the announcement of the Passion (vv. 31-33) and the sayings about losing one's life to save it and the necessity of carrying the cross if one is really to follow Jesus.[18]

Receptivity to the Good News or openness to faith in the Kingdom demands a basic underlying attitude on the part of the listener, namely, "poverty of spirit." As Jesus opens his inaugural discourse in the Sermon on the Mount, his first words are: "How happy are the poor in spirit; theirs is the kingdom of heaven" (Mt 5:3). Legrand maintains: "This readiness to accept the revolutionary pattern of living and thinking proposed by Christ is possible only to the poor, which does not mean only the economically destitute but all those who are crushed by the old order and its standards and feel the need of a radical change."[19] Only for these poor is Jesus' message good news. Because it is only those who either have nothing to lose or are willing to lose everything who are ultimately ready to take the risk of faith—a faith that follows a rabbi who finds freedom in serving and life through death on a cross.

Finally, then, in this one pericope of Mark's gospel account we find summed up the entire *first moment* of the evangelization process. "The Kingdom of God is at hand. Repent." Here we have the explicit proclamation of the Mystery of God's rule and Kingdom (which later on will become identified with Christ himself) and a direct invitation to adhere to the Good News or the Gospel. Explicit, also, is the human response of faith, which in its turn becomes the *second moment* in the process and mission of evangelization. However, for a better understanding of this entire mission, we must look now in more detail at the Evangelists' treatment and at the interpretation given to it by the apostolic Church in the New Testament.

C. THE GOOD NEWS ACCORDING TO THE EVANGELISTS

Mark is the only one of the four Evangelists to entitle his work "the gospel" yet he never uses the verb "to evangelize," whereas Luke (as has already been mentioned above) employs only the verb. Given the context of the early Christian community in which Mark wrote, his omission of the verb appears to be deliberate. While G. Friedrich has pointed out that this peculiarity has been "frequently noted but never explained,"[20] Legrand believes that "the linguistic impact of this usage of Mk draws the attention of the reader towards the Good News itself rather than its actual proclamation by Jesus."[21]

Luke's use of the verb emphasizes the action in which the *content* of the action itself tends to become obscured. Marxsen, consequently, makes the observation that in the case of Luke, to a certain extent, the use of the verb takes on "a quite general connotation, viz., that of 'preaching.' "[22] For Mark, the Good News itself is the focal point of attention. He is akin to Paul in seeing the Gospel as "the power of God saving all who have faith" (Rom 1:16). As Legrand sums it up:

> In the communication of the Good News, the heart of the matter is not the energy of the evangelizer but the power of the Gospel itself. In so far as the word evangelization would give the impression that it is man's activity that achieves results, it fails to do justice to the power of the Gospel itself. It is not the Church that gives force to the Gospel. It is the Gospel that gives the Church existence and dynamism.[23]

Having established this centrality of the content of the Good News, especially in Mark's account, it is appropriate to consider now the activity of proclaiming it as seen from the viewpoint of the Evangelists. News means communication. Thus, news is only news when it is announced. For the purpose of announcing the Gospel, Mark employs the verb "kerussein" (literally, "to herald"). Jesus "heralds" the Good News in Mk 1:14. Even Luke, who along with Paul often uses the verb "katangellein" ("to announce"), never applies it to Jesus, nor do we find Jesus using it in any of the gospel traditions. Luke employs the verb "to evangelize" some ten times in his account, tending, therefore, to restrict the activity of evangelizing to the oral proclamation of the message—as it is often more commonly understood even today. "Teaching the Gospel" never occurs, although "didaskein" is frequently used "to summarize the verbal aspect of Jesus' activity."[24] Furthermore, Jesus' "heralding" or "evangelizing" in the gospel accounts takes two forms, namely, words and deeds.

1. The Parables and the Sermon on the Mount: Good News in Words

Jesus' words and teaching in the gospel accounts are especially recorded in two important forms: the Sermon on the Mount and the parables. The Sermon on the Mount has often been misunderstood as "the New Law," just as the parables have at times mistakenly been categorized as moral exhortations. Luther considered the Sermon on the Mount to be an "impossible ideal," which served only to make humanity aware of its sinfulness and thus prepare people for salvation through faith alone. But according to J. Jeremias both the Sermon and the parables are proclamations of the Good News.[25]

The Sermon on the Mount is introduced with unusual solemnity. Matthew intends it to be Jesus' inaugural address for the Kingdom, "the explication of what he has called the proclamation of the reign or the good news of the reign."[26] The Sermon begins with the Beatitudes. Joy and happiness are proclaimed to all those who are awaiting the fulfillment of the promises of the prophets. The Beatitudes announce the dawning of a new age. "How happy are the poor in spirit; theirs is the kingdom of heaven" (Mt 5:3). This exhilarating experience of joy continues throughout the entire Sermon. In the various collections of sayings, both in Mt 5-7 and Lk 6:20-49, "the Gospel preceded the demand."[27] "Good works" (Mt 5:16), then, consequently proceed from one's conversion to belief in the Good News of the Kingdom which has brought about an entire reorientation of values.

The parables, too, seem to be primarily a continuation of the proclamation of the Good News. Despite the early Church's hermeneutic reading of them as illustrated exhortations, the studies of C.H. Dodd and J. Jeremias show that, once shorn of all later additions and reinterpretations, "all the Gospel parables are a defence of the Good News."[28] Legrand adds that "thus the parables of the Friend at Night and the Unjust Judge did not originally give lessons on prayer but proclaimed what Jeremias calls 'the Great Assurance': even if God seems to tarry, we can be sure that the Kingdom is going to be fulfilled."[29]

The parables also contain an amount of mystery as they announce the unpredictability of God's intervention and the overflowing abundance of his Love. At the same time they challenge one to metanoia, to have a radical change of heart, as is summarized in Mk 4:11-12: "The secret of the kingdom of God is given to you, but to those who are outside everything comes in parables, so that they may see and see again, but not perceive; may hear and hear again, but not understand." Jesus' speaking in parables was not intended to confuse his hearers. "If parables blinded men's minds and hearts, it was more because they refused the piercing challenge than because they could not understand intellectually."[30] For the "secret" is only revealed to those who accept God's Kingdom as announced by Jesus, along with the reversal of values that this implies and effects.

2. The Good News in Deeds: the Miracles and Exorcisms

Besides proclaiming the Good News in words, Jesus' deeds themselves incarnated the message. Much of his activity was symbolic in form, a veritable proclamation of God's Kingdom in action. "His sitting at table with sinners (Mk 2:15-17), his attitude towards the children (Mk 10:13-16) carry the same message as the Beatitudes: they embody in life attitudes the Good News to the Poor."[31]

Along this line special mention must be given to Jesus' miracles. They have often been understood as being strictly apologetic in scope, as external confirmations of Jesus' message. But if this was the sole purpose of the miracles, one has trouble explaining away Jesus' desire that some of them be kept secret (e.g., in Mt 8:4, 9:31, etc.). Scripture scholars today see the miracles themselves as vehicles of the message. "Side by side, word and miraculous deed gave expression to the entrance of God's kingly power into time."[32] The miracles themselves are revelations of God's power and love erupting into time on behalf of the poor, the suffering and the outcasts of society. They, too, then challenge one's standards of appreciation of people, one's willingness to accept the new and unpredictable ways of God's Kingdom.

Among the miracles of Jesus, the exorcisms loom large. These exorcisms are frequently passed over today as peculiar to the "demonic-cosmic" background of the Palestinian world which attributed all evil to the influence of inimical spirits and demonic powers. Even sickness and infirmities in those days were attributed to diabolical powers as is attested especially in Lk 13:10-17, where a woman "for eighteen years had been possessed by a spirit that left her enfeebled; she was bent double and quite unable to stand upright." And Jesus' healing in this instance is seen as an act of liberation: "was it not right to untie her bonds on the sabbath day?" (v. 16). Jesus is here looked upon as a Liberator. Elsewhere in Lk 11:20, Jesus' exorcisms are attributed to "the finger of God," which is evidently a reference to Ex 8:19, where this phrase signifies God's power at work in the freeing of his people from their bondage in Egypt.

Jesus' exorcisms proclaimed the Good News of liberation. Luke has Jesus in Nazareth at the beginning of his ministry reading from the scroll of the prophet Isaiah that the Lord "has sent me to bring good news to the poor, to proclaim liberty to captives . . . to set the downtrodden free" (Lk 4:18). Jesus' exorcisms thus announce in deed the fact that God's power is active in overcoming the forces of evil that hold people in bondage and alienation. Legrand observes:

> . . . it would be wrong to dismiss the whole matter of exorcisms as childish representation. In the language of those days, the possessions express man's alienated condition. The old Semitic conception is not so distant from modern philosophical analysis (cf Marxism, Freudism) which sees man alienated by forces which go far beyond the reach of the individual. The victory of Jesus, stronger than the might of those forces, is "gospel," good news that the forces that cripple man can be cast out . . . that a world gone beserk on account of sin is now reconciled with itself and with God.[33]

3. *The Identification of the Gospel and the Kingdom with Christ*

Beyond Jesus' words and deeds, the very style of his life conveyed the Good News of the Kingdom.

> The life attitudes of Jesus, are a parable in action on freedom, on sharing in God's unpredictability and his independence from man made restraining categorisations. Jesus speaks for God and yet he does not campaign for any of the "sacred values" of Judaism: he is no Sadducee upholding the Temple as the navel of the world, no Zealot fighting for the sacred land, no Essene withdrawing to the desert.[34]

Jesus does not ask his disciples to rally around any institution or cause, not even around his person as an object of cult or respect. He just asks them to sell everything, give the money to the poor and "come, follow" him (cf. Mt 19:21), leaving themselves totally available to the cause and the course of the Kingdom. Jesus does not refuse help or fellowship to anyoñe, neither the sick, nor sinners, prostitutes and tax-collectors, a Roman centurion, a Samaritan and a Syro-Phoenician woman.[35] And although Jesus himself never ventures far beyond the borders of Galilee and Judea, he welcomes all.

Jesus' words, deeds and style of life are so central to his proclamation of the Good News of the Kingdom that the Evangelists writing their accounts in the early post-resurrection period did not hesitate to identify Jesus with the Good News and the Kingdom. Mark does this in 8:35 and 10:29. Elsewhere among the Synoptic accounts, parallel identifications are found: "And everyone who has left . . . for the sake of my name (Mt 19:29), for my sake (Mk 10:29), there is no one who has left . . . for the sake of the kingdom of God" (Lk 18:29).[36] Thus, it gradually becomes recognized that the Gospel itself is realized in the person of Christ.

In John the identification of the Kingdom with Jesus is even more explicit. "In Jn 18:36-37 the 'Kingdom' and the 'Kingship of Christ' are parallel to his 'coming into the world to witness to the truth,' and he affirms the necessity of 'being of the truth' to hear his voice."[37] Hence, only those recognize his kingship who live a life of faith in him. This Christological interpretation is further required "to see" and "enter the Kingdom of God." This, also, is the interpretation given to the passage by John Chrysostom[38] and Cyril of Alexandria.[39] And finally in Jn 3:36 one reads: "Anyone who believes in the Son has eternal life, but anyone who refuses to believe in the Son will never see life." Thus, it is not only Jesus and the Kingdom that are here identified, but both in turn are identified with Eternal Life.

4. *The Newness of the Gospel*

The gospel accounts of the Evangelists reveal the Good News of God's intervention in Jesus. They recount for us Jesus' method of evangelization in words and deeds, in parables and miracles. They even show us that Jesus himself gradually became identified with the Gospel and the Kingdom. But what is there about this intervention of God in and through Jesus Christ that makes it different from his previous saving interventions in the holy men and prophets throughout the history of God's chosen people? Jesus announces that "the time is fulfilled" (Mk 1:15), that this is the definitive intervention and revelation of God long promised by the prophets. What then exactly constitutes the qualitative newness that makes this the unsurpassable revelation of God? An indication of the answer has already been given in treating of the radical nature of the Kingdom that inverts all human standards and ways of perceiving reality. A hint, too, is found in the unpredictability of God and the extravagance of his generosity that comprise a great part of the mysteriousness of the parables.

The newness of this revelation of God in and through Jesus Christ is probably best portrayed in Jesus' farewell discourse to his disciples as read in Jn 15:9-13:

> "As the Father has loved me,
> so I have loved you.
> Remain in my love.
> If you keep my commandments
> you will remain in my love. . . .
> I have told you this
> so that my own joy may be in you
> and your joy be complete.
> This is my commandment:
> love one another,
> as I have loved you.
> A man can have no greater love
> than to lay down his life for his friends."

The joy and happiness of the Good News find their "fulfillment" as Jesus announces the *extent* of God's love for us. The incredible newness of the Gospel proclaimed here is explained by Lyonnet:

> . . . if the Old Testament knew we must love all men as God has loved us, no one then could obviously have guessed to what point the love of God could go: to the point of becoming a man so as to be able to love them unto death, not only to the point of becoming the shepherd of Israel seeking after lost sheep (Ezekiel 34:11-16) but to the point of giving his life for his sheep. (John 10:11-16)[40]

Thus, the above-cited passage from John both heralds and challenges. It heralds the unimaginable happiness of sharing through Christ communion in the life of God himself, while at the same time it challenges one to a radical conversion: "This is my commandment: love one another as I have loved you."

As previously noted, Jesus proclaimed the Good News not only in words, but in deeds and with his very life as well. This he did to the very end, when the Cross became "the supreme act of evangelization." In the words of Legrand: "The cross was the ultimate parable of God's Revolution. There at last, the Word was made flesh and the message totally expressed no longer in words of lips but of flesh and blood."[41] St. Paul attests to this ultimate proclamation of the Good News when he writes to the Church at Rome: "What proves that God loves us is that Christ died for us while we were still sinners" (5:8). The radical conversion that Jesus demands of his disciples is fully incarnated on the Cross.

> "Anyone who wants to become great among you must be your servant, and anyone who wants to be first among you must be slave to all. For the Son of Man himself did not come to be served but to serve, and to give his life as a ransom for all." (Mk 10:43-45)

Yet the concluding accounts of the Evangelists emphasize that the Good News of the Kingdom, although fully proclaimed by a death on a cross, cannot end with death. As two of Jesus' disciples on the road to Emmaus were to learn from a Stranger they met on the way: "You foolish men! So slow to believe the full message of the prophets! Was it not ordained that the Christ should suffer and so enter into his glory?" (Lk 24:25-26).

D. THE RESURRECTION, EVANGELIZATION AND THE APOSTOLIC COMMUNITY

He is Risen!

Shortly after Jesus' death by crucifixion, rumors started circulating among his disciples and followers that he was alive (cf. Lk 24:23). The content of these rumors was soon confirmed by the Eleven and others among their membership who said, "Yes, it is true. The Lord has risen and has appeared to Simon" (Lk 24:34).

1. *The Meaning of the Resurrection*

Of major significance for our study is the fact that all four of the gospel accounts end with the risen Lord appearing to the Eleven and sending them on their mission (Mt 28:19; Lk 24:47-49; Mk 16:15; Jn 20:21, 21:15-17 and the symbolism of the catch of fish).[42] A study of the wording of the missionary mandates reflects the theological viewpoint of each gospel, but as Legrand observes:

> The main common point in the structure of these accounts is that they are situated in such a way as to constitute the conclusion of the Gospel.
>
> In Mt it is strikingly so and it gives Mt's conclusion a vibrant dignity which has made of this text a favourite in Christian liturgical and homiletic tradition.

Lk has added the narrative of the Ascension to the missionary mandate and so has the longer ending of Mk, probably under the influence of Lk. Lk may have done it to link up the Gospel with the book of Acts. . . . He may have done it to make the Ascension in Jerusalem the denouement of a Gospel which was built on the theme of the "ascension" towards Jerusalem. Anyway this addition of Lk does not detract from the final authority of Jesus' last words.

In Jn also something follows after the missionary commission in 20:21-23. In fact the whole episode of the doubting Thomas in vv. 24-29 sounds like an anticlimax after the final orders of the Master. But it would be a misunderstanding to see it as a little bit of gossipy information about an apostle. Jn does not intend to draw the attention away from the mission of the apostles. The conclusion of the Thomas episode in v. 29 shows that all along Jn had the mission in mind: "Blessed are they who have not seen yet believe." After the sending of the messengers, the text ends with an evocation of "all those who believe through their word" (Jn 17:20). Thomas is the type of all those who will be evangelized, of their difficulties to believe, of their eventual enlightenment and blessedness. Far from breaking the structure of the mission appearance the episode of Thomas underlines the essential point in it.

Legrand, then, emphatically notes the implication of this structural convergence:

> *It means that, in all the traditions underlying the six accounts and in all the Churches which had carried those traditions, it was understood that the ultimate significance of the Resurrection was to be found in the apostolic mission.*[43]

The Resurrection of Christ is the revelatory aspect of the one salvific Paschal Event (Passion-Death-Resurrection-Ascension) that is essentially vindicative and missionary in character. The Resurrection of Jesus, therefore, is not to be looked upon as a separate occurrence, a resumption of life after death, which provides an apologetic proof for his life and deeds, and which subsequently gives support and validity to a Christian belief in being saved by Christ's death on the Cross. "If Jesus is victorious *over* death, it is first of all because he is victorious *in* his death."[44]

The Resurrection reveals the eschatological authenticity of the

Kingdom that Jesus proclaimed during his whole ministry. God's ways, indeed, are not our ways. The Resurrection reverses the verdict of Jesus' trial by the legitimate civil and religious authorities.

> Among the authors of the New Testament, Jn particularly has brought out this aspect of the resurrection: the glorification of Jesus means that the Spirit will show how wrong the world was: actually the world took side against God himself by not believing in Jesus; he will show that Jesus is right since God has raised him up and taken him into his glory. Thus will be fulfilled the eschatological judgment in which God triumphs and the Prince of the world is defeated (Jn 16:8-11).[45]

Furthermore, the world's view of reality comes into question as what it calls death is revealed to be really life and what it considers to be life is death. "The Jesus who preached the Good News and gave the signs of man's liberation in his work, life and death remains a living reality."[46] It is this living presence that gives power and authority to the gospel mandate:

> "Go forth therefore and make all nations my disciples. . . . And be assured, I am with you always, to the end of time."(Mt 28:19-20, *NEB*)

2. *Evangelization and the Apostolic Community*

The power and dynamism of Christ's risen presence were soon to be experienced by his apostles and disciples in the Pentecost event. The arrival of the Holy Spirit promised by Jesus (cf. Jn 14:16, 26, 15:26, 16-17, 12-15) brought New Life, courage and boldness to the group of disciples, "making them witnesses not only in Jerusalem but throughout Judea and Samaria and indeed to the ends of the earth" (Acts 1:8). The history of the early Church's mission of evangelization begins here with the outpouring of the Spirit. Once again the theme of Good News resounds as Peter filled with the Holy Spirit quotes David in Ps 16:

> "I saw the Lord before me always,
> for with him at my right hand nothing can shake me.
> So my heart was glad
> and my tongue cried out with joy,
> my body, too, will rest in hope
> that you will not abandon my soul to Hades
> nor allow your holy one to experience corruption."
>
> (Acts 2:25-27)

Luke in the book of Acts gives us an overall view of the methods and process of evangelization in the apostolic community of the early post-Resurrection period. Receiving the Spirit is indispensable for continuing Christ's mission of proclaiming the Good News of the Kingdom as John, too, demonstrates well in his account of Christ's missionary mandate: " 'As the Father sent me, so I am sending you.' After saying this he breathed upon them and said: 'Receive the Holy Spirit' " (Jn 20:21-22). Luke describes the unique religious experience associated with the receiving of this gift in Acts 2:1-13. "A powerful wind from heaven" and "tongues of fire" symbolize this new theophany. The universalism of the gift of the Spirit is indicated by "the gift of speech" making the receiver capable of speaking "foreign languages." To the eyes of passersby, the lively spontaneity and enthusiasm engendered by this gift of the Spirit took on the appearance of inebriation.

Peter then addresses the crowd. This speech along with five others attributed to Peter in the book of Acts are all substantially the same in structure and content; there is no real theological development from one to the other (cf. 2:14-40; 3:12-26; 4:8-12; 5:29-32; 10:34-43). They follow the basic outline of Jesus' proclamation in Mk 1:14-15:

> The prophecies are fulfilled; God has shown his mighty works. The Messiah has come; he has been exalted to the right hand of God; he has given the Spirit, which according to the prophets, should come "in the last days" (Joel 2:28-32). The kerygma concluded with an appeal to conversion, the offer of forgiveness and of the Holy Spirit, and the promise of salvation, that is, "the life of the Age to Come" to those who enter the elect community.[47]

The material in the book of Acts appears to divide the early Church's efforts of evangelization into six stages of territorial expansion:

1. 1:1-6:7 —the Jerusalem Church;
2. 6:8-9:31 —the Church spreading through Judea, Galilee and Samaria with the conversion of Saul in Damascus;
3. 9:32-12:24 —the Church among the Gentiles with its foundation in Antioch;
4. 12:25-16:5 —Paul's missionary journey into Asia Minor;
5. 16:6-19:20 —extension of the Church to the political and cultural centers of Greece and Macedonia;
6. 19:21-28:31 —the Church arrives in the imperial capital of Rome.[48]

In the extension of its missionary task, the action of the Holy Spirit is constantly evident as conflicts, prejudices and exclusivistic tendencies are overcome in the early Christian community. The Spirit, too, gave shape to the early Church as its members "remained faithful to the teaching of the apostles, to the brotherhood, to the breaking of bread and to the prayers" (Acts 2:42).

Receiving the Spirit of the risen Christ, the disciples were brought together in a communion of life, which marked a sharing in the intimate life of the Trinity. This communitarian life of love and fellowship itself constituted an effective means of evangelization as it mirrored the fruits of Jesus' prayer: "Father, may they be one in us, as you are in me and I am in you, so that the world may believe it was you who sent me" (Jn 17:21).

Important to our understanding of the theology of mission and evangelization in this earliest stage of the infant Church is Luke's text of Acts 13:1-3:

> In the Church at Antioch the following were prophets and teachers: Barnabas, Simeon called Niger, and Lucius of Cyrene, Manaen, who had been brought up with Herod the tetrarch, and Saul. One day while they were offering worship to the Lord and keeping a fast, the Holy Spirit said "I want Barnabas and Saul set apart for the work to which I have called them." So it was that after fasting and prayer they laid their hands on them and sent them off.

From this text the primacy accorded the pneumatic, ecclesial and charismatic dimensions of missionary work comes to light. As Conzelmann describes it: "The Spirit dwells in the Church and is imparted through its means of grace and its office bearers."[49] Central in Luke's purpose is the ecclesial aspect. Legrand emphasizes this point when he writes: "From the outset, Luke wants to make it clear that Paul is not a free lancer experimenting on his own under the lone guidance of the Spirit. This guidance of the Spirit has an ecclesial dimension."[50]

The basic elements of an early apostolic ecclesiology are found here. The Church is the community of the Spirit, gathered together in "offering worship ('leitourgein') to the Lord." The five "prophets and teachers" named in v. 1 are apparently the governing body of the Antiochian Church. Legrand adds: "But precisely this governing body is made up of charismatic figures. It is not basically an administrative but a prophetical body, entrusted with the Word of God, open to the action of the Spirit."[51] The "call" of the Spirit (in the sense of a divine appointment) initiates the "work" of evangelization, while the Church through the rite of imparting the Spirit in the "laying upon of hands" sends forth her missionaries.

Finally, the terms "apostle" and "witness" are also important concepts in Luke's ecclesiology and theology of evangelization. The designation "apostle" (from "apostellein," meaning "to send as one's messenger") was originally restricted to the Eleven and Matthias (Acts 1:26) who alone fulfilled the requirements described by Luke in Acts 1:21-22, but later came to be used in a more generic sense in Pauline terminology. The concept of "witness" and its implications for evangelization will be developed below in a review of Johannine theology. In summing up the mission of evangelization in the apostolic period—a mission that was not at all extraneous to the early Christian community but that in fact brought it to a progressive realization of its own essential nature as church—Pathrapankal concludes:

> It was Jesus' intention to train a group of men who had learned in apprenticeship to him how to accept the rule of God for themselves, and how to extend it to their neighbours at home and abroad, in a spirit of service by serving them in love and with a genuine understanding of their concrete situations. Jesus saw his immediate task as that of creating such a community within Israel. He had the faith and conviction that it would transform the life of his own people, and that a transformed Israel would transform the nations of the world, thus bringing about God's plan to save the whole world, a plan God had inaugurated in the call of Abraham (Gen 12:1-3) and the election of Israel.[52]

E. A PAULINE THEOLOGY OF EVANGELIZATION

Paul bears the distinction of being the earliest Christian theologian. His letters, although by no means resembling organized theological treatises, do contain the basic elements of what can be called a distinctively Pauline theology of the saving Mystery as revealed in the Christ event. Most of Paul's letters antedate the four gospel accounts, and are, therefore, basically independent of the historical traditions of these later narratives. Central to Paul's gospel is his unique experience of the risen Lord whom he encountered on the road to Damascus (Acts 9:3-6). It was on the basis of this experience that he could say, "I am an apostle and I have seen Jesus the Lord" (1 Cor 9:1) though he would not hesitate to admit, "I am the least of the apostles; in fact, since I persecuted the Church of God, I hardly deserve the name apostle; but by God's grace I am what I am" (1 Cor 15:9-10).

1. *Paul's Gospel*

Paul uses the word "gospel" some fifty-four times in his letters (plus six times in the Pastorals), which is more than any other writer in the New Testament. Paul in his writings even refers to "my gospel" (Rom 2:16, 16:25, 2 Tim 2:8). By this he is not referring to a different gospel (cf. Gal 1:7), but rather to the manner in which he received it through a special revelation. Paul's "kerygma" finds its source in his personal encounter with the risen Lord and not in an account of the words and deeds of the pre-Paschal Christ. "Gospel" in Paul's writings more commonly refers to the *content* of his message, although he does at times employ the word to designate the activity of evangelizing. And the content of his message is no longer the "kingdom of God," but "the gospel of Christ" (1 Thes 3:2; Gal 1:7; Phil 1:27; etc.), "the gospel of our Lord Jesus" (2 Thes 1:8), or "the gospel of his Son" (Rom 1:9).

The Good News that Paul proclaims, nevertheless, "is not a mere series of revealed propositions about Christ that men must intellectually apprehend and assent to. Rather it is 'the power of God,' it is a force that is communicated to men. God exercised this power in the history of Israel, and the same power is now revealed in the Gospel."[53] Thus he writes in Rom 1:16-17:

> For I am not ashamed of the Good News: it is the power of God saving all who have faith—Jews first, but Greeks as well —since this is what reveals the justice of God to us: it shows how faith leads to faith, or as scripture says: *The upright man finds life through faith.*

And this power of the Gospel is associated with the Holy Spirit (1 Thes 1:5-6), "the pledge of our inheritance which brings freedom for those God has taken for his own" (Eph 1:14).

The Good News that Paul proclaims as "its herald, its apostle and its teacher" (2 Tim 1:10) is something that he first of all "received" as tradition, which he then in turn "hands down." His use of specific Greek terms for "to receive" and "to hand down" comprise the technical vocabulary of tradition, which parallels the rabbinical schools. It is with these same technical words that he introduces his gospel resume in 1 Cor 15:3-5:

> Well, then, in the first place, I taught you what I had been

taught myself, namely that Christ died for our sins, in accordance with the scriptures; that he was buried; and that he was
raised to life on the third day, in accordance with the scriptures; that he appeared to Cephas and secondly to the Twelve.

And in Gal 1:8 he calls down a curse upon anyone who would teach a
different gospel. With regard to Paul's role as herald, apostle and teacher of this Gospel, it becomes evident that

. . . he considered himself destined from his mother's womb
for this task (Gal 1:15; Rom 1:1; 1 Cor 1:17) and "entrusted"
with the gospel as with some prized possession (1 Thes 2:4; Gal
2:7). He became its "servant" (Col 1:23; cf. Eph 3:7) and felt a
"compulsion" (1 Cor 9:16) to proclaim it. He looked on his
preaching of it as a cultic, priestly act offered to God (Rom
1:9; 15:16). He was never ashamed of it (Rom 1:16); rather,
even imprisonment because of it was for him a favor (Phil 1:7,
16).[54]

2. *The Christocentrism of the Gospel Mystery*

For Paul, Jesus Christ is the Gospel: "For it is not ourselves that
we are preaching, but Christ Jesus as Lord" (2 Cor 4:5). And the Gospel
is "the message which was a mystery hidden for generations and centuries and has now been revealed to his saints. . . . The mystery is
Christ among you, your hope of glory" (Col 1:26-27). The Good News
in Paul, then, takes on the nature of revelation. It is the "mysterion"
(the "mystery" or "secret") now revealed; it adds an eschatological
nuance to the "gospel." The "mystery of Christ" for Paul, presupposing
the Jewish apocalyptic literature, involves creation, the history of the
world, and the eschaton, which are all now seen as embraced in the Father's magnificent plan of salvation for all the world (Eph 1:3-14).

The gradual unfolding of the Mystery begins with creation. "Ever
since God created the world his everlasting power and deity—however
invisible—have been there for the mind to see in the things he has
made," (Rom 1:20). But peoples "refuse to honour him as God or to
thank him" (v. 21). "Jews and Greeks are all under sin's dominion"
(3:10): the Jews for breaking the Law (2:23) and the pagans for not
obeying "the substance of the Law engraved on their hearts" (2:15). But
now the Good News of God's saving justice is proclaimed:

God's justice that was made known through the Law and
the Prophets has now been revealed outside the Law, since it is

the same justice of God that comes through faith to everyone, Jew and pagan alike, who believes in Jesus Christ. Both Jew and pagan sinned and forfeited God's glory [cf. 2 Cor 4:6— "the glory" now revealed "on the face of Christ"], and both are justified through the free gift of his grace by being redeemed in Christ Jesus who was appointed by God to sacrifice his life so as to win salvation through faith. In this way God makes his justice known; first, for the past, when sins went unpunished because he held his hand, then, for the present age, by showing positively that he is just, and that he justifies everyone who believes in Jesus. (Rom 3:21-26)

The Good News resounds as God's justice is made known in that "now after many falls comes grace with its verdict of aquittal" (Rom 5:16). "What is revealed in Christ is not God's vindictive justice; rather this term ("diakaiosune theou") refers to his salvific righteousness, a quality by which God manifests his faithfulness ("emet"), love ("hesed") and fidelity in acquitting, vindicating and accepting his people."[55] It is this firm belief and conviction that makes Paul cry out to the Philippians: "Rejoice in the Lord always; again I will say, Rejoice" (Phil 4:4— RSV).

Paul's reason for rejoicing is found in the Paschal Mystery, which reveals the extent of God's love for us, because "what proves that God loves us is that Christ died for us while we were still sinners" (Rom 5:8; cf. Eph 2:4-6). It is thus that "the language of the cross may be illogical to those who are not on the way to salvation, but those of us who are on the way see it as God's power to save" (1 Cor 1:18). Furthermore, there is cause for rejoicing in that "those who are on the way" to salvation, that is, those of us who have faith (cf. Rom 5:2), who have been "baptized in Christ Jesus, went into the tomb with him and joined him in death, so that as Christ was raised from the dead by the Father's glory, we too might live a new life" (Rom 6:4). Thus, "for anyone who is in Christ ["in Christ"—with "in the Lord," "in Him"—occurs 165 times in Paul's letters, designating the dynamic, ontological and eschatological status of the believer, in which Christ and the Christian enjoy as it were a symbiosis, a being together], there is a new creation; the old creation has gone, and now a new one is here. It is all God's work" (2 Cor 5:17).

3. *The Good News of Reconciliation and Freedom*

This "free gift of his grace" (Rom 3:24) which declares our acquittal and makes us a new creation in Christ is all God's doing. "It was God who reconciled us to himself through Christ and gave us the work of handing on the message of reconciliation" (2 Cor 5:18). Through "reconciliation" we once again share friendship and communion of life with God. "In a religious sense this word denotes the return of man to God's favour and intimacy after a long period of estrangement and rebellion through sin and transgression."[56] Thus, "God wanted . . . all things to be reconciled through him and for him, everything in heaven and everything on earth, when he made his peace by his death on the cross" (Col 1:20).

The pledge of God's love and friendship is the gift of the Spirit that has been poured into our hearts (cf. Rom 5:5). Through faith and baptism, the Christian receives the Spirit (Gal 3:2, 14 and 1 Cor 6:10), which is the "Spirit of Christ" (Rom 8:9; Phil 1:19; Gal 4:6). Through his reconciliation in Christ and the gift of the Spirit, the Christian believer becomes a "son of God" (Rom 8:14). "The proof that you are sons is that God has sent the Spirit of his Son into our hearts, the Spirit that cries, 'Abba, Father,' and it is this that makes you a son, you are not a slave anymore" (Gal 4:6-7; cf. Eph 1:14). As "sons" we are set free from the Law, sin and death (cf. Rom 8:1ff.). Thus it is with joy and confidence again that Paul writes to the Galatians: "When Christ freed us, he meant us to remain free. Stand firm, therefore, and do not submit to the yoke of slavery again" (5:1).

The Christian is now liberated from the Mosaic Law and from all the consequences that failure to keep it implied. Yet, Christian freedom cannot be equated with antinomian or libertine existence in which everyone can do whatever he or she feels like doing (cf. 1 Cor 6:12). Rather, the Love that is revealed in Jesus Christ becomes the Law of the Spirit, or the Law of Christ (Gal 6:2). It is not a new legal code, for "if you are led by the Spirit, no law can touch you" (Gal 5:18), but rather "the new inner force, source and guide of life by which the spiritual man lives; it is an ontological principle of vitality, whence springs the love which is the external manifestation of the internal principle and guiding force of the Christian's entire ethical conduct."[57] It is the Law of Love by which we "serve one another" (Gal 5:13) and "carry each other's troubles" (Gal 6:2; cf. Col 1:24).

For Paul, then, the "gospel of Christ" is the Good News of reconciliation and freedom. It is the gift of the Spirit, which makes us "sons of God," and frees us from the Law of sin and death. In the Spirit, too, we form one body, the Church (cf. 1 Cor 12:27-28) with Christ as its Head (Eph 5:23); and to this body the Spirit gives a variety of gifts (cf. 1 Cor 12:4ff). And the fruits the Spirit brings are these: "love, joy, peace, patience, kindness, goodness, trustfulness, gentleness and self-control" (Gal 5:22). The reconciliation and freedom which Christ effected through his Paschal Mystery are subsequently ecclesial—the Church is the "fullness" of the new creation (Eph 1:23)—universal and cosmic in scope and under the guidance of the Spirit (cf. Col 1:20; Rom 8:20-27).

Thus Paul's proclamation of the gospel mystery develops to the point where he sees it as the Good News of the "hidden plan" which God "so kindly made in Christ from the beginning to act upon when the times had run their course to the end: that he would bring everything together under Christ, as head (the "anacephalaeosis"), everything in the heavens and everything on earth" (Eph 1:9-10). It is finally reconciliation itself which becomes the *raison d'être* of proclaiming the gospel message, for as he writes to the Church at Corinth: "God in Christ was reconciling the world to himself, not holding men's faults against them, and he has entrusted to us the news that they are reconciled. So we are ambassadors for Christ" (2 Cor 5:19-20).

4. *Paul's Invitation to Faith and On-going Conversion*

Paul's letters were all addressed to believers who had already been converted to the Gospel of Christ. Paul's invitation to them is in a sense to become what they already are, namely, "new creatures" in Christ (Gal 6:15). The basis for Paul's invitation "to go on making ever greater progress" (1 Thes 4:10) is the gospel mystery into which they have been inserted at their baptism (Rom 6:1ff; Col 3:3-4): "let your behavior change modelled by your new mind" (Rom 12:2). Our growth in Christ depends on our living according to "the life of Christ who lives in (us)" (Gal 2:20; cf. Phil 1:21); "you must be rooted in him and build on him and held firm by the faith you have been taught, and full of thanksgiving" (Col 2:7). God intended us "to become true images of his Son" (Rom 8:29); "and you have put on a new self which will progress towards true knowledge the more it is renewed in the image of its creator" (Col 3:10). In a like manner Paul urges the Ephesians to continuing conversion: "You must give up your old way of life. . . . Your mind must be renewed by a spiritual revolution so that you can put on the new self that has been created in God's way, in the goodness and holiness of the truth" (Eph 4:22-24).

Paul's exhortations, then, "to lead a life worthy of your vocation" (Eph 4:1) arise from the Mystery of Christ in which we have been given New Life. In Christ we are members of his Body, the Church. "If we live by the truth and in love, we shall grow in all ways into Christ, who is the head . . ." (Eph 4:15). Since, too, in Christ we share in the mystery of his reconciliation and peace, Paul writes to the Church at Corinth, after having experienced a distressing situation in their regard (cf. 2 Cor 2:1ff.), "the appeal that we make in Christ's name is: be reconciled to God . . . we beg you once again not to neglect the grace of God that you have received" (5:20; 6:1). It is Paul's existential and concrete belief and firm conviction in the Mystery of Christ that lead him to pray to the Father for the Church at Ephesus' continual growth in its knowledge and awareness of the *extent* of this Mystery which is summed up in his prayer:

> Out of his infinite glory, may he give you the power through his Spirit for your hidden self to grow strong, so that Christ may live in your hearts through faith, and then planted in love and built on love, you will with all the saints have strength to grasp the breadth and the length, the height and the depth; until, knowing the love of Christ, which is beyond all knowledge, you are filled with the utter fullness of God.
>
> Glory be to him whose power, working in us, can do infinitely more than we can ask or imagine; glory be to him from generation to generation in the Church and in Christ Jesus forever and ever. Amen. (Eph 3:16-21)

To get some idea of Paul's methodology in primary evangelization, that is, his proclaiming the Good News to nonbelievers who have not yet heard of the Gospel, one must turn to Luke's account in the book of Acts. Luke preserves two such speeches: one at Antioch of Pisidia (Acts 13:16-41) and the other at Athens (Acts 17:22-31). Being Lucan interpretations, there arises some doubt as to how faithful to Paul they are in their approach. The one at Antioch addressed to the Jews of the Diaspora contains some distinctively Pauline themes, especially the reference to justification by faith (vv. 38-39). At Antioch, Paul gives a quick summary of God's intervention in Jewish history finishing with the Paschal Event of Christ, adding that "it is through him the forgiveness of your sins is proclaimed" (v. 38), and in an invitational sort of warning he quotes the prophet (Hab 1:5), "I am doing something in your own days that you would not believe if you were told of it" (v. 41).

At Athens, Paul tries a more philosophical, and definitely less successful, approach to the proclamation of the Good News while addressing the Council of the Areopagus. He issues a call to repentance (v. 31) before mentioning the Resurrection, but "at this mention of rising from the dead, some of them burst out laughing; others said, 'We would like to hear you talk about this again.' After that Paul left them, but there were some who attached themselves to him and became believers" (vv. 32-34). Paul's conviction and support for such primary evangelization find expression in his letter to the Romans, when, referring to a Scripture passage that says: "Everyone who invokes the name of the Lord will be saved" (10:13), he asks, "How could they invoke one in whom they had no faith? And how could they have faith in one they never heard of? And how hear without someone to spread the news? And how could anyone spread the news without a commission to do so? And that is what Scripture affirms: 'How welcome are the feet of messengers of good news' " (10:14-15).

F. THE JOHANNINE CONCEPT OF EVANGELIZATION

Although the concept of evangelization in the Johannine writings is still a much-debated topic—as is even the author's awareness of evangelization as an ecclesial task—it is clear that the Scripture scholars themselves are divided according to whether or not they view evangelization as the essential, constitutive mission of the Church, or as just one of the Church's many tasks. Matthew Vellanickal proposes that the Johannine concept of evangelization can best be approached through a comparison of vocabulary between the author of John and other New Testament writings:[58]

OTHER NEW TESTAMENT WRITINGS	JOHN: JN + 1 JN
Process of evangelization	
"paradidomi" (transmit)	"didomi" (give) 76+7
"kerusso" (preach)	"laleo" (speak) 60+3
"euaggelizomai" (evangelize)	"lego" (say) 266+6
"kataggello" (proclaim)	"martureo" (witness) 33+10
"diagello" (proclaim)	"krazo" (cry) 4
	"apaggello" (announce) 1
	"didasko" (teach) 9+3
	"anagello" (show) 4+1
	"apaggello" (announce) 1+2
Object of evangelization	
"euggelion" (Gospel)	"aggelia" (message) 2
	"aletheia" (truth) 25+20
	"logos" (word) 40+7
"kerygma" (preaching)	"rema" (word) 12
	"marturia" (witness) 14
Recipient of evangelization	
"paralambano" (receive)	"lambano" (receive) 46+6
	"akouo" (hear) 58+16
	"horao" (see) 31+8

Evident from a glance is the fact that the Johannine terminology is more general and less technical in nature. This actuality corresponds to the particular *sitz-im-leben* from which these writings arose—a kind of life situation which greatly influenced the development of specific views on the nature of the process of evangelization. The choice of this more general vocabulary quite naturally then gave expression to an enriched theological meaning. The process of evangelization in the Johannine works, as will be demonstrated, is integrally connected with the very essence of the Christian mysteries of Revelation, the Incarnation and the Church.

Parallel to Paul's rather factual resume of the gospel tradition in 1 Cor 15:1-4, one finds the following more personal and experiential summary in 1 Jn 1:1-3:

> Something which has existed since the beginning,
> that we have heard,
> and we have seen with our own eyes;
> that we have watched
> and touched with our hands:
> the Word, who is life—[lit., "the word of life"]
> this is our subject.
> That life was made visible:
> we saw it and are giving testimony,
> telling you of the eternal life
> which was with the Father and has been made visible to us.
> What we have seen and heard
> we are telling you
> so that you may be in union [lit., "fellowship"] with us,
> as we are in union
> with the Father
> and with his Son Jesus Christ.
> We are writing this to you to make your own joy complete.

At first it seems that the author of this epistle is reechoing Jn 1:1 ("In the beginning"), in v. 1, but in this instance one reads "since the beginning" rather than the ·"in the beginning" of the gospel account. So, rather than suggesting creation and the preexistence of Christ, the emphasis here is on "something . . . that we have heard . . . seen . . . watched . . . touched," namely, the revelation of God, that is "the eternal life which was with the Father and has been made visible to us." Unlike Jn 1:1, where the author intends to personify "word," the author here clearly wants to personify "life."

Jesus himself does not seem to be the ultimate origin of this process as if he were the unique object of this "seeing" and "hearing". He himself is presented as the subject of this process, namely, as the one who "sees" and "hears" the Father and "testifies" to it.[59]

Jn 3:31-32 reads: "He who comes from above . . . bears witness to the things he has seen and heard." Thus, the Johannine process of evangelization is not to be construed as a set of facts, but rather as a testimony to the Eternal Life, the fullness of the divine Mystery which reveals itself in the incarnate Word. The original conclusion of the Gospel According to John states: "These are recorded so that you may believe that Jesus is the Christ, the Son of God, and that believing this you might have *life* through his name" (20:31).

1. *The Word*

In John, the Word signifies the specific content of evangelization. "In the OT the word of God is God's manifestation, the revelation of himself, whether in creation, in deeds of power and grace, or in prophecy. All of these strains of thought are taken up by Jn, who shows that Christ the Incarnate Word, is the ultimate and complete revelation of God."[60] With the recognition that the Word has become flesh, the incredible has taken place. Man, striving and unable to reach the divine, has this gap bridged by the Incarnation. "Furthermore, the revelation of God is not to be found in the abstract contemplation of truths, but in the example and imitation of a life that has been led, the life of the Son of Man (Jn 12:23-26). In the life of the Son of Man, the glory of God has been revealed."[61]

"Your Word is truth" (Jn 17:17; cf. 1 Jn 1:8 and 10, Jn 8:31-32). According to R. E. Brown, "The Gr. 'aletheia' has the basic meaning of non-concealment; it describes what is unveiled."[62] In the Old Testament, "truth" can either refer to a moral element or serve as a synonym of *wisdom*; hence, "truth" can be associated with "mystery" and denote the revelation of God's hidden plan (cf. Wis 6:22). Thus, the precise reason Jesus came into the world was to bear witness to the Truth (Jn 18:37). Jesus and the Truth are identified (Jn 14:6), and it is this truth that is contrasted to the Law in Jn 1:17—"though the Law was given through Moses, grace and truth come through Jesus Christ."

"The word of life" (cf. 1 Jn 1:1-3) also was made visible in Jesus Christ. Jesus is "the life" (Jn 11:25, 14:6; Rev 1:18); "he is the divine Word spoken with the purpose of giving eternal life to men (1:4; 1 Jn 1:1-2) and it is for this purpose that the Son has come among men

(10:10; 1 Jn 4:9). . . . Belief in him is the only way in which men can receive God's life (3:16; 20:31)."[63] This Life is communicated to us through the Spirit. As Yahweh breathes his spirit or breath to give us natural life (Gen 2:7), so Jesus gives Eternal Life by breathing forth the Spirit upon his disciples (Jn 20:22). This Eternal Life is the very life by which God himself lives; it is qualitatively different from natural life. Death cannot destroy it (Jn 11:26); its only enemy is sin (1 Jn 3:15). This divine life is the object of Revelation—the content of Truth.

Jesus, the Word of Life and the Truth, is preeminently the revelation of God's love. No other New Testament author lays so great a stress on the virtue of love. "God's love is the motive of sending the Son into the world. But more than a motive, love is revelation itself. Even as God is love (1 Jn 4:16), Jesus is the incarnation of the divine love for man, embodying in himself this relation willed by God."[64] As in Paul (cf. Rom. 5:8), so, too, for John the extent of God's love finds its supreme revelation on the Cross: "A man can have no greater love than to lay down his life for his friends. You are my friends" (Jn 15:13-14; cf. 1 Jn 3:16). The kenotic nature of this love is shown when John begins his Passion account ("The Book of Glory"—chap. 13:1-20) with Jesus' washing the feet of his disciples. As Brown observes: "Verses 14-17 state explicitly that what Jesus did in the washing of the feet was an example of self-sacrificing humility to be imitated by them. . . . Thus, in the footwashing, Jesus humiliates himself and takes on the form of a slave."[65] It seems very likely here that the Johannine author intended to create a definite parallel with Paul's "kenosis" hymn of Phil 2:5-11. Jesus, the Word of Life and the Truth, bears witness to the extent of the Father's love, and his disciples are invited and encouraged "to do the truth" (Jn 3:21; 1 Jn 3:19). The "Word" and "Truth" in John is not simply the object of verbal preaching; rather it is the interior source and essential moral principle of the Life that we share with, in and through Jesus Christ, the Word of Life.

2. *Mission*

The concept of "mission" or "being sent" is integral to Johannine theology. In John, Jesus, the Spirit, and the Apostles are all "sent."

Jesus, as "the one who is sent" by the Father, is a constant theme in John, occurring some forty times in the gospel account alone.

All the redemptive work which Jesus has accomplished is nothing else than the fulfillment of the commission which he has received from the Father. For, Jesus came "to do the will of him who sent him" (Jn 4:34; 6:38f). He came to accomplish the work of his Father (Jn 9:4) and to speak what he had learned from him (Jn 8:26). What he teaches is not his own but the teaching of the Father who sent him (Jn 7:16) and he speaks whatever the Father has commanded him to say (Jn 12:49; 14:24). To believe in him is to believe in the Father who has sent him (12:44). He who sees him, sees him who sent him (12:45). Eternal life consists in knowing the only true God and him whom he has sent (17:3). The object of faith is the union of the Son with the Father (11:42; 17:8, 21, 25). In John the sending of the Son and his work on earth are the ultimate proof of God's love for us (3:16; 1 Jn 4:9f., 14).[66]

The experience of God as Father is central to Johannine theology (the name "Father" for God occurs 107 times in Jn + 12 times in 1 Jn). Jesus is the Mediator and missionary sent by the Father. Jesus employs two metaphors—"food" and "harvest"—to demonstrate the essential missionary character of his whole life from the Incarnation to his death and resurrection. "My food is to do the will of the one who sent me, and to complete his work" (Jn 4:34). And in Mt 9:37f. the "harvest" refers to the missionary activity of Jesus and the Apostles. In his concrete person, "gospel" and "missionary" merge into a dynamic unity as Jesus' life-mission is to reveal the Good News of the Father's love by bringing us the fullness of Life (Jn 10:10).

Jesus "sends" the Apostles, and their mission is intimately one with his—"As the Father sent me so am I sending you" (Jn 20:21)—just as he is one with the Father, and the Father and he desire to be one with them "so that the world may believe it was you who sent me" (Jn 17:21). In John's gospel the Holy Spirit is also "sent"; "the Holy Spirit, whom the Father will send in my name will teach you everything" (Jn 14:26), and "he will be my witness" (Jn 15:26). "Thus the Holy Spirit makes present in the apostles the life of the Father revealed and communicated in Christ . . . [and] the missionary existence of Christ is continued in the missionary existence of the apostles, of the believers and of the Church—through the Life of the Spirit."[67]

3. Witnessing: The "Spirit of Truth" and the Church

The word "marturein" (witnessing) becomes a full-fledged theological concept in John to designate the process of evangelization. The noun "witness" is found earlier in Christ's missionary mandate of Lk 24:48 and is carried over into the book of Acts: "You will receive power when the Holy Spirit comes to you, and then you will be my witnesses" (1:8). Luke's primary concern is proclaiming the story of Jesus and his resur-

rection from the firsthand knowledge of a personal encounter with the
risen Lord (cf. Acts 1:22; 10:39; and 2:32; 3:15 etc.). In John, witnessing
leaves the realm of historical facts and pertains simply to the person of
Christ and its significance.

> For an individual to discharge the function of witnessing
> to Jesus, acquaintance with the historical Jesus is not neces-
> sary. This is quite clear from 1 Jn 5:10 where it is said that he
> who believes in the Son of God has in himself God's testimony
> and the knowledge he thus has of Jesus' person and signifi-
> cance will enable him to function as a witness to Christ.[68]

One of the main words in John for describing evangelization is "lalein"
(to speak). Referring etymologically to the babbling and chattering especially of little children, it connotes the idea of intimacy. John often uses
it as a parallel to "marturein." When used by Jesus it is a "speaking," a
revelatory action, that demands a faith response (e.g., Jn 3:11, 34; 8:12;
9:37, etc.). All this points to the fact that "evangelization for John is no
mere verbal communication of the Good News but a sharing of the experience of God."[69]

The Father is the real subject of witness to Jesus in the Johannine
writings. In Jn 8:18, Jesus says: "I may be testifying on my own behalf,
but the Father who sent me is my witness, too" (cf. also Jn 3:11; 8:38;
12:49-50). The testimony of Jesus' works is also a testimony of the Father (Jn 5:36). The Father continues his testimony to Jesus down
through the ages in the sacramental activity of the Church which was directly and symbolically prefigured in those works. For the sacraments
themselves through the presence of the Spirit continue the Father's salvific work accomplished in Christ's Paschal Mystery. The Father also
witnesses to Jesus by working mysteriously within the hearts of men and
women urging them to believe in Jesus.

Receiving the Holy Spirit, as already mentioned above when referring to Acts 1:8, is essential to becoming a witness in the Lucan concept
of the term. So, in John, the Apostles' mission is "to continue the Son's
mission, and this requires that the Son should be present to them during
the mission, just as the Father had to be present to the Son during his
mission. This becomes possible only through the gift (Jn 20:22) whom
the Father sends in Jesus' name (Jn 14:26) and whom Jesus himself
sends (Jn 15:26)."[70] But in the Johannine theology of evangelization, the
Spirit assumes a particular role as the "Spirit of Truth" (cf. Jn 14:17,
15:26, 16:13; 1 Jn 4:6). He is the Paraclete whose task it is to bear witness

on Jesus' behalf (Jn 16:26). He continues Jesus' mission of revealing the Eternal Life which was with the Father from the beginning (cf. 1 Jn 1:1-3), and he "will remind you of all I have said to you" (Jn 14:26). As Brown describes it:

> . . . the one whom John calls "another Paraclete" is another Jesus. Since the Paraclete can come only when Jesus departs, the Paraclete is the presence of Jesus when Jesus is absent. Jesus' promises to dwell within his disciples are fulfilled in the Paraclete. It is no accident that the first passage containing Jesus' promise of the Paraclete (14:16-17) is followed immediately by the verse which says "I am coming back to you."[71]

The Paraclete's witness, however, is invisible (Jn 14:17). It is only through the witness of the disciples that his presence is made known. "The witness of the Spirit and the witness of the disciples stand in relation to each other much in the same way as the witness of the Father is related to the witness of the Son."[72] This introduces the communitarian and ecclesial element of witness in John, to which "the life of fellowship" in 1 Jn 1:1-3 obviously refers.[73] The "Spirit of Truth" is also the Spirit of Love (cf. 1 Jn 3:23-24; 4:12-13). By keeping Christ's commandment to love one another just as he has loved us, the world will come to know we are his disciples (Jn 13:34-35), and the community of life we share in union with the Father and the Son becomes evangelization (Jn 17:21). Thus, it must be said that the Church's main task lies in its becoming a credible witness and sign of Christ's presence with us yet. This it accomplishes only by making visible and incarnate in the world the life of kenotic love that we, as believers, share.

> In Jn, evangelization is inseparably related to the existence of the Church. This is because of the very nature of evangelization which according to John is the sharing of the experience of the Word of life and thus necessarily results in a life of fellowship and communion.[74]

SUMMARY

From the prophetic tradition of the Old Testament, the proclamation of "glad tidings" becomes the context of God's self-revelation and intervention in human history. Associated with Messianic expectations, these "glad tidings" ring out peace, happiness and salvation. Israel sees herself having a particular role to fulfill as a "light to the nations," becoming a living sign and witness to the holiness of God so that all the nations will come to acknowledge Yahweh as God.

In keeping with this prophetic tradition, after the arrest and imprisonment of John the Baptist, Jesus appears in Galilee proclaiming: "The time is fulfilled. The Kingdom of God is at hand. Repent, and believe the Good News" (Mk 1:15). The time ("kairos") is now. The long-awaited, direct intervention of God announced by all the prophets has arrived. The Kingdom of God is inaugurated as his power and sovereignty erupt in human history. Things almost too unbelievable to be true are about to occur. Men and women are challenged to do an about-face and to begin to look at reality in a new way. They are invited to forego all human securities and to put their complete faith and trust in this revolutionary pattern of living and thinking proposed by Jesus.

In the accounts of the Evangelists this itinerant rabbi proclaims the Good News by his words, deeds and the very style of his life. His parables announce to those who have ears to hear the unpredictability and utter extravagance of his Father's love for us. His miracles and exorcisms convey the message and the power of this liberating and healing love. His life itself incarnates the message as it finds its supreme expression on the Cross, proclaiming there to all the world the *extent* and lengths to which God will go to prove his love.

The Good News cannot and does not end in death, but in the glory of a new creation. Through Christ's Paschal Mystery we are reconciled to God and are liberated from the Law of sin and death. The primal enemies of humankind have lost their sway in the victory of Christ's Resurrection. Christ is alive. His risen presence gives power and authority to his final mandate: "Go forth therefore and make all nations my disciples . . . And be assured, I am with you always, to the end of time" (Mt 28:19-20).

At Pentecost the apostolic community receives power from on High in the outpouring of the Holy Spirit. Filled with new boldness and enthusiasm, the Apostles continue the mission of Christ by becoming his witnesses to the ends of the earth. In the Spirit the community of believers grows and is strengthened as they "remained faithful to the teaching of the apostles, to the brotherhood, to the breaking of bread and to the prayers" (Acts 2:42).

The first theological reflection upon this unique event is found in the letters of Paul. His kerygma, however, finds its source in his personal encounter with the risen Lord on the road to Damascus and not in an account of the words and deeds of the pre-Paschal Jesus. For Paul the Gospel is "the power of God," the revelation of his hidden plan ("mysterion") which finds its fulfillment in the Paschal Mystery of Christ. The Good News rings out as "in Christ" the justice of God is made known and his verdict of acquittal is proclaimed. "In Christ" the believer becomes a "new creature" experiencing God's gift of reconciliation and the freedom of the children of God. The fruits of the Spirit—love, joy, peace, patience, kindness, goodness, fidelity, gentleness and self-control—make us into an ever more perfect image of the Son. The Spirit, too, pours forth his gifts upon the Church, the Body of Christ and the fullness of the new creation, as God's plan moves forward to its final universal and cosmic completion in the "anacephalaeosis" of Christ. And thus, Paul's invitation to believers is to become ever more fully what they already are, namely, "new creatures" in Christ.

The gospel mystery finds enriched theological meaning in the Johannine Corpus, as Jesus becomes the subject of the process, the Word of Life who "comes from above" and "bears witness to the things he has seen and heard." Jesus himself is "the Way, the Truth and the Life" (Jn 14:6) who has become flesh to communicate this Eternal Life to us through the Spirit. The "Word" and the "Truth" is not simply the object of verbal preaching; rather, it is the interior source and essential moral principle of the life that we share with, in and through Jesus Christ, the Word of Life. Through faith and in the Spirit we become witnesses of Christ, as the life of love and fellowship we experience in union with the Father and the Son becomes evangelization. The process and mission of evangelization is inseparably related to the existence of the Church as she strives to become a more and more credible witness and sign of Christ's life and presence with us yet.

NOTES

1. Cf. Legrand, "Jesus and the Gospel," *GN&W*, 5.
2. Legrand, *GN&W*, 9-10.
3. Cf. *ibid.*, 10-11.
4. Quoted by Legrand in *GN&W*, 11.
5. For a discussion of this point, cf. Legrand, *GN&W*, 11-13. This section "B" and parts of section "C" are basically a summary of Legrand's exposition of these themes, pp. 11-45.
6. Cf. C.H. Dodd, "The Framework of the Gospel Narrative," in *New Testament Studies* (Manchester, 1953), 1-11.
7. Cf. Bultmann, *The History of the Synoptic Tradition* (Oxford, 1963), 126-151).
8. Legrand, *GN&W*, 13.
9. *Ibid.*, 14.
10. *Ibid.*, 16.
11. *Ibid.*, 17.
12. *Ibid.*, 18.

13. J. Guillet, *Jésus devant sa vie et sa mort* (Paris, 1971), 65-66, as quoted in Legrand, *GN&W*, 19.

14. Hünermann, "Reign of God," art. in K. Rahner *et al.*, eds., *Sacramentum Mundi* (New York, 1968) V 236. (Hereafter cited as *SM*.)

15. Legrand, *GN&W*, 20.

16. *Ibid.*, 22.

17. *Ibid.*

18. *Ibid.*, 24.

19. *Ibid.*

20. G. Friedrich, "euangelizomai," in G. Kittel, ed., *Theologisches Wörterbuch zum Neuen Testament* (Stuttgart, 1933ff.) Vol. 2, 727. (Hereafter cited as *TWNT*.)

21. Legrand, *GN&W*, 6.

22. W. Marxsen, *Mark the Evangelist* (Nashville, 1969), 117f.

23. Legrand, *GN&W*, 7; or as E.J. Mally writes in R.E. Brown, J.A. Fitzmyer, and R.E. Murphy, eds., *The Jerome Biblical Commentary* (London, 1968), 42:8 (hereafter cited as *JBC*), "in calling his book 'the gospel' Mark means that it is not primarily an account about Jesus but a proclamation of the Risen Christ in which he is again made present."

24. Cf. *ibid.*, 27.

25. Cf. J. Jeremias, *The Sermon on the Mount* (Philadelphia, 1963), 34; and *The Parables of Jesus* (London, 1963), 145.

26. L. McKenzie, "The Gospel According to Matthew," *JBC* 43:30; cf. Schnackenburg in *The Moral Teaching of the New Testament* (New York, 1965), 65, sees the Sermon on the Mount basically as the announcement of God's will which has been partly distorted and diminished by humankind in the Jewish conception of law.

27. Jeremias, *The Sermon of the Mount*, 35.

28. Jeremias, *The Parables of Jesus*, 145 quoted by Legrand in *GN&W*, 30.

29. Legrand, *GN&W*, 30, with reference to Jeremias, *The Parables of Jesus*, 153-160.

30. D.M. Stanley and R.E. Brown, "Aspects of New Testament Thought," *JBC*, 78:139.

31. Legrand, *GN&W*, 32.

32. Stanley and Brown, "Aspects," *JBC*, 28:126. Cf. also to Mt 11:4-6, where Jesus' answer to John the Baptist concludes the list of miracles with "and the Good News is proclaimed to the poor," thus implying that the miracles themselves are a constitutive part of the message.

33. Legrand, *GN&W*, 35.

34. *Ibid.*, 36-37.

35. Cf. Lk 10:30-37, 17:11-19; Jn 4:1f; Mt 8:5-10, 13; and Mk 7:24-30, etc.

36. Cf. Vellanickal, "The Biblical Theology of Evangelization," *SAS*, 59: "The same parallelism is found also in Mk 11:10 and Lk 19:38."

37. *Ibid.*

38. Cf. J.-P. Migne, ed., *Patrologia Graeca* 59, 146. (Hereafter cited as *PG*.)

39. Cf. *ibid.* 73, 241.

40. S. Lyonnet, "The Newness of the Gospel," *SAS*, 98.

41. Legrand, *GN&W*, 43.

42. Cf. Stanley and Brown, "Aspects," *JBC*, 78:154. Legrand, *GN&W*, 49, maintains a sixth such appearance in 1 Cor 15:3ff. "The apparition to the 500 brothers in v. 6 breaks the rhythm and must be Paul's own comment. If it is so, we have one more report concluding with the missionary appearance and a total of *six Resurrection accounts focussing on the mission.*"

43. Legrand, *GN&W*, 50-51. Italics in the original citation.

44. W. Guzie, *Jesus and the Eucharist* (Paramus, New Jersey, 1974), 89. Italics in original.

45. Legrand, *GN&W*, 55.

46. *Ibid.*, 60.

47. J. Pathrapankal, "The Early Church and Paul," *GN&W*, 71.

48. Cf. *ibid.*, 65-67.

49. H. Conzelmann, *The Theology of St. Luke* (London, 1960), 208.

50. Legrand, *SAS*, 129.

51. *Ibid.*, 131.

52. Pathrapankal, *GN&W*, 82.

53. *Ibid.*, 100-101.

54. Fitzmyer, "Pauline Theology," *JBC*, 79:28.

55. Pathrapankal, *GN&W*, 103.

56. *Ibid.*, 105. F. Mussner, "The Epistle to the Colossians," in J.L. McKenzie, ed., *New Testament For Spiritual Reading* (London and Sydney, 1970) Vol. 17, p. 118, points out that sinful humanity long regarded God as enemy, but in light of the Good News we must "give up the pagan idea that God is [our] enemy. Jesus' death on the cross is more than sufficient proof that God is man's friend and that he wants to be man's friend . . . God was not man's enemy, but man was God's enemy."

57. *Ibid.*, 110.

58. M. Vellanickal, "Evangelization in the Johannine Writings," *GN&W*, 125. *Note:* The development in this section "F" is basically a summary of Vellanickal's viewpoint, pp. 121-68.

59. *Ibid.*, 127.

60. B. Vawter, "The Gospel According to John," *JBC*, 63:40.

61. B. Vawter, "Johannine Theology," *JBC*, 80:23.

62. R.E. Brown, *The Gospel According to John*, Anchor Bible (Garden City, New York, 1966-70), 499.

63. *Ibid.*, 507.

64. Vawter, "Johannine Theology," *JBC*, 80:25.

65. Brown, *The Gospel According to John*, 558, 564.

66. Vellanickal, *GN&W*, 133-34.

67. *Ibid.*, 136.

68. *Ibid.*, 142.

69. *Ibid.*, 144.

70. *Ibid.*, 150.

71. Brown, *The Gospel According to John*, 1141.

72. Vellanickal, *GN&W*, 152.

73. For a discussion of Johannine ecclesiology, cf. Brown, *The Gospel According to John*, cv-cxi.

74. Vellanickal, *GN&W*, 163.

II
Historical Notes

Here we do not intend to present the entire history of the Church's evangelizing efforts. Rather, as the title of the chapter indicates, we only propose to offer some historical "notes" which will give us the tenor of the various shifts in the Church's outlook upon the process of evangelization down through the centuries. To this end, we will start with the patristic era with its close ties to the life-style and traditions of the primitive Church. Next, we will see major political, social and cultural changes radically alter the Church's role in Western civilization and usher in the "Era of Christendom." This development in turn gives rise to the "Age of Missionaries," whose outreach to pagan lands has been well documented over the years. For our purposes the "notes" will jump immediately to the twentieth century and the again radically changing socio-cultural scene of modern Europe, which forms a prelude to the Second Vatican Council and its reflection on the Church's mission in the modern world. Finally, we will review the contributions and conclusions of the Fourth Synod of Bishops which met in Rome in the autumn of 1974 to discuss the theme of the "Evangelization of the Modern World."

A. THE PATRISTIC ERA AND EVANGELIZATION

Poignantly aware that the New Life they shared "in Christ" was not just a matter of intellectual or rational assent to doctrinal propositions about a certain Jesus of Nazareth, the earliest Christians in apostolic times soon came to refer to their fellowship and communion of life with the risen Lord as "the Way" (cf. Acts 9:2; 18:25, 26; 19:9, 23; 22:4; 24:14, 22). Through repentance and baptismal faith, the Christian convert entered into a human community, into a society of those already called in Christ—the Church. "Koinonia" was the Greek term employed to describe this way of life, this common sharing and fraternal communion in love that bound these early Christians to one another. This gospel-life, its spirit and traditions, were handed down intact to successive generations of Christians in those first centuries now referred to as the Age of the Fathers of the Church, or the patristic era.

48

The writings and documents of these first generations which immediately followed the New Testament era, however, are few in number and hardly more than occasional. Inferences and conjecture must necessarily play a major role in reconstructing this primitive period of the Church. Not until the appearance of the works of St. Irenaeus (c. 180) and the Fathers of the Antiochene and Alexandrian schools in the early part of the third Christian century does one find the beginnings of a substantial and systematic reflection upon the life of faith shared by the members of the early Church. Nevertheless, it is not the intent of this particular section to attempt any sort of detailed historical analysis of the patristic period, but rather simply to try to demarcate in a very summary fashion the main phases of the continuation of the evangelization process which evolved from the apostolic community's understanding of its own *raison d'être*.

1. *Kerygma*[1]

In primitive Christianity this term distinguished "the proclamation of the word" from "catechesis" (religious instruction) and doctrinal teaching ("didache"). "Kerygma" is the substantive of the Greek verb "kerussein," which, as has already been pointed out, literally means "to herald." This same verb is used in Mk 1:14 to describe Jesus' proclamation of the Gospel. Thus we could probably best render the term "kerygma" today as meaning "to preach as Jesus did," since as a substantive it denotes both the act and the message.

Kerygma is basically an *event*. In the proclamation of the Gospel, Christ is not only proclaimed, but he is also made present in this proclamation. This is implied in Lk 10:16—"Anyone who listens to you listens to me." "Whatever forms the kerygma takes, it is always the expression of one thing only: the 'word of Christ' (Rom 10:17), which is the origin and medium and object of the whole kerygma (as event)."[2] The kerygma is thus a charismatic, dynamic and life-giving power summoning its hearers to confident faith and constituting the Church as the fellowship of those who hear and follow the Word of God.

In the sub-apostolic communities the kerygma evidently found its place in the liturgical celebrations of the community, for the earliest writings of the Greek and Latin Fathers of the Church, with their copious citations from Scripture, presuppose an audience familiar with the sacred text and the gospel mystery.[3] Yet, there were no Christian schools, no systematic catechetical instructions for children, no institutions, societies and fraternities, and no evidence of an organized missionary outreach.[4] The liturgy somehow substituted for these other institutions as it nourished the life of love and fellowship they experienced in union with the glorified Christ who lived and still lives in the Church through the Holy Spirit, who himself is the Spirit of Christ. In the liturgy of the early Church it could be said that Christ was "kerygmatically present."

> It is curious that the early writings practically never mention those many details and events which make up the "Gospel story." Christ was indeed a historical figure, but what stands out above all other things is that Christ was the Kyrios, and this Kyrios became a specific Christian conception with specifically Christian connotations: it implies the Incarnation, Passion, Resurrection, Ascension; it refers to the glorified God-man who sent the Holy Ghost at the founding of the Christian Church; it refers to Christ as the source and center of the Christian cult in which we are united with The Father in Him.[5]

The summoning presence, challenge and power of Christ in the kerygma remained a part of the Church's preaching throughout the patristic era until Gregory the Great (d. 604),[6] who seems to have had some inkling of the forthcoming transferal of imperial power, the "translatio imperii," which would radically transform Roman tradition and culture and in its turn mark the passage from Christianity to "Christendom" (to the "Respublica Christiana"). In the meantime, the nature of the kerygma was beginning to be modified as the Apologists of the second century adapted the content of their proclamations to the need of rebutting the calumnies circulated against the Christians, but essentially their task was a missionary effort aimed at the conversion of their pagan audience. A century later the Arian threat would give rise to the necessity of maintaining the Son's consubstantiality with the Father. This controversy, along with other Christological questions that would soon follow, led gradually to a shift of interest from the historical to the ontological—from the Christ of salvation-history, as Redeemer, the Good Shepherd, and Head of the Church, to the Christ of the abstract, intellectual formulas of the Nicaeo-Constantinopolitan Creed. As the era of Christendom dawned, Christ, when introduced, was presented solely as the object of preaching; he was no longer considered its dynamic origin and living medium as in the earliest kerygma.

2. *Catechesis and the Catechumenate*

Catechesis refers basically to religious instruction both doctrinal and moral. The Greek word "catechein" literally means "to resound" and includes the notion of oral teaching and the handing on of what has been received. In the New Testament the verb is employed to denote instruction about the content of faith (Gal 6:6) or the deepening of knowledge already acquired. "The NT itself is catechesis. The specifically Christian teaching which it contains is designated by a variety of words (. . . 'way,' 'doctrine,' 'tradition,' 'word')."[7] Catechesis, therefore, from the very beginning has been intimately associated with kerygma. The early Church never viewed this form of instruction primarily as a system of facts or a set of precepts, but saw it rather as the proclamation of a person and of events, in whom and in which God revealed himself and continues to reveal himself. After the New Testament era, a moral catechesis was set forth in such works as the *Didache* or *Teaching of the Twelve Apostles* with its theme of the two ways and the two "spirits" between which we must choose once and for all, and in the *Epistle of Barnabas* with its choice between the Way of Light and the Way of Darkness.

Only in the course of the second and third centuries does the terminology become more exact as "catechesis" takes on the technical sense of instruction given to someone preparing for baptism (cf. the *Traditio Apostolica* of Hippolytus, c. 215). In the third century the period of preparation lasted three years and took the form of a moral trial made up of religious and ascetical practices; finally, in the second degree, that of *proximate preparation* before Easter, the catechumen was introduced to dogmatic theology and the Good News of salvation. In the catechumenate of the fourth and fifth centuries, a preliminary catechesis was introduced accompanied by certain ceremonies. Only when the candidate was ready for baptism was he given a complete course of instruction or catechesis (*doctrinal*—centered on the Creed, and *moral*—a study of the Two Ways). Such instruction took place during the Lenten season.

During these three or four centuries, a number of catechetical works were produced. They assumed a more formal character after the Edict of Toleration (313). Among these are listed such works as the *Catechetical Lectures* of Cyril of Jerusalem; Ambrose's *De Sacramentis* and *De Mysteriis*, and the *Catechesis* of Theodore of Mopsuestia. The preparatory catechesis before baptism was gradually supplemented with a mystagogical catechesis for neophytes, e.g., Ambrose's *De Mysteriis*. An interesting discussion of catechetical method is found in St. Augustine's famous *De Catechizandis rudibus* (405); Augustine's primary aim was to get the catechumen to understand that Redemption was basically a work of love to which human love should respond by full and hearty obedience to the commandments of God.

The catechumenate as an institution began its decline toward the end of the fifth century as the practice of infant baptism increased. Catechesis was transferred to the post-baptismal period in the form of home instructions by parents and by liturgical homilies in church.[8] After the fifth century, the Germanic peoples were baptized (often as an entire tribe at once) after a catechumenate of only a few weeks. Christianity at this time arrived at the point where it became a religion of the masses. It was during this new era, known as "Christendom," that a mass Christianization process incorporated large numbers into the Church without their ever being evangelized. With the demise of the catechumenate, the term "catechesis" itself disappeared from the Christian vocabulary and with it passed away a primordial form of Christian teaching.

3. *Christian Gnosis*

The writings of the Fathers are permeated with the evangelical spirit of primitive Christianity. As opposed to gnosticism, the Fathers present a genuine Christian gnosis or "knowledge of God," which is Jesus Christ, the Risen One, through whom and in whom we are assimilated to God, participating in the very Life of the Trinity. As Jesus' gospel proclamation of the Kingdom of God becomes identified with Christ in the synoptic accounts and Paul, and with "Eternal Life" in John, so the Fathers continue to develop these latter Pauline and Johannine themes which constituted the very heart and core of the Church's early kerygma. Homilies, letters, apologetic writings and other manner of works proclaimed this *union* with Christ through a life of charity (*agape*). Louis Bouyer thus summarizes it:

> The whole of the Christian asceticism of the patristic era, in spite of the risks of deviation continually threatening it, remains basically simply the concrete realization of the cross which the Servant of Yahweh invited his disciples to take up and to carry after him. The mysticism of the Fathers is only the fruit of the knowledge of God, knowledge in the Scriptures, by the faith that takes hold of the whole of life, the faith to which God reveals himself in Christ as *agape* while he pours out precisely this *agape* through the Spirit of Christ, into the hearts of those who give themselves up unreservedly to the mystery of the Cross. Such remains the teaching of the last great bishops and doctors.[9]

The teaching of the Fathers is steeped in a concrete spirituality. They never look to the past trying to recapture some historical objectivity, but rather seek to make one aware of the genuine inexpressible reality that encompasses all human experience and "knowing"—Christ, the glorified Redeemer, who has lifted our humanity to a new being, to a new nearness to God.

The Apostolic Fathers (Clement of Rome, Ignatius of Antioch, Polycarp, Barnabas, the Shepherd of Hermas) demonstrate their continuity with the apostolic writings by using the epistolary form. They are chiefly concerned with handing on the kerygma of the apostolic age along with the practical moral efforts that this tradition calls for. Clement's epistle propounds this "gnosis" which causes us to recognize the wonderful harmony of the actions of God in history. At the same time Clement himself desires to lead his readers by the path of humility in faith to a realization of charity in the Church. Ignatius of Antioch always proceeds from the presence of "the suffering Christ" in the Eucharist to charity while viewing martyrdom as "the eternal consummation in 'incorruptible love' of union with God in Christ."[10] The *Epistle of Barnabas* locates the focus of gnosis in meditation on the Scriptures centered on Christ and his cross—a meditation which is no mere intellectual effort, but rather a living grasp of the realities of salvation.

The second century has been designated the era of the Apologists (Justin, Tatian, Athenagoras, Theophilus of Antioch, Tertullian). They were determined to prove the acceptability of Christianity to an educated pagan world as more and more men of learning and rank were receiving Christian baptism. Through the literary form of the "discourse," the dialogue and the petition, they tried to demonstrate that all the best in pagan thought and life finds its perfection and its real home in Christianity. Justin was the first to combine philosophical and religious experience. Yet, others following immediately upon Justin's footsteps would discourse on Christ as the "Logos" without having freed themselves from the Hellenistic deformations that surround this term. These, then, opened the way for the Arian heresy that would arise some two centuries later, and so already "we see outlined the temptation which was to be that of all Christian 'humanisms': that of a natural spirituality which the redemption would do nothing but restore and perfect, to the detriment of divine transcendence and grace."[11]

Toward the end of the second century, Irenaeus of Lyons inveighs against the Gnostic claim to the possession of a secret tradition. In his famous *Adversus Haereses* he maintains a concept of the Church centered on the experience of the Spirit and "agape" (III, xxxviii, 1); through the grace of the Spirit given to us by God, we are renewed in the image and likeness of God (V, viii, 1), and in his doctrine of the "recapitulation" of the whole human race in Christ, the "anacephalaiosis" of Eph 1:10 takes on new life in the patristic era (III, xvi, 6).

The theological schools of Alexandria and Antioch dominate the Christian teaching of the third century; the theological terminology developed here would later influence the Christological controversies of the succeeding century. The work of these schools is not yet so abstract that it loses contact with concrete spiritual realities. For Clement of Alexandria, the supreme state of gnosis is one in which we know the God of love by the fact that we love as he loves; thus, the true gnostic is one who has acquired the habit of doing good; he acts well rather than speaks well.

The edict of Milan (313) and *Cunctos populos* of Theodosius the Great (February 27, 380) would effect the status of Christianity within the Roman Empire. This ushered in the age of the great ecumenical councils as various schools of theology tried to expound the orthodox teaching in solving the Christological questions that now rocked the Church to its very foundations. Amid these controversies, Gregory Nazianzen was able to enunciate clearly for his time the Mystery (in its Pauline expression) at the very heart of the Christian faith:

> I must be buried with Christ, rise with Him, become Son of God. . . . This is what is the great mystery for us, this is what God incarnate is for us, become poor for us. He has come to make us perfectly one in Christ, in Christ who has come perfectly into us, to put within us all that he is. There is no longer man nor woman, barbarian nor Scythian, slave nor free man, characteristics of the flesh; there is now only the divine image that we all bear within us, according to which we have been created, which must be formed in us and impressed on us so strongly that it will suffice to make us known.[12]

A short while later St. Augustine would give the gnosis of the Greek Fathers a new twist. Augustinian wisdom would distinguish itself by its psychological, reflexive orientation: rather than the mystery of God in Christ, it would start with the mystery of ourselves, which God and Christ help us to unravel. Thus, speculating on the divine Trinitarian image in us, Augustine came to view our Christian charity as a participation in the charity proper to God, as love of the Love with which we have been loved. The emergence here of such anthropocentrism and psychocentrism will eventually lead to an alienation from the Eastern tradition. Finally, in the homilies of Leo the Great (d. 461 ?), the great Pauline theme of incorporation into Christ by faith and the sacraments is set out one last time in a language and style that is still magnificent.

From this all too brief survey of the major writers of the patristic era—a survey which really has not been able to take into account the divergent influences of the Greek and Latin cultures, nor the impact of the many historico-political events of the age—we can see that their major thrust centers about an exposition of Christian gnosis or wisdom viewed as an inner realization of living faith acting through charity. In fact, as we shall see later, early Christian morality was centered on human response in gratitude and love to the gospel message of God's magnanimous love, or divine grace, in Christ.

Evangelization in the patristic era focused on the exposition of that divine life which the Christian community was continually aware of sharing in its risen Lord. The proclamation of this gospel mystery took the forms of kerygma, catechesis and the interpretation of Christian gnosis (the *first moment* of the evangelization process). Christian witness (the *second moment* to be developed in Part II), especially the witness of the early martyrs, played no small role in the evangelization of the Roman Empire. As Harnack has observed: "It was characteristic of this religion that every serious adherent served also towards its propagation."[13] There has been found no record of early missionary enterprise in the sub-apostolic community. From the stringent requirements demanded of candidates for instruction, such as found in the *Church Order* or Hippolytus, "we get the impression that the Church built walls and barriers around herself, making it difficult for the heathen to enter."[14] Still, by the beginning of the fourth century, there were an estimated seven million Christians in a total population of fifty million in the Roman Empire; geographically, the Church had penetrated Gaul, Spain and the marginal zones of Germany and Britain in the West and as far as Edessa in the East. These early centuries of Christianity display a vision which is dominated by what St. Augustine came to call the "Total Christ," communion with whom in an ecclesial community of shared faith provided the focal point of the Church's life and worship and the terminal point of the evangelization process. During this era, however, the stage had already been set for the radical transformation of Christianity into "Christendom."

B. THE ERA OF CHRISTENDOM AND THE AGE OF MISSIONARIES

In 380, by an imperial decree of Theodosius the Great, the Catholic Church became the official religion of the Empire. *All* citizens necessarily and under pain of legal sanctions became Christians, and gradually the law of the Church began to coalesce with the law of the Empire so that the religious and political foundation of the "Respublica Christiana" was laid. A new volume in Church history and in the evangelization process was being prepared.

The first major development in Christianity after this historic turning point is described in the words of Bouyer:

> It was not by chance that anchoritism, the retreat to the desert, spread so suddenly just as the State made its peace with the Church. There is certainly a very close connection between these two contemporaneous historical facts. When a world in which Christians as such were separated and proscribed was succeeded by a world in which they came to be in honor, but a world whose Spirit had hardly changed for all that, the best Christians, by instinct, would freely choose the state of proscription no longer imposed on them by circumstances. In a world which no longer treated them as enemies they would feel obliged to live as enemies of the world; they sensed too well that, without this, they would become its slaves.[15]

With the cessation of persecutions and martyrdom, monasticism quickly became the ultimate form of Christian witness. From these new monasteries would go forth the missionaries and evangelists of the medieval world.

With the collapse of the Empire and the appearance of new nations among the Germanic peoples after the fifth century, new principles of evangelization were introduced. In the Roman Empire, as Jungmann observes,

> . . . the Church applied the principle that the conversion should take place from the inside to the outside, and from below to above; this certainly was one way to a thorough reformation of life. With regard to the new peoples an opposite principle was applied: from the outside to the inside and from the top to the bottom: hence a more or less external change of adherence preceded firm conviction and inner reformation, and the people had to learn a new way of life from their converted leaders.[16]

Whereas originally in the primitive Church evangelization preceded admittance to baptism, in the era of Christendom the process would be reversed, but not without subsequent deleterious effects on the quality and fervor of spiritual life in the new Christian communities.

As the organization of the Empire waned, the Church admitted to her fold new populations who had no education nor culture of their own. Amid ignorance, pagan customs and different languages, the new converts were in no sense familiar with the Gospel; "they had no inkling of theology, let alone the theological implications of 'Christ' and 'Church'; they knew nothing of the traditions that molded Christianity so far."[17] The missionaries sent out to these new peoples could hope for little more than having them learn by rote the Our Father and the Creed. A spiritual life based on Scripture was rapidly replaced with more popular forms of religious piety based on the cult of local saints, miracles and relics. Participation in liturgical and sacramental acts was reduced to a mere matter of obligation.

The consequences of the theological and doctrinal controversies of the fourth and fifth centuries now made their presence felt. As Christ's divinity came more and more to the fore, his mediatorship role slipped farther and farther into the background. A study of the letters of St. Boniface, the great missionary apostle to the Germanic peoples, proves that: "The joyful awareness of being children of God does not control his attitude."[18] Celtic monasticism brought on the impact of an ascetic way of life.

> This influence became more decisive for the culture and education of the broad masses in medieval times than the oft-praised literary and scholastic influence of the Benedictines. . . . The Christian character of the world had to be made evident in the field of morality: the monks, therefore, were concerned to provide religious practices to accompany every moment of life and with the aid of strict sanctions to secure the observance of the moral law. The principles of this morality were found in the prescriptions of the Old Testament in both the decalogue and the ritual laws.[19]

Cathechesis in the Middle Ages depended largely on the strength of the Christian family and the communal life, but with the passage of time the sense of community would grow weaker and weaker, and an individualistic piety would come to predominate. A gradual but perceptible change in the religious spirit and practice tended toward an overemphasis on the external elements of religion. The existential anchoring of moral theology and spirituality disappears as Mystery is objectified and the Host becomes "God." The centrality of the Eucharist in Christian life and worship was lost sight of, replaced by a superstitious confidence in the Blessed Sacrament. Abuses occurred in liturgical and sacramental practice while local councils were concerned about indulgences, pilgrimages and relics. Catechetical synthesis disintegrated with the medieval fascination for numbers with its subsequent arbitrary and artificial classifications: seven sacraments, seven capital sins, seven works of mercy, seven petitions in the Lord's Prayer, etc.[20]

When emphasis on the Incarnation revived, it took a new form differing from that of the patristic era. The Franciscan movement succeeded only in making Jesus in his poverty and suffering as such (the "Christus secundum carnem") an object for compassion and imitation, thus not quite recapturing the "Total Christ" of the early Church. Theological reflection and speculation tended more and more towards symbolism and to the philosophical and the abstract. According to Sloyan the appearance of the *Elucidarium*, a theological summary attributed to Honorius, head of the school of Autun in the twelfth century, "marks the death and burial of the Patristic tradition in catechetics, just as it brings to the fore the theological answer-man who, while he says he deals in mysteries, does not seem to be aware of any." The theological picture, however, was not all black; "there was still a powerful succession of sober and wise traditionalists who were fully aware of the dangers implied in the indiscriminate symbolism which became a fashion—from Florus, the deacon of Lyons, who conducted a major ecclesiastical battle with Amalarius of Metz, to Raban Maur and Walafrid Strabo, who stood firmly by the Gregorian tradition, and so to Thomas Aquinas."[21]

In the era of Christendom one might say that the process of evangelization literally took an objective turn for the worst. The emphasis on "mystery," "Life" and "community" that played such a predominant part in the patristic era had all but disappeared. The Church's mission of evangelization was now narrowly confined to missionary outreach into pagan lands. Meanwhile, in the "Christian" culture of Western Europe, baptism and the other sacraments seemed at times to be little more than rites of sociological attachment performed more for the privileges associated with them than as the means of access to the transcendent reality embodied in them. The discoveries of new lands and peoples in the fifteenth and sixteenth centuries opened a new era in missionary activity. The age of worldwide missions had dawned and the process of evangelization became identified solely with the conversion and baptism of "pagan" peoples. Not until the Second Vatican Council (1962-65) would a more comprehensive understanding of the Church's mission of evangelization once again begin to emerge.

C. VATICAN II

A number of documents promulgated by the Second Vatican Council, especially *Lumen Gentium, Gaudium et Spes*, and *Ad Gentes*, have reopened the way to a more comprehensive understanding of the Church's mission in the world. With *Lumen Gentium*, a renewed ecclesiology began to focus the Church's attention on her essential mission of showing forth to the world the mystery of Christ (cf. *LG* 8). A distinction had to be made, therefore, between the mission of the universal Church and the Church's "missions" (cf. *AG* 5&6). The original groundwork for the Council's conclusions must be sought amid the developments in the field of ecclesiology during the first half of the twentieth century.

1. *A Prologue to Vatican II: The Emergence of Mission in Ecclesiology*

For a long time, since the great discoveries of the sixteenth century stimulated the missionary movement, the Church's efforts at evangelization played almost no part in her theological self-understanding. Preoccupied with the Reformation and Counter-Reformation while maintaining a compartmental view of the world—a view which placed Christians and the Church in one hand so to speak, and missionary countries and pagans in the other—the Church herself found little opportunity to promote an integrated theology of ecclesial mission.[22] Not until the early twentieth century, when the collapse of Christendom and the effects of a growing industrialization and secularization became evident, did theologians begin to reflect in earnest upon the role of the Church in the modern world. The term "mission" was now utilized not only to describe the task of preaching the Gospel to "the heathen," but also to denote the new exigency of "reevangelizing" the so-called "Christian" nations.

This new application of the term "mission" was inspired by the problem of the Church in the contemporary world. Three real-life phenomena which sprang up in response to the new problematic took the forms of Catholic Action (with its slogan: "We shall make our brothers Christian again"), the priest-worker movement, and the ecumenical movement. Theologians soon tried to demonstrate how all three were actually congruent with the Church's mission.

In his first writings between 1932 and 1937, Yves Congar delineates three different aspects of the ecclesial mission: "the symbol of the Church in the world, a symbol to be transformed; her mission in life and in the diversity of cultures in which she should be embodied; the real nature of the laity, whose mission appears in a new light requiring a gradual reappraisal of ministry."[23] With Congar theologians began to forsake apologetics and started to look at the Church from the viewpoint of unbelievers, not in order to refute them but to understand them. In *Chrétiens désunis* (1937), Congar maintains that catholicity is apostolic.

As P. Haubtmann would later write: "The Church in the past traced by Congar is missionary, not by practical necessity in order to meet transitory historical circumstances, but by her essence, by her very way of living. The mission exists everywhere, in countries referred to as missions as well as Catholic countries."[24] Mission was thus understood as synonymous with the life of the Spirit in the Church, which Congar would ultimately link to the traditional theme of Incarnation, developed so lucidly by J. Moehler in the previous century: "The Church then is Jesus Christ always renewing himself, reappearing in human form: *she is the permanent incarnation of the Son of God.*"[25]

Starting from the sociological situation, M.-D. Chenu proposed the formula *the Church in the state of mission* to describe that point where the Gospel affects the world in its process of development. It succinctly expressed the ecclesiological dimension experienced by the priest-worker movement. Mission is, thus, the realm of faith which takes responsibility for the growth of humanity, so that it becomes "the communitarian growth of the grace of God, in Christ."[26] Like Congar, Chenu links mission with Incarnation; following the Johannine tradition, he holds that Christ returned to his Father at the very moment when he was incorporating himself in the human condition until death, linking himself to all who would be recapitulated in him, and not only afterward as an extrinsic recompense for one's actions. Recognizing the failure thus far of the institutional parish to accomplish this mission, Chenu threw his support behind Catholic Action as the appropriate means.

Later, Karl Rahner would trace the de-Christianization of the West through the Reformation, the Renaissance and the Enlightenment which occurred at just that moment when the Church became worldwide in its outreach. The implications here point to a necessity inherent in salvation history, namely, that the Church "must" everywhere become a Church of the *diaspora,* "a Church which lives in the midst of a multitude of non-Christians, a Church consequently embedded in a cultural, civic, political, scientific, economic, artistic context which is not the work of Christians only."[27] The Church of the diaspora becomes a Church with active members, a Church of laypersons who feel genuinely responsible as individuals; she must then have a more religious and a more interior-looking face because as an organization in this new situation her power can no longer be exercised widely and directly on the political level.

Alongside these developments, three other theological considerations with a decisive impact on missiology also came to the fore during these years: (1) the possibility of salvation outside the Church; (2) the value of implicit faith by which a non-Catholic would in fact be an "Anonymous Christian"; and (3) practical doubts concerning the results of missionary endeavors already undertaken and the authenticity of the conversions made.[28] As a consequence of all this ferment, the idea of mission came under heavy challenge. No one definition or concept of mission enjoyed the unanimous acceptance of missiologists, although the classical notion of the "implantation of the Church" understood in an institutional sense by the great missiologists Schmidlin and Charles had by now become clearly inadequate. De Menasce contributed to the basic evolution on the missiological plane when in 1939 he wrote in *L'Annuaire Missionnaire Catholique de la Suisse:* "There is among all Christians endowed with grace an ordering more or less explicit toward the missionary intention of the Church, which has the same extension as the salvific will of Christ." Later the works of C. Journet and A. Chavasse would bring missiology into the very heart of ecclesiology;[29] and Le Guillou would link the mission of the Church with ecumenism. In the thought of Le Guillou, "mystery" in the Pauline sense formed the basis of mission and unity in their mutual relations: "Only that conception of mystery puts the Church in a fully theological perspective: it can thus be seen in the ensemble of God's plan, as well as in its pastoral and missionary dynamism, centered around the cross and the eucharist, all tending toward eschatology."[30] With this the stage was set for the declarations and distinctions promulgated in the documents and decrees of the second Vatican Council.

In the decades immediately preceding Vatican II, the popes did not remain aloof from this weighty question of the Church's mission in the world. Pius XI reinserted mission into ecclesiology when in *Quae Nobis* (Nov. 13, 1928), he gave impetus to the Catholic Action movement by stating: "Catholic Action does not differ from the divine mission entrusted to the Church and from its apostolate." In seeking to dialogue with the world, John XXIII would bring to the fore a more dynamic concept of the Church, whose mission he saw as preparing the way for the unity of the human race "in order that the earthly city may be brought to the resemblance of the heavenly city where truth reigns, charity is law, and whose extent is eternity."[31] During the Council, Paul VI would further elaborate on this theme of dialogue with the world in his encyclical *Ecclesiam Suam* (1964). It is thus that Le Guillou can conclude: "From Pius XI to Paul VI the problem of the Church's mission has been stated with increasing precision with respect to the development of the world, and has been viewed with more understanding; this process in various ways gives the Church a new bearing."[32]

2. *Lumen Gentium: The Mission of the Church*

The opening words of the Dogmatic Constitution on the Church set forth the theme and purpose of the program of reform envisaged by the Council. "Christ is the light of the nations," and the Church radiates this light "by proclaiming the gospel to every creature"; therefore, "this Council wishes to set forth more precisely to the faithful and to the entire world the nature and encompassing mission of the Church" (*LG* 1).

The constitution of the Church, however, will not succeed in presenting in any sort of systematic way the specific mission of the Church. In order to understand the Church's doctrine on this matter, one has to glean the various indications scattered throughout this document and the other decrees of the Council. "By her relationship with Christ," the opening article of *Lumen Gentium* declares, "the Church is a kind of sacrament or sign of intimate union with God, and of the unity of all mankind" (*LG* 1). The Church's mission, therefore, must be sought in the mission of Christ who was sent by the Father and came

—to inaugurate the kingdom of God on earth (*LG* 3&5);
—to re-establish all things (*LG* 3);
—to be a light to the nations (*LG* 1&3);
—to reveal the Father's will to men (*LG* 2);
—to effect a new and perfect covenant between God and men (*LG* 9);
—to preach the good news to the poor, heal the contrite of heart, save what was lost (*LG* 8);
—to achieve redemption through obedience (*LG* 3), in the poverty and amid persecution (*LG* 8);
—to be the source of salvation for the whole world (*LG* 17).[33]

This mission of Christ, and likewise that of the Church, is described in the terms of salvation history and God's plan for the world and not in any abstract notions of nature-supernature categories. "By an utterly free and mysterious decree of His own wisdom and goodness, the eternal Father created the whole world. His plan was to dignify men with a participation in His own divine life" (*LG* 2). With regard to the mission of the Church, understood generally, we find the following formulations in this document:

—to be for the whole race a sure seed of unity, hope, and salvation (*LG* 9);
—to be an instrument of redemption for all (*LG* 9);
—to be for each and all the visible sacrament of saving unity (*LG* 9);
—to be the universal sacrament of salvation (*LG* 48);

—to proclaim the kingdom of Christ and God, to establish it
among all the nations, and to be the germ, beginning and
instrument of this kingdom (*LG* 5);
—to reveal to the world the mystery of Christ (*LG* 8).[34]

The Church in its reality is primarily a mystery and a spiritual
community ("communitas spiritualis," "koinonia," "the People of
God"). As a mystery, the Church, "by an excellent analogy . . . is compared to the mystery of the incarnate Word" (*LG* 8), reechoing J.
Moehler's concept cited above. As a "koinonia," biblical images and
analogies are applied to describe it (cf. *LG* 6). "Just as the assumed nature inseparably united to the divine Word serves Him as a living instrument of salvation, so, in a similar way, does the communal structure
of the Church serve Christ's Spirit who vivifies it by way of building up
the body (cf. Eph 4:16)" (*LG* 8). Thus, in Christ and in the Spirit, the
Church must carry out its mission of proclaiming the Kingdom of Christ
and of God in establishing it among all peoples.

In article No. 17 the Council Fathers relate the Church's missionary mandate to the doctrine of the Trinity—this theology of mission
is further developed in *Ad Gentes*—and declare that "the obligation of
spreading the faith is imposed on every disciple of Christ according to
his ability." In Chapter IV, article No. 35, we read:

So too the laity go forth as powerful heralds of a faith in things
to be hoped for (cf. Heb 1:1) provided they steadfastly join to
their profession of faith a life springing from faith. This evangelization, that is this announcing of Christ by a living testimony as well as by the spoken word, takes on a specific quality
and special force in that it is carried out in the ordinary surroundings of the world.

Lumen Gentium, therefore, confirms the Church's essentially missionary
nature, and as we have just seen also gives a broad range of indications,
but no specific clarification, as to what exactly constitutes the Church's
mission. The necessity of proclaiming the Kingdom of Christ and of
God is substantiated and even extended in its scope, but precisely what
this involves is not clearly delineated.

3. *"Gaudium et Spes": The Church and the World*

Chapter IV of the Pastoral Constitution on the Church in the Modern World considers the Church "inasmuch as she exists in the world,
living and acting with it." In this relationship with the world, the Church

envisions herself serving "as a leaven and as a kind of soul for human society as it is to be renewed in Christ and transformed into God's family" (*GS* 40). Thus the Council Fathers declared:

> Christ, to be sure, gave His Church no proper mission in the political, economic, or social order. The purpose which He set before her is a religious one. But out of this religious mission itself come a function, a light, and an energy which can serve to structure and consolidate the human community according to divine law. As a matter of fact, when circumstances of time and place create the need, she can and indeed should initiate activities on the behalf of all men. This is particularly true of activities designed for the needy, such as works of mercy and similar undertakings. (*GS* 42)

The Church's mission to the world finds its theological validation in the New Testament, especially in Paul's Letter to the Ephesians, where sovereignty is attributed to Christ who is the head both of the Church (1:18, 22) and of all things (1:22). "Thus two domains are marked out, one absolutely universal in scope, comprising the whole of creation, the other formed of men who accept the gospel and which is, properly speaking, the Church: two concentric circles, as it were, which coincide by their common dependence on the same head, the same supreme authority, Christ."[35] *Gaudium et Spes* accents this aspect when in article No. 45 it develops Paul's doctrine on the recapitulation of all things in Christ (Eph 1:10), the Alpha and the Omega. A further theological impetus comes from eschatology. As Congar explains: "The end of the ages has already begun, for the foundation of the restoration of all things has already been laid in Jesus Christ. This fact imposes on Christians the duty of working in the world to establish an order in harmony with the gift of truth and grace which they have received in Jesus Christ."[36] The interpretation of the Church's mission of evangelization is thus broadened in *Gaudium et Spes*, for the Church present in the world as the "universal sacrament of salvation" (*LG* 48) is now viewed as the historical, social, visible and public form assumed by God's comprehensive, salvific will. The Church's entire function, then, is to serve this saving plan by proclaiming the gospel both in word and deed, for "by thus giving witness to the truth, we will share with others the mystery of the heavenly Father's love" (*GS* 93).

4. *"Ad Gentes": The Church's Mission and 'Missions'*

The Council's Decree on the Missionary Activity of the Church explicitly states: "The pilgrim Church is missionary by her very nature" (*AG* 2). Taking its theological cue from *Lumen Gentium*, the present decree would affirm that the Church takes her origin from the mission of the Son and the mission of the Holy Spirit, in accordance with the decree of God the Father. In other words, "through the incarnation and the Pentecostal event, the Father's saving will has become present and visible in the world. The Church has its ground in the Life of the Trinity, and by its very nature is missionary."[37]

The document then proceeds from this theological starting point to posit a major distinction between mission understood "in the broader sense" and mission "in the more restricted sense":

> *In the broader sense:* The mission of the Church, there-fore, is fulfilled by that activity which makes her fully present to all men and nations. She understands this activity in obe-dience to Christ's command and in response to the grace and love of the Holy Spirit. Thus, by the example of her life and by her preaching, by the sacraments and other means of grace, she can lead them to the faith, the freedom, and the peace of Christ. Thus lies open before them a free and trustworthy road to the full participation in the mystery of Christ.
>
> This mission is a continuing one. In the course of history it unfolds the mission of Christ Himself, who was sent to preach the gospel to the poor. (*AG* 5)
>
> *In the more restricted sense:* "Missions" is the term usual-ly given to those particular undertakings by which the heralds of the gospel are sent out by the Church and go forth into the whole world to carry out the task of preaching the gospel and planting the Church among peoples or groups who do not yet believe in Christ. These undertakings are brought to comple-tion by missionary activity and are commonly exercised in cer-tain territories recognized by the Holy See.
>
> The specific purpose of this missionary activity is evange-lization and the planting of the Church among those peoples and groups where she has not yet taken root. (*AG* 6)

Having thus described these two types of mission, the decree itself makes a distinction among the three classes of people who are the sub-jects of the general mission of the Church—Catholics, other Christians, and non-Christians: "Thus, missionary activity among the nations differs from pastoral activity exercised among the faithful, as well as from undertakings aimed at restoring unity among Christians" (*AG* 6).

Later, in Chapter II on "Mission Work Itself," the decree emphasizes the value of Christian witness in proclaiming the Gospel.

> For, wherever they live, all Christians are bound to show
> forth, by the example of their lives and by the witness of their
> speech, that new man which they put on at baptism, and that
> power of the Holy Spirit by whom they were strengthened at
> confirmation. Thus other men, observing their good works, can
> glorify the Father (cf. Mt. 5:16) and can better perceive the
> real meaning of human life and the bond which ties the whole
> community of mankind together. (*AG* 11)

Among the "good works" elaborated by the Council Fathers are "the
proper regulation of the affairs of economic and social life," "the education of children and young people," "waging war on famine, ignorance,
and disease," and the prudent cooperation of the faithful in "projects
sponsored by public and private organizations, by governments, by international agencies, by various Christians agencies, and even by non-
Christian religions" (*AG* 12). It is thus that, "in imitation of the Incarnation and through the communication of God's love, Christian development work is an integral part of the Church's mission and therefore of
evangelization."[38] Christian witness becomes a revelation without words,
a proclamation of the Good News through life and deeds.

In summary, the documents and decrees of the Second Vatican
Council incorporated much of the theology of the Church's mission that
was developed in the years and decades immediately preceding its convocation. Numerous references to an expanded concept of the ecclesial
mission are present in these decrees and several important distinctions
were made. But no systematic theological synthesis of the Church's mission of evangelization ever issued from the pages of the Council. In fact,
new questions would arise concerning the place of Christian witness and
development not only in the Church's missionary undertakings, but also
in the *total* mission and process of evangelization.

D. Synod of Bishops (Rome 1974)

The years immediately following the close of Vatican II were
fraught with activity. Life both in the Church and in the world did not
stand still while the decrees of the Council were being implemented.
Newspaper headlines kept track of a world in a constant state of rapid
change and turmoil: racial conflicts in the United States and Africa;
student demonstrations in Europe and America, violence in the cities;
wars in Vietnam and the Middle East, and political and civil strife in

Ireland; Watergate; poverty, famine and exploitation in the Third World; revolutions in Africa and Latin America; increasing emphasis on economic, industrial and technological expansion; the population explosion, the ecology and energy crises, etc. Amid all this the Roman Catholic Church was keeping house: implementing reforms in her institutional and liturgical life, seeking dialogue with other Christians, non-Christians and atheists in a world constantly becoming more and more secularized and pluralistic. Large numbers in so-called Christian countries were abandoning their practice of the faith while in Africa millions more were being converted to the same faith. Theological reflection and speculation now centered on the place and meaning of God and the Church in the "secular city" and the modern world. Vatican II had given some indications of what that place and role should be, but a great number of questions still remained unclear and unanswered. How does one go about preaching the Gospel in a "post-Christian" era? What is the relationship of evangelization to human development? to a people's quest for peace, justice and liberation? What does the Gospel have to say to a pluralistic, secular age? to ecumenical endeavors among Christians? and to non-Christian religions? To all these questions the Council had succeeded in doing little more than opening the door.

Meanwhile, new political theologies of the world, liberation, revolution and development made their debut in Europe and the Third World. In his message on World Mission Sunday, October 18, 1970, Pope Paul VI elaborated on the difference between evangelization and development:

> It would be unthinkable for us believers that missionary activity should make earthly reality its only or principal end, and lose sight of its essential goal: namely, to bring all men the light of faith, to give them new life in baptism, to incorporate them into the Mystical Body of Christ, to teach them to live like Christians, and to hold out an existence beyond this earthly one. It would likewise be inadmissible for the Church's missionary activity to neglect the needs and aspirations of developing peoples and, because of its religious orientation, to omit the basic duties of human charity. We cannot forget the Gospel's solemn teaching on the love of our needy and suffering neighbor reiterated by the Apostles, and confirmed by the Church's whole missionary tradition.[39]

The following year the Synod of Bishops' statement on *Justice in the World* (Rome, 1971) declared in no uncertain terms: "Action on behalf of justice and participation in the transformation of the world fully appear to us as a constitutive dimension of the preaching of the Gospel, or, in other words, of the Church's mission for the redemption of the human race and its liberation from every opppressive situation."[40]

Proclaiming the Gospel is now clearly seen to involve incarnating it in the hearts, minds and daily lives of the Church's members as they struggle to give Christian witness amid humankind's hopes and desires for justice, peace and a better world. This same theme is taken up by the Declaration of the International Theological Conference on Evangelization and Dialogue in India (October 1971):

> We live in a momentous period in history when a new civilization is being born before our very eyes. We live in a world in which man strives to be the master of his own destiny, seeking liberation from every form of oppression and slavery. We believe that the universal spirit of Christ, the Lord of History, is undoubtedly present in the evolution that is taking place today, and that we are called upon to discern the signs of the times and to participate with all men of good will in building up the universal brotherhood of love.[41]

It was thus amid this fermentation of world events and theological thought that Pope Paul VI chose as the topic of discussion for the Fourth Synod of Bishops meeting in Rome in 1974 the theme "Evangelization of the Modern World"—a theme he hoped would spark a spiritual renewal within the Church, which for nearly a decade now had been preoccupied with the external reforms of its institutional and liturgical structures and with an updated image of itself to be presented to the modern world.

1. *Preparations for the Synod and the Opening Address*

From the suggestions of the various episcopal conferences around the world, the Synod Secretariat compiled a working paper of topics for discussion during the Synodal meetings. The working paper was divided into two parts: (I.) "The Exchange of Experiences," and (II.) "Connected Theological Questions."[42] Topics that were submitted for discussion under Part I included: the propensity for more intense spiritual life (as witnessed in the sudden rise and popularity of the Cursillo, encounter, and charismatic movements among the faithful), presbyteral and parish councils, the role of the laity, youth, lapsed Catholics, ecumenism, work for human promotion and liberation, the communications media, and liturgical renewal.

In the part on "Connected Theological Questions," first consideration was given to the role of the Holy Spirit in evangelization. Under the topic of "Evangelization Itself," the following clarifications were made: "The 'gospel' does not *per se* and directly signify a certain book, nor a doctrine, nor a law, but the knowledge of this new unheard of reality, definitive and transcendent, that radiates in the person of Jesus Christ"; and the word "evangelization" was defined as "the complex of activities by which men are brought to share in the mystery of Christ in the proclaimed gospel." These activities are then enumerated as (1) the preaching of the word, (2) the testimony of life, and (3) the administration of the sacraments. "The *sacramentality* of evangelization consists first of all precisely in this: the Holy Spirit uses the Church as an organ and an instrument of his action in the world." Finally, the aspects of conversion and salvation were treated as the purpose and goal of evangelization respectively.

Pope Paul VI, in his opening address to the Synod on September 27, 1974, spoke first of the necessity of evangelization and stated: "Evangelization, therefore, is not an occasional or temporary task but a permanent and constitutive necessity of the church: from the command, 'Go therefore and teach all nations' (cf. Mt 28:18-20, Mk 16:16) of the founder, to the incisive word of Paul, and to that equally firm statement of Peter and John: 'We are not able to keep silent about that which we have seen and heard' (Acts 4:20), the mandate continues consistently and cogently down to the most recent council."[43] He then elaborates on the universality and the specific finality of this task. Under the topic of finality and religious purpose, Pope Paul VI, citing *GS* 42, reiterated a point he had made before: "There is no opposition or separation, therefore, but a complementary relationship between evangelization and human progress. While distinct and subordinate, one to the other, each calls for the other by reason of their convergence to the same end: the salvation of man." He concludes by recommending to the Synod's reflection their task of bringing "face to face the traditional concept of the work of evangelization and the new trends, which seek their justification in the Council and the changed conditions of the times."

2. *First Part: Exchange of Experiences*

Discussion of the topic of evangelization began on the morning of September 28, with "panorama" reports of the situations on the five continents.[44] *Africa* reported that Christianity there is growing at double the population rate. Major concerns centered around the adaptation of Christianity to African culture and the Church's continued exertion of its moral authority within those nations still favoring colonialism, apartheid and racial rivalries. Unresolved questions for the African church included relations with Muslims and the evangelization of those peoples who still have never heard the Gospel. The countries of *Latin America* are fundamentally Christian and Catholic in their cultural and religious heritage. The present historical context of the continent centers about a number of phenomena: "an advance toward progress; emargination and unjust dependence; legitimate aspirations to freedom, peace, justice, solidarity, and common brotherhood; dramatic temptation to violence." Amid all this, the Latin American church seeks to be a sign and instrument of Christ's Paschal presence. One report was presented on *North America—Australia—Oceania*. With cultures as varied as these included in a single report, a variety of observations and problems were recorded. Secularization and its accompanying pluralism emerged as a common phenomenon along with concern for the "image" of the Church, both in regard to its official and institutional aspects and to the style of life conveyed by its members, especially the clergy. The present situation in *Asia* is one characterized by rapid transformation and social change brought on by secularization and industrialization. Asiatic countries experience dire poverty which is often aggravated by natural factors. The Church in this situation constitutes a minority amid the other great religions which look upon Christianity as a colonial import. Christian resources on this continent are limited and minimal. The concluding report of the day described a *Europe* that lives in a secularized, "post-Christian" era divided between the "liberal ideology" of the West and the "Marxist ideology" of the East. Many of the reports from the European episcopal conferences stress the need to have a Church which "gets away from itself and concentrates everything on Christ and men."

The oral and written interventions in the week that followed stressed primarily the witness value of a genuine faith-life incarnated in day-to-day living. In a pluralistic, secular age—an age of rapid transport and multimedia communications—the witness of a genuine Christian life speaks more loudly than any number of gestures and words. Cardinal Darmujuwono, Archbishop of Semarang, Indonesia, pointed out: "As an external witness, it is therefore necessary for evangelization to start from concrete circumstances of time and place without changing into a 'transplatio' of the Church from without, but into an 'implantatio' of the Word of God which becomes incarnate in a well-defined socio-cultural context. It then truly becomes dialog."[45] Most of the other interventions manifested different modes of this same point. Cardinal Duval, Archbishop of Algiers, explained: "Essentially, evangelization is an act of love toward God, but also toward our neighbor to whom we wish to show the love of God."[46] Father Pedro Arrupe, Superior General of the

Society of Jesus, maintained the same sort of witness value in the evangelical radicalism of religious life. Bishop Worlock of Portsmouth, England, applied the same theme to work with youth; Cardinal Alfrink to the exercise of authority; Cardinal Tarancon, Archbishop of Madrid, and Brother Charles Henry Buttimer, Superior General of the Brothers of Christian Schools, to the role of the institutional church; Archbishop Lorscheider of Fortaleza, Brazil, to the witness of "pastoral experience of the poor, simple Bishop—one who is open to everyone freely. Distance from the people—often provoked by the bishop himself who still lives like a prince—is of no little harm in evangelization";[47] Archbishop Quinn of Oklahoma City to the witness of the Church's minister; and Monsignor Job, Vicar Capitular of Ibadan, Nigeria, to the total development of the human being—body and soul.

Other important aspects of evangelization brought out in the interventions of the first week included the essential role of an active prayer-life as presented by Cardinal Krol of Philadelphia in regard to youth, and by Archbishop Picachy of Calcutta who stated: "At a time such as we are living in, the Church must above all become contemplative and gradually, day by day, she needs to allow herself to be changed by the Holy Spirit through prayer, contemplation and assiduous listening to the Word of God."[48] Liberation from sin and sinful social structures received the attention of Cardinal Suenens, Archbishop of Brussels, and Archbishop Florez of Cuzco, Peru. Bishop Deskur, President of the Pontifical Commission for Social Communications, spoke on the role of the media in evangelization, while Archbishop Tortola of Parana emphasized the primacy of the family in the evangelization process.

A synthesis of the first week was presented on October 4 by Cardinal Cordiero, Archbishop of Karachi. At the beginning, the Cardinal outlined the methodology of the Synod, stating: "It is necessary to move from concrete realities as God is properly present in this context and reveals Himself to us. These realities will be like 'signs of the times' which should be read, scrutinized and interpreted in order to understand God's designs for the present and to draw from them a theology of evangelization which allows us to agree on the method and programming of evangelization."[49] Among the concrete realities of the present situation were listed: the great world religions renewing themselves while in some places being aided by government support; the "popular religiosity" widespread among Christians and non-Christians; new nations gaining independence in Africa; poverty and material underdevelopment in the Third World; industrialization, urbanization and the growing influence of science and technology; atheism and the Marxist ideology.

With regard to the image of the Church, both positive and negative elements were cited. Among the positive were devotion to one's rightful mission, care for the poor, education work, medical and hospital activities. Negative elements included its Western or foreign aspects, identification with the established order, a certain legalism and authoritarianism, and insufficient reflection of Christ's image. Other aspects of the Church's life discussed included the positive role played by small communities and charismatic groups, the need to give a witness of unity, the value of the local church and indigenization with the creation of indigenous theologies. Finally, all agreed that evangelization is the duty of everyone in the Church and the means to be employed in this task centered around (1) social communications, (2) presbyteral and pastoral councils for planning and implementation, and (3) biblical and catechetical renewal along with the celebration of the liturgy adapted to different local cultures.

3. *Second Part: Connected Theological Questions*

On October 8, Cardinal Wojtyla, Archbishop of Cracow, presented the theological part of the Synod's theme. He began by stating:

> The various questions which will go to make up this report can be considered under the light of one main question: in what sense does evangelization itself constitute a theological theme, and how is it to be treated from the theological viewpoint. This is a topic which under its pastoral theological aspect is of great importance for bishops. Indeed, the entire people of God awaits a clear explanation since in a way, evangelization constitutes the very life of the Church and its prime activity.[50]

The theological elements then brought into consideration commence with Christ's mandate, the promise of the Holy Spirit and the certainty of faith, "which then passes from the theoretical plane of orthodoxy to the concrete plane of orthopraxis." The emphasis here shifts to the ecclesial dimension and the role of the Magisterium:

> The mandate conferred on the Apostles stretches even into the Church of today. It is the Church, in fact, which believes and evangelizes, and together it is believed and becomes evangelized. . . . Announcing the mystery hidden by the centuries in God, the Church announces itself as the sacrament or sign, and the instrument, in Christ, of that intimate union with God and the unity of the whole human race. That announcement is but

an invitation to enter into authentic communion with the People of God, living in fruitful fullness in the Church of Christ.

Under this ecclesial dimension special emphasis is placed on the celebration of the Eucharist, for "evangelization's root and the basis of its effectiveness always remains in the *Mystery of the Cross.*" Finally, a theological concept of the world (based on *Gaudium et Spes*) is presented. Linked under this concept are the themes of conversion-liberation and eternal salvation-human promotion, which are related to the Gospel precept of charity, "of love of God and love of one's neighbor: the last judgment on man and eternal salvation depend on obedience to this precept."

Interventions on this part and the reports of the "circuli minores" (language groups) did little more than highlight various theological points that had already been made. Abbot Rembert Weakland discussed the positive elements favoring theological and liturgical pluralism "in the unity of faith."[51] Many others reemphasized the necessary role played by Christian witness and by work on behalf of human development and liberation in the process of evangelization. The centrality of prayer and the interior life were accented by Archbishop Bernardin speaking on behalf of English language group "A" and Cardinal Marty of Paris, who added: "To be truly evangelizing the Church must be a Church of prayer and Bishops should be teachers of prayer."[52] Cardinal Willebrands, President of the Secretariat for Christian Unity, spoke of the integral relationship between work for ecumenism and evangelization, stressing that "unity in the perfect ecclesial community is a sign of the authenticity of Christ's mission";[53] and Bishop Matagrin of Grenoble, France, speaking for French language group "C," raised the problem of "whether the Eucharist is the *end* of or the *way* to unity; one would hope for greater liberty for the local churches in the matter of eucharistic hospitality."[54] Some discussion on the discernment of the Spirit and reading "the signs of the times" was also brought to the Synod floor. And Bishop Albert Descamps, Secretary of the Pontifical Biblical Commission, developed three scriptural themes: (1) Jesus preached the coming of the Kingdom of God; (2) Christ is the model of apostolic style; and (3) Christ described various attitudes necessary to listen to the word of God: poverty of spirit, childlike simplicity, trust in the Messiah and the heavenly Father.[55]

4. *Declaration of the Synod and Closing Address*

On October 22, a draft of the final document was handed to the

Synodal Fathers for their approval. It was divided into a preamble and four parts:

I) Evangelization in Itself: the Service of the Gospel for the Work of the Church
II) Evangelization and Human Promotion
III) Various Groups Questioning the Church Today
IV) Evangelization as the Work of the Entire Church

When the votes were counted, *only* Part I received the approval of the majority. This part established the theological sources and elements involved in the Church's mission of evangelization. Starting with the role of the Holy Spirit, it declares that salvation comes from Christ alone, who through the means of the Church, the Sacrament of Salvation, continually renders the Incarnation and the work of salvation actual. Next the need for conversion and the interior life is developed, and, finally, the various means of evangelization are described: witness, preaching, catechesis, and the mass media.

Since time was too short for redrafting the rejected proposals, the Synodal Fathers, on October 23, decided on the appropriateness of preparing some sort of final declaration in the form of a message addressed to the whole Church. This declaration,[56] issued by the Synod on October 25, attempted to manifest some fundamental convictions and a few of the more urgent guidelines needed to promote and deepen the work of evangelization. Reechoing the Pope's opening address, the Synodal Fathers confirmed anew that "the mandate to evangelize all men constitutes the essential mission of the Church." They then emphasized the necessity and universality of this mission which must involve every "real Christian." Next, they state:

. . . this work demands incessant interior conversion on the part of individual Christians and continual renewal of our communities and institutions. In this way, faith will become stronger, purer and more intimate and we will become better fit and more credible as witnesses of the faith through the coherence of our individual and social life with the gospel which we must preach.

Such conversion requires intimate union with God through prayer, contemplation on the Word of God and frequent participation in the sacraments.

The Declaration also warns of the difficulties and obstacles placed in the way of evangelization by secularism, atheism and religious persecution. The rapid and radical change in the conditions of our times requires that communication of the Gospel "takes place through word, work and life, each closely connected, and is determined by various almost constitutive elements of the hearers of the word of God: that is, their needs and desires, their way of speaking, hearing, thinking, judging and entering into contact with others." Next the relationship of evangelization and ecumenism is discussed, and, finally, the relationship between liberation and evangelization:

> . . . the church, supported by Christ's gospel and fortified by his grace can harness such dedication to the elimination of deviations, and so the church does not remain within merely political, social and economic limits (elements which she must certainly take into account) but leads toward freedom in all its forms—liberation from sin, from individual or collective selfishness—and to full communion with God and with men who are like brothers. In this way the church, in her evangelical way, promotes the true and complete liberation of all men, groups and peoples.

In his closing address on October 26, Pope Paul VI congratulated the Synod on its efforts,[57] remarking that he realized that the breadth and complexity of the theme did not allow for its exhaustive study in such a short time. His overall evaluation was positive. He enumerated seven points of consensus:

(1) the clarification of the overall relationship of human advancement to evangelization;

(2) the responsibility of *every* Christian to partake in the mission of evangelization;

(3) the relationship between evangelization and genuine Christian witness;

(4) the unanimous respect for human and religious values existing in non-Christian religions and non-Catholic confessions;

(5) the realization of the fact that the Church at the same time is the object and the subject of evangelization;

(6) the conclusion that local churches, in communion with the universal church, are co-responsible for the evangelizing mission;

(7) the action of the Holy Spirit in the work of evangelization, as "the soul of the Church."

In summing up the positive elements of the Synod, the Pope stated: "In a word, there has been a call to greater responsibility on the part of

all, to more prayer, to a deeper interior life, to a greater spirit of poverty, self-denial, genuine love for the Church and souls, to greater fidelity
to God's Word."

The Pope then moved on to the mention of some points, especially
among those that came out of the "circuli minores," that must be better
defined and subjected to further study. Among these are the relationship
between the particular churches and the Apostolic See; the correct understanding of theological pluralism; and the relationship of various individual aspects of human advancement, social progress, etc., to the announcement of the Good News.

Thus, the Fourth Synod of Bishops convoked to discuss the theme
"Evangelization of the Modern World" came to a close. As far as developing a systematic theological synthesis of evangelization, the Synod
proved to be only virtually successful. It did, nevertheless, provide a new
input of concrete experience and reflections which contributed to broad-
ening the overall context in which the Church's mission of evangelization must be understood. In the end, the Synod Fathers found it fitting
to entrust the entire fruits of their discussions and labors to Pope Paul
VI to await further impetus from him.

5. *Evangelii Nuntiandi—Paul VI (December 8, 1975)*

A year after the close of the Synod, Paul VI issued an Apostolic
Exhortation, *Evangelii Nuntiandi*, addressed "To the Episcopate, to the
Clergy and to All the Faithful of the Entire World on Evangelization in
the Modern World."[58] Having completed his study and reflection upon
the work of the 1974 Synod, Pope Paul divided his "meditation" into
seven chapters:

     I: From Christ the Evangelizer to the Evangelizing Church
    II: What is Evangelization?
   III: The content of Evangelization
   IV: The methods of Evangelization
    V: The beneficiaries of Evangelization
   VI: The workers of Evangelization
  VII: The spirit of Evangelization

This rather extensive reflection on "the essential mission of the Church"
contains much that is of theological import. Intending it in a meditative
vein, Paul VI starts with the Apostolic community's faith-experience of
Christ the Evangelizer as recorded in the gospel accounts. His approach
here markedly differs from the Synod's methodology which proposed
starting with concrete realities in order to draw from them a theology of

evangelization (cf. above, 71). Pope Paul chose instead to begin with eliciting and analyzing the New Testament's understanding of its evangelizing mission. From there he proceeds to adapt the fruits of this reflection to the concrete realities of the contemporary situation, all the while continuing to maintain close contact with the scriptural sources.

Realizing the complexity of the evangelizing action, Paul VI warns against formulating any facile definition of it:

> Any partial and fragmentary definition which attempts to render the reality of evangelization in all its richness, complexity and dynamism does so only at the risk of impoverishing it and even distorting it. It is impossible to grasp the concept of evangelization unless one tries to keep in view all its essential elements.[59]

These elements he later enumerates as: "the renewal of humanity, witness, explicit proclamation, inner adherence, entry into the community, acceptance of signs, apostolic initiative."[60] Describing the purpose of evangelization, he writes: "The Church evangelizes when she seeks to convert, solely through the divine power of the message she proclaims, both the personal and collective consciences of people, the activities in which they engage, and the lives and concrete milieux which are theirs."[61]

Pope Paul sees the content of evangelization centered on the Kingdom of God with the evangelizer bearing witness first of all to the Father's love revealed by Christ in the Holy Spirit.[62] Next he brings into play necessary secondary elements which are subject to changing circumstances, such as the relationship between evangelization and human advancement, stating that "the man who is to be evangelized is not an abstract being but is subject to social and economic questions."[63] Pertaining to the methods of carrying out this mission, Paul VI discusses the witness of life, preaching, catechetics, the mass media, personal contact, the role of the sacraments, and popular piety. The beneficiaries of evangelization included everyone, Christians and non-Christians, nonbelievers and the nonpracticing; he saves a rather lengthy paragraph under this particular area for an evaluative critique of "small communities" (*communautés de base*) elaborating on their pros and cons.[64] Reaffirming the teaching of Vatican II, the Pope then demonstrates that the Church is missionary in her entirety. Be it the universal Church, local churches, bishops, priests, religious, laity, families, young people—all Christians everywhere are called to proclaim the Good News according to their particular vocation.

Finally, Pope Paul discusses the "spirit of Evangelization" referring to the interior attitudes by which the Holy Spirit animates those who work for evangelization. Just as the descent of the Spirit upon Jesus at his baptism manifests his election and mission, so today the same Holy Spirit is "the principal agent of evangelization."[65] "But," the Pope continues, "it can equally be said that he is the goal of evangelization: he alone stirs up the new creation, the new humanity of which evangelization is to be the result, with that unity in variety which evangelization wishes to achieve within the Christian community." It is the Spirit, too, who causes people to discern the signs of the times, so that they can penetrate the heart of the world with the Gospel and animate it with the love of God.

Evangelii Nuntiandi—while dedicated by Paul VI to the commemoration of three events: the end of the Holy Year, the tenth anniversary of the closing of Vatican II, and one year after the Synod of Bishops met to discuss the theme of evangelization—is more truly a fitting conclusion to the work of the Synod of Bishops. Here Paul VI accomplishes what that Synod had to leave unfinished, namely, to piece together a sufficiently systematic theological description of the Church's evangelizing mission.

SUMMARY

Christians, in the ecclesial communities of the first Christian centuries, continued to share the spirit, traditions and way of life handed down to them from apostolic times. For them Christ was the glorified and risen Lord, present in their midst. In his Name they were baptized and came to share the divine life of the Father, Son and Spirit. In his Name they gathered together to offer prayers, to listen to the readings from Scripture and to celebrate the Eucharist. By means of the "kerygma," the "catechumenate," and the teaching of the Fathers (Christian "gnosis"), they were built up, instructed and transformed into a community of faith, hope and love. Martyrdom for them at that time became the ultimate *witness* and union with Christ. The whole patristic era was dominated by a vision of the "Total Christ," communion with whom in an ecclesial community of shared faith provided the focal point of the Church's life and worship and the terminal point of the evangelization process.

Already during the patristic era, however, the seeds of a radical transformation in Christianity had been sown. Theodosius the Great's imperial decree of 380 laid the foundation of "Christendom" or the "Respublica Christiana." Persecutions ceased and monasticism now flourished as the ultimate form of Christian witness. The masses were soon to be baptized with little or no catechetical preparation. During the time of the transferal of imperial power entire German tribes were baptized at once, and missionaries could hope for little more than their learning the Our Father and the Creed. Christ's divinity, because of earlier Christological controversies, was now emphasized to the point where his humanity passed into the shadows. Christian worship and the spiritual life tended more and more toward objectification and external expressions. Evangelization no longer centered on the kerygma, but rather it was now solely identified with the conversion and baptism of "pagan" peoples—an orientation it would maintain throughout the centuries of worldwide discoveries and explorations.

This narrower concept of evangelization officially prevailed in the Church until the Second Vatican Council. In the early twentieth century, European theologians began to reflect on the contemporary situation that saw formerly Christian countries becoming de-Christianized with the growth of industrialization, urbanization, and the rise of secularism and atheism. The birth, too, of Catholic Action, the priest-worker movement, and ecumenism gave new impetus to resituate the notion of mission within ecclesiology. New research in this latter field soon showed that the Church herself as mystery and communion is primarily and essentially missionary. Vatican II gave an official stamp to these latest conclusions in ecclesiology by its promulgation of *Lumen Gentium*, the Dogmatic Constitution on the Church. *Ad Gentes*, the Council's Declaration on Missionary Activity, helped to clarify the situation somewhat by making a distinction between the Church's mission and "missions" (*AG* 5&6), and the Pastoral Constitution on the Church, *Gaudium et Spes*, set some guidelines for the Church's mission in the modern world. No systematic theological synthesis of evangelization, however, was ever developed by the Council.

The decade following the close of Vatican II was a time of rapid change and transformation both in society and in the Church. As new nations in Africa and older ones in Latin America were seeking independence and liberation from exploitation and colonial rule, the whole question of the relationship of human development and evangelization came to the fore within the Church. The Council's reforms of the Church's institutional structures and liturgical life were being implemented, yet the people seemed to be searching for something deeper, more spiritual and interior. It was at this time that Pope Paul VI chose as the topic of discussion for the Fourth Synod of Bishops to meet in Rome in the autumn of 1974 the theme of the "Evangelization of the Modern World." For four weeks the Pope and bishops met. There was a lively exchange of experiences, but the Synod, too, was unable to put together a comprehen-

sive and systematic theological synthesis of evangelization. Yet, somehow, the pendulum now appeared to have come full swing from the
patristic era. The Church now seemed to be standing at the very thresh-
old of a great spiritual-moral renewal based upon the gradual rediscovery of the evangelical spirit and life which she herself shares in communion and fellowship with her glorified and risen Lord—Jesus Christ.
Finally, with the publication of *Evangelii Nuntiandi* on December 8,
1975, Paul VI endeavored to give a new impetus to this evangelical renewal and mission.

NOTES

1. The term "kerygma" has been resurrected in the last few decades in an
attempt to resolve the modern "crisis of preaching," which reproaches contemporary preaching for being too abstract, moralistic and lifeless (cf. D. Grasso,
Proclaiming God's Message [Notre Dame, Indiana, 1965], x-xiv). It was as a
solution to this crisis that Jungmann proposed the development of a *Verkün-
digungstheologie*, or kerygmatic theology in *Die Frohbotschaft und unsere Glau-
benverkündigung* (Regensburg, 1936). See also *The Good News Yesterday and
Today*, an abridged translation of *Die Frohbotschaft*, (New York 1962).

2. E. Simons, "Kerygma" *SM*, III, 245; cf. also, H. Schlier, "The Chief
Features of the New Testament Theology of the Word of God," *Concilium* 33
(New York, 1965), 9-19.

3. Cf. R.E. McNally, *The Unreformed Church* (New York, 1965), 65-67.

4. Cf. J. Jungmann, *The Early Liturgy* (Notre Dame, Indiana, 1959), 74,
166.

5. T.L. Westow, *The Variety of Catholic Attitudes* (New York, 1963), 19.

6. Cf. Jungmann, *The Good News*, 25: "Again and again Gregory's
thought turns to the glorified Redeemer, who at the side of His Father, is our
support and helper—not a piece of past history but the highest actuality, toward
whom we constantly strive." Westow in *The Variety of Catholic Attitudes*, 36,
observes that "after Gregory's death, the West for three centuries and more
failed to produce a single outstanding thinker or theologian. Such means as missionaries could use in their work of conversion were: the more or less established
tradition of the liturgy in the celebration of the Mass and the Divine Office, the
stories of saints and their miracles, a tendency toward a more or less individualistic spiritual life as it developed in some monastic circles, the new devotional
fashions based on such works as the *Peregrination Sylviae*, which revealed the
material reminders of Christ's life in Palestine to the Western world in the
fourth century, and the suddenly popular traffic in relics. . . ."

7. J. Audinet, "Catechesis," *SM* I, 264.

8. Cf. G.S. Sloyan, "Religious Education: From Early Christianity to
Medieval Times," in *Shaping the Christian Message*, idem., ed. (New York,
1958), 21.

9. L. Bouyer, *The Spirituality of the New Testament and the Fathers*
(New York, 1963), 537.

10. *Ibid.*, 184, 201.

11. *Ibid.*, 211.

12. "Orat., VII: In lauden Caesarii," 23; *PG*, xxxv, 785.

13. A. Harnack, *Die Mission and Ausbreitung des Christentums in der ersten drei Jahrhunderten* (1902), 267f.

14. Jungmann, *The Early Liturgy*, 74-75.

15. Bouyer, *Spirituality*, 305-6.

16. Jungmann, *The Early Liturgy*, 251.

17. Westow, *The Variety of Catholic Attitudes*, 31.

18. E. Iserloh, "Die Kontinuität des Christentums beim Obergang von der Antike zum Mittelalter," in *Trierer theol. Zeitschrift*, LXIII, 1954, 193-205.

19. A. Mirgeler, *Mutations of Western Christianity* (New York, 1964), 69.

20. Cf. M.E. Jegen, "Cathechesis, II (Medieval and Modern)," *The New Catholic Encyclopedia* (New York, 1967) III, 210-17. (Hereafter cited as *NCE*.)

21. Westow, *The Variety of Catholic Attitudes*, 41-2, and a footnote reference to *Summa Theologica*, III, q. lxxxiii, ad 1, where "St. Thomas discusses the annual celebration of the *Passio Domini*, which, in his quotation from St. Augustine, he identifies with the Pascha, in the true early patristic tradition. He then says: '*Sed tempore passionis recolitur passio Christi solum secundum hoc quod in ipso capite nostro fuit perfecta.*' "

22. M.-J. Le Guillou, "Mission as an Ecclesiological Theme," *Concilium*, XIII (New York, 1966), 82.

23. *Ibid.*, 92.

24. P. Haubtmann, *Semaine religieuse de Paris* (October 26, 1963), p. 1031.

25. J.A. Moehler, *Symbolism* (London, 1843), 6-7.

26. M.-D. Chenu, *La Parole de Dieu II: L'Evangile dans de temps* (Coll. Cogitatio Fidei II) (Paris: Ed. du Cerf, 1964), 489.

27. K. Rahner, *The Christian Commitment* (New York, 1964), 33-4. H. Urs von Balthasar, making a rapid summary of the development of the Church since the Middle Ages, writes: "Many people today are ready to give their life for the Church and the world. . . . They need a theology which views Christian life as service, mission and participation in the source of energy where the Church attains completion. If a theology clearly thought out along these lines could be achieved and also popularized by its adoption into Christian teaching, Christian communities could radiate this new force over the world." Cf. "Raser les bastions," in *Dieu Vivant* 25 (1953), 32.

28. J. Masson, "Vatican II and Post-Conciliar Theology of Evangelization," *SAS*, 41.

29. Cf. C. Journet, *L'Eglise du Verbe incarné II: Sa structure interne et son unité catholique* (Paris, 1951), 1223-53; and A. Chavasse, H. Denis, J. Frisque, R. Garnier, *L'Eglise et apostolat* (Paris/Tournai, 1954).

30. M.-J. Le Guillou, *Le Christ et l'Eglise—Théologie du mystère* (Paris, 1963), 15, as quoted by idem., in "Mission," 117.

31. John XXIII, "Opening Speech to the Council" (Oct. 11, 1962), in *Abbott*, 718.

32. Le Guillou, "Mission," 89-90.

33. Cf. B. Kloppenburg, *The Ecclesiology of Vatican II* (Chicago, 1974), 98.

34. *Ibid.*, 99.

35. Y. Congar, "Pastoral Constitution on the Church in the Modern World, Part I, Chapter IV," in H. Vorgrimler, ed., *Commentary on the Documents of Vatican II* (New York, 1966), V, 205. (Hereafter cited as *Vorgrimler.*)

36. *Ibid.*, cf. *GS* 43.

37. S. Brechter, "Decree on the Church's Missionary Activity," in *Vorgrimler*, IV, 114.

38. J. Schütte, "Evangelization and Development in Light of Conciliar and Post-Conciliar Theology," *SAS*, 383.

39. Paul VI, "Message for World Mission Sunday," dated June 5, 1970, in *The Pope Speaks*, 15 (1970-71), 105-6. (Hereafter cited as *TPS.*)

40. Synod of Bishops, *Justice in the World*, (Typis Polyglottis Vaticanis, 1971), 6.

41. "Declaration of the International Theological Conference on Evangelization and Dialogue in India," (Nagpur, Oct. 6-12, 1971), *SAS*, 1.

42. Cf. "Evangelization in the Modern World"—Synod Working Paper, Rome Synod Secretariat (unofficial trans.), *Origins* IV (Aug. 29, 1974), 147-53.

43. Paul VI, "Opening Address to the Synod of Bishops," in *L'OR(E)*, 41 (Oct. 10, 1974), 6. This same text along with the Closing Address, the Declaration, Synodal statement on Human Rights and Reconciliation, and the oral and written interventions of the American representatives can be found in the booklet, *Synod of Bishops—1974*, USCC (Wash. D.C., 1975).

44. Cf. *Synodus Episcoporum—Assemblea Generale 1974* (Comitato per L'Informazione), Bulletin No. 2 (Sept. 28, 1974). (Hereafter cited as *SE.*)

45. *SE* No. 5 (Oct. 2), 3.

46. *SE* No. 3 (Sept. 20), 13.

47. *SE* No. 7A (written intervention, Oct. 3), 3.

48. *SE* No. 4 (Oct. 1), 9.

49. *SE* No. 8 (Oct. 4), 1.

50. *SE* No. 9 (Oct. 8), 2.

51. *SE* No. 10 (Oct. 9), 2.

52. *SE* No. 17 (Oct. 17), 6.

53. *SE* No. 13 (Oct. 11), 6.

54. *SE* No. 11 (Oct. 11), 10.

55. *SE* No. 14 (Oct. 12), 9.

56. Cf. "Declaration of the Synodal Fathers," in *L'OR(E)*, 45 (Nov. 7, 1974), 3, for all quotations from this message.

57. Cf. "Holy Father's Address at the Conclusion of Synod of Bishops," in *L'OR(E)*, 45 (Nov. 7, 1974), 8-10, for all quotations from this address.

58. *Evangelii Nuntiandi*, par. 1-5. (Herafter cited as *EN.*)

59. *EN*, par. 17.

60. *EN*, par. 24.

61. *EN*, par. 18.

62. Cf. *EN*, par. 8: "Only the Kingdom therefore is absolute, and it makes everything else relative." Also, pars. 26 and 34.

63. *EN*, par. 31.

64. Cf. *EN*, par. 58.

65. *EN*, par. 75.

III
Theological Reflections

The Second Vatican Council's Decree on the Missionary Activity of the Church stated that: "The pilgrim Church is missionary by her very nature. For it is from the mission of the Son and the mission of the Holy Spirit that she takes her origin, in accordance with the decree of God the Father" (*AG* 2). Pope Paul VI and the Fourth Synod of Bishops (1974) later declared that evangelization constitutes the Church's "essential and primary mission." In order, therefore, to locate the starting point of the evangelizing mission, we must trace our steps backwards beyond time and history to that primal, divine surge by which God, in an utterly free and mysterious decree of his own wisdom and goodness, chose to enter into a love-filled dialogue and to impart himself to the world. As G. Thils has described it:

> This is a single impulse and from time immemorial, God awakens and quickens the world, mankind; and so doing he outlines like a filigree tracery in this movement the dominant traits of what may be called his one eternal plan. What is his aim? To bring about the perfecting and fulfilment of the human community and of the universe "in His image and likeness" mysteriously but authentically, so that the fellowship of fullness of life may one day be established between Him and man, and in Him among all men. This project is primal and fundamental, it is wholly one of light, joy and peace. Yet in so far as men are weak, sick, enslaved and sinful—in so many ways at so many levels—this same impulse of the Father, the Lord and the Spirit strengthens us, heals us, liberates and restores us: it is a capital and indeed indispensable work, but one that is nonetheless secondary and subordinate since it wholly tends toward fulfillment, the perfecting of all created things.[1]

This loving self-communication of God constitutes the entire economy of salvation and has a Trinitarian structure.[2] This is the "gospel mystery" Paul speaks of, "a mystery kept secret for endless ages, but now so clear that it must be broadcast to pagans everywhere to bring them to the obedience of faith" (Rom 16:26)—a mystery revealed in Christ through the Spirit (cf. Eph 3:4-6).

God's communicating himself in love and revealing his gracious plan has been perceived to be "good news." Thus, the psalmist cries out:

> Sing Yahweh a new song!
> Sing to Yahweh all the earth!
> Sing to Yahweh, bless his name.
>
> Proclaim his salvation day after day,
> tell of his glory among the nations,
> tell his marvels to every people. (Ps 96:1-3)

Indeed, God's loving design, which provides the basis for all his work and activity "ad extra," can be said to constitute the context of evangelization.

In this chapter we want to bring together the various elements that elucidate this one divine plan, once referred to during the early Christian era as "the mystery of simplicity."[3] We want to attempt above all to maintain that unity of the gospel mystery which is often lost and hidden among the complexities of its individual aspects. Theological reflection arises from the human situation to which God reveals and gives himself. Theology, understood in this sense, seeks to categorize and systematize our knowledge of God-revealing-and-communicating-himself to the human race. It is not concerned with metaphysics and the study of God "sub ratione Deitatis," but with the ongoing dialogue in which God and human persons are co-subjects.[4] To this end we shall summarize some of the contemporary reflections of dogmatic theology upon the mysteries of Revelation, Grace, the Church and Sacraments which in turn serve to explicate the *first moment* of the evangelization process, namely, the proclamation of the gospel mystery.

Since the divine economy of salvation has a Trinitarian structure, its implementation should follow therefrom. The utterly free and mysterious decree of God the Father is revealed through the Word (thus revelation is concerned with the *signifying* mission and its Christological aspect—cf. Rom 17:25), and is accomplished in the Spirit (here grace explains the *unifying* mission and its pneumatic aspect—cf. 1 Cor 12:12-13). Both aspects are never really separate. Revelation itself is a gift of grace, and the Spirit is operative in revelation. Yet the doctrines of revelation and grace present us with the two fundamental aspects of God's one plan. The two aspects carry over into our experience of the Church and the sacraments and are combined in the Church's fundamental mission of evangelization.

A. REVELATION

From an anthropological perspective, revelation denotes that fundamental insight from which a human person's awareness of ultimate transcendent Reality arises. Christians see it primarily as a Christological encounter, since it pertains to the Word of God, who is the mediator of all divine self-communication for "through him all things came to be, not one thing had its being but through him" (Jn 1:3). This encounter is in actuality a process of unveiling and recognition "because God in whom we live and move and exist was always there, and always there *first*."[5] It comprises the experience of a transcendental relationship that seeks expression in categorical terms. Thus the word of God (Hebrew, "dabar") in the Old Testament has both a dynamic and noetic aspect. R. Latourelle observes: "On the one hand, the word of God creates the world, imposes His law, sets history in motion; and on the other hand it manifests the will of God, his salvific plan. The word of God infallibly effects what it says."[6] This can be clearly seen from the different forms that the self-revelation of God assumes.

1. *Religious Experience*

The saints, mystics and spiritual writers down through the centuries, while affirming that God is knowable, at the same time bear witness to the fact that he is incomprehensible.[7] When we turn to the mystics, such as Julian of Norwich or John of the Cross, who "saw God," we hear them "speak of their knowledge as an 'entrance into unknowing,' and John described the object of his search and his finding simply as 'I-don't-know-what' (non sé qué)."[8] This incomprehensibility of God means "that God is not 'grasped' like any other object of knowledge and that any human knowledge of God is only mediate and indirect."[9] The authentic revelation of God, therefore, is not first and foremost a matter of the intellect but a matter of spirit, a dialogue of love between persons. This fact has important implications for one's spiritual-moral life and for evangelization and the proclamation of the gospel truth. In the words of Thomas Merton:

> God has revealed Himself to men in Christ, but He has revealed Himself first of all as love. . . . Only he who loves can be sure that he is still in contact with the truth, which is in fact too absolute to be grasped by the mind. Hence he who holds to

the gospel truth is afraid that he might lose the truth by a failure of love, not by a failure of knowledge.[10]

The reflection of fundamental theology upon religious experience reveals that "in religious matters love precedes knowledge."[11] As B. Lonergan points out: "Before it enters the world mediated by meaning, religion is the prior word God speaks to us by flooding our hearts with his love."[12] God reveals himself to us primarily as a loving presence. *Cor ad cor loquitur.* Personal presence takes knowledge out of an epistemological context. "Ordinarily, the experience of the mystery of love is not objectified. It remains in subjectivity as a vector, and overtow, a fateful call to dreaded holiness."[13]

2. *The Cosmic Word*

The sacramentality of creation is one of the great themes of Sacred Scripture and the Eastern churches. The Old Testament psalms have heaven and earth and all things singing the glory of God (Ps 14, 96, 97, 104). St. Paul explicitly affirms God's revelation of himself to the whole human race in the splendor of creation: "For what can be known about God is perfectly plain to them since God himself has made it plain. Ever since God created the world his everlasting power and deity—however invisible—have been there for men to see in the things he has made" (Rom 1:19-20). As already noted, St. John tells us that all that is and all that has life came to be through the Word and "without Him nothing was made" (Jn 1:1-4).

Furthermore, God created us in his image (Gen 1:26; Wis 2:23). "Male and female he created them" (Gen 1:27). In the Trinitarian image of God the human person was created not as a solitary, but as a social being, "and unless he relates himself to others he can neither live nor develop his potential" (*GS* 12). God thereby inscribed his law in our hearts (Rom 2:15), revealing to us what is just and good. Through creation God makes himself known to *all* humankind.[14]

3. *Salvation History*

In a certain general sense all of history is salvation history, since history is the prerequisite and the channel through which God's manifestation of his self-revealing love reaches the human heart. History is the necessary a priori human context within which the divine plan of salvation becomes known. In a general sense such knowledge can remain noncategorical and unarticulated and is equivalent to the spiritual dynamism inherent in the universality of divine grace. In a more specific sense salvation history "signifies the story of God's saving action in history as interpreted by the prophets and apostles and as recorded in the Bible."[15]

Salvation history in this latter sense more clearly demonstrates the dynamic and noetic aspects of revelation as it assumes the double form of words and deeds. Vatican II's Dogmatic Constitution on Divine Revelation thus describes it: "This plan of salvation is realized by deeds and words having an inner unity: the deeds wrought by God in the history of salvation manifest and confirm the teaching and realities signified by the words, while the words proclaim the deeds and clarify the mystery contained in them" (DV 2). Strictly speaking, this salvation history begins with the Mosaic covenant and the Exodus event. The Jewish people first came to experience God as a savior. It was only in reflecting upon this saving event that the Hebrew mind eventually came to recognize God as the Creator. The Old Testament, then, interprets and explains in the terms of salvation those greater and lesser events in the history of God's Chosen People that are discerned by the sacred writers and prophets to be of salvific import. The word of God becomes the interpretative element of these events, as the knowledge grows clearer and clearer.

In this historical process of interpretation by the words of God himself—the specific characteristic of the special history of salvation—God's offer of grace to man and man's more and more manifest acceptance of it move parallel on to the eschatological climax which determines the meaning and outcome of all history. At this point offer and acceptance of grace, and their interpretation by God's own words, attain their historical and indissoluble unity, in the person of the Word become man.[16]

4. *The Incarnation*

The Christocentric nature of all revelation, basically hidden through the history of salvation to this point, is fully manifested when the Word becomes flesh. Incarnation is the primary law of revelation! God's revelation of himself is essentially incarnational.

Then, after speaking in many places and varied ways through the prophets, God "last of all in these days has spoken to us by his son" (Heb 1:1-2). For He sent His Son, the eternal Word, who enlightens all men, so that he might dwell among men and tell them the innermost realities about God (cf. Jn 1:1-18). Jesus Christ, therefore, the Word made flesh, sent as "a man to men," "speaks the words of God" (Jn 3:34), and

completes the work of salvation which His Father gave Him to
do (cf. Jn 5:36; 17:4). (*DV* 4)

Salvation history in both the general and more specific sense arrive at
their culmination here. The former, in principle though perhaps not de
facto, becomes absorbed in the latter, for Christ is the absolute point of
unity between grace and revelation.

The entire economy of salvation, which originates from the desire
of the divine will to enter into a loving dialogue and relationship with us
through a total communion of life, finds its fulfilment in the Word made
flesh. Thus, in commenting on *Dei Verbum*, J. Ratzinger observes:

> . . . in the New Testament; instead of words, we have *the*
> Word. Christ no longer speaks merely of God, but he is him-
> self the speech of God; this man is himself and as an entity the
> Word of God that has made himself one of us. Thus the per-
> fection of revelation in Christ is here removed from the do-
> main of positivist thinking: God does not arbitrarily cease
> speaking at some point in history and at some point of his dis-
> course, although there would be much more to say, but Christ
> is the end of God's speaking, because after him and beyond
> him God has, as it were, said himself. In him the dialogue of
> God attained its goal; it has become union.[17]

God's self-giving love for us, which, indeed, was there from the beginning, becomes *the* Gospel (the Good News) in Love Incarnate, who is
Emmanuel, that is, God-with-us (cf. Mt 1:23). As we have noted already, Jesus Christ is the divine Word spoken who has come for the purpose of giving us Eternal Life (cf. Jn 1:4; 10:10, and 1 Jn 1:1-2; 4:9). So
it is that in him the *extent* of God's love ("agape") for us is fully
revealed (cf. Jn 15:13; Rom 5:8) when he emptied himself ("kenosis")
and accepted even death on a cross (cf. Phil 2:6-8), thereby fulfilling
God's will to reconcile all things, everything in heaven and on earth
through him and for him (cf. Col 1:20).

Jesus Christ is Love Incarnate (1 Jn 4:8 and Jn 1:14, also *GS* 22)—
the "agape-kenosis" or kenotic love. In him God's will takes on flesh
(cf. Mt 26:42; Jn 6:38). Word and deed (the noetic and dynamic aspects
of revelation) are united as the "kenosis" becomes the ultimate expression of God's self-emptying love.[18] Out of such kenotic love comes the
further revelation of eternal life as Jesus' resurrection becomes one of
the most decisive turning points in salvation history. Rising in "the spirit
of holiness that was in him" (Rom 1:4), Jesus is the "new Adam" (1 Cor
15:45), the prototype of the transformation of the human race. In the

Paschal Mystery, the revelation of the divine economy of salvation reaches its climax as all of God's promises throughout the history of salvation find their fulfillment. "The word of resurrection becomes the bestowal of reconciliation, of the life and love of God himself, as they are revealed in Jesus Christ (2 Cor 5:20, 6:2; 1 Jn 1:2, 3:5, 8, 4:7ff.)."[19] Jesus himself, thus, has been denominated the "primordial dogma" of Christianity.[20] In him and through him divine life and Love is given and made known.

Revelation constitutes God's loving dialogue with humankind. Its primary law is incarnation as it seeks ever more and more concrete expression from creation through salvation history to the Word made flesh, Jesus Christ. Revelation thus attempts to signify in terms of human comprehensibility and experience that which, because of its luminous and infinite magnitude, must always remain a veiled and inexpressible Mystery for finite creatures. As dialogue, revelation addresses the human person, moves one to conversion and challenges one to a personal response of living faith. Faith completes revelation and makes it truly a dialogue of being and life. As Hugo Rahner has explained it:

> Revelation is always a communication of knowledge and being. It is faith and new life. This new life begins with faith as its starting point, and, vice versa, faith is the activity of this new way of life, the activity of supernatural being. But this new life is a participation in the life of the Trinity (and so also a participation in the knowledge about this life), hence in the eternal, spiritual life of God.[21]

Divine revelation as a dialogue of love constitutes spiritual intercourse and a real communion of persons. It conveys both knowledge and grace —God's gift of himself to us.

B. GRACE

Through the mission of the Son, the Word of God become flesh, the divine economy of salvation was fully revealed to humankind. It was Christ's Paschal Mystery which made known God's loving design to invite us to participation in his own divine life. This New Life, constituted by God's self-communication, is a free gift attributed to the power and mission of the Holy Spirit. It is grace. The Greek word "charis" (grace) in common usage connoted charm, benevolence, mercy and gratitude. Thus, before its adoption by the apostolic Church, this word "already meant both the condescension of the giver and the thanks of the favored."[22] In its Christian context, "grace" consequently refers to "God's loving presence and man's transformation in it."[23] P. Fransen further elaborates on this Christian concept: "Essentially, grace consists in this: that God, the Blessed Trinity, loves us. The trinitarian love consists in the union of the Father, Son and Holy Spirit with us; or better their drawing us into the intimacy of their own trinitarian life by uniting us with themselves."[24]

For a long time in the Western Church, the doctrine on grace had become disassociated with its source in Christ and the activity of the Holy Spirit. Karl Rahner affirms: "There are whole tracts 'De gratia Christi' in which for all practical purposes, and seen as a whole, the word 'Christus' appears only in the title. These tracts simply presuppose as self-evident, or mention only briefly, that this grace is 'merited' precisely by Christ himself."[25] And J. Jungmann affirms: "In the early Church the doctrine about grace—in so far as this was not contained in the doctrine on Christ . . . —was taught, by preference, under the rubric of 'the Holy Spirit.' In Baptism the Holy Spirit was bestowed on the faithful as an uncreated gift and he remained in them as the motive power of their new life."[26] The placement of the theological tract of grace here was determined by the Trinitarian structure of the Creed. Peter Lombard would later identify grace with the Holy Spirit, but after much discussion in the thirteenth and fourteenth centuries, his thesis was rejected. Scholastic theology would maintain that grace could only be appropriated to the Holy Spirit. Subsequent dogmatic inquiry concerned itself only with actual grace—and that understood solely in abstract, metaphysical categories—as a necessary prerequisite for positing a moral act. Our return to a biblical vision of grace, in this particular section, will show its necessary relationship to Christ's Paschal Mystery and the mission of the Holy Spirit.

1. *Grace: Its Christological Origin*

Christ, as we have already seen, is the absolute point of unity between grace and revelation. He is the mediator of all grace. St. Paul writes: "If it is certain that through one man's fall so many died, it is even more certain that divine grace, coming through one man, Jesus Christ, came to so many as an abundant free gift" (Rom 5:15; cf. also 1 Cor 1:4). St. Paul never really described the full theological concept of grace, but he "linked its function indissolubly to the death of Jesus Christ in his notion of the history of salvation; then, he situated it for believers in the process of justification and baptism; and finally, he interpreted this 'charis' as a call to special moral or apostolic service."[27]

The revelation of grace has its source in the Paschal Mystery (cf. Rom 8:32). In its power and inwardness this grace is associated with the

Holy Spirit (cf. Rom 5:5), for the Spirit is the principle of resurrection. Again, St. Paul teaches: "If the Spirit of Him who raised Jesus from the dead is living in you, then he who raised Jesus from the dead will give life to your own mortal bodies through his Spirit living in you" (Rom 8:11; cf. also, 1:4). Thus, this Spirit is referred to as the "Spirit of Christ" (Rom 8:9, Phil 1:19; Gal 4:6), and as "another Advocate" (Jn 14:16) who is another Jesus, the presence of Jesus when Jesus is absent. This relationship of the Spirit to Christ and its origin in the Paschal Mystery is clearly demonstrated by Vatican II's Dogmatic Constitution on the Church:

> Christ, having been lifted up from the earth, is drawing all men to Himself (Jn 12:32, Greek text). Rising from the dead (cf. Rom 6:9), He sent His lifegiving Spirit upon His disciples and through this Spirit has established His body, the Church, as the universal sacrament of salvation. Sitting at the right hand of the Father, He is continually active in the world, leading men to the Church, and through her joining them more closely to Himself and making them partakers of His glorious life by nourishing them with His own body and blood.
>
> Therefore, the promised restoration which we are awaiting has already begun in Christ, is carried forward in the mission of the Holy Spirit, and through Him continues in the Church (*LG* 48).

Commenting on the seeming identification of Christ and the Spirit, such as in Paul's formula "The Lord is Spirit" (2 Cor 3:17), M. Schmaus maintains that this is purely a dynamic and not an ontological identity. "Christ is active through the Holy Spirit, so that Christ and the Spirit do not constitute two separate principles of activity, but combine as one."[28] In the Resurrection, Christ became "spiritual." Indeed, Christ's whole ministry and work of redemption was accomplished in the Spirit (cf. Jn 1:32-33) and through him the Spirit flows forth into all who believe (cf. Jn 7:37-39; 19:34).

The purpose of grace is also fundamentally Christological. The graced person through participation in the divine life becomes Christlike. St. Paul clearly emphasizes this particular point when he writes: "I have been crucified with Christ, and I live now not with my own life but with the life of Christ who lives in me. The life I now live in this body I live in faith: faith in the Son of God who loved me and who sacrificed himself for my sake. I cannot bring myself to give up God's gift ('charis')" (Gal 2:20-21). In the Letter to the Romans we read that God has called us and chosen us specially long ago "to become true images of His Son" (Rom 8:29); and this follows from the fact that "the baptized man has become with Christ 'a single being' ('sumphytos' Rom 6:5). In baptism is given to us the Spirit of Christ, in whom Father and Son love one another and love men so that Paul does not hesitate to define the Christian, a son of God, in terms of the gift of the Spirit"[29] (cf. Rom 8:14). By grace we are transformed into "images" of Christ, who is the paradigm of humanity, the perfect model of the kind of love God expects from human persons, for "if we live by the truth and in love, we shall grow in all ways into Christ who is the head by whom the whole body is fitted and joined together" (Eph 4:15-16). This Christ-likeness, as now becomes evident, is more perceptible in the community of the faithful as a whole than in any individual member.

In Pauline theology, the goal of grace is the recapitulation of all things in Christ (Eph 1:9-10). Thus, one of the early titles given Christ is that of the "New" or "Second Adam" (cf. Rom 5:15-19; 1 Cor 15:21f, 25). "Because *Adama* means not one individual man (*ish*) but man in the sense of mankind the title Second Adam implies a new model for what mankind can be. It suggests that men can find a new corporate unity in Jesus. It does not suggest that any individual can be exactly like Jesus, but rather that Jesus extends the power (grace) to grow to be like him and to be one in him to mankind."[30] In one Spirit and through a variety of gifts ("charismata") we form Christ's body, the Church (I Cor 12:4, 27). The grace of reconciliation and freedom which originates from Christ's Paschal Mystery is essentially ecclesial—the Church is the "fullness" of the new creation (Eph 1:23)—universal and cosmic in scope and under the guidance of the Spirit (cf. Col 1:20; Rom 8:20-27).

2. *New Life*

In Paul's letters and elsewhere in the New Testament, especially in John, we find a number of synonyms to designate this new existence in grace. The most common ones are: life, spirit, new creation, filial adoption, the interior man. The fundamental Johannine term employed to describe the reality of Christian existence is "life." Christ is the "Word of Life" (1 Jn 1:1), the revelation of Eternal Life which was with the Father from the beginning and has now been made visible. The purpose of this revelation is that we may have fellowship with the Father and the Son, and that our joy may then be complete (1 Jn 1:2-4). In other words, Jesus unveils for us and communicates to us the mystery of divine life whose essential element is love (Jn 14:23-24), the fruit of the Holy Spirit (Gal 5:22) who is the "bond of love"[31] between the Father and the Son, and "the Spirit of life, a fountain of water springing up to life eternal (cf. Jn 4:14; 7:38-39)" (*LG* 4). The implications gleaned from scriptural references concerning this New Life are summarized by J. L. Segundo:

> It is clear that possessing God's life is a creative summons to a new life in love (1 Jn 2:5-6). In that life John and Paul point to the features which proceed from God's own life: opposition to death (Rom 6:12-14), to literalism (Rom 7:5-6) and to the legalism centered on works (Rom 8:3-13). This life is Spirit, the great divine breeze or breath (Lat. "spiritus") that blows in us and bears us up (Jn 3:8). This new existence has all the freshness of an absolutely new start; it is a new creation (2 Cor 5:17; Gal 6:15), a new birth (Jn 3:3). But in order for this new reality to open up in man's existence, within a universe that dominates and overwhelms it, the Spirit that gives breath and life must transform us from slaves into free and operative creators. It does this by giving us and making us feel the spirit of sonship (Rom 8:14-21; Gal 4:6; 1 Jn 3:1-3), and by establishing us, not juridically but existentially, as heirs and lords of the universe (Gal 4:1-3). Only in this way will we cease to be dominated by external things and by fear. Only in this way does our inner self open up to full spontaneity (Rom 7:21), so that gratuitousness wells up in man as well.[32]

Through the gift of the New Life of grace, we are transformed into a "new creature" (2 Cor 5:17). By faith through Jesus we have been justified (Rom 5:2) and "have already gained our reconciliation" (Rom 5:11). For this reason the Council of Trent spoke of grace "inhering" in the soul (*D* 800, 821), thereby intending to state the fact that "justification consists, through genuine rebirth, in the constitution of a new creature, of a temple really inhabited by the Spirit of God himself, of a human being who is anointed and sealed with the Spirit and born of God; and that the justified person is not merely 'regarded' forensically 'as if' he were just but truly *is* so (*D* 799f., 821)."[33]

Furthermore, in view of this New Life constituted by God's loving dialogue in which he communicates himself to humankind, the classical designation of the three theological virtues of faith, hope and charity as a simple "habitus" which modify the operative faculties of intellect and will seems to fall short of the biblical vision of reality. Scripture relates the Spirit to each of the virtues: to faith (cf. Acts 6:5, 11:24; 2 Cor 4:13), to love (cf. Rom 5:5), and to hope, the "pledge of the Spirit" (2 Cor 1:22, 5:5; Eph 1:4). These three "infused virtues" are "ontological energies" which emanate from the grace of the Spirit; they empower one's whole personality and comprise the soul of all the other virtues. In a holistic view this triad may even be better rendered as "faith-hope-charity," naming one ideal state. "Collectively the three virtues designate the state of a person existing (in this world) in the perfect kind of personal relationship primarily with God and secondarily with his fellow men and the rest of reality."[34] They constitute the one basic orientation, the dynamic gift-call, which the divine dialogue imparts along with new life to its human partner and co-subject. All these various aspects are integral to the healing (forgiving) and elevating effects produced within us by God's loving self-communication of himself ("sanctifying grace") through our rebirth in water and the Spirit (cf. Jn 3:5). This doctrine is thus summarized by St. Paul in his Letter to Titus:

> But when the kindness and love of God our saviour for mankind were revealed, it was not because he was concerned with any righteous actions we might have done ourselves; it was for no reason except his own compassion that he saved us, by means of the cleansing water of rebirth and by renewing us with the Holy Spirit which he has so generously poured over us through Jesus Christ our savior. He did this so that we would be justified by his grace, to become heirs looking forward to eternal life. (Titus 3:4-7)

3. The New Law

The gift of New Life in the Spirit, this divine self-communication, constitutes a new interior dynamism and a principle of action in us which Scripture terms the "Law of Christ" (Gal 6:2; 1 Cor 9:21), and "the law of liberty" (Jas 2:12; 1 Pt 2:16, 2 Pt 2:19). St. Paul writes: "The law of the Spirit of life in Christ Jesus has set you free from the law of sin and death" (Rom 8:2). This "new law," however, is not intended to be a new legal code, because elsewhere the same Apostle writes: "If you are led by the Spirit, no law can touch you" (Gal 5:18). It becomes evident, therefore, that "Paul was not opposing the Mosaic law to another law, but to grace: if sin no longer exerts control over you, he explained, 'you are not under the law but under grace' (Rom 6:14)."[35] His frequent use of "law" instead of "grace" most likely referred to the prophecy of Jeremiah, who stated: "This is the covenant I will make with the House of Israel when those days arrive—it is Yahweh who speaks. Deep within them I will plant my Law, writing it on their hearts. Then I will be their God and they shall be my people" (Jer 31:33). Ezekiel later took up the very same theme but substituted the word "spirit" for "law" (cf. Ez 36:27). Describing the uniqueness of this "new law," S. Lyonnet observes: "The law of the Spirit is by its very nature radically different from the old law; it is no longer a code, even if 'given by the Holy Spirit'; not a simple, external norm of action, but what no other code of laws as such could be, a principle of action, a new, interior dynamism."[36]

This new law is often referred to as the "law of love" (cf. Gal 6:2).[37] It must be interpreted, though, in the sense of the Johannine clarification, "this is the love I mean: not our love for God, but God's love for us when he sent his Son to be the sacrifice that takes our sins away" (1 Jn 4:10), for the external commandment of love (Jn 13:34) would itself be lethal without the interior dynamism of grace (God's love for us). In the words of J. Dedek: "Without the power of the grace of the Holy Spirit the moral precepts of the New Testament are no better than the moral precepts of the Old Testament. Not only are they not salutary; they are as deadly as the Mosaic law."[38] Christ-in-us is the principle of this new law; he is the revelation of the *extent* of God's love for us and in us (Jn 15:13 and 17:26)—the "agape-kenosis" or self-emptying love. From this, and this only, flows his new commandment: "Love one another as I have loved you" (Jn 15:12).

A consideration of the new law must also at this point bring to light the teaching function of grace. John's gospel account has Jesus tell his disciples: "The Advocate, the Holy Spirit, whom the Father will send in my name, will teach you everything and remind you of all I have said to you" (Jn 14:26). The Spirit does not bring a new gospel. His role is essentially subordinate to the revelation brought by Christ. But Lyonnet adds:

> . . . this teaching of Christ must not remain external to the believer: St. John stresses the necessity of making it interior, by accepting it with an ever more intense faith. This is the meaning of such typically Johannine expressions as "to abide in the doctrine of Christ" (2 Jn 9), "to abide in His word" (Jn 8:31; see also 15:7-8). This is exactly where the action of the Spirit is—he too "teaches". He teaches what Jesus taught, but causes it to enter into men's hearts. There is, therefore, a perfect continuity in revelation: coming from the Father, it is communicated to us by the Son, but it attains its fullness when it enters into the most intimate part of our being through the action of the Spirit.[39]

The Spirit, then, is referred to as the "Spirit of Truth" who will remain with Christ's disciples after Christ's departure; for "when the Spirit of truth comes he will lead you to the complete truth, since he will not be speaking from himself but will only say what he has learnt" (Jn 16:13). His task ultimately is to offer an explanation of a previous revelation and to continue to make it present down through the ages. The "Spirit of Christ" in us is the dynamic principle, source and norm, of love and truth. Thus, it is in this sense that he is the "new law" of grace.

4. *The Universality of Grace*

The Fathers of the Second Vatican Council explicitly affirm the universality of God's gift of grace in *Lumen Gentium:* "Those also can attain to everlasting salvation who through no fault of their own do not know the gospel of Christ or His Church, yet sincerely seek God and moved by grace, strive by their deeds to do His will as it is known to them through the dictates of conscience" (*LG* 16). In other words, the Council Fathers intimate that in one's conscience, the innermost depth and core of one's being, whether categorically or non-categorically, each and every person "hears" and perceives the gift-call of God (the Word of God) addressing him or her in a loving dialogue of self-communication. Elsewhere the same Council affirms that through the Incarnation, "the Son of God has united Himself in some fashion with every man" (*GS* 22). This essential and obligatory openness and disposition of all human persons to grace is referred to by theologians as the "potentia obedientialis" and the "supernatural existential."

This universal prevalence of grace was overshadowed in classical theology which posited a certain dualism by dividing reality into "natural" and "supernatural" spheres. This distinction was originally proposed to emphasize the gratuitousness of God's gift of grace. But as J. L. Segundo explains: "The purely natural is a limit concept, i.e., a possibility which must be kept in mind always to appreciate and remember that the gift is a gift. But it is not a concept that has real, historical content, i.e., a concept which points to something which can possibly be found or imagined concretely within our history."[40] The universal salvific will of God is attested to in the New Testament, especially in the classical text 1 Tim 2:5-6, where it is stated that God "wants everyone to be saved and reach the full knowledge of the truth. For there is only one God, and there is only one mediator between God and mankind, himself a man, Christ Jesus, who sacrificed himself as a ransom for them all."[41] And although the doctrine of the universality of grace has never been solemnly defined, it can no longer be denied in light of Vatican II's statement that "we ought to believe that the Holy Spirit in a manner known only to God offers to every man the possibility of being associated with the paschal mystery" which is the only way to share in the grace of Christ's saving death and resurrection (*GS* 22, cf. also *AG* 3). It thus becomes evident that God's grace is somehow given to all men and women of every time and place.

The doctrine of the universality of grace then ties in both with the sacramentality of creation and with salvation history understood in its general sense, for they posit the a priori context, set the stage as it were, for the divine-human dialogue. Grace is bound up with history since the Blessed Trinity is present in our world in a living manner throughout all the ages of time. "All through centuries-old silence prior to the coming of man, God was there, Father, Son and Holy Spirit. God is totally other than the world, and yet, He is its most secret root and deepest source of life. 'And the Spirit of God hovered over the waters' (Gen 1:2), as prime origin of its existence and as its ultimate meaning."[42] Then, with the appearance of the human race, the divine-human dialogue of love began, culminating in Christ, "the summit, the consummate actualization of the divine presence in our history."[43] The early Church seemed to have captured the ultimate meaning of God's presence throughout history when it spoke of the "ecclesia ab Abel," from the first just man,[44] and of the "logos spermatikos," present in the world since its beginning.[45] The universality of grace must then not be interpreted only synchronically, but also diachronically—throughout all of time. B. Häring maintains that "in fact, history taken as a whole becomes history truly only because it is rooted in the transcendent. . . . It was fashioned by the creative Word of God and entrusted to man to be formed and moulded by him. In every historic event man must, therefore, seek to understand the word which God speaks to him."[46]

Christ, the risen and glorified Lord, is also the Lord of History (Rev 21:5-6) who through love and the energy of his Spirit is guiding it to its completion and fulfillment in him.

> For God's Word, through whom all things were made, was Himself made flesh and dwelt on the earth of men. Thus he entered the world's history as a perfect man, taking that history up into Himself and summarizing it. He himself revealed to us that "God is love" (1 Jn 4:8). . . . To those, therefore, who believe in divine love, He gives assurance that the way of love lies open to all men and that the effort to establish a universal brotherhood is not a hopeless one. . . . Appointed Lord by his resurrection and given plenary power in heaven and on earth, Christ is now at work in the hearts of men through the energy of His Spirit. He arouses not only the desire for the age to come, but by that very fact, He animates, purifies, and

strengthens those noble longings too by which the human family strives to make its life more human and to render the whole
earth submissive to this goal (*GS* 38).

The Spirit of Christ, his truth, his love and life-giving grace, are present
in various manners and degrees throughout all of creation gathering and
unifying all things, both in heaven and on earth, for their final recapitulation in him, "when he hands over the kingdom to God the Father" (1
Cor 15:24).

C. THE CHURCH AND SACRAMENTS

The Holy Spirit, "the bond of love" between the Father and the
Son, is the principle of life in the Church. Of its very nature grace is
Trinitarian and, therefore, constitutive of interpersonal communion. As
a divine gift-call, grace orients us to intimate union with God and to
fellowship with one another through a shared spirit.[47] The Church, then,
can only be understood within the entire context of revelation, within the
context of the mission of the Son (Incarnation) and the mission of the
Holy Spirit (Pentecost), (cf. *AG* 2). The self-donation of God revealed
in Jesus Christ, in the "agape-kenosis" of the cross, is an act of reconciliation (cf. Col 1:20) which seeks to gather ("ek-klesia") all men and
women into a fellowship and community of divine life (cf. 1 Jn 1:3). In
the words of *Lumen Gentium:*

> It has pleased God, however, to make men holy and to save
> them not merely as individuals without any mutual bonds, but
> by making them into a single people, a people which acknowl-
> edges Him in truth and serves Him in holiness. He therefore
> chose the race of Israel as a people unto Himself. With it He
> set up a covenant . . . All these things, however, were done by
> way of preparation and as a figure of that new and perfect cov-
> enant which was to be ratified in Christ . . . [who] instituted
> . . . the new testament, in His blood (cf. 1 Cor 11:25), by
> calling together a people made up of Jew and Gentile, making
> them one, not according to the flesh but in the Spirit." (*LG* 9)

The Church and its liturgy take their origin from the Paschal Mystery
of Christ, as "one of the soldiers pierced his side with a lance; and immediately there came out blood and water" (Jn 19:34).[48] Yet it is exactly
here established simultaneously as a *call* ("And when I am lifted up
from the earth, I shall draw all men to myself"—Jn 12:32) and a *sending* (cf. Jn 19:34 above, where the "water" from the side of Christ is

symbolic of the gift of the Spirit).[49] Essentially, the Church is a "missionary convocation"; she is called together in order that she may be sent. Bernard Häring, in his work *The Sacraments and Your Everyday Life*, aptly describes and clarifies this twofold process of *convocation-mission* by noting that through the Church "Christ continues his revealing presence—although not in a sense of monopoly, as if he might not be present also beyond her structures. He works throughout the whole history, but he has chosen the Church, has bestowed on her the Holy Spirit abundantly, and has sent her, that she may be ever more a unique sacrament of union with God and the unity of mankind, in Him and through Him." In this particular section, therefore, we will bring together the various aspects of the Church's life and worship through which she becomes associated with the mission of the Son and of the Holy Spirit in their bringing to fulfillment the divine economy of salvation.

1. *The Church as a Mystery of Communion*[50]

The Church is seen as a mystery of communion because she takes her origin from Christ, the Incarnate Word, who is the fullness of revelation making known the Mystery hidden in God throughout the ages, but now revealed through the apostles and prophets (cf. Eph 3:3-9)—the mystery of Christ who through his cross has united both aliens and Jews in one single Body creating one single New Man in himself and restoring peace by reconciling them with God (cf. Eph 2:13-16). This "single Body" is referred to by the Fathers of Vatican II as the "new People of God" (cf. *LG* 9 and 1 Pet 2:9-10) whom they go on to describe as a messianic people:

> That messianic people has for its head Christ, "who was delivered up for our sins, and rose again for our justification" (Rom 4:25), and who now, having won a name which is above all names, reigns in glory in heaven. The heritage of this people are the dignity and freedom of the sons of God, in whose hearts the Holy Spirit dwells as in His temple. Its law is the new commandment to love as Christ loved us (cf. Jn 13:34). Its goal is the kingdom of God, which has been begun by God Himself on earth, and which is to be further extended until it is brought to perfection by Him at the end of time. Then Christ our life (cf. Col 3:4), will appear, and "creation itself also will be delivered from its slavery to corruption into the freedom of the glory of the sons of God" (Rom 8:21). (*LG* 9)

The Church can be described as a mystery of communion because she is imbued with the hidden presence of the Trinitarian God. She is the new People of God "made one with the unity of the Father, the Son, and the Holy Spirit."[51] Indeed, the very life of the Blessed Trinity animates the Church from within and holds her together in unity. She comes forth "from the eternal Father's love" (*GS* 40), his utterly free and gracious plan (*LG* 2; *AG* 2). Then, she was "founded in time by Christ the Redeemer" (*GS* 40) whose mission was to reconcile the whole human race by bringing us into union with himself in a certain spiritual solidarity (cf. *AA* 8). Finally, the Church is "made one" in the mission of the Spirit (*GS* 40). Numerous references to the Holy Spirit's mission are scattered throughout the documents and decrees of Vatican II. In *Lumen Gentium*, art. 4 alone, "we are taught that the Holy Spirit

> —perpetually sanctifies the Church;
> —gives life to men who are dead from sin;
> —dwells in the hearts of the faithful as in a temple;
> —prays in them;
> —bears witness to the fact that they are adopted sons;
> —guides the Church to knowledge of the truth;
> —unites the Church in fellowship and service;
> —directs her through various hierarchical and charismatic gifts;
> —adorns her with the fruit of his grace;
> —perpetually renews her;
> —leads her to perfect union with her spouse."[52]

This presence of the Spirit in the Church is compared analogously to the mystery of the Incarnate Word. "Just as the assumed nature inseparably united to the divine Word serves Him as a living instrument of salvation, so, in a similar way, does the communal structure of the Church serve Christ's Spirit, who vivifies it by way of building up the body (cf. Eph 4:6)" (*LG* 8). So it is from the mission of the Holy Spirit that the Church receives her life and unity.

Christ inaugurated the Church by preaching the Good News of the coming of God's Kingdom (*LG* 5). The concept of "kingdom" itself denotes the Church's social and communal nature. Yet the Church is not identifiable with the Kingdom of God; she is only "the kingdom of Christ now present in mystery" (*LG* 3). The Church lives now in the in-between time of Christ's first and second comings, in the already and the not-yet. The Church is a pilgrim people on the way to a glorious union with her risen Lord (cf. *LF* 48). Meanwhile, " 'like a pilgrim in a foreign land, [she] presses forward amid the persecutions of the world and the consolations of God,' announcing the cross and death of the Lord until He comes (cf. 1 Cor 11:26)" (*LG* 8). Through this Paschal Mystery her members are molded in the image of Christ (cf. Gal 4:19) and form a body of which he is the head. Through this incorporation into Christ, the Church is "the fullness of him who fills the whole creation" (Eph 1:23). This constitutes an eschatological reality awaiting Christ's return in glory, yet now "stamped with the seal of the Holy Spirit of promise, the pledge of our inheritance" (Eph 1:13-14). As a mystery of communion, the Church is grace *par excellence*, a share in the inner divine life of the Blessed Trinity. As a "koinonia," or a fellowship of those who are in Christ, the Kingdom of God begins to take shape in the Church, its earthly sacrament. "Thus the Church, at once a visible assembly and a spiritual community, goes forward together with humanity and experiences the same earthly lot which the world does. She serves as a leaven and as a kind of soul for human society as it is to be renewed in Christ and transformed into God's family" (*GS* 40). She is becoming the true and everlasting people of God, the new Israel, the people of the promise and the inheritance.

2. *The Church as Sacrament of Salvation: Presence and Witness*

In the opening paragraph of Vatican II's Dogmatic Constitution on the Church, the Council Fathers wrote that "by her relationship with Christ, the Church is a kind of sacrament or sign of intimate union with God, and of the unity of all mankind" (*LG* 1). Later they would refer to her "as the universal sacrament of salvation" (*LG* 48) "simultaneously manifesting and exercising the mystery of God's love for man" (*GS* 45). Through her intimate association with Christ her head, the Church continues to make known to the human race the self-communication of God's love revealed in the Incarnation and Paschal Mystery of Jesus. As a "koinonia" or fellowship gathered together in the Spirit of Christ, the Church is a sign and witness of Christ's mission from the Father (cf. Jn 17:21).

The Church can rightly be considered the consciousness of humanity as it were, making known the hidden reality of God's gift of himself which passes our way without people knowing it. She is a word and sign for the whole world proclaiming the presence of the mystery of Christ in the Spirit. The Church is a sign of the presence of Jesus' Paschal Mystery, for he, her head, her glorified and risen Lord, *still* bears on his hands, feet and side the marks of his life-giving passion and death (cf. Jn 20:25-27). Christ reigns as the Lamb who was slain (Rev 5:6). The Paschal Mystery thus reveals the fundamental dialectic that underlies the whole process of evolving love ("agape-kenosis") between human beings; it constitutes the structure of any and all human progress. The

Paschal Mystery is the revelatory summit of the "mystery of simplicity," of the divine economy of salvation. Its revealing power continues in our world through the loving presence and witness of the Church, a people baptized into the Paschal Mystery (cf. Rom 6:5-11) and sharing fellowship and a union of being and life in and with the crucified and risen Lord.

The Christian community is a sacrament of the personal presence of God who dwells at the depths of all human experience. It is a sacrament of Christ who, in his humanity, is the sacrament of God. Consequently, it is a sacrament of the Spirit of Christ, who, as the Spirit of truth, is present and active within the Church transforming her members into the image of Christ and thereby making them heralds and witnesses of the gospel truth with all that it entails for the eschatological future of the world. The Church as witness was one of the major themes of the Second Vatican Council. The word "witness" recurs more than a hundred times in the conciliar documents. Through her active participation in Jesus' Paschal Mystery, which she both lives and also celebrates in her liturgy, the Church becomes an existential witness to the unity and love that come to the world through our redemption in Christ. Only thus is she able to be a "light of the world" (cf. Mt 5:14) reflecting the Light of Christ who is indeed the Light of all nations ("Lumen gentium"). Finally, to accomplish its sign-bearing mission, Christ established his Church "as a visible structure" (*LG* 8), providing it with "those means which befit it as a visible sacrament of saving unity" (*LG* 9). In her, the grace of God, his all-loving self-communication, is made manifestly present in time and space and becomes accessible to everyone.

3. *The Sacraments*

This visible community, according to the Council Fathers, "subsists in the Catholic Church, which is governed by the successor of Peter and by the bishops in union with that successor" (*LG* 8). The spiritual life and unity we share in and with Christ are celebrated and nourished within this Catholic Church by seven outward signs or rites that tend to open us to the mystery of Christ in an ever-growing dialogue of grace and faith. Therefore, the life of this visible community continues to be shaped by these expressions or articulations of the one Mystery that repeatedly raise it to a heightened level of memory and consciousness. These seven sacraments engage a person in the divine-human dialogue by positing a response to God's love and by unfolding the implications of this saving Mystery for the lives of individuals and communities. Through these seven symbolic and ritual acts, Christ continues to *gather* his followers for the purpose of *sending them out* as heralds of God's loving design for the world.

In essence the sacraments are a ritual incarnation of the Good News. In the words of B. Häring: "They are gospel, gladdening news, a message of love, and thus an effective challenge and commandment to treasure in our hearts this message and give thanks for the gift they bestow." As symbolic actions they give visible expression to the invisible divinity present and communicating himself to us. In the teaching of the Fathers of the Church and in the Greek Orthodox theology, the operation of the sacraments was attributed to the action of the Holy Spirit. The Epiclesis prayer in each sacrament was specially addressed to the Spirit inviting him to fill the water and chrism and the sacred actions with his power and grace. In the earliest theology of the Church, the sacraments could never be considered apart from the creative, effectual presence of the Father in the Son through the power of the Holy Spirit. They made present in visible finite forms the Good News of the ineffable mystery of God's loving design for the world.

The sacraments are visible signs of God gathering his people into the Body of Christ, the Church, where the Trinitarian indwelling seeks to find a concrete expression in a visibly recognizable communion of fellowship and love. In this way the Father prolongs the work of redemption in Christ and in the power of His Spirit. But besides being the Body of Christ, the Church is also his Bride, and the sacraments, too, are prayers and public acts of worship expressing our personal faith-response to the divine gift-call. Yet our prayers and acts of worship themselves are grace—"grace existentially accepted and lived up to, grace that comes to life in faith and charity."[53] St. Paul himself tells us that we are not able to address the Father except in the Holy Spirit (Rom 8:15-16; Gal 4:3); and this must be viewed in light of the ancient tradition of the closing words of the liturgical orations: "through Jesus Christ our Lord." Our whole life of prayer and worship itself can only be attributed to our share in the inner life of the Trinity—"a share shrouded on earth in the obscurity of faith."[54]

As gospel the seven sacraments are centered on the Paschal Mystery, the revelatory summit of God's redeeming love for humankind. The Christian community's celebration of them incorporates it ever more fully into the Paschal Christ and through him into the unsurpassable mystery of God's love for us and the inner Trinitarian Life we share. The sacraments constitute meaningful life-moments of heightened awareness and transforming integration within God's universal dispensation of salvation. In them Christ, the *primordial* sacrament of our encounter with God, continues to be redemptively present as Emmanuel (God-with-us), bringing the power of the Gospel to the critical moments of our individual life-histories and to our collective gathering in his Name.

In baptism we are sacramentally incorporated for the first time into the Paschal Mystery of Christ (Rom 6:3-4) and thereby into the visible community of the Church which seeks to follow him by walking in the newness of life and hope it receives in the Spirit's freeing it from the law of sin and death (Rom 8:2). "Baptism is, therefore, at once an act of liberation, rebirth and incorporation."[55] Through spiritual rebirth the baptized person is set free from the selfish enslavement of sin to live the New Life of union with God in the supporting fellowship of the Christian community. He or she is baptized into the people of the new and eternal Covenant who bear the priestly and prophetic responsibility of continuing to make present Christ's mission of proclaiming the Good News to all the world. The baptized person is later sacramentally perfected and strengthened in this special mission by the gift of the Holy Spirit at confirmation in a kind of personal Pentecost which turns him or her outward in witness and service to the world.

The Eucharist, "which is the fount and apex of the whole Christian life" (*LG* 11), draws us into communion with Christ's Paschal Mystery, both nourishing us with the Bread and Cup of our New Life and holding out before us the promise of our resurrection unto Life everlasting (cf. Jn 6:54). The Eucharist is the sacramental sign of the revelatory summit of what God is doing in our world. It is the efficacious memorial of Jesus' redemptive death on our behalf (cf. Jn 15:13). Through it the living Christ is in our midst unleashing in our lives the great event and dynamic force of his life-giving death, and assimilating "his body, the Church, to the offering he the head made on the cross."[56]

Partaking of one Bread and one Cup, we become one Body in him, making us of the same mind (cf. Phil 2:5) by drawing us into the same attitude of offering and self-dedication to God (the "agape-kenosis"). The Eucharist thus sacramentally constitutes the heart and core of God's loving design for us and our grateful acceptance of this divine self-giving; it is the sacramental embodiment of the divine-human dialogue, and, therefore, has been called "the fount and apex of the whole Christian life" (*LG* 11). All the other sacraments bring this Mystery to bear on the crucial moments of human life.

In the sacrament of reconciliation, the New Life lost or diminished by sin is once more restored and/or strengthened by the penitent's reinsertion into the sphere of God's mercy and love, and "if the person has not sinned in a decisive way, the emphasis will be on expressing one's longing for healing and a more thorough integration of all one's attitudes, desires and tendencies into the central orientation of one's heart to God."[57] This reconciliation is also a reintegration into the community after separation and/or damage brought about by personal sin, and a sign of the need for on-going conversion in its individual members and in the Church as a whole. In the sacramental anointing of the sick, "the whole Church commends those who are ill to the suffering and glorified Lord, asking that He may lighten their suffering and save them (cf. Jas 5:14-16)" (*LG* 11). Through the grace of healing brought by Christ a person who is physically ill, whether by sickness, injury or the debility of advanced age, receives the help to suffer in union with Christ and to pass with him into a newness of life—whether in this world or beyond death.

Christian marriage is a sacramental sign of Christ's covenantal love for humankind. "Christian spouses, in virtue of the sacrament of matrimony, signify and partake of the mystery of that unity and fruitful love which exists between Christ and His Church (cf. Eph 5:32)" (*LG* 11). Christian matrimony thus constitutes a lifelong sign of Christ's Paschal Mystery (cf. Eph 5:25) as "each partner expresses to the other the self-forgetting and redemptive love that Christ manifested in going to death on our behalf." This covenantal love and fidelity mirrored in Christian marriage is geared to the creation and growth of new life in both the procreative and spiritual sense. The married partners' selfless dedication to one another and to their children is a sign of God's gift of himself to us and a dynamic sign-bearing witness to all of humanity of the ultimate meaning of life that comes to us through faith in Christ.

Finally, through sacramental ordination members of the faithful are "appointed to feed the Church in Christ's name with the Word and grace of God" (*LG* 11). Ministry in the New Testament appears basically as a "ministry of reconciliation" (2 Cor 5:18) by men set apart for the proclamation of the Good News. For this service men are specially called, and then through ordination itself, are "*incorporated* into the body of those holding ministerial responsibility and authority in the Church."[58] Thus *designated* and *consecrated* by ordination for roles of leadership in the Church, these men are marked as builders of the Christian community bringing people together in the obedience of faith (cf. Rom 1:1-6) and being a sign by their very identity of God's reconciling presence in the world. Through proclaiming the Word and serving or presiding at the eucharistic table, these ordained ministers lead the faithful into the sacramental celebration and realization of the Paschal Mystery in our lives.[59] They thereby gather together the Christian community by ritually incorporating it into God's loving design, and thus nourish and prepare it through prayer and worship for its mission of evangelization—a mission which is an obligation "imposed on every disciple of Christ, according to his ability" (*LG* 17).

D. THE PROCESS OF EVANGELIZATION

Jesus originally gathered together his disciples in order to send them out as messengers of the Good News (cf. Mk 1:17; 3:13-14). After his resurrection they were sent to continue Christ's mission of proclaiming the Gospel through the power of the Holy Spirit. In the Johannine account of the missionary mandate we read: " 'As the Father sent me, so I am sending you.' After this he breathed upon them and said: 'Receive the Holy Spirit' " (Jn 20:21-22). At Pentecost the Church was sent to gather the nations into one fold under one Shepherd, Jesus Christ (Jn 10:16), bringing them together in his Spirit into a communion of Life which will mark the fulfillment of the Father's eternal and all-loving plan. In this, the in-between time, the Church is essentially and fundamentally constituted to continue the revelatory mission of the Son in the grace and power of the Holy Spirit by incarnating through her very life and presence in the world this divine, evangelical economy. The Church is gathered-sent for the sole purpose of proclaiming the Good News in word and deed. Evangelization is her essential, primary mission, and a permanent, constitutive necessity of the Church (as we have already seen illustrated from the statements of Pope Paul VI and the work of the 1974 Rome Synod of Bishops). The Church evangelizes and is evangelized by simultaneously continuing to proclaim the Gospel to every nation and striving to become ever more and more a sacramental or incarnate image of her Head, Jesus Christ, the Paschal Lord of all creation.

The Church's mission of evangelization is her categorical insertion into and assumption of a continuing process that reaches back into metahistory—into God the Father's utterly free and loving design to communicate and reveal himself to us through the missions of the Son and the Holy Spirit. The whole economy of salvation is an evangelical process. We cannot speak, therefore, of a theology of evangelization as such. Evangelization, rather, constitutes the entire context within which theological reflection occurs. The various theologies, such as that of revelation, of grace, etc., take place within this evangelical context and attempt to elaborate and systematize the many rich and varied elements and aspects of the one divine economy, the "mystery of simplicity."[60] We hope, therefore, in this particular section, neither to propose nor develop a theology of evangelization, but rather only to uncover and indicate the principal dynamics and elements at work within this process or mission.

1. *The Necessity of Evangelization*

Proclaiming the Gospel, as we see in the New Testament, is both a duty and a command. Jesus himself felt compelled by the necessity of preaching it: "I must proclaim the Good News of the Kingdom of God . . . because that is what I was sent to do" (Lk 4:43). Jesus in his person is and remains the Word of God, the Good News incarnate, and the first and greatest evangelizer. But after his resurrection he gave the mandate to his disciples: "Go out to the whole world; proclaim the Good News to all creation" (Mk 16:16). St. Paul later wrote to the Corinthians, "preaching the gospel . . . is a duty which has been laid on me; I should be punished if I did not preach it!" (1 Cor 9:16); and to Titus: "by the command of God our savior, I have been commissioned to proclaim it" (Titus 1:3). Through the centuries from the time of the apostles, the Church has continued to fulfill this divine mandate. But this evangelizing mission does not depend solely on Christ's extrinsic command. "As is clear from the missionary life of Jesus and his disciples, it flows from the very nature of life in the Church, the command being the expression of what the Church ought to do in order to be what she is."[61] Preaching the Good News is an act of worship and praise (cf. Rom 1:9), and evangelization constitutes the Church's very *raison d'être.*

The Church is *gathered-sent* in order to give glory and praise to God the Father through the Lord Jesus Christ in the Spirit by making known all the wondrous works he has accomplished on our behalf (cf. Eph 1:6, 12, 14). In the words of Paul VI: "Evangelizing is in fact the grace and vocation proper to the Church, her deepest identity. She exists in order to evangelize, that is to say in order to preach and teach, to be the channel of the gift of grace, to reconcile sinners with God, and to perpetuate Christ's sacrifice in the Mass, which is the memorial of his death and Resurrection."[62] Here Pope Paul links the necessity of evangelization with the Eucharist, the Church's communal act of praise and thanksgiving. Because the Gospel of Christ is indeed good news, the Church must proclaim it in joyful gratitude (cf. Col 3:16-17). This she does in word and sacrament, especially in the eucharistic celebration where she gathers together the People of God sharing *one* Bread and *one* Cup in anticipation of the banquet feast of the coming Kingdom. The duty of evangelizing, thus, pertains primarily to the Church as a whole, because in the words of *Lumen Gentium:* "It has pleased God . . . to make men holy and to save them not merely as individuals without any mutual bonds, but by making them into a single people, a people which acknowledges Him in truth and serves Him in holiness" (*LG* 9). The Church thus constituted as koinonia becomes a sign or sacrament proclaiming the Good News and the presence of God's saving love. Then, from this community of shared life in Christ, the individual members are sent to spread the faith according to their particular vocation and ability (cf. *LG* 17).[63]

Furthermore, as we have stated previously, incarnation is the first law of revelation. God's self-communication through his Word (which is both dynamic and noetic) seeks explicit formulation. God wants humankind to arrive at full knowledge and awareness of his plan to save all men and women through self-emptying love. "This hidden wisdom of God which we teach in our mysteries is the wisdom that God has predestined to be for our glory before the ages began. . . . These are the very things that God has revealed to us through the Spirit . . . to teach us to understand the gifts he has given us" (1 Cor 2:7-12; see also, Eph 3:9-11). It is for this reason then, that Pope Paul affirms in *Evangelii Nuntiandi:*

> . . . the presentation of the gospel message is not an optional contribution for the Church. It is the duty incumbent on her by the command of the Lord Jesus, so that people can believe and be saved. This message is indeed necessary. It is unique. It cannot be replaced. It does not permit either indifference, syncretism or accommodation. It is a question of people's salvation. It is the beauty of Revelation that it presents. It brings with it a wisdom that is not of this world. It is able to stir up by itself faith—faith that rests on the promise of God. It is truth. It merits having the apostle consecrate to it all his time and energies, and to sacrifice for it, if necessary, his own life.[64]

God is Love. His grace, presence and activity pervade all of created reality. When we discourse on human love we often employ the adage that actions speak louder than words. Without words our actions are sometimes left unnoticed, or even misinterpreted and misunderstood. So it is with God's loving design for the human race. Were it not for revelation, the proclamation of the Gospel and its sacramental incarnation, first in Christ and then in his Church, the divine evangelical economy would for the most part remain hidden to our minds (cf. 1 Cor 2:7-8). So, all the while acknowledging that all men and women may come to a religious awareness of the reality of God through all sorts of experiences, the Church firmly maintains that it is only through revelation, Jesus Christ, his Gospel and the Church that God the Father and his loving design for us can become known with compelling clarity. And thus, Paul VI states in *Evangelii Nuntiandi:* "Even in the face of natural religious expressions most worthy of esteem, the Church finds support in the fact that the religion of Jesus which she proclaims through evangelization, objectively places man in relation with the plan of God, with his living presence and his action; she thus causes an encounter with the mystery of divine paternity that bends over to humanity."[65]

2. *Proclaiming the Good News*

The starting point of the evangelization process, as has already been noted, is God's loving plan, and the revelation of this evangelical economy continues today in the mission of the Church. The Church was founded and established for this very reason. Her existence in the world attests to the actual presence of the Trinitarian Life communicated by Christ in his Spirit. Experiencing this Life, living it and inviting others to share it, the Church evangelizes. Through her very Life in the Spirit, she invites men and women to a new relationship among themselves and with God in Jesus Christ.

Seeking to share this Life with others, the proclamation of the gospel truth and mystery takes place through both words and deeds. This was the method of proclamation employed by Jesus and the early Church, which is confirmed in the book of Acts, especially in the introduction where St. Luke writes: "In my earlier work, Theophilus, I dealt with everything Jesus had *done* and *taught* from the beginning. . . ." (Acts 1:1). The apostolic Church itself was equally dependent on kerygma ("didache") and koinonia (cf. Acts 2:42). Proclaiming the Gospel is more than just an oral or verbal announcement, more than just a repetition of a statement formulated in the past in a particular historical, cultural, social context. Proclaiming the Gospel is an incarnational process of witness and a shared life; it is the communication of the love of God—"preaching in words and communicating in life and deeds the all-redeeming and all-embracing love of Christ."[66]

The purpose and finality of the whole process of evangelization find their end in leading men and women to conversion and making them disciples of Christ. Evangelization calls for a certain "break" in a person's life, an about-face which demands that one look at reality in a new way; that one discover the meaning of existence in God's gift of himself alone and that one, then, live his life as a faith-response glorifying God in spirit and truth. Conversion means embracing the Kingdom of God before anything else by accepting the primacy and sovereignty of the divine Trinitarian self-communication in our lives. In so doing we become disciples and witnesses of the Word or Truth which is Jesus Christ, through whom alone we are reconciled to God and find salvation from sin and death.

Jesus proclaimed the gospel mystery using the medium of both words and deeds. He came into the world "to bear witness to the truth" (Jn 18:37), and at one point he maintained in the presence of his disciples: "I am the Way, the Truth and the Life" (Jn 14:6). He in his person is the Truth, the non-concealment of Mystery. Truth is revealed in and through a person, because Truth is a personal, relational and Trinitarian Mystery. God alone is Ultimate Reality and Absolute Truth. Thus, truth evades categorization; it cannot be encapsulated by mere words, formulas and doctrinal statements.

Evangelization, which depends solely on the external word of preaching, teaching or doctrinal formulas, is clearly inadequate. God is not revealed by words alone, no matter how accurate their content. "Hence evangelization is not a mere theoretical teaching about Christ, an apologetic argument about Christianity, but a sharing of the Christian experience—a testimony to the transforming interpersonal relationship brought about between man and God, and among men by and in Jesus Christ."[67] To categorize this latter necessary element of witnessing to the gospel truth, some contemporary theologians have coined the word "orthopraxis"[68] as a complement to "orthodoxy." Orthopraxis may consequently be referred to as the "orthodoxy of action"; it seeks to actuate the truth.[69]

The Scriptural and theological evidence point to the fact that *genuine* orthodoxy expresses itself in a twofold manner: one is orthopraxis, and the other is in the correct formulation of doctrine (which alone has been more commonly referred to as "orthodoxy"). Christian revelation, as we have seen, is not a compilation of revealed truths but a person (cf. *DV* 4). Jesus Christ has been called the "primordial dogma" of Christianity. Genuine orthodoxy is consequently incarnational (it is the "Way"[70]), whereas "orthodoxy" pertains only to the realm of right conceptualization, right words and correct formulas. Precisely because so many Christians today embrace only such an "orthodoxy," the Second Vatican Council warned that "this split between the faith which many profess and their daily lives deserves to be counted among the more serious errors of our age. . . ." (*GS* 43). From the Scriptural and doctrinal point of view, it even becomes evident that orthopraxis shares a *prima inter pares* relationship with "orthodoxy."

(a.) *Proclamation by Deed (orthopraxis).* The prophetic tradition of the Old Testament often emphasized the pragmatic side of faith in Yahweh. The prophets attacked all ritual practice (the confessional element of religion and thus "orthodoxy"), which was not related to moral conduct (orthopraxis)—cf. Is 1:11, 15:17; Jer 7:3-4; Mi 6:7-8; Amos 6:23-24. Also the concept of the word ("dabar") of Yahweh in the Old Testament has a definite pragmatic character to it—a *dynamic* aspect as well as a noetic aspect. One can even observe a certain chronological primacy of the dynamic over the noetic. God first reveals himself by his divine interventions in the history of a people which are later reflected upon and realized as being moments of salvific import.

Jesus is *the* Prophet in the New Testament. He continues the prophetic emphasis on orthopraxis over "orthodoxy." In the Sermon on the Mount, he teaches his disciples: "It is not those who say to me, 'Lord, Lord,' who will enter the kingdom of heaven, but the person who does the will of my Father in heaven" (Mt 7:21). In the Parable of the Two Sons (Mt 21:28-31), obedience to the will of the Father takes precedence over lip service or a spoken response. In the account of the Last Judgment (Mt 25:31-46), the Son of Man takes no cognizance of any kind of intellectual knowledge or any familiarity with the Law. Orthopraxis is all that counts. In the Parable of the Good Samaritan (Lk 10:29-37) the priest and Levite were considered to be "orthodox" persons, yet the protagonist, the unorthodox one, is the only one of the three to have Jesus' approval, and this he wins because of his orthopraxis.

Doing God's will, in fact, in Jn 7:17 is posited as a prerequisite for coming to know the doctrine of Jesus.[71] Finally, the greatest example of orthopraxis is the act by which our redemption is accomplished: "A man can have no greater love than to lay down his life for his friends" (Jn 15:13); "by one man's obedience many will be made righteous" (Rom 5:19). Jesus was not satisfied with simply telling us the Good News of his Father's love for sinners; he proved it on the cross (cf. Rom 5:8). "There, at last, the Word was made flesh and the message totally expressed no longer in words of lips but of flesh and blood . . . the cross is the supreme act of evangelization."[72]

The Pauline Corpus of the New Testament continues to place a primary emphasis on doing the right thing. Although the term "orthopraxis" is foreign to the New Testament writings, we do find "orthopodein" (Gal 2:14) and "orthotomein" (2 Tim 2:15), which basically have the same connotation. Orthopraxis is also indicated elsewhere in Paul: (a) "in the obedience of faith" (Rom 1:15; 16:26);[73] (b) "doing the truth in love" (Eph 4:15);[74] (c) "You have shown your faith in action, worked for love" (1 Thes 1:3);[75] (d) "knowledge" geared toward love (1 Tim 1:5; 1 Cor 8:1). Then, in 1 Tim 5:8 the truth accepted through deeds guarantees the orthodoxy of one's faith: "Anyone who does not look after his own relations, especially if they are living with him, has rejected the faith and is worse than an unbeliever." In the Johannine writings we find an integral connection between truth and action (cf. Jn 8:44 and 1 Jn 1:6).[76] In Jn 8:29 Jesus himself testifies that there is a causal relationship between God's remaining with one and that person's doing what is right. Echoing the prophetic tradition, the Letter to the Hebrews replaces ritual sacrifice with self-sacrifice in doing God's will (cf. Heb 10:5-7). And the Letter of James puts heavy emphasis on *doing* what the word tells us (1:22); "true religion" for the author is orthopraxis (cf. 1:27).

The evidence from Scriptures, as can be seen, places great emphasis on the need "to do the truth," "to do the will of God," to live our faith in praxis. The actual confession of faith in words, while important and necessary, is actually secondary to "doing the truth in love." The truth is not primarily affirmed in intellectual assent, but rather in practice and action—right action (orthopraxis), for Scripture also affirms that objectively correct action alone is not enough. "If I give away all that I possess, piece by piece, and if I even let them take my body to burn it, but am without love, it will do me no good whatever" (1 Cor 13:1-3). Orthopraxis is the incarnation of "agape-kenosis."

Furthermore, when we take into consideration the doctrinal assertions of the Church, especially with regard to the sacramentality of creation, the universality of grace, God's universal salvific will, and the Incarnation, we see implicitly affirmed this *prima inter pares* position of orthopraxis in relation to "orthodoxy." We have already dealt with these doctrinal aspects. In summary, the Fathers of Vatican II affirming the universality of God's gift of grace stated: "Those also can attain to everlasting salvation who through no fault of their own do not know the gospel of Christ or His Church, yet sincerely seek God and *moved by grace, strive by their deeds to do His will* as it is known to them through the dictates of conscience" (*LG* 16).[77] God's Word is revelation and self-communication, whose first law is incarnation—the Incarnation of Love ("agape-kenosis"). In incarnation, the act of love (orthopraxis) takes primacy over the verbal explanation and conceptualization of the event ("orthodoxy"), although the latter is necessary to clarify the former. Thus, genuine orthodoxy necessarily expresses itself both in orthopraxis and "orthodoxy," but orthopraxis has primacy, for without it "orthodoxy" is nothing more than mere words.

(b.) *Proclamation by Word ("orthodoxy").* The necessity of the oral or verbal element in the process of evangelization is by no means diminished. The Church's mission of proclaiming the gospel mystery and of being a sign of the presence of God's saving love fully revealed in Jesus Christ demands orthodox formulation, "because human action is in every sphere inconceivable without the element of theoretical implication. Similarly, Christian orthopraxis is also inconceivable without the element of theoretical Christian knowledge and, in that sense, orthodoxy."[78]

Correct formulation of the truth revealed in Christ and taught by the Church is indeed a necessity. This exigency is attested to by the New Testament on numerous occasions, especially in the pastoral letters of Paul: "Anyone who teaches anything different, and does not keep to the sound teaching which is that of our Lord Jesus Christ, the doctrine which is in accordance with true religion, is simply ignorant and must be full of self-conceit—with a craze for questioning everything and arguing about words" (1 Tim 6:3-4; cf. also, 2 Tim 1:13; 4:3; Titus 1:9, 13; 2:1, 8). In his Letter to the Galatians, Paul warns and reiterates: "If anyone preaches a version of the Good News different from the one you have already heard, he is to be condemned" (Gal 1:9). The need, too, of verbal proclamation of the gospel mystery is confirmed by Paul in Rom 10:17, where he maintains that "faith comes from what is preached." Precisely here the phenomenology of the spoken word comes into play. R. Latourelle writes:

> Karl Bühler distinguishes a threefold aspect in word: 1. The word has *content*. It signifies or represents something: it names an object, it formulates a thought, a judgment, it recounts a fact (*Darstellung*). 2. The word is *interpellation*. It is addressed to someone and tends to provoke a response in him, a reaction. It acts like a call, a provocation (*Appell, Auslösung*). 3. Finally, the word is the unveiling of the person, the manifestation of his interior attitude, of his dispositions (*Ausdruck, Kundgabe*). To sum up, we might define a word as being the activity through which one person *addresses* and *expresses* himself to another person with a view towards *communication*.[79]

In the verbal proclamation of the gospel mystery, the divine self-communication, seeking to become incarnate in a purely human context, thus takes into consideration the objective structuring of human dialogue and employs it in mediating the divine-human encounter.

The spoken word in evangelization constitutes an objective, external grace, as it were, addressing the human power of reasoning, the mind or intellect, in counterdistinction to the prior inner dynamism of love (grace) which addresses and reveals itself to the heart (*Cor ad cor loquitur*). In other words, the revelation of God's Word is primarily an *event*, expressed both in words (the noetic element: written and spoken language) and deeds (the dynamic aspect: His love). "Orthodoxy" and orthopraxis are equally necessary expressions of God's revealing and self-communicating Word; yet, "orthodoxy" is really secondary in importance (and often in time) as a concrete explanation of what has occurred, is occurring, or will occur. The act is the primary of the two, even though the act might not be correctly understood, or understood at all, without the formulated explanation. Thus the Church's mission of evangelization incarnates and continues to make sacramentally present the missions of the Son (the revealing Word) and the Spirit (the unifying, inspiring and creative dynamism of divine love).

Evangelization, as verbal communication, took the forms of kerygma (preaching), catechesis (moral and doctrinal instruction) and gnosis (apologetical and other theological reflections) in the early Church. But none of these forms was separated from the dynamic element of new life "in Christ" which the early Church experienced and shared in fellowship or koinonia. Today, these same three forms still hold their validity, although they are greatly aided in their present tasks with modern technological developments effecting the instruments of social-communications and with discoveries in the life sciences regarding the listening subject.[80] The *kerygma* remains as important as ever, especially in the liturgical assembly. As proclamation of the gospel mystery it is not just words nor the presentation of facts, but a creative act. "It is a word which gives meaning, and in the very disclosure of meaning there is new life."[81] Through preaching the Word, the presence of Christ in the community is unveiled, and the listener is addressed and challenged to an ever greater response of faith and gift of self. Its goal is a personal encounter. "Catechetical training is intended to make men's faith become living, conscious, and active, through the light of instruction" (*CD* 14). *Catechesis*, or religious instruction, also has to be evangelical in scope. In seeking to present the doctrinal and moral content of faith ("fides quae"), it must first start by attempting to open the heart to the divine-human dialogue of love ("fides qua") "without which the pure and simple content of the faith cannot be grasped."[82] The Good News and the unfolding of the evangelical economy of salvation provide the entire framework or context from which both doctrinal and moral instruction must proceed. In both preaching and catechesis a biblical approach is needed which unveils the gospel mystery through the use of appealing narratives, stories and parables—the teaching techniques of Jesus himself.[83] Finally, Christian *gnosis* today would refer to the whole general form of "theology" ranging from personal spiritual reflection to formal systematic treatises and courses in theology.[84]

Proclamation of the gospel mystery by word and deed combine to form the *second moment* of the evangelization process, that is, Christian witness, which itself in turn becomes a most effective proclamation of the Good News. Our faith-response, or living adherence to the Gospel, incarnates this evangelical mystery in time and place. The various facets of this faith-response will be developed in Part II. Here we are only concerned with the proclamative or sacramental aspect of living the Good News. For our proclamation and witness to be effective, however, the mediating role of discernment in the evangelization process must first be analyzed.

3. *Discernment: Encountering the Spirit of Christ in the Signs of the Times*

Given the universality of God's all-loving self-communication, which through Jesus Christ in His Spirit still remains hidden but to the eyes of faith, the Church in this in-between time has need to discern his presence at work in the world. Thus Jesus chided the Pharisees and Sadducees for not discerning the "kairos" of the present moment: " 'In the evening you say, "It will be fine; there is a red sky," and in the morning, "Stormy weather today; the sky is red and overcast." You know how to read the face of the sky, but you cannot read the signs of the times' " (Mt 16:2-3). Likewise today, if Christ is indeed *already* the Lord of History, "then he is in the midst of the world already and was there long before Christians even thought about the matter. Consequently, the church's job is not to take him there, but to find him there, i.e., to discern how and where he is already at work in the world."[85] This very tenet was maintained by the Second Vatican Council which stated:

> The People of God believes that it is led by the Spirit of the Lord, who fills the earth. Motivated by this faith, it labors to decipher authentic signs of God's presence and purpose in the happenings, needs, and desires in which this People has a part along with the other men of our age. For faith throws a new light on everything, manifests God's design for man's total vocation, and thus directs the mind to solutions which are fully human. (*GS* 11)

Being able to discern the Lord's presence in the signs of the times requires vigilance, wisdom and prudence. Hence, the need is great for watchfulness in prayer and for the utilization of all those means that Providence today puts at our disposal, especially the contributions to our self-understanding proffered by the human or life sciences, anthropology, psychology and sociology. In the First Letter of John, the author warns: "It is not every spirit, my dear people, that you can trust; test them, to see if they come from God" (1 Jn 4:1). The reason for such testing of the spirits was stated by Paul: "Satan himself goes about disguised as an angel of light" (2 Cor 11:14); and so, Paul lists the gift of discernment of spirits among the "charisms" (1 Cor 12:10). Such perception has its origin in love (cf. Phil 1:9-10) which possesses an instinct for spontaneously embracing the proper attitude: "Love is always patient and kind; it is never jealous; love is never boastful or conceited; it is never rude or selfish . . . (1 Cor 13:4ff.). This is the height of Christian wisdom, maturity or perfection, for the "teleioi" (the "mature" or "perfect"—cf. 1 Cor 2:6) are spiritual persons "who receive the Spirit that comes from God, to teach us to understand the gifts he has given . . . A spiritual man . . . is able to judge the value of everything, and his own value is not to be judged by other men" (1 Cor 2:12, 15). A "spiritual person's" life incarnates, as it were, the divine gift of faith-hope-love (cf. Eph 1:15-19).

The Spirit of the risen Christ, the Paschal Christ, the Christ of the "agape-kenosis" is the Spirit of truth whom Christ has sent to teach us all things and to remind us of all that he has said (Jn 14:26); he will remain with us forever (Jn 14:16). Guided by Christ's Spirit we will not yield to self-indulgence, "since self-indulgence is the opposite of the Spirit. . . . What the Spirit brings is very different: love, joy, peace, patience, kindness, goodness, trustfulness, gentleness, and self-control" (Gal 5:17, 22). Jesus, in his eschatological discourses in the synoptic accounts, calls for vigilance or wakefulness (Mt 24:42; Mk 13:33; Lk 21:34) and prudence (the parable of the Conscientious Steward—Mt 24:45-51; the parable of the Ten Bridesmaids—Mt 25:1-13; and the parable of the Talents—Mt 25:14-30). Such vigilance and prudence has need of prayer (Mt 26:40-41; Mk 14:37-38; Lk 22:46), which itself is a gift of the Spirit: "For when we cannot choose words in order to pray properly, the Spirit himself expresses our plea in a way that could never be put into words" (Rom 8:26).

Discerning the signs of the times is a spiritual gift given to the Church in this in-between time while waiting for the Parousia or Christ's Second Coming. Given the ambivalence in varying degrees of social, cultural, political and economic activities and of scientific and technological developments, the gift of discernment is a prerequisite for the Church's mission of evangelization which must take seriously the words of Paul: "This may be a wicked age, but your lives should redeem it" (Eph 5:16). The signs of the times, then, "are 'openings' for the gospel, points at which the world, being more 'penetrable,' more easily allows Christianity to enter."[86] Scrutinizing these "openings" in our contemporary world, according to B. Häring, requires employing "the unre-nounceable instruments" of "anthropology, the comparison of cultures, psychology, both individual and social, and also depth psychology. The Church cannot evangelize the world without making full use, obviously wise use, of the new sciences."[87]

The primacy of prayer, both personal and communal, remains, for if it is the Church's mission to awaken all people to the presence of the Mystery in which they live, she cannot hope to fulfill it unless she herself remains fully awake. Contemplative prayer constitutes such a wake-fullness or awareness of the presence of the Spirit. In whatever human context, prayer opens us to the Spirit of truth, the Spirit of the Paschal Christ (the "agape-kenosis") present and active in the world. "Prayer becomes the simple response of the servant listening attentively for ways to be of service, to become an instrument of peace and witness to God's all embracing reign, while respecting the unique personal freedom of fellowmen."[88]

The pervasive immanent presence of the Spirit of Truth also defines the teaching role or magisterial function of the Church. The variety of the gifts of the Spirit are given as a benefit to the whole Church, and each of them contributes to form one Body because they all come from the same Spirit (cf. 1 Cor 12). Since the gifts are given for the benefit of the whole Church, it is the Church's role to regulate these spiritual gifts (cf. 1 Cor 14:26-33). Likewise, the Good News is not given to a single apostle, but is confided to the whole community; and it is entrusted to the Church not for the purpose of conserving it in abstract formulas, "but so that it may be maintained alive in evangelization and witness to the faith."[89]

4. Witness: Incarnating the Good News in the Contemporary World

The gospel mystery is proclaimed by both word ("orthodoxy") and deed (orthopraxis), and the two together combine to form the element of Christian witness, which itself becomes evangelization as others ask us to give an explanation for the hope that is in us (cf. 1 Pt 3:15).[90] Through the gift of discernment and the life of prayer and liturgical worship, the Christian community incarnates the mission of the Spirit of Truth in a particular time and place by making visible in its fellowship the divine, Trinitarian self-communication—the divine evangelical econ-omy or "mystery of simplicity." The Church, thereby, becomes a sacra-mental presence in a given milieu revealing this Mystery and inviting men and women to share in this communal life or koinonia of the Spirit. Also, striving to realize Jesus' commandment of love (Jn 13:34-35) and his desire for unity among his disciples, the Church, too, becomes a sign inviting all humankind to faith in Christ and his mission from the Father (cf. Jn 17:21). Christ came to earth so that we may have life, and the only true life is to know the Father and Jesus Christ whom he has sent (Jn 17:3). The Church, thus, only fulfills her mission of evangelization inasmuch as she becomes a witness to the presence of this New and Eternal Life.

The Church must witness to the Paschal Mystery present and active in the midst of our world, for it is only through living this Mystery of the "agape-kenosis" that the transforming power of love is revealed to all the world. Without this concrete, practical love and fellowship, the proclamation of the Word would remain empty, ineffective, and even, in a certain sense, incredible. Living this Mystery and incarnating it, however, requires discerning the signs of the times which are open to receive it. As was pointed out in Chapter Two, the demise of Christendom and the concomitant growth of pluralism and secularism within Western civilization over the last century prompted the Church's reevaluation of its evangelizing mission. It is not our purpose in this section to seek to interpret the signs of the times in contemporary society; that will be attempted with regard to the American scene in the last part of this work. But since this radical transformation in the make-up of the structure of modern Western society has so affected the Church's mission in today's world, we will here briefly mention the necessary implications that such rapidly growing pluralism and secularism have for Christian witness as the primary means of evangelization today.

The West today considers itself to have advanced into a "post-Christian" era; it views itself as living in a "liberated," critical age which has transcended Christianity. Thus, in this pluralistic world, talk about God and the dignity of the human person becomes just one of many varied positive views of humankind. The Christian view, on its theoretical level, cannot possibly evoke universal appeal in modern contemporary society. E. Schillebeeckx observes:

> Despite all the pluralism, then, there is in positive views of man, the element of common search to realize the constantly threatened humanum. . . . This critical negativity, or negative dialectics is the universal pre-understanding of all positive views of man. It is not really in the first place knowledge, but a praxis which is motivated by hope and within which an element of knowledge can be formulated in a theory as discernible.[91]

We can reach an agreement on the inhuman that exists in human experience, and such experience provides an appropriate insertion point for evangelization through Christian witness which is primarily incarnated in the orthopraxis of kenotic love. Such orthopraxis does not advocate a Christian activism or pragmatism, nor does it espouse that cold, calculating super-organized efficiency of the modern business world which, though admirable, remains soulless and unattractive. Christian orthopraxis primarily witnesses to the presence of self-emptying love through its continual sacrifice for and on behalf of men and women.[92]

Such a Christian witness combined with a "critical negativity" of the inhuman forces and structures existing in contemporary society can prove to be a faithful continuation of the prophetic tradition. For the Church must proclaim the Good News with prophetic "parrhesia" or boldness (cf. 2 Cor. 3:12), never yielding to an easy irenicism, nor adjusting her doctrine and moral message to the spirit of the age. Thus, Christian faith here bears witness both in hope and love, for there lives a certain innate trust in the heart of the human person, a glimpse of the ultimate meaning of life, which tells him or her that it cannot all be totally meaningless. Finally, it is Christian eschatology which should give substance to these human hopes. As E. Schillebeeckx explains:

> Eschatology does not allow us to cash in on the hereafter, but it is something to be achieved responsibly by all the faithful within the framework of our terrestrial history. . . . This salvation must already be achieved now in our history, in the world, and so this history becomes itself a prophecy of the final transcendent *eschaton.* It is the promise of a new world, a powerful symbol which sets us thinking and above all acting. The credibility of this promise lies in the renewal now of our human history.[93]

In a pluralistic, secular world our lives themselves must become evangelization as we put on the love of Christ revealed in the orthopraxis of the Cross. For this to occur we must become true disciples of Jesus. A radical conversion is here essential, so that we ourselves will be willing to take up the cross (cf. Mk 8:34) and live according to the New Life (the dynamic power of grace) that has been so freely bestowed on us in Christ Jesus our Lord.

SUMMARY

The loving design of God the Father to give himself and communicate himself to all humankind is accomplished through the mission of the Son, the revealing Word, and the mission of the Holy Spirit, the dynamic, inner word of Love and creative power of New Life. This divine plan constitutes an evangelical economy having its source in the Father's free, gracious and all-benevolent will. It is the Mystery hidden for generations but now revealed in Jesus Christ—the "mystery of simplicity," God's *one* plan of salvation by which he reconciles us to himself by giving us a share in his very own Life. The revelation and actuation of this divine economy inaugurates a process of evangelization, a process into which Christ inserted his disciples when he commanded them to go out and preach the Good News to all nations and to baptize them into the mystery of this New Life and this self-emptying Love. The Church is, thus, gathered-sent to proclaim the Gospel in word and deed, becoming a sacrament to all peoples of the life and fellowship we share in Christ's Spirit. Evangelization is the Church's primary, constitutive mission, her very *raison d'être*.

Through revelation the evangelical economy becomes known. God addresses, unveils himself, and communicates himself in a divine-human dialogue which seeks to become ever more and more incarnate, culminating in the Paschal Mystery of the Word-made-flesh. The revelatory summit of the divine economy finds its supreme expression on the Cross—God's complete gift and humankind's total response, a divine-human dialogue of "agape-kenosis," reconciliation and peace. Through the grace of the Holy Spirit, we are brought to share the divine Trinitarian Life. We are united in Christ's Spirit to form one Body, the Church, who has as its Head the Paschal Lord of history in whom, through whom, and for whom all things were created. In the Spirit we are transformed into "images" of Christ, who is the paradigm and perfect model of the kind of love God expects from us. Through the Spirit revelation is communicated in its fullness in the most intimate part of our being where it becomes a principle of action, a new interior dynamism. Our very participation in this New Life constitutes the new "law of the Spirit." All men and women of all ages, places and time are called by this grace, this immanent and yet transcending presence of Trinitarian Life. But Christians are specially called by this grace to be concrete signs and witnesses of what God is doing in the world. The Church is gathered-sent to be a "universal sacrament of salvation"; she is a "mystery of communion" bringing people together into intimate union with God and into fellowship with one another in a shared Spirit. Through her liturgy and sacramental life she consciously celebrates the Mystery of her very life, the Paschal Mystery of Christ, uniting us to it and bringing it to bear on the critical human moments of individual and community life. Through her liturgy the Church is evangelized, so that she may go out as a sign and witness to proclaim the Good News to all the world.

Thus, the Church's mission of evangelization is her actual insertion into and assumption of a continuing process that finds its origin in God's loving plan. This mission is both an external mandate and an intrinsic necessity, because it is only through revelation, Jesus Christ and the Church that God the Father and his evangelical economy can become known with compelling clarity and be embraced by us in faith, hope and love. This divine Mystery of God-revealing-and-communicating-himself must be proclaimed by both word and deed, for the gospel truth is a Reality that must be experienced and lived, otherwise it remains just a matter of theory or mere words offering little that is meaningful or efficacious to fellow human beings. Words and deeds then combine to form the element of Christian witness, whereby our lives, guided by the Spirit, incarnate the evangelical economy in a particular time and culture. Through the Spirit's gifts of prayer and discernment we are enabled to scrutinize the signs of the times and, thereby, find "openings" for bringing this gospel mystery to bear on the everyday realities of our contemporary world. Thus, the Church must become a witness of the divine "agape-kenosis" present and active in our midst. Living this mystery we evangelize as we invite all men and women to see what we see and to share what we share—the very Life and Love of the Father, Son and Holy Spirit.

NOTES

1. G. Thils, "Pivotal Positions on 'Evangelization' and 'Salvation,'" *Lumen Vitae* (Eng. ed.), 30 (March 1975), 75.

2. The doctrinal formulas of the early Christian Creeds were also arranged according to this same Trinitarian structure.

3. Cf. the *Passio Sanctorum Scillitanorum*, July 17, 180, in Africa. The Christian Speratus addressed the proconsul: "If you will give me a quiet hearing, I will tell you of the mystery of simplicity." (Footnote No. 4, McNally, *The Unreformed Church* [New York, 1965], 58). Back in 1950, J.A. Jungmann wrote that what is particularly lacking in the faithful is "a sense of unity, seeing it all as a whole, and understanding of the wonderful message of divine grace. All they retain of Christian doctrine is a string of dogmas and moral precepts, threats and promises, customs and rites, tasks and duties imposed on unfortunate Catholics, while the non-Catholic gets off free of them." ("Theology and Kerygmatic Teaching," *Lumen Vitae*, 5 [1950], 258.)

4. Cf. Jungmann, *The Good News Yesterday and Today* (New York, 1962), 9: "But Catholic theology is not merely the development of a single con-

cept, even that of God Himself. It is rather *the presentation of a way* which unites heaven and earth."

5. J.L. Segundo, *Our Idea of God* (Maryknoll, New York, 1974), 22.

6. R. Latourelle, *Theology of Revelation* (New York, 1966), 30.

7. This too has been the traditional teaching of the Magisterium down through the ages. Knowability of God: Vatican I (*D* 1806, cf. 1785; *DS* 3026, 3004); Vatican II, *DV* 6. Incomprehensibility of God: Lateran IV (*D* 428); Vatican I (*D* 1782).

8. J. Powers, *Spirit and Sacrament* (New York, 1973), 6.

9. *Ibid.*, 20.

10. T. Merton, *Conjectures of a Guilty Bystander* (Garden City, New York, 1965), 44.

11. B. Lonergan, *Method of Theology* (New York, 1972), 123.

12. *Ibid.*, 112.

13. *Ibid.*, 113.

14. Cf. Vatican I (*DS* 3002); Irenaeus, *Adversus Haereses*, IV, 20, 7; *PG* VII, col. 1037: *"Gloria Dei vivens homo: vita autem hominis visio Dei."* And the great Scholastics viewed creation in terms of participation, enriching the principle of causality.

15. A. Dulles, "Revelation," in G. Dyer, *et al., An American Catholic Catechism* (New York, 1975) no. 8, p. 4. (Hereafter cited as *AACC*.)

16. A. Darlap, "Salvation," *SM*, V, 418.

17. J. Ratzinger, "Dogmatic Constitution on Divine Revelation, Chapter I," *Vorgrimler*, III, 175 with a footnote reference to K. Rahner, "The Development of Dogma," *Theological Investigations*, I (1961), pp. 39-78; p. 49: "Nothing new remains to be said, not as though there were not still much to say, but because everything has been said, everything given in the Son of Love, in whom God and the world have become one."

18. Since in the hypostatic union Jesus is both God and man, E. Schillebeeckx describes this ultimate revelation from its anthropological perspective in: "The 'God of Jesus' and the 'Jesus of God,' " *Concilium*, 93 (New York, 1974), 125: "God's sublime and definitive revelation thus occurred in his silent but extremely intimate nearness to the suffering and dying Jesus, who experienced, in his suffering and death, the depths of the human predicament and at the same time his inseparable belonging to God. This is what cannot be theoretically included within a rational system—it can only be the object of faith."

19. N. Schiffers, "Revelation," *SM*, V, 345. See T. Guzie, *Jesus and the Eucharist* (New York, 1974), 88 and 91, for an interpretation of the Paschal Mystery from its anthropological perspective: "The paradox of christian faith, the well known stumbling block and piece of foolishness, is that life and true union with God is to be found in the death of a man and union with his death. . . . Christian faith does not affirm that life is *resumed* after death. It affirms something much more profound, namely that life comes *out of* death."

20. Cf. R. Modras, "The Elimination of Pluralism between the Churches through Pluralism within the Churches," *Concilium*, 88 (New York, 1973), 78: "Christian revelation is not a compilation of revealed truths but a person (Constitution on Revelation, 6). For this reason, and in virtue of the original union and totality of revelation in him, Jesus has been called the 'primordial dogma' of Christianity."

21. H. Rahner, *A Theology of Proclamation* (New York, 1968), 21.

22. K. Berger, "Grace," *SM*, II, 410.

23. C.R. Meyer, "Grace," *AACC*, No. 1, 56.

24. P. Fransen, *The New Life of Grace*, (London, 1969), 55.

25. K. Rahner, *Theological Investigations*, Vol. 2 (London, 1963), 113.

26. Jungmann, *The Good News*, 47.

27. Berger, "Grace," 412.

28. Cf. Schmaus, "Holy Spirit," *SM*, III. 56.

29. S. Lyonnet and I. La Potterie, *The Christian Lives by the Spirit* (New York, 1971), 205-6.

30. M. K. Hellwig, "Christology," *AACC*, No. 21, 71.

31. Cf. Fransen, *The New Life of Grace*, 57, where he notes: "the Spirit is 'the bond of love', the divine amen to the primordial gesture of love which the Father makes in the Son."

32. J.L. Segundo, *Grace and the Human Condition* (Maryknoll, N.Y., 1973), 10-11.

33. K. Rahner, "Grace," *SM*, II, 418.

34. N. Rigali, "Faith, Hope and Charity," *AACC*, No. 10, 196.

35. Lyonnet and La Potterie, *The Christian Lives by the Spirit*, 157.

36. *Ibid.*, 158. St. Thomas Aquinas wrote in his *Summa theol.*, I-II, q. 106, A.1, corp: *"Principaliter lex nova est ipsa gratia Spiritus Sancti, quae datur christifidelibus."*

37. Cf. St. Thomas Aquinas, *In 2 Cor 3:6: "Spiritus Sanctus, dum facit in nobis caritatem, quae est plentitudo legis, est testamentum novum"* (lect. 2; ed. R. Cai, no. 90).

38. J. Dedek, "The Moral Law," *AACC*, no. 6, 171-2.

39. Lyonnet and La Potterie, *The Christian Lives by the Spirit*, 64.

40. Segundo, *Grace*, 69. Relating it analogously to human experience, he writes further: "What it comes down to—and this is a major point relating to the whole topic of grace—is that we are not accustomed to gifts like this one. For us the very idea of gift entails the notion of *scarcity*. In our minds the natural is associated with that which abounds; it is what everyone has. In our ranks, gifts always constitute privileged moments. So we set about looking for grace, convinced that if it is a gift, it must be missing at some point in our lives or the lives of others. And by comparing presence and absence we hope to find the line of separation where pure nature lies on one side and the supernatural on the other."

41. Other pertinent texts include: 1 Tim 4:10; 1 Jn 2:22; Mk 10:45; Rom 11:32.

42. Fransen, *The New Life of Grace*, 151.

43. *Ibid.*, 154.

44. Cf. St. Gregory the Great, "Sermons on the Gospel," 19, 1: (J.-P. Migne, ed., *Patrologia Latina* [1844ff.], 76, 1154 B; hereafter cited as *PL*); St. Augustine, "Sermon," 341, 9, 11: (*PL* 93, 1499).

45. St. Justin, 2 Apol 6, 3; 8, 1; 10, 1-3.

46. Häring, *The Law of Christ* (Cork, 1960) I, 89.

47. Cf. Powers, *Spirit and Sacrament*, 108-9: "The Church of the Christ is *ekklesia*, a community gathered together by God. But . . . this is a matter of a shared spirit, a shared vision, a shared experience and a shared life whose center and context is the risen Jesus, with all this implies for our experience of ourselves, our world, our history . . . the Spirit of God, the Spirit of Christ is borne

and shared by people like ourselves. . . ."

48. Cf. D. Mollat, *The Jerusalem Bible*, commentary on the verse: "Many of the Fathers, not without good reason, interpret the water and blood as symbols of baptism and the Eucharist, and these two sacraments as signifying the Church which is born like a second Eve from the side of Adam." See also, A. Grillmeier, "The Mystery of the Church, Chapter I," in *Vorgrimler*, I, 141-42.

49. Cf. R. McAfee Brown, *Frontiers for the Church Today* (New York, 1973), 109-10: "The tendency in the past was to stress summoning, the church as the community that gathers together. (*ek-klesia* means those who are 'called out' from the world.) What is now being stressed is a sending, which must be understood as an integral part of summoning: the church is summoned for the sake of being sent. This has been true since the beginning. The marks of the summoned church in Acts 2:42—teaching, fellowship, breaking bread, and prayer—were set in the context of the apostles being sent into the world." See also M. Buber, *I and Thou* (New York, 1971), 164: "All revelation is a calling and a mission. . . ."

50. R. Latourelle, *Christ and the Church: Signs of Salvation* (New York, 1972), 128, writes: "Of all the themes to which the Second Vatican Council addressed itself, that which renews most deeply our vision of the Church is precisely this theme of the Church as a mystery of communion. It orients and inspires the whole of the constitution *Lumen Gentium*. . . . The ecclesiology of communion especially alive and fruitful in the Churches of the east, has been in the west, not disowned or ignored, but for a long time left in the shade, in favor of an ecclesiology of institution, hierarchy and authority."

51. Cf. *LG* 4. In the Second Vatican Council's Decree on Ecumenism we find that "The highest exemplar and source of this mystery [the mystery of the unity of the Church] is the unity, in the Trinity of Persons, of one God, the Father and the Son in the Holy Spirit" (*Unitatis Redintegratio*, Second Vatican Council's Decree on Ecumenism [Nov. 21, 1964], 2. Hereafter cited as *UR*).

52. B. Kloppenburg, *The Ecclesiology of Vatican II* (Chicago, 1974), 30-1. For further elaboration on the Spirit's mission elsewhere in the conciliar documents of Vatican II, see 31-2.

53. Fransen, *The New Life of Grace*, 85. See also, *Sacrosanctum Concilium*, Second Vatican Council's Constitution on the Sacred Liturgy (Dec. 4, 1963), 33: "For in the liturgy God speaks to His people and Christ is still proclaiming His gospel. And the people reply to God in both song and prayer." (Hereafter cited as *SC*.)

54. *Ibid.*, 86.

55. Wicks, "Christian Sacraments," *AACC*, no. 3, 113.

56. *Ibid.*, no. 6, 162.

57. *Ibid.*, no. 7, 128.

58. *Ibid.*, 143.

59. Cf. *Optatum Totius*, Second Vatican Council's Decree on Priestly Formation (Oct. 28, 1965), 8, which while outlining the spiritual formation of seminarians notes: "They should live His paschal mystery in such a way that they know how to invite into it the people entrusted to them." (Hereafter cited as *OT*.)

60. Cf. G. Thils, "Pivotal Positions on 'Evangelization' and 'Salvation,' " *Lumen Vitae* (Paramus, N.J., 1971), 76: ". . . there is in fact but a single and unique economy of salvation, the object of evangelization."

61. Vellanickal, *SAS*, 68.

62. *EN*, par. 14.

63. Cf. Powers in *Spirit and Sacrament*, 111: "Thus *ekklesia*, the calling and gathering which being the Church of Christ means, is at the same time a sending, a driving of the Christian outside himself, outside the community of shared belief to tell the world that Jesus is risen from the dead, to ask the world of men if they can see what we see."

64. *EN*, par. 5.

65. *EN*, par. 53.

66. J. Schütte, "Evangelization and Development in the Light of Conciliar and Post-Conciliar Theology," *SAS*, 381.

67. Amalorpavadass, "Theology of Evangelization in the Indian Context," *SAS*, 37-8.

68. The first author to use this term was J. B. Metz in "Gott vor uns. Statt eines theologischen Arguments," in H. Unseld, ed., *Ernst Bloch zu ehren. Beiträge zu seinem Werk* (Suhrkamp, Frankfurt, 1965), 233, 241. (Cf. E. Cambon, *L'ortoprassi* [Roma, 1974], 20.)

69. Cambon, *L'ortoprassi* (Rome, 1974), 19.

70. For Christianity as the "Way" see Acts 9:2; 18:25, 26; 19:9, 23; 22:4; 24:14, 22. Thus J. Ratzinger in his *Introduction to Christianity*, (London, 1969), 64: "If Platonism provides an *idea* of the truth, Christian belief offers truth as a *way*, and only by becoming a way has it become man's truth. Truth as a mere perception, as a mere idea, remains bereft of force; it only becomes man's truth as a way which makes a claim upon him, which he can and must tread."

71. Elsewhere in the gospels Jesus puts the emphasis on *doing* the right thing: practicing what one preaches (Mt 23:4); doing the Father's will (Mt 12:50); reconciliation in preference to worship (Mt 5:23-24); service (Mt 10:43-45); "bearing fruit" (Mt 13:8-9; 25:14f.; 7:16-20; Jn 15:16).

72. Legrand, *GN&W*, 43, 45.

73. Cf. Fitzmyer, "Pauline Theology," *JBC*, 79:125.

74. Cf. M. Zerwick, *The Epistle to the Ephesians* (London, 1969), 113-4.

75. Cf. T. Forestell, "The Letters to the Thessalonians," *JBC*, 48:14.

76. Cf. R. Bultmann, "aletheia," G. Kittel, ed., *Theological Dictionary of the New Testament*, I (Grand Rapids, 1964), 245, 247. (Hereafter cited as *TDNT*.)

77. Emphasis added.

78. E. Schillebeeckx, *The Understanding of Faith* (New York, 1974), 59.

79. R. Latourelle, *Theology of Revelation* (New York, 1966), 316, with footnote: K. Buehler, *Sprachtheorie* (Jena, 1934), 2, 28-33. Corresponding to this threefold aspect of the word are the three persons of the verb: the word expresses (first person), addresses (second person), recounts (third person).

80. Cf. *EN*, par. 42.

81. V. Elizondo, "Biblical Pedagogy of Evangelization," *American Ecclesiastical Review*, 168 (October 1974), 527. (Hereafter cited as *AER*.)

82. B. Häring, *Evangelisation Today* (Slough, England, 1974), 11. Cf. also, *EN*, par. 44.

83. H. Weinrich, "Narrative Theology," *Concilium*, 85 (New York, 1973), 50, observes: "Christianity, however, did not remain a story-telling community. In its meeting with the Hellenistic world it lost its poetic innocence. In Greek culture, storytelling (myth) had long been subordinated to argument (logos)."

84. Cf. Sacred Congregation for the Clergy, *General Catechetical Directory* (USCC, Wash. D.C., 1971), 19, where treating the "Ministry of the Word in the Church" (no. 17) divides it into *four* forms: evangelization, or missionary preaching; the catechetical form; the liturgical form; and the theological form. I prefer to view missionary preaching and the liturgical form as two aspects of the *kerygma*, both having as their intent an invitation to a personal encounter. The term "evangelization" is more applicable theologically in describing the entire context within which the "ministry of the Word" is situated along with the element of Christian witness, since Christ proclaimed the gospel in both words and deeds.

85. R. McAfee Brown, *Frontiers*, 43; see also 45: "We must take seriously the suggestion of the French theologian George Casalis, which was later incorporated into a number of World Council documents. The traditional way of thinking of God in the world, Casalis says, has been through the sequence, *God-Church-World:* i.e., *God* makes himself known to the *church*, so that the church can make him known to the *world*. But, says Casalis, the real sequence should be *God-World-Church:* i.e., *God* is already at work in the *world* and the *church* is that part of the world that recognizes what he is doing there and tries to align itself and all people with his purposes so that they can be brought to fulfillment." Cf. also, *EN*, par. 75.

86. R. Latourelle, *Christ and the Church: Signs of Salvation* (New York, 1972), 203.

87. Häring, *Evangelisation Today*, 10.

88. B. Häring, "Prayer in a Secular Age," *Faith and Morality in a Secular Age* (Garden City, New York, 1973), 200-26; 219.

89. Häring, *Evangelisation Today*, op. cit., 93. Cf. also, *EN*, pars. 15 and 78.

90. Cf. J.-P. Jossua, "Christian Experience and Communicating the Faith," *Concilium* 85 (New York, 1973), 56-67, who suggests "the pathway of experience" or the witness of genuine Christian living as a way of inviting people to enquiry.

91. E. Schillebeeckx, *The Understanding of Faith: Interpretation and Criticism* (New York, 1974), 10.

92. Cf. L. Ratus, "Theology of Presence As a Form of Evangelization," *SAS*, 422: "Keeping these two aspects of the Incarnation in mind—solidarity and self-immolation—we are somewhat in a position to understand what the evangelical form of 'presence' involves. An apostle, who wishes to be 'present', as Christ was 'present', to the world must be prepared to undergo the Christic experience of *kenosis*. No true presence is achieved without the initial attitude of self-emptying, by which the disciple dispossesses himself of all that which may alienate him from the human situation of his environment and from proclaiming the Good News in and through his life. . . . The apostolate of presence cannot be lived unless one is prepared, like Christ, to share with deep solidarity the particular features of the condition—social, economic, cultural—of one's fellowmen. . . . By being 'present', we are to be 'one with them', suffering from what makes them suffer, loving what they love, aspiring as they aspire for greater truth and justice." Such a concrete form of evangelization by "presence" has been undertaken in the United States by the Glenmary Home Missioners—cf. D. Byers and B. Quinn, *Evangelists to the Poor* (Washington, D.C., 1975).

93. Schillebeeckx, *The Understanding of Faith*, 10.

PART II
Evangelization: Living the Good News

We have just analyzed in Part I the *first moment* of the evangelization process, namely, the proclamation of the Good News. Here in Part II our attention now turns to the fundamental components in the *second moment* of this process, that is, living the Good News. For in listening to the Gospel proclaimed, the hearer encounters Christ, the incarnate Good News. Meeting Christ, a person is challenged to believe what one hears and to place one's full trust and confidence in him whom he or she has encountered. In other words, the proclamation of the Good News, whether in word or deed, challenges and invites a person to conversion and discipleship. A person's faith-response to God's gift-call constitutes a new "Way" of perceiving reality and of living one's life accordingly. The immanent-transcendent presence of the Father, Son and Holy Spirit confronts us where we are and invites us to enter into a loving dialogue of shared life. Through the proclaimed Gospel and the grace of the Holy Spirit, God gives himself to us in kenotic love while at the same time inviting us to a reciprocal self-donation. Our loving acceptance (itself a gift of grace) of the divine self-communication finds its incarnate expression in a life of Christian witness. Adhering to the Gospel and living it in gratitude thus forms the foundation of the Christian "Way," which itself constitutes a genuine proclamation of the gospel mystery.

"Moral theology" as a separate discipline was nonexistent in the early Church. Its history, in fact, only begins after the Council of Trent. The early Church, nevertheless, was fully conscious of the moral implications of its faith-response to the Good News. But for these first Christians the Gospel was first of all considered to be the Good News of salvation, the proclamation of the unheard-of mystery of God-revealing-and-communicating-himself to us in love. It was by no means a code of ethics, nor was it primarily concerned with moral behavior. Yet, they realized that a person's wholehearted response in faith, hope and love must be put into practice. Thus appeared the Christian "Way" as both a "teaching" ("orthodoxy") and a "mode" of living (orthopraxis). A Christian's behavior was viewed as the incarnate expression of his or her faith. The "moral theology" of the early Church, in other words, was

based upon "doctrine" and the "spiritual life." Thus, discoursing on the
letters of St. Paul, F. Mussner observes that

> Nearly all of St. Paul's epistles have two parts, one which is
> theological and doctrinal, while the other deals with practical
> behavior. The theological and doctrinal exposition always pre-
> cedes the ethical considerations. It offers us a discussion of
> God's saving activity as it is revealed in history in Christ; this
> is the foundation of Christian life; it gives us the facts of that
> life. The obligations of the Christian life, the imperative it im-
> poses, with its moral demands and the need for truly Christian
> behavior, are a consequence of this. Christianity must never be
> confined to the level of "theory". The message we have re-
> ceived must be put into practice. This was one of Jesus' great
> concerns in his preaching.[1]

Here in the second part of this work we want to present and systematize the various factors of the *second moment* of the evangelization
process that comprise our living out the Mystery that the Good News
explicitly proclaims. Christian life based on the Gospel is a spiritual-
moral life, for it is in the Spirit that Christians, already redeemed and
reconciled "in Christ," are called here and now to become the "new humanity" (Col 3:9-11). This connotes a process of growth. In the fellowship of the believing community, we "mature" in Christ (Eph 4:13-16)
and become ever more and more transformed into his image. Thus,
Christian morality is in actuality a by-product of this spiritual growth or
maturing process. The fundamental factors involved in this process remain essentially the same because they constitute the stuff of the human
condition vis-à-vis Ultimate Reality; they are the elemental components
of the divine-human relationship, which in Christian life are categorized
by a gospel-worldview. The *second moment* of the evangelization process, then, concerns itself with our moral-spiritual life. Our faith-
response in love and hope in this context gives witness to the gospel mystery. At the same time a renewed "moral theology" or a "theology of
Christian living" is called for in order to demonstrate further the evangelizing potential of our faith-life and to emphasize better the necessary
dependence of Christian ethics and spirtuality upon the Christ Mystery.

For our purposes here in this second part of our study, we will
parallel our development of the *first moment* of the evangelization process in Part I by first returning to the faith-experience of the apostolic
community as recorded in the New Testament. In so doing we will both
situate the faith-response of Christian life within the context of the proc-

lamation of the Good News, and also, at the same time, comply with the mandate of the Second Vatican Council for the renewal of "moral theology." The Council Fathers stated:

> Other theological disciplines should also be renewed by livelier contact with the mystery of Christ and the history of salvation. Special attention needs to be given to the development of moral theology. Its scientific exposition should be more thoroughly nourished by scriptural teaching. It should show the nobility of the Christian vocation of the faithful, and their obligation to bring forth fruit in charity for the life of the world. (*OT* 16)

By inserting the theological discipline of "moral theology" into the wider context of the gospel mystery and Christian life, the fundamental categories of this special science, which up until recently have been based upon the abstract philosophical and legalistic principles of the Counter-Reformation period and presented in the form of a "casuistry manual" for confessors administering the sacrament of penance, will of necessity become enriched, expanded and reorganized. The renewal of "moral theology" in this manner will, indeed, show its intimate relationship to and dependence upon the other theological disciplines of scripture, dogma and spirituality.

Christian life in the early Church of both the New Testament era and sub-apostolic period depended upon an inherent synthesis of doctrinal belief, spiritual life, and moral behavior. Our study of this integral Christian life-style will be entitled "The 'Way' of the Early Church" (Chapter IV). Paralleling Part I, we will here have little to say historically beyond the sub-apostolic times because the same social, cultural and political transformation that affected the methods of proclaiming the Good News in that era also had a similar impact on the dissolution of this early Christian "Way" of life.

Immediately following our look at the early Christian "Way," we will undertake an analysis of the "Fundamental Evangelical Categories for Contemporary Christian Living" (Chapter V). Set astir by the major social, cultural, political and technological transformation of modern times which fostered the concomitant demise of Christendom, theological thought and speculation, especially during the first half of the twentieth century, was forced to raise a large number of new and pertinent questions regarding the place and mission of the Church in the contemporary world. The Second Vatican Council (1962-65) eventually sought to clarify and to put into perspective a goodly portion of this new situation, while at the same time it mandated the reform and renewal of many theological disciplines and ecclesiastical institutions.

Recognizing the positive value of the new secular sciences for theology, the Council Fathers stated:

> In pastoral care, appropriate use must be made not only of theological principles, but also of the findings of the secular sciences, especially of psychology and sociology. Thus the faithful can be brought to live the faith in a more thorough and mature way. . . . Let them blend modern science and its theories and the understandings of the most recent discoveries with Christian morality and doctrine. Thus their religious practice and morality can keep pace with their scientific knowledge and with an ever-advancing technology. (*GS* 62)

Therefore, in developing our fundamental evangelical categories of a contemporary Christian "Way," in this *second moment* of the evangelization process we will consider not only Scripture and the tradition of the early Church, but also the human or life sciences along with philosophy (cf. *OT* 15) and the "manual" tradition of the recent past. The theological reflections of this chapter will gather together within a gospel-worldview the primary elements of the Christian's faith-response as they are being currently analyzed by some recent proponents of a contemporary "moral theology." They will provide us with the basis for a "theology of Christian living" whose main concern is incarnating the gospel mystery in our lives. Living the Good News will thus be seen to carry sacramental value and evangelizing power.

NOTE

1. F. Mussner, "The Epistle to the Colossians," in *New Testament for Spiritual Reading*, J. McKenzie, ed., (London and Sydney, 1970), 95. For the integral relationship between doctrinal and moral teaching see E. McDonagh, "The Study of Christian Theology," *Invitation and Response* (New York, 1972), especially pp. 16-17: "The genesis of the division between dogmatic and moral theology and the alliance between moral theology and canon law form an interesting if complex chapter in the history of theology. For St. Thomas and the scholastics the division did not exist. His *Summa Theologica*, which affirms in its first question the unity of theology, sets out to cover the whole range of Christian theology including its moral implications. What has been isolated as a matter of moral theology is dealt with mainly in the Second Part of the *Summa*, but one would be unfaithful to the mind of St. Thomas to isolate this as a tract on moral theology. For him all theology was one and must be treated as such."

IV

The "Way" of the Early Church

This study, thus far, has shown that "the proclamation of the Good News" ("kerygma") is primarily an *event* in which the hearer encounters Christ, who is himself the Word of God and the risen Lord. The Christian's faith-response, therefore, is not a mere intellectual assent to revealed "wisdom" or "knowledge" (cf. 1 Cor 8:1). It is instead a total personal commitment (a covenantal relationship) in love and hope to Christ the Lord through whom and in whom we are given "new life" and become members of the "new humanity." Such integral Christian faith is constitutive of a new dynamic and ontological reality. It opens the way to a personal dialogue between divine and human co-subjects, and the relationship therein established finds its genuine expression in a concrete mode of existence or "Way" of life. It is for this reason, then, that certain local communities in the New Testament era referred to Christianity itself as the "Way" (cf. Acts 9:2; 18:25; 19:9, 23; 22:4; 24:14, 22). We, therefore, have adopted this designation in the title of this chapter to emphasize specifically this dynamic, living and integral character of the faith-response of the early Church. The "Way" in fact is the one New Testament term that best encompasses all that we mean here and now when we speak of the *second moment* of the evangelization process. Our purpose herein will be to establish and analyze the principle factors that constituted the "Way" of the early Church: first, in the apostolic period of the New Testament, and then, in the sub-apostolic era of the first Christian centuries.

A. The Church of the New Testament

The faith-experience of the apostolic community, as recorded in the Synoptic gospels, attests to Jesus' proclaiming the Kingdom of God during his earthly ministry. But the small group of believers who gathered around the apostles in the immediate post-resurrection period soon came to the realization that the Kingdom Jesus preached was, indeed, an eschatological, heavenly reality that had already begun on earth with the founding of the Church.

Certain themes or categories by which they explicate this reality often recur in the New Testament writings. Thus these early Christians held that *"in Christ,"* the now risen and exalted Lord, and in the manifestly new presence of the Spirit among his disciples since Pentecost, the "new humanity" was being created, the Kingdom was being formed. The "power of the gospel" was released as it gathered the Church to become the Body of Christ and the new "Israel of God" (Gal 6:16). Convoked "in Christ" the "ekklesia" became a *"koinonia,"* a fraternal communion of life in faith, hope and love. And just as Christ preached repentance and faith as prerequisites for entrance into the Kingdom, so likewise did the apostolic Church call for *conversion* before receiving new members into its fellowship through the reception of Christian baptism and the gift of the Spirit (cf. especially Acts 2:38). Through baptism, the new Christian in imitation of Christ's death dies to his or her former sinful self (cf. Rom 6:6) and rises to New Life with God. This neophyte becomes a "spiritual man" ("pneumatikos"), a true *disciple* or follower of Christ. As a disciple, then, the Christian continues to sever oneself from *sin.* He or she "matures" in Christ, and his or her very life bears witness to Jesus and the Gospel (cf. Rev. 12:17). In this particular section, we want to bring into focus and expand upon these various elements that played such a major role in the evangelization itself of the New Testament Church.

1. *"In Christ" the Second Adam*

St. Paul in referring to the risen Christ writes: "The last Adam has become a life-giving spirit" (1 Cor 15:45). The outpouring of the Spirit, in fact, constituted the basic religious experience of the early Christian community. The Pentecost event gave birth to a new reality, a new "Way" of living. In the power of the Spirit the Church was born and a "new humanity" began to take shape (cf. Eph 2:15; Gal 6:15); the Good News itself became incarnate in the local community of believers.

The Pauline concept of the "Second Adam," referring explicitly to Christ, is also a collective designation denoting this "new humanity," or *an evangelized mankind.* Christ, being the unique Mediator of the New Covenant (cf. Heb 8:6) is, as Son (Heb 1:2), the ultimate revelation of God's faithfulness and love, and, as the "Second Adam" (Rom 5:15-19), mankind's perfect response of obedience (Rm 5:19) and love. His obedience has ratified the New Covenant reconciling us to God and to one another and granting us a share in the intimate Life of the Father, Son, and Spirit (divine grace). In Christ, the Second Adam, all is now grace and a "new creation." The spiritual-moral life of the Christian is in essence constituted by this new Christological, pneumatological, and ecclesiological reality. To facilitate our analysis, however, we will here first discuss the combined Christological and pneumatological aspects of this Life, and then, under the title of *"koinonia,"* its ecclesiological phase.

Humankind's faith-response, our spiritual-moral life, is itself a gift from God. It is a matter of the Spirit and the New Life we share in Christ. The various theologies of the New Testament employ many different images and concepts that arise out of Old Testament sources to describe this new reality that has now suddenly become manifest in the "Christ Spirit."

Considering, first of all, Christ as humankind's perfect response in love and obedience to God the Father, we see the recurrence throughout the writings of the New Testament of the Deutero-Isaian theme of the "Suffering Servant", which in Paul evolves into the concepts of the Second Adam and the new creation. Jesus is the "Son of Man" who "did not come to be served but to serve, and to give his life as a ransom for many" (Mk 10:45). Mark's gospel account connects the role of Servant and Covenant as Jesus utters the words over the chalice at the Last Supper saying: "This is my blood, the blood of the covenant, poured out for many" (Mk 14:24).[1] This association of Christ's death with the "new" covenant (Heb 8:13) brings to the fore further prophetic images of a "new heart," a "new Law," and a "new Spirit," (cf. Jer 31:31-34; Ezk 36:26f.). Christ's Paschal Mystery, indeed, marks the beginning of a whole new creation through which the world is becoming evangelized.

This theme of the "new creation" as a new "Way" of living is common to the theologies of both John and Paul. The beginning of the Johannine gospel account specifically links the new creation to the coming of Christ (the Incarnation). Christ has come that we might have Life in all its fullness (cf. Jn 10:10), and those who are reborn "through water and the Spirit" enter the Kingdom of God which in John is identified with Eternal Life (Jn 3:5). In Johannine theology, the new creation originates in Christ and in the Spirit and is connected with the parallel themes of rebirth and eternal life. Jesus is "the way, the truth, and the life" (Jn 14:6), "the resurrection and the life," and whoever believes in him shall not die (Jn 11:25). Furthermore, "eternal life" connotes a definite moral imperative in Johannine thought. In the gospel account we read: "And eternal life is this: to know you the only true God, and Jesus Christ whom you have sent" (Jn 17:3); and the First Letter of John will add: "We can be sure we know God only by keeping his commandments" (1 Jn 2:3).

These same themes of regeneration and new life, which are indeed indicative of the *second moment* of the evangelization process, recur in the Pauline Corpus. By our baptism into Christ's death and resurrection, our sins are forgiven and we are given New Life "in Christ" (Rom 6:1-11), for "Jesus was put to death for our sins and raised to life to justify us" (Rm 4:25). In fact, the baptized person has become with Christ "a single being" (Rm 6:5). "Recreated by Word and Spirit, man has become a new being (Titus 3:5) whose moral behavior is radically transformed."[2] This grace of the Holy Spirit has now become the dynamic vital and moral principle of our new "Way" of life. Thus, as C. Spicq points out: "The Christian life—a symbiosis with the Lord, to borrow a term from biology (Rom 6:8; Col 2:13)—will be nothing other than the living and putting into effect of this baptismal grace, a continuous, progressive death to sin and a life of renewal and victory."[3]

The Pauline theme of Christ, the Second Adam, is furthermore implicitly related to the covenantal character of our new way of life. Paul writes: "As by one man's disobedience many were made sinners, so by one man's obedience many will be made righteous" (Rm 5:19). Here Christ's obedience connotes his mediatorship of the New Covenant established in his blood (cf. Heb 10:9-10). In the words of D. Stanley: "As Second Adam, Paul perceived, Christ had perforce to break the old sinful solidarity that bound man to his first parent. The significance of Christ's death, then, was a dying to sin (Rm 6:10), to the law (Gal 2:19-20), to death itself (1 Cor 15:26; Rm 6:9."[4] In designating Christ as the Second Adam, Paul takes the theme of the "Suffering Servant" to a higher synthesis. For Paul, Christ's resurrection is not so much a vindication of his death or a reward for his transcendent obedience—a view suggested by the Servant theme—but rather "for our justification" (Rom 4:25).[5] Christ's perfect response of love and obedience justifies us. As the Second Adam, he is indeed the Head of "the new humanity," the People of the New Covenant. The Second Adam "has become a life-giving spirit" (1 Cor 15:45). And his Spirit is our new law (cf. Rm 8:2); it dwells in our hearts (cf. Eph 3:17), crying out, "Abba, Father" (Gal 4:6). Thus, all the prophetic promises of a New Covenant are fulfilled (Jer 31:31-34; Ezk 36:26f.). In Christ, the Second Adam, humankind is renewed and the Good News continues to be incarnated.

It becomes evident that when speaking about the Christian "Way" of life, Christ and the Spirit cannot be really separated. In actuality, the Christological and pneumatological aspects of this New Life form a dynamic, although not an ontological, identity. It is in the Spirit that Jesus himself effects his earthly ministry: preaches the Good News to the poor (Lk 4:18), confronts the devil (Mt 4:1) and frees his victims (Mt 12:28), and has access to the Father (Lk 10:21). He promises his disciples that after he departs the Spirit will take his place as their Paraclete (Jn

14:16; 16:7). In the theologies of John and Paul the Spirit is the source of New Life, a dynamic vital force (Jn 3:5-8; Gal 5:25). In the Johannine gospel account, the Spirit empowers the apostles to forgive sins (Jn 20:22). In Pauline thought he is the vital principle of the Church, the Body of Christ (Eph 4:4), and the principle of power, love and self-control (2 Tim 1:7). In 1 Pet 1:2 the Spirit is the agent of holiness.

Paul, more than any other New Testament author, has developed a rather elaborate theology of the Spirit effecting our New Life in Christ. For Paul, it is in the Spirit of the risen Christ that we become "a spiritual person" (cf. 1 Cor 2:15), because it is through the Spirit that we are given power for the development of our inner selves (Eph 3:16). The Spirit is, in fact, the fundamental vital and operative principle of our own continuing evangelization. As Spicq observes: "He is the very source of our spiritual life, so much so that the new morality, contrasting markedly with Israelite morality which was based on the Commandments, is a life that responds to the movement of the Holy Spirit."[6] It is the Spirit who shows us the way to live (cf. Gal 5:18). He is the new Law (Rom 8:2) which takes the place of the law of sin and death. Herein is found our liberty, as we are endowed with the freedom of the children of God (Rom 8:15), for "where the Spirit of the Lord is, there is freedom" (2 Cor 3:17). In the Spirit we are sons of God (Rom 8:14). "Because Christians have received the Holy Spirit and live according to his light and in his love, their new morality becomes a morality of sonship. They act as befits sons of such a Father!"[7] We are led to assume the attitudes of God, to act as he acts, that is, out of love. The law of the Spirit is, indeed, the law of love (cf. Gal 5:14), for "the love of God has been poured into our hearts by the Holy Spirit which has been given us" (Rom 5:5). This divine love ("agape-kenosis," cf. Eph 5:1-2) is infused in us so that we can love one another as God loves us. The Christian's spiritual-moral life is the way of love:

> Avoid getting into debt, except the debt of mutual love. If you love your fellowmen you have carried out your obligations. All the commandments: "You shall not commit adultery, you shall not kill, you shall not steal, you shall not covet," and so on, are summed up in this single command: "You must love your neighbor as yourself." Love is the one thing that cannot hurt your neighbor; that is why it is the answer to every one of the commandments (Rom 13:8-10). Serve one another in works of love, since the whole Law is summarized in a single command: "Love your neighbor as yourself" (Gal 5:14). You should carry

one another's burdens and fulfill the law of Christ (Gal 6:2).
Over all these clothes . . . put on love (Col 3:4); you have all
clothed yourselves in Christ. (Gal 3:27)

This love of the Holy Spirit uniting the individual to Christ is, also,
the cohesive principle of the Christian community, the Body of Christ
(cf. 1 Cor 12:12-13), but this leads to the topic of our next section.

2. *Koinonia*

Although the immediately preceding section may seem to have been
concerned only with the Christ-and-Spirit-related aspects of the individual Christian's spiritual-moral life, it must again be emphasized that
these elements do not exist in the New Testament in isolation from the
ecclesial community. They are all parts forming an integral whole (i.e.,
the divine evangelical economy or the "mystery of simplicity") which
cannot really be viewed separately except as is done here for the purpose
of making logical distinctions.

Nicholas Crotty emphasizes the communal character of early
Christian life in his article "Biblical Perspectives in Moral Theology":

> For the Christian convert, baptismal repentance and baptismal
> faith meant an introduction into a human community, into a
> society of those already "in Christ." It was this community
> and society that provided him with a concrete and living norm
> of behavior: the Way. What was most characteristic of this
> way of life was the fraternal communion in love that bound the
> members one to the other. This was a *koinonia*, a common
> sharing in all the riches of divine life that belonged to Chris-
> tians by reason of their redemptive union in Christ.[8]

In Christ and in the Spirit these first Christians realized they shared
fellowship and life with the Trinity and with one another. The divine
love ("agape-kenosis"), which had been fully revealed in Christ's Paschal Mystery, was now infused in them by the power of the Spirit, forming them into a living organism, the Body of Christ (1 Cor 12:12-30).
Their spiritual-moral life, consequently, was not seen merely in the perspective of the recreated individual, but of a recreated humanity. The
moral imperatives of this Christian way of life can be aptly described as
"a *koinonia* ethic: a standard of conduct for men in fellowship."[9] Their
responsible activity sought not individual betterment or gain, but only
the good of the Kingdom as proclaimed by Jesus.

In Christ and in his Spirit, the Church is gathered-sent from among the peoples; it is "ekklesia." But in its own self-consciousness the Church is "koinonia," a spiritual-moral fellowship sharing the fullness of New Life with her risen Lord. During his earthly ministry Jesus proclaimed the Good News of the Kingdom. In his glorification as "Lord" this Kingdom was revealed as a transcendent spiritual reality with its inauguration on earth having already begun through the new presence of his Spirit in the community of his followers. As risen Lord, Christ is the Second Adam, the Head of a new humanity, which forms his Body. Christ is the true Messiah of the "true Israel" (Gal 6:16), the people of the New Covenant. In him resides the fullness of divinity (Col 2:9), which he bestows upon his followers, thereby filling his Church with the fullness of the new creation (Eph 1:23). He holds the Church together in unity, sharing with it fellowship and life, and conferring upon it the gifts ("charismata") of the Spirit. He is the principle of life, cohesion, and growth.

The Church's existence as koinonia is based upon its fellowship with Christ (cf. 1 Cor 1:9). Through faith and baptism we are "all one in Christ Jesus" (Gal 3:28); yet the achievement of this union comes primarily in the "breaking of the bread" (Acts 2:42). The Church as koinonia is essentially a eucharistic community.

> The blessing-cup that we bless is communion (koinonia) with the blood of Christ, and the bread that we break is a communion (koinonia) with the body of Christ. The fact that there is only one loaf means that, though there are many of us, we form a single body because we all have a share in this one loaf. (1 Cor 10:16-17)

The various theologies of the New Testament pinpoint different aspects of the divine-human koinonia. Christ gives us a share in his divine nature (2 Pet 1:4) even as he himself shares our human state in its weakness (Heb 2:14). The book of Acts recounts the mysterious identity of Christ and his Church (Acts 9:4) while describing the "brotherhood" or "fellowship" of the earliest community (Acts 2:42-47). In Pauline theology, there is "one Body," "one Spirit," and one hope into which all of us are called, just as there is "one Lord, one faith, one baptism, and one God who is Father of all, over all, through all and within all" (Eph 4:4-6). Of course, for Paul, as we have just seen, our communion with Christ is primarily achieved in the eucharistic body, and through the operation of the Spirit (2 Cor 13:13; Phil 2:1). In the captivity epistles the metaphor of the Body of Christ, with Christ as its Head, attains its full Pauline development, and in Ephesians, particularly, the theology of the Church comes to its maturation.[10] Although the Johannine writings never mention the word "church" (*ekklesia*), the concept of "koinonia" is explicit (especially, 1 Jn 1:3). And the entire gospel according to John reads almost like a treatise on the Church's inner life. "His allusions to a new exodus (Jn 3:14; 6:32f.; 7:37ff.; 8:12) call to mind a new people of God, which the biblical images of bride (3:29), of flock (10:1-16), and of vine (15:1-17) directly describe."[11]

"Koinonia" itself essentially implies a new way of living, such as is described in Acts with regard to the earliest Christian community: "These remained faithful to the teaching of the apostles, to the brotherhood, to the breaking of bread and to the prayers. . . . The faithful all lived together and owned everything in common. . . ." (Acts 2:42-47). Incorporated into Christ and the gospel mystery by baptism, the new Christian joins this brotherhood, which seeks to "become the perfect Man, fully mature with the fullness of Christ himself" (Eph 4:16). Their common life is thus nourished in the eucharistic assembly, as they seek to grow in the image of the Son (cf. Rom 8:29; 2 Cor 4:18). Continuing to grow and mature in Christ by sharing in the Paschal Mystery of kenotic love, we who have died to our former sinful selves, therefore, "must give up our old way of life" (Eph 4:12) and let our behavior change, modelled on our new mind (Rom 12:2). Christ's example of self-emptying service (cf. Jn 13:15) associated with his Paschal Mystery gives rise to his commandment that we love one another as he has loved us (13:34) by laying down his life for us (15:13). And Christ's glorified presence now empowers us to love in this new way. To Paul, the concrete implications of this Mystery and communion are clear:

> You, of all people, must give all these things up: getting angry, being bad-tempered, spitefulness, abusive language and dirty talk; and never tell each other lies. You have stripped off your old behavior with your old self, and you have put on the new self which will progress towards true knowledge the more it is renewed in the image of its creator. (Eph 3:8-10)

Christian living in the New Testament is fundamentally a koinonia existence. It is based upon relationships—communion with the Father, Son, and Holy Spirit, and brotherhood or fellowship with one another. Thus, the two greatest commandments as revealed by Christ are love of God and love of neighbor (Mt 22:37-39; Mk 12:28-31; Lk 10:25-28).

During his earthly ministry Christ preached the Kingdom of God as *the* Absolute in man's life. The ethics of the Kingdom inform the moral life of the koinonia. One must be willing to give up everything to attain it (cf. Mt 13:44ff.). Jesus inaugurated the Kingdom on earth by entrusting it to his "little flock" (Lk 12:32). It then takes on the earthly appearance of the Church founded on Peter to whom he gives "the keys to the kingdom of heaven" (Mt 16:18ff.). True to apostolic tradition the primitive Church preserved Jesus' discourses on the Kingdom, which teaching in turn served as the spiritual-moral code of the *koinonia*. And conversion was the first requirement for citizenship in the Kingdom (cf. Mk 1:15).

3. *Conversion*

John the Baptist appeared in the wilderness of Judea preaching: "Repent, for the kingdom of heaven is close at hand" (Mt 3:1). Soon afterwards Jesus started his public ministry, reechoing the same words (Mt 4:17). Then, on the day of Pentecost, Peter stood up and addressed the crowd, exclaiming: "You must repent, and everyone of you must be baptized in the name of Jesus Christ for the forgiveness of your sins, and you will receive the gift of the Holy Spirit" (Acts 2:38). Repentance and conversion constitute the fundamental theme of the prophets, John the Baptist, Jesus, and the early Church.

Based on the Hebrew word "shûb," conversion implies a "return"; it is an action word requiring active conduct. According to R. Schnackenburg, "what underlies it is the image of a road: we turn back from the wrong direction, and take a new road."[12] The Baptist emphasizes this new way of life as essential to conversion, when he challenges the Pharisees and Sadducees coming for baptism: "But if you are repentant, produce the appropriate fruit, and do not presume to tell yourselves, 'We have Abraham for our father' " (Mt 3:9). John's preaching aimed at the moral conversion of the Jewish people in order that they might escape the anger of God in the coming judgment. But Jesus' motive for preaching differed; conversion was a thankful response for the salvation already offered by God. "With Jesus, metanoia includes belief in the message of salvation and becomes an expression of joy and confidence in salvation"[13] For Jesus, conversion also implies a new way of living, as Matthew's gospel demonstrates with the Sermon on the Mount (Mt 5:7).

In the New Testament two Greek words are employed to describe this repentance and conversion: "metanoein" and "epistrephein." They are virtually synonymous. "Metanoein" stresses more the inner attitude, or change of heart, while "epistrephein" tends to emphasize practical conduct. Our concern here is principally with the latter, although we cannot really separate the two altogether. Both actually are gifts of grace flowing from divine initiative, as is conveyed by Jesus' attitude toward sinners (Mt 9:10-13; Lk 15:2) and his parables of the shepherd in search of the lost sheep (Lk 15:4ff.) and of the prodigal son, which in reality spotlights the Father's love and mercy (Lk 15:11-32), more than the son's return to his Father's house. The practical follow-up to conversion, as Jesus intended it, is manifested in Zacchaeus' willingness to give away half his belongings to the poor and to make fourfold amends to all whom he had wronged (Lk 19:5-8), and in the sinful woman's washing of Jesus' feet at Simon the Pharisee's house (Lk 7:36ff.). In both incidences, their actions are sparked by gratitude for the salvation and forgiveness which Jesus brings.

Poverty of spirit is the first beatitude (Mt 5:3), and Jesus indicates that its opposite, self-righteousness, usually associated with contempt for others, sets up the greatest obstacle to conversion. To illustrate this point, he tells the parable of the Pharisee and the publican (Lk 18:10-14); he also disapproves the attitude of the elder brother who stayed away from the feast given for his brother's homecoming (Lk 15:25f.) and of the discontented laborers in the vineyard (Mt 20:1-15). To communicate the necessary and correct attitude, Jesus holds up as an example the little children, stating: "Unless you change and become like little children you will never enter the kingdom of heaven" (Mt 18:3). Thus R. Schnackenburg sums it up:

> Genuine repentance, the repentance that opens to itself the kingdom of God, is only possible when a man knows he is small and slight as a child before God (Mt 18:3). In his sight we are always unprofitable servants (Lk 17:10); we are always his debtors (Mt 6:12). But if we ourselves realize this, then the saying that "God exalts the humble" will be proved true in us (cf. Lk 14:11, par.; 18:14; see also Jas 4:10 and 1 Pt 5:6).[14]

Conversion and the way of life it implies is related to koinonia. It concerns our fellowship with God and with our neighbor, and the attitude or stance we assume in living out these relationships. The early Church in the New Testament sees conversion as a spiritual rebirth accompanying faith and baptism as prerequisites for membership in the community of Christ. Through conversion we are truly evangelized; we obtain the forgiveness of our sins and thus walk as children of God in the newness of his Life. It is God's gift to Israel (Acts 5:31) and to pagans as well (Acts 11:18) urging them "to prove their change of heart by their deeds" (Acts 26:20).

In the writings of Paul and John, "the conversion call recedes into the background—outwardly as a concept; but in effect it remains present,

implicit in the call to have faith, and effective in the moral imperative."[15] Paul continually urges the young churches to live a life worthy
of their vocation and of the "new man" they are in Christ. Although the
two Greek words for conversion are absent in John, the concept they
embody is clearly evident. The Johannine idea of faith is all-embracing.
It includes obedience (Jn 3:36) and keeping Christ's words and commandments (Jn 8:15; 12:47; 14:21, 23). Conversion is also implied in the
sharp contrasts John sets up between life and death (Jn 5:24) and between darkness and light (Jn 8:12). For the most part, the New Testament authors speak of initial conversion, the first change of heart issu-
ing in an integral faith-response.

Another form of conversion, a second conversion, constitutes the
theme of the Book of the Apocalypse. There the seer, expecting an imminent parousia, challenges the still young churches to repent of their
waning fervor and their weakening love (cf. Rev 2:4-5; 3:3, 19, etc.). The
further concept of an on-going conversion, as such, is all but absent, although Jesus does warn about the danger of backsliding (cf. Lk 11:24-
26), and Paul speaks of the inner man being "renewed day by day" (2
Cor 4:16). Paul's emphasis, however, is on making ever greater progress
in our new life (1 Thes 4:10) by doing the truth in love, and thus growing
in all ways into Christ who is the Head of the body, the Church (cf. Eph
4:15-16). The requirements of our continuing conversion or our on-going
evangelization, as envisioned by the early Church, will now be discussed
under the heading of discipleship.

4. Discipleship

Faith reflects the positive side of conversion. "Repent. Believe the
Good News" (Mk 1:15). Faith constitutes a way of living one's life in
gratitude for God's gift of salvation. It means "to believe in the message
about the Kingdom of God that Jesus brings, not in a cold, uncommit-
ted way, but by accepting in a positive fashion everything it involves for
each human being personally."[16] Faith, thus, establishes a person's relationship of trust, hope and love in a communion of life with the living
God. Paul congratulates the Thessalonians for living out just such a
relationship, stating: "[We] constantly remember before God our Father
how you have shown your faith in action, worked for love and per-
severed through hope, in our Lord Jesus Christ" (1 Thes 1:3). Through
the gift of faith and a constantly greater faith-response, the Christian
believer is integrated ever more fully into the divine evangelical plan.
From the viewpoint of the apostolic community, faith implies becoming
a "disciple" or follower of Christ.

In the gospel accounts the disciples of Jesus differ from the disciples of other rabbis of their time, primarily with regard to their relationship to their master. Intellectual aptitude is not one of the requirements for Jesus' disciples; he is not first of all concerned with handing on to them a series of doctrines. They became his disciples in response to his call (Mk 1:17-20; Jn 1:38-50) and as a gift from the Father (Jn 6:39; 10:29; 17:6, 12). He says to the disciple: "Follow me!" Becoming a disciple of Jesus meant taking up a whole new way of life and attaching oneself to his person (e.g., Mt 8:19-20). They could never hope to attain his dignity. They were always to remain his disciples, renouncing their families and possessions and taking up their crosses (cf. Lk 14:25-33). They were to become his witnesses through their faith in him.

Through the gift of the Holy Spirit in faith and baptism, one enters the community (koinonia) of believers (cf. Acts 2:38), and thus becomes a "disciple." For faith implies obedience (cf. Rom 1:5; 16:26) and, therefore, discipleship. Through faith a person is united with Christ (2 Cor 3:15; Gal 2:16, 20) and in the Spirit becomes a son of God (Gal 3:26). Sonship and discipleship are integrally related. Matthew quotes Jesus as saying: "You must therefore be perfect just as your heavenly Father is perfect" (Mt 5:48). Hence there appears an inner connection between being children of God and imitating God. Discipleship involves faith and the imitation of God or the following of Christ. In other words, the Christian's response of integral faith-hope-love involves trust and confidence, obedience and service. It constitutes complete dedication to the will of God and to his Kingdom. It is in light of our citizenship in the Kingdom that Jesus' moral demands come down to us. In Johannine theology real faith is also intimately connected with love of Jesus (Jn 16:27) and obedience to his commands (Jn 14:15, 21; 15:10). Consequently, the disbelief of the Jews is attributed to their moral guilt (Jn 3:19ff.; 5:40ff.; 8:41ff.; 15:24ff.).

For Jesus the obedience required of faith means more than the legal observance of the Law. "Jesus refused to regard man's relationship to God as a relationship in law."[17] For him obedience is first an interior reality, a matter of the heart and of a person's relationship to God and to his or her neighbor. "Jesus demanded interior disposition as the decisive factor in moral action. He made the heart the center of the moral personality."[18] The Sermon on the Mount in Matthew's gospel serves as the charter for the Kingdom, and it is there we hear Jesus exclaim: "A good man draws what is good from the store of goodness in his heart; a bad man draws what is bad from the store of badness. For a man's words flow out of what fills the heart" (Mt 6:45, see also, Mk 7:14ff.). The Sermon closes with Jesus relating the parable of the house built on rock which is a call to us not only to listen to his words, but to put them into action (Mt 7:24-27). The Sermon itself illustrates the radical obedience to the holy will of God which Jesus demands of all who hear his message. The will of God, rather than external conformity to a law, thus becomes the guiding principle for moral action in the early Church.

The motive that Jesus proffers for his radical demands of discipleship and obedience to the will of God is primarily the promise of the Kingdom of God and its blessedness. "Theirs is the kingdom of heaven" is the motive with which he frames the Beatitudes (Mt 5:3, 10). Indeed, Jesus' moral demands constitute Good News; they lead to our sharing in God's eschatological reign of peace, justice, salvation and joy. This reward, too, is a gift from God, something that can never be merited. For the disciples of Christ, the will of God is embraced in loving and hope-filled gratitude.[19] For in the gift of the Spirit, following upon Jesus' resurrection, the early Church experienced the fulfillment of Christ's promises (cf. Acts 2:33, 39). Once again, Jesus' radical demands are seen as Good News, for not only does he command, but in sending the Spirit he also imparts the capability of fulfilling his commandments. Thus, as N. Crotty has described it:

> Christian hope does not mean envisaging our earthly existence as if it were a sort of examination with marks and a prize to be awarded at the end. It is not that we look forward to a gift to be made simply in the future. The gift has already been made, and the motive for our moral endeavor lies in the fact that we must do honor to this gift of God. What we aim at is not so much the obtaining of mercy (which in Christ is ours already) as the expressing of gratitude for mercy.[20]

In the gospel accounts, however, Jesus does frequently talk of reward and punishment (e.g., Mt 10:15; 11:22, 24; 12:36). They are motives by which he urges his hearers to seek God alone, to inquire of his will and to reflect upon their own salvation. But he relates these motives always to the coming of God's reign, which we are expected to identify with our longing for salvation. Thus, the coming of God's Kingdom and his glorification remain the primary motive for "following Christ" in the apostolic Church. Emulating God's love and serving him in gratitude and praise become the joyful task of all Christ's disciples.

For the early Church the disciples' original relationship to Jesus during his earthly life served as the archetype for their imitation of him, for following on his way. The oft-cited passage in this regard is Mk 8:34: "If anyone wants to be a follower of mine, let him renounce himself and take up his cross and follow me." Jesus' original circle of disciples was expected, not just to tag along after him as the multitudes often did, but to enter into a life-companionship with the Master. In the immediate post-Resurrection community such a close following in his Spirit became a concrete possibility for every believer, even if this latter had never met Christ in the flesh during his earthly ministry. For baptized into Christ's Death and Resurrection, the new Christian shared a symbiosis of life with him and at the same time received the gift-call which empowered one to live a way of life according to his or her faith and new being. Thus, St. Paul writes the Colossians: "You must live your whole life according to the Christ you have received—Jesus the Lord; you must be rooted in him and build on him and held firm by the faith you have been taught, and full of thanksgiving" (Col 2:6-7).

Discipleship, in the Church of the New Testament, constituted a new spiritual-moral reality, a new way of living one's life. In Johannine theology this new spiritual reality of sharing life in Christ, like branches on a vine (cf. Jn 15:1-17) means bearing fruit in love, and following his example of self-emptying service (Jn 13:15). Paul reiterates the same truth in the kenosis hymn of Phil 2:5-11, and the primitive Church in the book of Acts attempts to put it into practice, as for example in their daily distribution of food to the poor, which they looked upon as a service of love ("diakonia," cf. Acts 6:1). In the theology of Paul, assimilating the "image" of Christ (Rom 8:29) replaces the concept of following him or imitating him, and being thus renewed in his image restores sound moral judgment to the "new man" (cf. Col 3:9-10). In the Spirit we are children of God, freed from the slavery of sin and alive for God in Christ Jesus. We are Christ's disciples proclaiming his presence among us to all humankind and we follow him and invite others to follow him by walking in this newness of Life. Yet Paul warns against unspiritual interests (Rom 8:5ff.) and becoming enslaved to sin once again (Gal 4:9).

5. *Sin*

Unbelief is sin (cf. Jn 16:9). The refusal to believe in Christ and to accept his words, (i.e., the refusal to be evangelized), is the sin par excellence (cf. Jn 1:5, 10). "If I had not come, if I had not spoken to them, they would have been blameless; but as it is they have no excuse for their sin" (Jn 15:22). Sin is a refusal to believe the Gospel of Jesus Christ; it is likewise a rejection of the divine indwelling, for "anyone who lives in God does not sin" (1 Jn 3:6). Further, it is lawlessness (1 Jn 3:4), refusing to do God's will; it is unrighteousness (1 Jn 5:17), the denial of divine justice. Ultimately, sin is a refusal to love and to be loved (cf. 1 Jn 4:15-16). Therefore, summing up the concept of sin in Johannine theology, de la Potterie writes: "Each sin in different degrees arises from a lessening of faith. Thus, in a certain sense, sin is a rejection of the great realities of salvation, a free acceptance of Satan's dominion, a sinking into darkness."[21] Sin constitutes the negative response to the Good News, the rejection of the Kingdom and the refusal of koinonia.

Although the author of 1 Jn maintains that: "No one begotten by God sins" (1 Jn 3:9, see also, 3:6), the concrete experience of the early Church testifies to the fact that the power of sin had not yet been definitively broken. It was still able, in certain circumstances, to come back into their lives (e.g., Acts 5:1-11; 1 Cor 5:1-5). So, with Christian realism, the same author also writes: "If we say we have no sin in us, we are deceiving ourselves and refusing to admit the truth" (1 Jn 1:8). Yet, in so doing he is not really contradicting himself because, "the Christian who is called by grace, born again by the power of God in baptism and committed to holiness of life is placed in a state of tension by the very fact of life in this world, and we can never really get rid of this tension."[22] Fully aware of this situation, Jesus breathes forth the Spirit upon the apostles giving them the power to remit sins (Jn 20:22).

Christian freedom is a gift of the Spirit; "where the Spirit of the Lord is, there is freedom" (2 Cor 3:17). It is a call (Gal 3:5) to which a person is responsible under grace. In fact, the Letter of James speaks of "the perfect law of freedom" (1:25), of actively putting into practice the word of God ingrafted in our hearts (cf. Jas 1:21). The disciple is called to fulfill "the law of Christ" (Gal 6:2). For Paul freedom is not so much "freedom *from*" as it is "freedom *for*": freedom *from* Law *for* the Gospel, freedom *from* the flesh *for* the spirit, freedom *from* sin *for* grace, and freedom *from* death *for* life.[23] So Christian freedom is not a license or pretext to do whatever one wills (1 Pt 2:16), but Paul's teaching on this subject was at times misinterpreted (e.g., Rom 6:1, 15). Freedom is, moreover, adherence to the truth (Jn 8:32), and in its fullness Christian liberty is received only as an eschatological gift (cf. Rom 8:23). In the meantime, this freedom is threatened by sin as St. Paul observes:

> The fact is, I know of nothing good living in me—living, that is, in my unspiritual self—for though the will to do what is good is in me, the performance is not, with the result that instead of doing the good things I want to do, I carry out the sinful things I do not want. (Rom 7:18-19)

In this theology Paul distinguishes sin ("hamartia," in the singular) from sinful acts, that is, faults ("paraptoma") or transgressions ("parabasis"), without intending, however, to lessen the gravity of the latter.

Hamartia, or sin in the singular, refers to that power or force in the world which is hostile to God and his Kingdom, and sinful acts (faults and transgressions) are an expression and exteriorization of this condition. Paul himself throughout his letters includes lists of these latter acts that Christians must avoid (1 Cor 5:10f.; 6:9f.; 2 Cor 12:20; Gal 5:19-21; Rom 1:29-31; Col 3:5-8; Eph 5:3; 1 Tim 1:9; Titus 3:3; 2 Tim 3:2-5) at the risk of being excluded from the Kingdom of God (cf. 1 Cor 6:9; Gal 5:21). For Paul, to sin means to walk according to the "flesh," to submit to all that is transient and perishable (e.g., 2 Cor 10:3; Rom 7:14; Gal 3:3). Paul furthermore portrays sin as a personal, demoniacal being (Rom 5:12, 21; 6:17; 7:14, 20), and here he does not intend just a metaphorical and rhetorical use of language, but rather the description of an existential reality.

In the Synoptic gospels Jesus speaks of sin as coming from the heart of man, and maintains that it alone makes a person unclean (Mt 15:18-19; Mk 7:20-22). In the Parable of the Prodigal Son, sin is equated with the son's wandering from his father's house (Lk 15:18, 21). In all its forms sin is a turning away from love which resides in the heart, the source of all personal awareness and encounter. The heart for the Semites was the seat of moral judgment. We now attribute this function to one's conscience. The gospels never mention "conscience" as such. Paul, nevertheless, frequently employs the term "syneidesis,"[24] which is not yet entirely identical with what we call "conscience" nowadays.

"Syneidesis" as described by Paul has the fundamental meaning of awareness (cf. 2 Cor 4:2, 5:11; Rom 13:5); although in 1 Cor 10:25, 27 and 28 he employs it to refer to moral scruples. "Most often conscience is characterized as a 'witness' (Rom 2:15, 9:1; 2 Cor 1:12); it accompanies our actions as an incorruptible witness within us, and can also be called upon to attest to the truth of our assertions."[25] Every person has a conscience (Rom 2:14f.), and it is the ultimate authority in moral judgment, even when it judges wrongly (Rom 14:23b). Thus, Paul tries to make Christians aware of true moral values (Phil 1:9; Col 3:13; Eph 4:32; Gal 5:15), encouraging them to examine themselves (1 Cor 11:28; 2 Cor 13:5; Gal 6:4) and to seek constantly the will of God (Rom 12:2; Eph 5:10). To this end he employs the word "dokimazein" ("to test"), in the sense of perceiving what is morally best, or the most Christian thing to do, in a given context. This right-perception is rooted in mutual love (cf. Phil 1:9). Indeed, our Christian freedom itself must be viewed in the context of love (Gal 5:13), with conscience deciding "what is useful and beneficial for our neighbor (1 Cor 6:12; 10:23), what is likely to edify him or scandalize him."[26] Failure to be aware of this and to act upon it is itself sin—the rejection of Christ (cf. Mt 25:31-46). Yet, despite the ever-present threat of sin and the power of evil, the early Christian community never became despondent. Always fresh in their minds was the Gospel and victory of Christ: "In the world you will have trouble, but be brave: I have conquered the world" (Jn 16:33).

B. THE SUB-APOSTOLIC COMMUNITY

From all that we can piece together from the few and infrequent writings of the immediate New Testament era, and from the subsequent teaching of the Fathers, the Church of this period continued to live as *the* community of the risen Lord and Savior. As R. E. McNally described it:

> In the first centuries after the close of the apostolic age the Christian consciousness of its close alliance with God and its special role in His universal plan of redemption is in clear evidence. As a believing and worshipping community the unity of the faithful in creed, code and cult was of the highest importance, for it was rooted in the oneness of Word and Sacrament; and it expressed the Church's special ethos as God's unique Kingdom of the last days.[27]

Although often threatened by persecutions, interior dissensions and heresies (especially Gnosticism), Christianity during these early years more than anything else continued to be a new "Way" of life in which the Kyrios and the Eucharist predominate. The life of the community centered on the mysteries of Christ. Authentic Pauline teachings—such as the saving victory of Christ over the powers of sin and death; the opposition between the new man risen with Christ and the old man, dead in Adam; the mysticism of the Spirit—remained alive and vital.

The spiritual life of the community continued as the constant theme of this period. The Christian's moral behavior flowed from the community's shared life in the Christ Spirit. Writing of this period, T. L. Westow observes: "The spiritual life, the life of prayer, the life of perfection swung, during the early centuries between the two poles of the communal celebration of the Eucharist and the communal achievement of martyrdom."[28] Both these poles pertained to a new way of living in koinonia. As Westow continues:

> The Christians are a community, live as a community, write to each other as members of a community, are martyred as representatives of a community, pray as a community. The very fact of being constantly subjected to possible outbreaks of persecu-

tion reinforces this sense of the community. Even their failures in moral problems of life are principally failures to maintain the "concord and harmony" of the community. The other moral failures are usually grouped in lists, from St. Paul on, with little preference for one sin or another.[29]

Shared life and union with God through Christ in the koinonia, arriving at its ultimate perfection in martyrdom, constitute the very heart of the early Church's spiritual-moral life. Systematic doctrinal and moral treatises are in the main nonexistent, although some practical applications arising from this new kind of life are proposed by individual authors.

The earliest post-New Testament writings describing this early evangelization process incarnated in the Christian way of life come to us from the Apostolic Fathers, whose teachings faithfully reflect genuine apostolic tradition. Their exhortations constantly refer to Scripture as they call Christians to the imitation of Christ. Their writings convey an ever-present awareness of the new order or the new way of life that has come into existence with Christianity. The Letter of Clement of Rome to the Church at Corinth (c. 97 A.D.) serves as a good example of this period. It was written as a moral exhortation to peace and unity following upon an outbreak of dissension and rivalry within the local church. Describing the original state of community life in the Church at Corinth, Clement writes:

> Moreover, you were all in a humble frame of mind, in no way arrogant; practicing obedience rather than demanding it: happier in giving than in receiving . . . it was his [Christ's] words that you carefully locked up in your hearts, and his sufferings were before your eyes. Thus all were blessed with a profound and radiant peace of soul, and there was an insatiable longing to do good, as well as a rich outpouring of the Holy Spirit upon the community.[30]

Clement then proceeds to warn them about the dangers of jealousy and envy which have been splitting the community (Chapter 4). He calls the Corinthians to conversion, which he sees as a grace won for them by the blood of Christ (Chapter 7)—an obvious reference to the eucharistic life which they are meant to share. Later in his letter (Chapters 19-34), paralleling St. Paul's listing of family virtues to be put into practice and of sinful acts to be avoided, Clement calls the Corinthians to holiness based upon gratitude for God the Father's "super-abundant gifts and blessings of peace" while looking forward to their future resurrection of which the Lord Jesus Christ is the first fruits. Good works are to be seen as the normal consequence of their new life in faith. Later, he echoes Paul's hymn to love (1 Cor 13:4-24) using it as the basis of Christian moral life: "He who has love in Christ must observe the commandments of Christ. The binding power of the love of God—who is able to set it forth?"[31]

Incorporation into the Life of the Lord Jesus Christ through baptism and through the faith and love of the eucharistic community constitute the major theme of the Letters of St. Ignatius of Antioch. For him the Christian's spiritual and moral life form a single reality in union with Christ:

> The carnal cannot live a spiritual life, nor can the spiritual live a carnal life, any more than faith can act the part of infidelity, or infidelity the part of faith. But even the things you do in the flesh are spiritual, for you do all things in union with Jesus Christ. . . .[32]

Later in this same letter, Ignatius asks the Church of Ephesus to pray for the conversion of everybody, adding: "Give them an opportunity, at least by your conduct, of becoming your disciples."[33] For Ignatius the spiritual-moral life of the community, a life of faith and love, is founded on the Eucharist:

> Take up the practice then of kind forbearance and renew yourselves in faith, which is the flesh of the Lord; and in love, which is the blood of Jesus Christ. Let none of you bear a grudge against his neighbor (*Trallians* 8). Here is the beginning and end of life: faith is the beginning, the end is love; and when the two blend perfectly there is God. Everything else that makes for right living is consequent on these. No one who professes faith sins; no one who professes love hates . . . (*Ephesians* 14). Be concerned about unity the greatest blessing (*To Polycarp* 1).[34]

Throughout his letters, then, he constantly recommends frequent participation in the Eucharist, "for when you meet frequently in the same place, the forces of Satan are overthrown and his baneful influence is neutralized by the unanimity of your faith."[35]

St. Polycarp of Smyrna, the second century bishop and martyr who was a disciple of St. John, takes as the theme of his Letter to the Philippians obedience to God's will in keeping the commandments; his ethical doctrine urges the imitation of Christ in loving our neighbor, especially imitating the patience of his passion and death.

Other writings during this period, which are of unknown authorship, offer a compendium of Christian ethics while discoursing of the Two Ways: one of Life and one of Death (*Didache*, 1:1-6:2); that of light and that of darkness (*Letter of Barnabas*, 18:1-21:9). *The Shepherd of Hermas* also utilizes the Two Ways (cf. *Mandates* 6&8). The Two Ways seems to be an ancient teaching aid common to Egyptians, Greeks, and Jewish sages. Matthew records Jesus himself employing this literary device in the Sermon on the Mount (cf. Mt 7:13-14). Furthermore, the moral instruction of the *Didache* is based on a life of faith and genuine spirituality, looking forward to the resurrection of everyone (cf. Chapter 16). The author of the *Letter of Barnabas* recommends life in Christian koinonia as a sure defense against temptation, for pondering there the Word of the Lord, a "labor of joy," facilitates one's observance of the Lord's commandments (Chapter 10). Finally, the *Shepherd of Hermas* (c. 150 A.D.) discourses on the nature of sin as the desire of wickedness coming from the heart, and the subsequent need of a second penance. The second part of this work presents twelve precepts which serve as a compendium of Christian moral teaching based on the recognition of the gift of faith and the power of grace that God dispenses for our living a new way of life.

Irenaeus of Lyons, a disciple of Polycarp of Smyrna, appears as the major theologian toward the end of the second century. In his *Adversus Haereses* and *Demonstration of the Apostolic Preaching*, he deals with numerous doctrinal concepts including the Trinity, Christology, Mariology, ecclesiology, the Eucharist, eschatology, etc. For Irenaeus, moral perfection is achieved through our cultivating the image of God within us. Through participation in the life of the Church and her sacraments administered in the name of Christ, the new Adam is substituted for the old, and the process of the recapitulation of all things in Christ moves toward its completion. Inveighing against the powerlessness of the Fates to control human destiny, Irenaeus insists again and again on our freedom of conscience.

The writings of the early Fathers of the Church during the first two centuries reveal a Christian way of life—an evangelizing process—based on a genuine, concrete spirituality. For them Jesus Christ is Lord and Head of the Church. He is the Second Adam in whom they have been baptized. Through faith shared in the Christian community, they mature in his image and are empowered by his Spirit to live in a new way by keeping his commandments of love, while gratefully looking forward in hope to the recapitulation of all things in Christ at his final coming. The

Christ-event, especially the Paschal Mystery, forms the heart and core of the community's spiritual-moral life. Gathered together in the unity of the Eucharist, a new manner of living in gratitude and praise for all God's blessings becomes a reality. Although backsliding and sin are still a distinct possibility for the Christian, a second conversion becomes conceivable and practicable. The Church as "koinonia" remains the hub of this new way of living.

The later Church Fathers continue to concentrate their attention on the spiritual-moral life of the Christian community. The African Fathers of the third century attempt to resolve the practical problems of Christians forced to live in a pagan world. Adamant in their condemnation of paganism, they tend toward rigorism in their interpretation of the moral demands of Christian living. Among them appear the first monographs on individual moral questions, e.g., Tertullian's *De spectaculis, De cultu foeminarum, Ad uxorem*; St. Cyprian's *De habitu virginum, De dominica oratione*, etc. In the East at the same time the Alexandrian School (founded as a preparation for martyrdom as well as for baptism) attempts to reconcile the positive aspects of pagan philosophy with the divine wisdom of the Word ("Logos spermatikos"). From these endeavors arise the first organic and systematic expositions of Christian doctrine and morals. Thus, St. Clement of Alexandria writes:

> The gnostic who has acquired the habit of doing good, acts well rather than speaks well; he asks to suffer together with the sins of his brothers; he prays for the confession and conversion of his neighbors, he desires to have his dearest friends share his own proper goods—and such are all his friends. Thus causing the seeds deposited in him to grow, according to the agriculture ordained by the Lord, he remains without sin; he is master of himself and he lives by the spirit with his compeers in the choirs of the saints even though he is still on earth. (VII *Stromata* 12, 80)[36]

Clement refers to "deification" as the supreme state in which we come to know God by loving as he loves (cf. V *Stromata* 1, 12).

The awareness of a concrete spirituality and way of life based on the presence of the risen Lord in the Christian community of faith, hope and love continues to influence the writings of the third and fourth century Fathers, although they, at the same time, employ different philosophical and cultural categories in their attempts to describe this one reality and thus evangelize their contemporaries. Their adoption, nevertheless, of the language and concepts of Hellenism eventually leads to the emergence of the great theological and Christological controversies and heresies of the fourth and fifth centuries. Neo-Platonic and Stoic categories also prevail in their development of Christian ethical ideals, while the mystical treatises of Plotinus provide the vocabulary for a new Christian contemplative "Way." A philosophical dualism thus begins to slip into Christian life and thought, and this, along with an overemphasis on Christ's divinity in the face of the Arian conflict, gradually begins to sever the original theological unity of the Christian "Way."

With the social and cultural transformation in Christian life brought about by the imperial decree of Theodosius in 380, monasticism soon replaces martyrdom as the way to perfect union with Christ the Lord. New elements come into play in this situation, as T. L. Westow explains:

> It is one thing to endure sufferings and finally death itself, inflicted by powers other than our own, it is quite another thing to arrive at spiritual perfection without this passive element, and to grow in this perfection through a slow, grinding process of spiritual, moral, and psychological transformation, a transformation, moreover, in which one remains, when all is said and done, alone with one's own conscience, one's own judgment, one's own limits and worst of all, with one's own self.[37]

Many Christians with a well-balanced sense of proportion arose to the new occasion, as the *Conferences* of Cassian attest. The life of the Church was greatly enriched as a person came to know oneself both as an individual and as a member of the community.

> Yet, was the average, ordinary Christian capable of supporting the strain within himself of the communal and individual forces within him? Was the society in which he lived capable of providing him with the peace, the balance and the insight which he needed? The new individualism could enrich the membership of the Church; it could also disrupt it. But before it could mature in the West this psychological growth was arrested by several centuries of barbarism.[38]

With the rise of monasticism a second, more perfect "way" of being Christian was held up to the faithful. Those who chose this "way of perfection" left behind the average, ordinary Christians to traverse the lesser way. Eventually, when combined with neo-Platonic categories of thought and mysticism, it would set up a two-class system in the Christian community's spiritual-moral life. Before this occurred, however, the later Western Fathers, especially St. Augustine, continued to view the Christian spiritual-moral life in the context of the "Total Christ." Association with him in the eucharistic community of faith, hope and love brings one to share in the divine Trinitarian life, and constitutes the *élan vital* of the Christian way of living. With the collapse of the Roman Empire and the spread of Christianity to the peoples of the new German nations, the era of Christendom arrived. The methods of evangelization were radically changed as there was little hope of bringing these illiterate new peoples to an understanding of "Christ" and the "Church." This objectification process gave way, then, to externalism, ritualism, and legalism in the matters of Christian life.

SUMMARY

The faith-response of the primitive Church to the divine gift-call of grace, revealed in the proclamation of the Good News and in the person of Jesus Christ, was no mere act of intellectual assent. Rather, it was an integral, personal response of shared faith lived out in hope and love. For the Christian community, this faith-response implied living a whole new "Way" of life—a life of fraternal communion or fellowship (koinonia). The risen Lord, whose presence in the Spirit was experienced in their midst, served as the dynamic source of this life and unity. He was the Second Adam, the first fruits of the new humanity. In him God's Kingdom (i.e., the divinely initiated process of evangelization) had been inaugurated on earth and was now moving toward its eschatological completion. The Church saw itself as the People of the New Covenant, the "true Israel." In Christ, the Second Adam, they experienced a new heart, a new law, a new Spirit, indeed, a whole new creation.

This faith-experience of the primitive Christian community also constituted a whole new spiritual-moral reality, the "Way." Led by the Spirit the new Christian, through conversion and baptism, became a "spiritual person." One's behavior was expected to change accordingly, as he or she renounced the sinful self and started to live life in conformity with a "new heart." The gift of faith and conversion established the Christian neophyte in a whole new set of relationships with God and neighbor. Grace is constitutive of relationships, and, therefore, the moral life of which it is the source is based on an ethics of koinonia. In faith the new convert sought to live his or her life in gratitude and praise of God for the blessings of salvation. Through one's membership in the Church, one became a disciple of Christ, "following" the Master in obedience and love. The gospel accounts preserved Jesus' words and deeds, his teaching of the Kingdom. The Sermon on the Mount in Matthew's gospel served as a sort of charter for the Kingdom, and thus as a blueprint for evangelizing the primitive Church's spiritual-moral life. The radical demands Jesus made on his disciples were seen as Good News, for along with his commandments he imparted the capability of fulfilling them in his Spirit. The power of sin, nevertheless, remained a threat in the early community. Seen primarily as the refusal of salvation offered in Jesus Christ, as the refusal to enter into relationship with God and neighbor, sin continued to endanger the Christian's new-found freedom. Yet Christ's victory over the "law of sin and death" filled one with courage and hope, and the certainty that ultimately sin and death themselves will be destroyed forever.

The Church of the sub-apostolic era continued to view its faith-experience as constitutive of a new "Way" of life. The few writings from this period were primarily concerned with the spiritual-moral life of the community. The Eucharist and martyrdom formed the two poles between which this life of communion with Christ the Lord evolved. Systematic doctrinal and moral treatises, for all practical purposes, were nonexistent, although compendiums of ethical teaching based on the Two Ways of Life and Death did appear in writings such as the *Didache* and the *Shepherd of Hermas*. The spiritual life of the community remained the predominant theme of the Apostolic Fathers. Faith and love, unity and peace within the life of the local churches were the major concerns of the letters of St. Clement and St. Ignatius of Antioch. During the third century, the African and Alexandrian Fathers attempted to propose different ways of approaching the pagan world in which Christians had to live. Some of them, however, were not left uninfluenced by neo-Platonic and Stoic categories of philosophical thought. Later, when persecutions ceased and Christianity became the official religion of the Roman Empire, monasticism replaced martyrdom as the way to perfect union with the risen Christ. The Church's understanding of the evangelization process would thus change as the Christian "Way" gradually split in two: the "way of perfection" via the evangelical counsels and the contemplative life for monks and religious, and the "ordinary way" of observing the commandments for the average Christian believer. Before this dichotomy was fully established, however, the later Western Fathers, especially St. Augustine, continued to emphasize communion of life with the "Total Christ," the Head and source of the Church's spiritual-moral life.

NOTES

1. Cf. D. Stanley, *The Apostolic Church in the New Testament* (Westminster, Maryland, 1967) 321: "The notion of a death 'for many' is the dominant theme of Isaiah 53."

2. Leon Dufour, ed., *Dictionary of Biblical Theology*, 345. (Hereafter cited as *DBT*.)

3. Spicq, *St. Paul and Christian Living* (Dublin and Sydney, 1963), 43.

4. Stanley, *Apostolic Church*, 345.

5. *Ibid.*, 346.

6. C. Spicq, *St. Paul and Christian Living*, 58.

7. *Ibid.*, 62-63.

8. *Theological Studies*, 26 (December 1965), 587. (Hereafeter cited as *TS*.)

9. *Ibid.*, 588.

10. Cf. Schnackenburg, *Moral Teaching in the New Testament* (New York, 1965) 183. The Pauline metaphor of the Church as a living spiritual temple is also closely associated with that of the Body of Christ (cf. 1 Cor 3:10-17; 2 Cor 6:16ff.; Eph 2:20ff.).

11. Leon-Dufour, *DBT*, 63.

12. R. Schnackenburg, *Christian Existence in the New Testament*, 2 vols. (Notre Dame, Indiana, 1968), I, 36.

13. Schnackenburg, *Moral Teaching in the New Testament*, 28.

14. *Ibid.*, 30.

15. Schnackenburg, *Christian Existence*, I, 55.

16. Schnackenburg, *Moral Teaching in the New Testament*, 34.

17. Schelkle, *Theology of the New Testament* (Collegeville, Minn., 1970) III, 33.

18. Schnackenburg, *Moral Teaching in the New Testament*, 69.

19. *Ibid.*, 149. Schnackenburg comments: "No one who correctly understands the gospel of the reign of God can make the search for the kingdom of God and his justice into an egotistical struggle for personal reward. In the first place we must remember that it was God who took the first step with the mission of Jesus and his preaching of salvation, and that man can and should only make a humble and grateful response. The coming of the perfect kingdom thus remains wholly and solely the act of God."

20. Crofty, "Biblical Perspectives in Moral Theology," *TS*, 592-93.

21. Lyonnet and de la Potterie, *The Christian Lives by the Spirit* (New York, 1971), 52.

22. Schnackenburg, *Christian Existence*, II, 120.

23. Schelkle, *Theology of the New Testament*, III, 142.

24. The word appears in the writings of Paul some twenty times as compared with only ten times in the rest of the New Testament, cf. Schnackenburg, *Moral Teaching in the New Testament*, 288.

25. *Ibid.*, 289.

26. Spicq, *St. Paul and Christian Living*, 74.

27. McNally, *The Unreformed Church* (New York, 1965), 20.

28. T.L. Westow, *Variety of Catholic Attitudes* (New York, 1963), 26.

29. *Ibid.*, 22-23.

30. *To the Corinthians* 2; J. Quasten and J.C. Plumpe, *Ancient Christian Writers* (Westminster, Md., 1961ff.), I, 10. (Hereafter cited as *ACW.*)

31. *To the Corinthians* 49; *ACW*, I, 39.

32. *To the Ephesians* 8; *ACW*, I, 62.

33. *To the Ephesians* 10; *ACW*, I, 64.

34. *To the Trallians* 8; *ACW*, I, 77. *To the Ephesians* 14; *ACW*, I, 65. *To Polycarp* 1; *ACW*, I, 96.

35. *To the Ephesians* 13; *ACW*, I, 65.

36. As quoted by L. Bouyer, *The Spirituality of the New Testament and the Fathers* (New York, 1963), 275.

37. Westow, *Variety of Catholic Attitudes*, 27-28.

38. *Ibid.*, 30.

V

Fundamental Evangelical Categories for Contemporary Christian Living

The dichotomy that crept into the Christian way of life with the advent of the era of Christendom continued unabated for the most part until the opening of the Second Vatican Council. The heavily legalistic and philosophical approach to "moral theology" in the counter-Reformation period had been contested for some thirty years prior to Vatican II, but new trends in this area were unable to win official ecclesiastical approbation. Indeed, the authors who prepared the preconciliar schema "De ordine morali" maintained, according to P. Delhaye,

> . . . the objective and absolute nature of the moral order. This is said to exist in God and to be communicated to men in two ways. The first is that of the commandments of the natural law as confirmed by Christ. The second is the evangelical law, whose tenor depends on three counsels. This moral theology would seem to have two levels (as the Reformed churches objected in regard to the post-Tridentine Roman Church). It is hardly surprising that there is no mention of charity, since causistic moral theology had constantly opposed it. But the *De ordine morali* went even further, and actually expressed fear that a moral theology of charity would mean no more than verbalism, sentimentalism and an abandonment of moral precepts.[1]

The text, however, was rejected in November 1962 by the conciliar majority. New "periti" were later chosen and set to work on *Gaudium et Spes*. Integrating recent developments in biblical studies, and being greatly influenced by other movements within the Church (theological, liturgical and ecumenical), these latter cast aside the defensive posture and the legalistic and rationalistic attitudes of the former causistic moral theology. In its place they proposed an integrated vision of Christian life, based upon a coherent synthesis of doctrinal beliefs, spiritual and li-

turgical life, and moral behavior. The presentation of *Gaudium et Spes*
was further enhanced through the utilization and recommendation of
fruitful contact with new developments in the secular sciences (especially
in the field of the life sciences: psychology, sociology and anthropology)
and with contemporary trends in modern philosophy.

The Christocentric focus of Vatican II provided the focal point for
the evangelical renewal of "moral theology," or what could even more
appropriately be called a "theology of Christian living." In Christ and in
the Spirit, Christian life is essentially a gift (cf. *LG* 7). "It is . . .
through the gift of the Holy Spirit that man comes by faith to the contemplation and appreciation of the divine plan" (*GS* 15); and "Christ,
the final Adam, by the revelation of the mystery of the Father and His
love, fully reveals man to man himself and makes his supreme calling
clear" (*GS* 22). Thus, a renewed moral theology was assigned the task
of showing "the nobility of the Christian vocation of the faithful" (*celsi-
tudinem vocationis fidelium in Christo—OT* 16). The Council Fathers
promoted the reintegration of the Christian "Way" by boldly proclaiming the universal vocation of all Christians to holiness, "to the fullness
of Christian life and to the perfection of charity," whatever their rank or
status (*LG* 40). Furthermore, they refuted an individualistic ethic
(*GS* 30) as was indeed fostered by the Nominalistic tendencies of the
"manual" approach to Christian morality. In fact, they distinctly elaborated on the communitarian character of the Christian calling (*LG* 9)
as evidenced by the work of Christ himself and his founding the Church,
which is his Body, as "a new brotherly community," where "everyone,
as members one of the other, would render mutual service according to
the different gifts bestowed on each" (*GS* 32).

This new vision proposed by the Council Fathers was extended to
their treatment of the traditional categories of fundamental moral theology (the "De Principiis" of the manuals: human act, law, conscience, sin
and virtues). The objectivity of "De Principiis" centered around the
human act considered as an entity onto itself, which tended then to
reduce the person to the mere subject or producer of the act. The Council, however, restored to theology the very objectivity of the human person as he or she freely responds to the call of God in the depths of the
individual personality (cf. *DH* 11). Indeed, the first three chapters of
Gaudium et Spes outline a Christian anthropology based on the dignity
of the human person. Regarding the category of "law," "Vatican II
does not forgo the use of the word 'law,' but in the very wide sense in
which Paul speaks of the law or 'principle of faith,' (Rom 3:27) and the
law of Christ (Gal 6:2). Hence, the conception of the law as a framework replaces the idea of the precise law (see, e.g., *LG* 9; *GS* 22, 24, 28,

32, 38, 41, 42, 43, 48, 50, 51, 78, 89)."[2] Implied in this view is the genuine Thomistic concept of God's grace or love as the primary law of the New Covenant. All extrinsicism is precluded as Christian consciences enlightened by the Spirit (*LG* 12) take up the law and become the innermost standard of human activity (*GS* 16, 19; *DH* 3). Rather than viewing sin as a violation of law, the Council Fathers returned to a more biblical perspective in seeing it as both a power with cosmic implications and as the refusal on a personal level to respond to God's call with its consequent deleterious effect of blocking the path to human fulfillment (*GS* 13, 37). Lastly, the virtues, too, are seen from a Scriptural viewpoint as gifts and fruits of the Holy Spirit promoting a more human way of life (*LG* 40). Indeed, the Fathers of Vatican II show how the whole of man's life is primarily integrated into the process of evangelization as it is transformed by the grace and power of the Good News accepted in faith:

> The Good News of Christ constantly renews the life and culture of fallen man. It combats and removes the errors and evils resulting from sinful allurements which are a perpetual threat. It never ceases to purify and elevate the morality of peoples. By riches coming from above, it makes fruitful, as it were from within, the spiritual qualities and gifts of every people and every age. It strengthens, perfects and restores them in Christ. (*GS* 58)

To this end the Holy Spirit grants the grace of conversion (a fundamental evangelical category nonexistent in the manual tradition), so that the gift of faith may lead everybody to "a progressive change of outlook and morals" (*AG* 13; see also, *SC* 9). These few brief references gleaned from the various Council documents further indicate the evangelical direction desired by Vatican II for the renewal of the fundamental categories of moral theology.

In the years following the close of the Council and in the ecumenical spirit promoted by it, Christian theologians have raised the question of the specifically Christian character of morality.[3] In other words, granted the universality of grace through creation and the Incarnation (*LG* 16; *GS* 22), people everywhere are seen to participate in the same gift-call. Dialogue with humanists and non-Christians has revealed that, indeed, they most often share with us the same basic motives, attitudes, goals, dispositions and virtues. Thus developed the popularity of the Rahnerian notion of "anonymous Christianity," a hapless term which nevertheless has been ably utilized by some to convey the existential grounding of all genuinely human activity in the unitive natue of Ultimate Reality. In order not to give offense to our non-Christian partners in the discussion, who might rightly resent being thus labelled, and in order to maintain the specific worldview implied in the term "Christian," we might better dialogue about our "overlapping experiences of Ultimate Reality."

Much of the discussion surrounding the question of a specific Christian ethics and/or morality has in fact been bogged down in semantic problems. J. Walters in an article entitled, "Christian Ethics: Distinctive or Specific?" attempts to sort out the major linguistic stumbling blocks.[4] We here employ this author's distinctions between "specific" (connoting exclusivity) and "distinctive" (connoting only a characteristic quality typically associated with a given reality); and between "ethics" (denoting and pertaining to first or fundamental principles) and "morality" (referring to actual human conduct derived from ethical principles). Until now we have made frequent use of the term "moral theology" which has been the canonized phrase for bringing together both ethics and theology in the Catholic tradition, while "Christian ethics" has served as its equivalent in the Reformed.[5] But in view of the argument advanced thus far in this work, namely, that God-reveals-and-communicates-himself to us in an on-going process of evangelization mediated in and through the mystery of Christ, it would seem more appropriate for us to describe our personal faith-response to this divine evangelical economy in terms of a "theology of Christian living." The study of this latter discipline may then be fittingly divided into "Christian ethics" meaning "ethics viewed from a Christian perspective" (treating the fundamental categories arising from a gospel-worldview) and "Christian morality" (treating of practical behavior in light of the Christian view of ethics).

Given the view that Absolute Reality is ultimately one, and therefore the underlying existential unity of humankind, ethics as such is one and universal, but it is further understood and interpreted from different cultural, philosophical and religious thematic perspectives. The specifically Christian perspective views the experience of Ultimate Reality in the light of a biblically inspired understanding of the human person and the world which culminates in the Good News of Jesus Christ. In our study so far, we have seen that Christian revelation understands this Reality to be personal and relational and as having freely chosen to reveal-and-communicate-himself to us in one divine evangelical economy, the "mystery of simplicity," which climaxed in the Paschal death-resurrection-ascension of Jesus Christ and h:s sending of the Spirit.

This gospel-worldview is particular to Christianity. For the believer, the Good News is the revelation of a "new" transforming and transcending power breaking into our consciousness (mind, heart, and total personality) and history. To the eyes of faith, "Jesus Christ is Lord"; he is the Second Adam and the Head of the "new creation." For one who has faith the gospel mystery is an actual reality which in-forms and thereby transforms the Christian believer's intentionality, attitudes, dispositions, and consequently his or her whole way of living. This faith in the Good News is alone specific in the determination and thematization of Christian ethics and its fundamental categories. Thus, it is only under these terms that we may speak of a "specific Christian ethics." In this same vein, we may even talk further of a "specific Catholic morality," which is derived from these fundamental Christian categories inasmuch as they are understood and applied from the particular viewpoint of the Roman Catholic tradition. Beyond faith in the gospel mystery (i.e., this whole divine-initiated process of evangelization), other aspects of Christian ethics are merely distinctive, such as love of one's neighbor and enemies, relationship to a Transcendent Reality, appreciation of the authentically human, a "prophetic" social-critical function, etc.

Our intention in this chapter is to examine from the contemporary viewpoint of the Roman Catholic tradition those fundamental categories of Christian living ("ethics") which arise out of a gospel-worldview and consequently insert the believer into the on-going process of evangelization. They are evangelical categories conceptualized in view of the new reality of the gospel message and of our faith-response to it and are elements common to the earliest Christian tradition. Returning to the summary of Jesus' preaching in Mk 1:15, we find the following six categories either explicit or implied: person-in-Christ; conversion; faith-response in love and hope; law of Christ; conscience; and sin.

(1) *"The time is fulfilled"*—declares the direct intervention of God promised in the eschatological times; God "has now committed himself, regardless of human failure, to the advent of the new man in the person of His Son"[6] (*person-in-Christ*).

(2) *"The kingdom of God . . ."*—refers to the primacy of God's reign (his grace and love) and is in the gospels identified with Christ himself (*law of Christ*).

(3) *". . . is at hand"*—expresses an invitation to one who is free to judge and decide for himself (*conscience*).

(4) *"Repent"*—denominates the nature of the response (*conversion*).

(5) *"And believe the Good News"*—describes the expected positive response (*faith-response in love and hope*), while implying . . .

(6) . . . the possibility of a negative response or refusal (*sin*).

All these categories are explicitly found in the tradition of the early Church (cf. above, Chapter IV), and most of them appear in some form or other in the post-Tridentine "manual" tradition. We will now look at them from the perspective of a contemporary Catholic moral theology, which seeks to dialogue with the modern world while calling it to realize its place within the evangelization process (the divine evangelical economy). The starting point for our arrangement of these six categories will be the "New Man" revealed by the Gospel (*person-in-Christ*) who is called to citizenship in the Kingdom (*conversion*) by responding in faith to the Good News (*faith-response in love and hope*); this faith-response, then, requires that the Christian live according to the law of grace (*law of Christ*) revealed in one's heart (*conscience*), which, however, remains always free to reject God's offer of salvation (*sin*).

A. PERSON-IN-CHRIST

In the gospel-worldview, the human person is seen, first of all, as created through Christ in "the image and likeness of God" (Jn 1:3 and Gen 1:26) by reason of creation, and as consequently being restored, and hence re-created a second time, to the "image of the Son" (Rom 8:29) by reason of redemption in Christ.[7] God is seen as revealing and communicating himself to us by means of the divine *gift-call*.[8] Indeed, God first created humankind by calling us forth in love to personhood and relationship in the divine Trinitarian image while placing within us the wherewithal to freely respond. The human person is, thus, constituted as a concrete spiritual-material unity. We are further created as social and sexual beings placed within a given cultural and historical context (*GS* 12) and have been given mastery over all creation (Ps 8:5-6). A human being, then, is a historical phenomenon who grows and develops through the realization of the divine-human dialogue within history. In the end, defiled by sin, we learn through the Paschal Mystery of Jesus Christ, the Second Adam, that there is "implied a certain likeness between the union of the Divine Persons, and in the union of God's sons in truth and charity. This likeness reveals that man . . . cannot fully find himself except through a sincere gift of himself" (*GS* 24). All these factors unite to constitute a human being as a personal subject in Christ, and this reality then provides us with genuine and normative objectivity for a theology of Christian living.

1. *Made in the image of God*

(a.) *By reason of creation* a biblical and theological anthropology views man and woman as made "in the image and likeness of God" (Gen 1:26), as social beings, since "male and female he created them" (Gen 1:27). And God blessed them saying: "Be fruitful, multiply, fill the earth and conquer it" (Gen 1:28). The book of Genesis here underlines the fact that while man and woman are like God, they are not equal to God. This divine likeness is neither merely physical nor strictly spiritual, but rather refers to the totality of our being regarded as a spiritual-material unity. Thus constituted, the human person is a creative and social being capable of freely entering into personal relationships with others, including God himself.

God gave us a task to accomplish by working in collaboration with him. Humankind, by the fact of its creation through the Word "spoken" by God, is essentially meant for dialogue. As M. Oraison observes: "The human race is called by infinite love to a role of response; in fact it is an exigency of his very existence. Hence within the human race itself there must be mutual and intersubjective call and response."[9] This dialogic and relational structure of human beings created in God's image comes into clearer focus with Christ's revelation of the perfect communication that exists between Father, Son, and Spirit (e.g., Jn 14:10; 16:13). Scholastic theology, thus, later described the Divine Person as "Relatio Subsistens"; they are constituted as persons not because they are separate entities, but precisely because of their relationships to one another. This koinonia "ad intra" is perceived by us only because it has been revealed "ad extra" in the divine evangelical economy through God's creative and redemptive relation to humanity, which in biblical terminology is expressed by the word "covenant." Many contemporary schools of philosophy (personalistic existentialism, phenomenology, etc.) and the life sciences (depth psychology, sociology and anthropology) have also accented this primary importance of interpersonal relationships.

(b.) *By reason of redemption* in Jesus Christ, the gospel views all human persons as being reborn in the Spirit and as being chosen by God to become "true images of his Son" (Rom 8:29). By Christ's Paschal Mystery we are reconciled to God and restored to the level of sonship. Christ, the Second Adam, through his perfect response of obedience and love, inaugurates a new and lasting Covenant; he reestablishes the divine-human dialogue that was broken off by the first Adam's sin. Christ came, indeed, to bear witness to the truth. Absolute Truth as revealed by him is "Abba, Father"; it is a person. In fact, it is a Trinity of per-

sons, for Jesus himself is the Truth (Jn 14:6), and he and the Father send
the Spirit of Truth (Jn 14:17). Christ, in his Paschal Mystery, reveals
that God is first of all self-emptying, self-giving and self-communicating
Love ("agape-kenosis") and that everyone is called to respond to and
share in this loving Mystery which underlies, penetrates and sustains all
created reality.

The "new man" in Christ grows in true knowledge and progresses
in the image of his creator (Col 3:10) inasmuch as he opens himself to
the transcending and transforming power of the Mystery of kenotic love.
"In loving concern for others, we are and become truly ourselves. The
paschal mystery emphatically teaches us this truth."[10] In living this
Mystery (cf. Lk 9:23-24) we are assimilated to God who is love (1 Jn
4:7-8); we become in fact "partakers of the divine nature" (2 Pet 1:4).

(c.) *By reason of both creation and redemption the human person
is constituted as a person-in-Christ.* "For in him were created all things
in heaven and on earth" (Col 1:16); in the Word spoken by God human
beings are called forth in love to an existence of "response-ability" and
relationship. In the Word, the human person is created for dialogue.
Being called through the divine self-communication of love, we are invited to responsible love. Indeed, we are given a vocation to responsibility;
created, in other words, as moral subjects or persons in an I-Thou-We
relationship. Here is found the essence of personhood. Made in the
image of God, humankind's dignity and freedom are constituted by our
being called to responsible relationships of love. God's call leaves each
of us free to refuse. In fact, in Adam the gift of this divine self-communication in love was refused. Humankind sinned. We rejected God's
call to participate in divine life, and thus acted contrary to our essence
as persons.

In Christ, the God-man, we were "re-personified" in the freedom of
the children of God. In the Paschal death-resurrection-ascension of
Jesus and his sending of the Spirit, humankind was restored to sonship.
Christ, the Second Adam, gives our perfect response of obedience and
love, delivering us from the slavery of the law of sin and death. The
divine-human dialogue inaugurated with the creation of Adam and Eve
is reestablished. God's love, mercy and forgiveness are revealed in Christ
through the free gift of "grace with its verdict of acquittal" (Rom 5:16).
Reconciliation is effected in Christ's Paschal Mystery, the revelatory
summit of God's love for us, which is at the same time humanity's perfect response of love and obedience. "Man's self-giving and sharing like
God's self-manifesting and inviting are achieved in Christ."[11] Through
faith in the Good News of Jesus Christ we are transformed into a "new
creation" and elevated to the status of divine sonship sharing in the

communication of intimate Trinitarian Life. In Christ we are once more fully relational beings; we are once again given the gift-call (grace) of true personhood in the "image of our creator."

(d.) *The sacramental aspect* of our life in Christ now finds its appropriate place. By reason of his Incarnation and Paschal Mystery, Christ is the true and primordial sacrament of the divine-human encounter. Through the sacramental life of the Church, Christ continues to communicate to us a share in his very own life. More than "sacred things" or "means" (as defined in the "manual" tradition), the sacraments are heightened moments of effective ritual encounter between Christ and believer; they are at once signs and sources of reconciliation and/or a deepening personal relationship with the Divine Persons and with the Christian community. Meeting Christ in the Sacraments, we are assimilated to the Truth of life, the Mystery of kenotic love. Thus, B. Häring writes:

> A sacramental outlook to life commits us to the paschal mystery. We share in the life of Christ, and this means readiness to pay the cost of discipleship. Christ has redeemed us into his personalism by sacrifice, by his death, and the price of this discipleship is sacrifice. We are truly united in his sacrifice only when we put to death all egocentric concern. The struggle is between the "old man" in us and the new creation. Without this struggle, without denial of the selfish self, there is no hope that we will become new persons conformed to Christ. But this mortification will liberate, not stifle our true self. It will do away with all those things that hinder the purification and growth of love, so that, in solidarity with Christ, we can join in his redemptive love for our brethren in the building up of his mystical body. We open ourselves to God and to others in a life of dialogue. This is the essence of sacramental spirituality.[12]

The sacraments are the Christian community's faith-response of worship and praise. By them we express our gratitude and joy for the gift of divine grace and love revealed in Jesus Christ. Yet, at the same time, they constitute God's gift of himself to us, thereby inspiring and empowering us to correspond ever more fully to the image of the "new man" in which we have been remade. The sacraments, then, are the signs and sources of our spiritual-moral life, and our following of Christ is grounded in our sacramental oneness with him. "Christian life implies a fusion of divine and human initiative."[13] Thus, F. Böckle speaks of the "sacramental co-cultivation of the life of Christ,"[14] emphasizing the fact that it is an organic, and not a mechanical process. Developing this particular point, the New Testament employs the image of the vine and the branches. "The power (of the Holy Spirit) in the vine (Christ) produces in its branches (the faithful) its fruit."[15] Through the sacramental life of the Church, we are consciously united with Christ in all of our activity, and develop our personhood in the truest sense. Christian living, in turn, assumes a sacramental value as it bears witness to all the world of the Christ-life within us.

2. *An Embodied Spirit*

Created in the image of the Incarnate Word, a human being viewed as a *person-in-Christ* is a spiritual-material unity, an embodied spirit. Called forth to loving response as a relationship-oriented being, the human person is more than a physical or biochemical composition.

> Physically and biochemically, humans may perhaps fall under the same laws as animals and be classified as a particular animal species, but in their whole approach to life and in their self-expression they show themselves very different. Their manner of communicating with one another and their attitude to their surroundings show that there is a form of life in them which surpasses the form of life in any other being on earth.[16]

Influenced by Plato and other Greek philosophers, not a few Christian theologians have spoken of "man" as composed of a "body" and a "soul" in a manner which envisions these two aspects being related to one another as a container is to contents. One has only to think of a false spirituality and a false asceticism which under Stoic influence considered the body depraved and sought to repress passions and emotions by purely spiritual-intellectual contemplation. A gospel-worldview honors our bodily existence and respects its powers and passions. Indeed, it reveals that "the Word became flesh," and thus embraced a human bodily existence.

By the offering of "his body and blood," Christ revealed the extent of God's love for us and returned humankind's perfect response of love and worship. And in his resurrected body, he remains forever the Head and first-fruits of the new creation. Thus, B. Häring maintains: "Man's body is not a thing but an embodied word, a message and an appeal."[17] A human does *not have* a body; he or she *is* a living body. Our corporeal-spiritual dynamism establishes each of us as a unique and subjective existential reality open to intersubjective relationships and, therefore, constitutive of personhood. One of the fundamental affirmations of recent anthropological studies is the psychosomatic unity of the individual human subject. "Psychic life at all its stages is expressed on the somatic register as much as in self-consciousness."[18] Given this unity based on clinical evidence and methodological observation and affirmed even by Thomas Aquinas through philosophical reasoning, we see how one's physical and psychological states can either help or hinder the growth and expression of one's full personhood.

3. Radically Free

Made to the "image and likeness of God" as a corporeal-spiritual being, a human being is a conscious subject gifted with radical freedom. Through the gift of freedom the human person is capable of self-transcendence and personal fulfillment, and with it he or she shapes history, society and culture, as well as being influenced and shaped in turn by them. As a *person-in-Christ* one's basic freedom of self-determination is exercised under the grace and guidance of the Holy Spirit. In the core of our being, in our noncategorical and unreflexive consciousness, we stand open to the Transcendent, to his gift of self-communication and love. Drawn by the gift of grace, a person either raises a radical "Yes" in full Christian freedom, or withdraws into oneself and proclaims a firm "No" in a negative self-commitment.

Christian freedom, then, is acquired through the radical acceptance of the gift of grace (cf. 2 Cor 3:17). By rebirth through water and the Spirit, Christians live as children of God; they can cry out, "Abba, Father." They are no longer slaves, but sons and daughters. They have been freed *from* the threats of sin, law, and death; and freed *for* God in love. "The highest degree of freedom is the perfect love of God in which man makes himself free from whatsoever resistance to being led by the Holy Spirit and thus comes to self-mastery in obedience, in his service to God."[19] This is the Christian paradox: freedom consists in total self-abandonment to the Spirit, implementing the words of Christ: "For anyone who wants to save his life will lose it; but anyone who loses his life for my sake will save it" (Lk 9:24). This Christian freedom again is a transcendental process of which we can have no adequate objective knowledge (cf. *DS* 1534f.) and is not to be equated with freedom of choice in particular moral acts, which we will treat of shortly. It is rather one's stance as a subject in a personal encounter with Transcendent Subjectivity communicating himself to us in love. This basic Christian freedom finds expression in the continuing activation of the moral direction of our lives, or in other words, in genuine Christian living.

4. *A Human-in-community*

Furthermore, to be a human person means to be a human-in-community, and to be a *person-in-Christ* means to be a member of his Body, the Church. Relationships, as we have already seen, constitute the essence of personhood. Recent interest in the theology of community has been stimulated by the concerns of the contemporary secular world. Sociological, philosophical and political thought in modern times has more and more focussed its attention on men and women as community beings. The Church has followed in pursuit in this regard, as is evidenced by the social encyclicals of John XXIII (*Pacem in Terris* and *Mater et Magistra*) and Paul VI (*Ecclesiam Suam* and *Populorum Progressio*). Indeed, a major shift away from the impersonal, individualistic and institutionalistic approach to Christian life within the Church occurred at Vatican II. *Lumen Gentium* describes the Church primarily as a community, a people bound together in Christ by bonds of love.

The Indian theologian R. Panikkar attributes the individualistic tradition in Western culture to a complex process of a "medieval nominalism grafted into the Cartesian system and mingled with other insights of the European protestant era."[20] Tracing the etymology of the word "person" back to the Latin *persona*, and the Greek *prosopon*, meaning literally a theatrical mask, he observes:

> The mask, the *persona* does not individualise, but personifies, i.e., robes our individuality from us and consequently allows us to play our role and to overcome our individualistic inhibitions, throwing us into the web of interrelations of human existence. Every human being has a different *persona* which allows him to perform the role for which he has been called into existence. Every man is a "personified" image of God, his Creator, in the traditional Christian worldview.[21]

The biblical view of humankind sees a person encountering God and being called to salvation in community by being incorporated into God's people. Both the Old and the New Testaments witness to the fact that God approaches us and gives himself to us in community, and that he intends humans to be builders of community (cf. the story of the Tower of Babel, and Christ's founding the Church as the New Israel).

A human being, once again, by reason of creation, is an embodied spirit and a social-sexual being capable of expressing the whole self in an interpersonal way, and thereby able to build community. Modern day psychology and sociology both point out that to meet a person is, indeed, to encounter a community which has formed him or her and of which he or she is a member. In the words of E. McDonagh, "to be human means to belong to some community, to be a product of it and to contribute to it, to share its destiny, its language, and its way of life to some minimal degree."[22]

5. *An Historical, Social and Cultural Being*

A human-in-community is, also, an historical and social-cultural being. Diachronically and synchronically one is deeply affected by the time-space continuum. Located in a given society and culture at any given time, the human person is greatly shaped and influenced by the historical background of his or her family and community, and by the current social, political, economic and cultural context out of which arises a distinctive set or system of values. A continuing dialectic between human persons and history-society-culture is in progress. History is humankind "in fieri" (becoming), in the process of constant growth and self-realization. History is where God calls us and communicates and gives himself to us. Thus, the divine-human dialogue in the Judaeo-Christian perspective has a history, a "salvation history," of which the Bible is a faith-record. B. Häring explains:

> God sends his invitation through history as an appeal to historic activity. But the response to the invitation ultimately is addressed to the Lord of History who transcends history. Thus history in every instance of the present, in every Now, in the *kairos*, is confronted by transcendence.[23]

Each person, too, has his or her own personal history of which he or she is a product and whose future remains a task or a project. Our humanity is not given to us complete at birth. It is rather a potentiality we must realize through the interplay of our conscious freedom, personal responsibility, and the objective factors of our own particular situation. Some of these latter factors are of a social-cultural nature, while others pertain to our own self-knowledge and physical-psychological condition. Describing "culture" in its general sense, the Council Fathers of Vatican II state that it includes

> . . . all those factors by which man refines and unfolds his manifold spiritual and bodily qualities. It means his effort to bring the world itself under his control by his knowledge and

his labor. It includes the fact that by improving customs and institutions he renders social life more human both within the family and in the civic community. Finally, it is a feature of culture that throughout the course of time man expresses, communicates, and conserves in his works great spiritual experiences and desires, so that these may be of advantage to the progress of many, even the whole human family. (*GS* 53)

In sum, it becomes quite evident that the starting point for our consideration of the "moral subject" in a theology of Christian living is much more than the static and abstract classical definition of "man" as a "rational animal." From the perspective of the evangelization process, the "new man" or *person-in-Christ* in his or her contemporary context is a concrete, existential reality, who approaches any given situation or moment of decision ("kairos") with his or her own personal biography containing the integration of a great number of significant factors and events. Among these latter are included one's biological, psychological, religious and spiritual maturity; one's present state of physical and mental health; one's social, economic and family status; one's educational background and particular vocation in life (lawyer, salesperson, public servant, etc.); in other words, all those factors that derive from a human person's basic make-up as a spiritual-corporeal unity, and as a radically free, community-oriented, social (including sexual), cultural and historical being.

B. CONVERSION

God addresses a human person's radical freedom and calls every one of us there to come home to him. Conversion may thus be described as God's gift-call to genuine orthodoxy, to believe the Good News, to place one's complete trust and confidence in the Absolute Truth therein revealed. In biblical parlance it involves an about-face in turning from idols and returning to the one true God. It is God's call and gift of himself in Truth and Love (Word and Spirit) inviting us in our spiritual-corporeal, social and historical nature to make a wholehearted, free and conscious response in faith, hope, and love. Our positive response to this gift-call roots us in the divine evangelical plan and bestows on us citizenship in the Kingdom. The *event* of conversion in the early Church was marked by the reception of baptism, which is at one and the same time a rebirth to a New Life in water and the Spirit and an incorporation into the believing community; thus, the New Testament basically tends to view conversion as a one-time event. Contemporary Christians for the most part have received infant baptism and thus the ultimate decisions and attitudes of their life in Christ are seemingly taken as a matter of course.

Today, conversion is seen more as a gradual and on-going process. Indeed, our understanding of basic freedom considers it to be a gift that requires an almost constant reaffirmation through continuing activation. It involves growth toward Christian maturity through an ever-greater conscious acceptance and realization (knowledge) of the gospel mystery as revealed by Jesus Christ and in which we live, move and have our very existence. Conversion, then, primarily means accepting the grace of God-revealing-and-communicating-himself in Jesus Christ. This implies: (1) turning away from idols and false images of God and believing in the Good News of Jesus Christ, which alone reveals what God is really like ("orthodoxy"); (2) accepting his rule and Kingdom with all our hearts by placing our complete trust and confidence in his dynamic and loving presence; and (3) putting this faith-experience into action by "doing the truth in love" (orthopraxis).

1. *Returning to the True God*

The Hebrew concept of conversion ("shub") implies a "turning back" after having taken a wrong direction; thus, the prophets of the Old Testament call the people to forsake their idols and to return to Yahweh. Jesus invites his hearers to "repent and believe the Good News." Voltaire once wrote: "God made man in his image and likeness and man has paid him back."[24] Conversion is a call to modern men and women to return from their idols and ideologies and from their misconceptions and false images of God to the True God made manifest in Jesus Christ. As in Voltaire's time, so today, we continue to remake God in our own image for our own finite purposes. Among these are the childhood images we receive of God, often unknowningly conveyed by our parents and elders. When the young adult, according to T. Burtchaell,

> . . . emerges from his years of youth altogether, he discovers —sometimes with resentment—that God has been used as a sanction for all those who were responsible for his discipline. When he used to cavort a bit maliciously at home, his mother might reach the end of her patience and threaten "When Daddy comes home, he'll take care of you." But if mommy and daddy are both at their wits end, then there is always the eternal spanking to which they can and do allude.[25]

Since a human person is a historical being, there is a growth in our ever-deepening understanding of God, both individually and collectively. This factor calls for an on-going conversion in order that our conceptualization of God may ever more properly conform to the truth of the Gospel according to our capacity for grasping it at any particular stage of maturity. Thus, some contemporary theologians point out three developmental stages in a person's concept of God: (1) the primitive stage of "magical understanding" or "systematic control"; (2) the more developed stage of "religious understanding" or "idealization"; and (3) the mature stage of "dynamic understanding" or "personal process."[26] The most primitive stage is immanentistic and consigns God in the main to sacred objects and rites, the disrespecting of which would invite some unknown punishment. The second stage exaggerates the Divine Transcendence and places God somewhere wholly "out there" or "up above," making him a totally extrinsic principle and an "ideal" to be imitated. The mature level of religious development grasps God as an immanent-transcendent Mystery. "This is the stage where death and resurrection become an interior part of our personal histories, not just a process carried through on our behalf by someone else."[27] It thus becomes evident that our understanding and conceptualization of God must constantly mature and keep pace with the rest of our personal developmental process, lest we find ourselves rejecting as the true God an "image" of God we can no longer believe in.

Other distortions of the image of God come from our own self-seeking ambitions and projections, both individual and collective. L. Segundo maintains that

> . . . by deforming God we protect our own egotism. Our falsified and inauthentic ways of dealing with our fellow men are allied to our falsifications of the idea of God. Our unjust society and our perverted idea of God are in close and terrible alliance.[28]

We subtly recreate the "image" of God to our own liking in order that he might not disturb our comfortable existence. Our desire for privacy and to be left undisturbed by our neighbor leads us to worship an image of God who is a self-sufficient individualist who espouses a like morality. A "will to power" creates a rationalistic concept of God who is stand-offish, static and indifferent, leaving the governance of the world's affairs to the rigid control of those who in their greed have been able to seize the strings of power. Still others view God as the Absolute Problem-solver, who is to be petitioned when all human knowledge and resources have come to no avail, and who is then quickly dismissed when we can once again make it on our own. Other false notions of God have been unwittingly propagated by certain "popular" styles of non-evangelical preaching: God as the Just but Exacting Judge, the Supreme Law-giver, God who is depicted as less approachable and less compassionate than human beings themselves. Beyond these and other falsifications of the image of God, there are idols and ideologies which often take first place and have all but replaced God in some people's lives: economic success, power, fame, careerism, sex, secularism, Marxism, Western materialism, pragmatic utilitarianism, conservatism and liberalism, etc.

Jesus' call to conversion and belief in the Good News is the gift of the true God-revealing-and-communicating-himself to us and inviting us to turn back from all our false idols and misconceptions of him. Jesus alone reveals to us the almost unbelievable Good News that the true God is far better than our greatest hopes and wildest imaginings could ever conceive him to be. Thus, T. Burtchaell, in describing the particular purpose of the Son's mission, states:

> What the very adventure of the Son in our man-flesh strives to convey is that there is a welcoming love, an unconditioned acceptance, a relentless and eternal affection in the Father which so far exceeds our own experience that even the selfless career and death of Jesus can only hint at it. The very substance of our faith is in the belief and hope that behind this hint lies love beyond measure.[29]

The Gospel, indeed, gives us a genuine and orthodox view of God. There Jesus reveals that God is primarily self-emptying and self-communicating love; he is essentially relationship and, therefore, personal. He is "Abba, Father"; he is Spirit and Truth, He is all-merciful, compassionate and forgiving. He is faithfulness and love. He is very near and dwells with us; he loves even sinners and goes to all extents to reach out to them and bring them back from their sinful ways. He is all this and more. These, then, are characteristics of the true God whom Jesus proclaims in the Gospel and invites us to believe in, to place all our hope, trust and confidence in, by accepting as Absolute his rule and kingdom in our lives.

2. Accepting God's Rule and Kingdom

As revealed in Jesus Christ, the Kingdom is the dynamism of God's love. Only the Kingdom is Absolute; it is the beginning and the end point of the entire evangelization process. It is grace (gift-call)! It is the

power of God erupting in time. The Kingdom confronts us where we are
Now (kairos), addresses us in our basic liberty, and calls us to an awareness of faith, to make a fundamental decision orientating our lives toward God (toward koinonia and relationship, or other-centeredness),
thereby initiating or re-confirming our personal evangelization in truth
and love and inserting us ever more fully in the one divine evangelical
economy.

The human person, however, remains free to refuse this gift-call
and to retreat into his or her own individualistic world (into self-centeredness, or the biblical "self-righteousness"). The underlying disposition or attitude emphasized by Jesus in the gospel narratives as a
prerequisite for accepting God's rule and sovereignty in one's life is
childlike simplicity or "poverty of spirit." Such a radical openness resembles the eager and heightened expectations of a child looking depen-
dently for good things to come from the hands of a friendly adult, whom
the little one is confident will not disappoint. Thus C. Curran observes
that "Jesus' anger is reserved for those who are not open to receive the
gift of salvation—the Pharisees and the rich. Jesus cursed those who
were hypocrites and smugly self-sufficient."[30] On the other hand, he welcomes the poor, sinners, and children who are not afraid to admit their
dependence and need for mercy, love, and all good things.

Accepting the will of God, his rule and Kingdom, requires a deep-
rooted faith and trust. It allows no room for nourishing and clinging to
false securities, for setting up "defensive blocs" against the dizzying
demands of relationships and love. As M. Oraison observes:

> What is at stake here is my internal security; and while it will
> be upset continually, this is what fundamentally constitutes
> progress. It allows me to recognize myself as a "self" absolute
> in my existence, but totally relative; proud, but lowly; irrevers-
> ible, but imperfect. My real security can be found only in a
> constant insecurity accepted as the inevitable condition of my
> progress in consciousness and relatedness.[31]

Radical faith and commitment to the Kingdom involve a risk. Christian
living is a venture-into-the-unknown. To accept the gospel mystery of
self-emptying love ("agape-kenosis") means to shoulder the Cross.

> The love in a Christian fashion is to sign a blank cheque. It is
> to leave the comfort of the known, the comfortable if enslaving
> known, for the hazardous but eventually liberating unknown.

It is to take up one's cross and follow Jesus. He who loves after his example will no doubt suffer after his example. To love in his unconditional way is to be crucified. What is done sacramentally in memory of his death until he comes finds another expression in the love-life called Christian life.[32]

To opt for citizenship in the Kingdom implies believing the Good News, the Mystery of Christ revealing God-giving-and-communicating-himself to us in truth and love. Our awareness and acceptance of this Mystery means more than just an intellectual assent—it involves the whole person; it involves loving God with all our heart, with all our soul, with all our mind, and with all our strength, and loving our neighbor as ourselves (Lk 10:27). Conversion and believing the Good News of the Kingdom of God mean basically orientating our whole lives, and fully committing ourselves, to doing the truth in love.

3. *Doing the Truth in Love*

Since in the divine evangelical economy God reveals and gives himself to us in Word and Spirit (in truth and love), our faith-response to this gift implies that we let him recreate and transform us in his image. We, therefore, must worship him in Spirit and Truth (Jn 4:23) and we must live by the Truth in love (Eph 4:15). Indeed, it is in our worship and liturgy that our idea of God becomes purified and is ever more and more conformed to the Truth, to the orthodoxy of the Gospel. "Liturgy in the Christian Church is a recalling and realising of the self-giving of the Son to the Father made possible by the gift of the Spirit."[33] Through the liturgy, in word and sacrament, we ourselves are evangelized as we are brought to an awareness and recognition of the true God present in our midst. It is impossible on Sunday to offer genuine praise and thanksgiving to God for all his gifts to us as Father if throughout the week we have not recognized our brothers and sisters in Christ as gift also.

Our liturgy, indeed, should be looked upon as a momentary celebration of the true and continuing worship and gratitude of which every minute of our lives must be an incarnate expression. In accordance with the Trinitarian structure of the divine economy and of the evangelization process which is revealed and communicated to us in words of truth and deeds of love, it follows then that genuine orthodoxy involves not only a true categorical awareness of the gospel mystery but also its concomitant implementation and incarnation in orthopraxis. Conversion, as we have seen in its biblical perspective, is both "metanoein" (a change of heart) and "epistrephein" (practical conduct). If, in fact, Absolute Truth is essentially personal and loving relationships, in brief we can conclude that "one behaves morally when one responds in an other-centered way; one behaves immorally when one behaves in a self-centered way."[34] "I give you a new commandment: love one another; just as I have loved you, you also must love one another. By this love you have for one another, everyone will know that you are my disciples" (Jn 13:34-35).

Conversion means placing all our hope and confidence in the one true God who saves us by acquitting us of our sins and giving us a share in his very own Trinitarian (personal) Life. Believing the Gospel means accepting Christ's revelation of this Mystery both in the kerygma and in the orthopraxis of the Cross. Through the Cross of Christ, we have been reconciled with God and with one another; through our continuing appropriation and realization of this Mystery ever present in our midst, we share a symbiosis of life with Christ, and in him bear fruit in love. Christian living thus resembles an organic process of growth and maturation, as in Christ we overcome the sinful tendencies of our historical condition and participate with him in the work of bringing about the final stage of the Kingdom of God. The contemporary Christian must remain ever open to whatever form the call and dynamic presence of this Christ Mystery takes in the here and now. We must constantly attempt to read and to discern the "signs of the times," in order to participate better in the on-going process of evangelization and to bear witness to the truth in word and deed.

> Through conversion to the reign of God the Christian has become a new creature in the life-giving Spirit and must now walk according to the new life that he has received in Christ Jesus. Anyone who meditates on the scriptures has to eliminate any type of quietism or denial of the importance of man's faith-issuing works.[35]

C. FAITH-RESPONSE IN LOVE AND HOPE

A person's positive response to the divine gift-call of conversion and faith enrolls one as a citizen of the Kingdom, or in the even more biblical terminology of the primitive Church, it makes one a "disciple." Discipleship meant complete dedication to the will of God and to his Kingdom, which the follower of Christ embraced in loving and hope-filled gratitude. It implied an active faith, persevering in hope while bearing fruit in love (cf. 1 Thes 1:3). Accepting the Good News in complete trust and confidence, the believer is expected to live it out in obedience and service, thereby giving witness to the hope that is in him or her. The Christian's faith-response lived out in love and hope bears witness to the Gospel and continues the process of evangelization by giving it an incarnate expression in human activity. The aspects which comprise this incarnating the Good News in Christian orthopraxis will be our concern in this particular section. This will involve looking at the fundamental category of the "human act" from the perspective of a contemporary gospel-inspired worldview, rather than from the classical abstract, static and objectivistic approach espoused by the "manual" tradition of the recent past. Genuine Christian living is necessarily permeated with the Spirit's gift of faith-hope-love (the "infused theological virtues"), which constitutes the believer's basic orientation toward God and comprises the soul of all virtuous activity.

1. *The Obedience of Faith*

United with Christ in faith and baptism, the *person-in-Christ* is also one with him in offering humankind's perfect response of obedience and love. This "obedience of faith" (cf. Rom 1:5; 16:26) is an interior reality, a matter of the heart and of a person's relationship to God and to one's neighbor. I. Hermann writes,

> . . . to the extent that it is obedience, faith appears to be a consent to a future under new auspices—that is, consent to an experiment in which someone who has come to his first encounter with faith lives on the basis of its truth, and can come to possess that truth in his own life, as his own.[36]

Faith itself must be living and active in order to be authentic. We must do the Truth; "orthodoxy" only finds its fulfillment in orthopraxis. Faith-in-action alone corresponds to the actual structure of the divine evangelical economy, revealed to us in words of truth and deeds of love.

The discrepancy between the faith we profess and the lives we lead has no little effect today on the credibility of the gospel we preach. The Second Vatican Council emphasized this precise point:

> Hence believers can have more than a little to do with the birth of atheism. To the extent that they neglect their own training in the faith, or teach erroneous doctrine, or are deficient in their religious, moral, or social life, they must be said to conceal rather than reveal the authentic face of God and religion. (*GS* 19)

The activity of love ("agape-kenosis") is the essential element of faith; it alone unveils the truth (orthodoxy) of the Mystery which permeates and sustains all creation. It alone returns true worship and praise to God. The Letter of James clearly teaches us that true worship and religion consists less in cultic service than in active love. Faith active in love alone corresponds to the Trinitarian (personal, and therefore communal) structure of Christian life. "Faith active in love radically defeats individualism and egotism; it is the harvest of the Spirit's presence in the baptized (cf. Rom 5:5) which makes him a member of the one Body of Christ (1 Cor 10:17 and 12; Rom 12:4-5; Eph 4:2-6)."[37] It seeks to bring about the unity of humankind and the cosmos in Christ, and thus makes visible the God who is love. Finally, faith is to be obeyed as the ultimate personal norm of moral activity, for St. Paul maintains that all which is not done from faith is sin (Rom 14:23).

2. *The Primacy of Love*

The divinely initiated process of evangelization which climaxes in the Good News of Jesus Christ reveals that God may be appropriately and primarily described as the Mystery of kenotic love ("agape-kenosis"). God communicates himself to us in the Truth which is self-emptying Love. "This is grace, the new life which man enjoys as a gift because it is a personal relationship with God made possible by God's gift of himself, by God's love, which is God (1 John 4:16)."[38] God loving us, thus, changes us making us both lovable and loving. When love is mutual, unity is achieved and a community (koinonia) is formed. The Gospel reveals, and so too the entire evangelization process itself, that our salvation is primarily accomplished through God's great love drawing us into intimate communion and fellowship by granting us a share of his own divine Trinitarian Life.

When we have been united to Christ through faith and baptism, the power of his love is active within us for he is the Head and we are his Body; he is the Vine and we the branches. In this way we become capable of keeping the two great commandments of love, which he teaches as summing up the entire Law and the prophets. Clearly grasping this Mystery, St. Paul thus writes: "In short there are three things that last: faith, hope and love; and the greatest of these is love" (1 Cor 13:13).

> The supremacy of charity in the Christian life and amongst the virtues is incontestable as far as the evidence of revelation goes. In the theological understanding of this, there have been various stages of development. A climax was reached in medieval theology with St. Thomas. His description of charity as mother, basis and root of all virtues received its full doctrinal

expression in his teaching on charity as the form of the virtues.[39]

This divine love in-forms all the other virtues: honesty, chastity, justice, and the rest. It is both the source and the end, too, of all genuine Christian activity, which itself, in one degree or another, is necessarily an incarnate expression of Christ's Paschal Mystery. Baptized into the passion, death and resurrection of Christ, our lives are meant to be a living out of this Mystery. Indeed, our share in it, which is appropriated to us in the sacraments, must be translated into our everyday activities. This continuing incarnation of the divine Mystery of love is essentially both a personal and community (ecclesial) task, since as members of Christ's Body we form a "new man" in him.

3. *Hope in God's Promises*

Believing in the Good News of God's faithful and all-merciful love revealed to us in the Christ mystery alone breaks open the iron circle that binds and condemns all human activity in cyclic futility. All our activity is infected by selfishness and sin, and appears ultimately consigned to death. But God's love manifests itself in this sinful world, as in Christ the powers of sin and death are defeated, and the risen Lord himself is acclaimed as the One who was, is and will come. Through his Paschal Mystery, a new creation comes to light. God's promises are fulfilled as Christ reveals the "new and everlasting covenant" between God and us, sealed in his blood. Men and women, despite their sinfulness and failure to love God and neighbor, are still assured of acceptance and forgiveness. Thus, E. McDonagh observes:

The bitter realisation of one's own failure must be balanced by this assurance of God's love and forgiveness. The first faltering movement of return in faith receives further impetus in the hope of forgiveness for past failures and of divine support in future difficulties.[40]

The hope of humanity has a certain built-in eschatological tension, but it cannot be rooted in our dreams of future accomplishments which themselves cannot help but be tainted by sin and self-seeking. Humanity's hope rather is grounded in God's promises, in what he has already done for us and continues to do for us who share a fellowship of life with him through Jesus Christ the Lord of history. This hope is a community hope, given to us who are members of his Body, the Church, and partners in the New Covenant. As B. Häring sums it up: "Hope is faith and love on pilgrimage; it is not something apart from faith or love."[41]

4. *Christian Orthopraxis*

The pragmatic side of faith manifests itself in genuine Christian living. Orthopraxis can be defined as "orthodoxy"-in-action, as living and doing the truth in faith-hope-love. This orthopraxis bears ethical testimony to the Good News, and so plays a firsthand role—if not *the* major role—in evangelization today. Incarnating this Christian faith-hope-love in our everyday activity remains our most serious moral obligation, but at the same time it is often our most difficult one because of a certain inherent tendency in the contemporary world to separate the religious and secular spheres of life (cf. *GS* 43). Our human activity is a kind of sacrament of our selfhood, of the person we are and are trying to become.

> By grace and the infused virtues God has taken possession of man's interior being, his "heart." The "heart of man" has become the mysterious locale of all that is human; human goodness is rooted here, as is evil. The hidden dynamism of the heart *will* express itself in exterior actions, and these actions in turn fill the treasury of the heart. In his human conduct man reveals what he is ("You will know them by their fruits," Mt 7:16); by his conduct man determines and shapes his own *being*.[42]

The earlier post-Tridentine "manual" approach to moral theology set up the "human act" itself as the objective focal point of moral activity. The "manuals" thus tended to espouse an act-centered, rather than a person-centered, morality. Their whole approach was abstract, essentialistic and legalistic. They defined a moral act as "an act done freely and with advertence to its relation to the norm of morality." One finds no consideration here of a gospel-worldview that focuses on doing the Truth in the faith-hope-love imparted to us by God's gift of himself to us in grace. The "manual" view of Christian moral life is hard to square with the evangelization process we have seen thus far in this study. In the gospel-worldview, Christian living is not concerned with the realization of an abstract ideal, but centers on a concrete personal response determined by the gift of grace and measure of faith given to each one (cf. Rom 12:3).

On the transcendental, noncategorical level of one's personality, the human person is called forth in basic freedom. There we encounter God as a co-subject and fundamentally orientate ourselves to him and others, or withdraw into self-centeredness. But, on the categorical level of free choice and human activity, a person is much more limited. Free will is not an independent reality in charge of the person; it is rather an aspect of the integral human totality. Thus, C. van der Poel observes:

> What we want to point out is that human freedom is very limited. It can express itself only within the limitations of the physiological, biological, biochemical, psychological and sociological conditions of this specific individual. We do not mean to imply that a human action is simply a necessary consequence of such conditions. But these conditions are essential elements of the human reality, and if man is the master of his own activity, then he cannot determine himself *outside* these conditions. His corporeal aspect is as essentially human as his spiritual aspect.[43]

Human self-determination, furthermore, presupposes knowledge, and hence we see the importance of kerygma and orthodox teaching. (Thus, an important question in moral theology has always been how much knowledge can be reasonably expected of a person in a given situation.) Absolute Truth is revealed in the Gospel as an interpersonal relationship expressed in "agape-kenosis" or kenotic love. Consequently, Christian orthopraxis in a given context and the evaluation of human and moral activity must be judged accordingly.

> In making a moral evaluation of a human action it is not merely the material result which is decisive, nor is it merely the intention of the agent, since the intention only establishes the human meaning of the action. It is the reality of the human action together with its impact upon the well-being of the individual and human society which is the norm for moral evaluation.[44]

Only when viewed in its totality can the interpersonal importance of a human action become evident. Christian orthopraxis in a gospel-world-view finds its interpersonal and normative value primarily in the "law of Christ," which is the grace of the Spirit, God-revealing-and-communicating-himself to us in an on-going process of evangelization, thus bringing about the reconciliation and recapitulation of all things in the Lord Jesus Christ.

D. THE LAW OF CHRIST

In the words of St. Thomas Aquinas: "The 'new law' is principally the grace of the Holy Spirit, which is given to the Christian believer."[45] The Gospel is grace. It is the "power of God" (Rom 1:16), the divine gift-call entering the most intimate part of us, summoning us in Christ and through his Spirit to the obedience of faith (cf. above pp. 94-96). It is the revelation of God sharing with us his own Trinitarian Life and directing us toward himself by the power of his self-emptying love. God's gift of himself in the on-going process of evangelization carrying out his saving economy is the dynamic interior norm that transforms us into ever more perfect images of his Son. This, then, constitutes the Law of Christ, the Christ Spirit living and working within us, which on a secondary level finds concrete expression and verbalization in commandments and precepts.

1. *The New Law of Grace and the Natural Moral Law*

The grace of the Holy Spirit, according to St. Thomas Aquinas, is the primary law of Christian living. "The grace-given being-in-Christ of each individual is being and task, fact and obligation at once."[46] It is, as we have emphasized all along, a divine gift-call. It is a divine invitation to love which itself empowers us to love. The Good News of Jesus Christ is the revelation both of this call and of the divine will, which is now no longer seen as something external to man, but as written on his heart (cf. Jer 31:31ff.). "Thus we are no longer under the law, but in the law: we are *ennomoi Christou* (1 Cor 9:21). Only in this analogous sense can we speak of the law of Christ, of Christ as lawgiver (*D* 1571)."[47] The absolute divine will, which Jesus reveals, finds its expression in the twofold precept of love of God and neighbor. St. Paul, indeed, speaks of the "law of Christ" as finding its fulfillment in our bearing one another's burdens (Gal 6:2).

"Love is . . . the answer to every one of the commandments" (Rom 14:10). The "law of Christ" is the law of love, which itself cannot be truly formulated and objectified; it always transcends our best efforts to fulfill it. "It is a summons (paraenesis) towards a point which always lies beyond our grasp, a call to perfect love with our whole heart and soul. . . ."[48] Sharing life in Christ, who is Love Incarnate, we participate in his very own love which reconciles us to God and to one another by healing our divisions and bringing peace. Christ's life and love within us both empowers and propels us to assume his attitudes, thus making them our own through our appropriating the mystery of his kenotic love. His Spirit, thereby, produces within us the harvest of "love, joy, patience, kindness, goodness, fidelity, gentleness, and self-control" (Gal 5:22). Through his Spirit we all become sons and daughters of the Father, and as such are related to all men and women as brothers and sisters. Thus, once again, we see grace (the primary law of the new covenant) as being constitutive of relationships. Our living the Good News proceeds according to the axiom: *actio sequitur esse*. Reconciliation and relationships are the primary moral task of a person who has been evangelized and is thus living in the law of Christ. "In spatial terms moral action is not staying in some place (in the 'state of grace'), it is going to some place (towards the Father and the brother)."[49] This sort of moral dynamism is present in the hearts of all people, even if categorically they do not accept the Good News and refer to it by some other name. Hence, theologians over the centuries have come to speak of a universal natural law.

St. Thomas defined natural law as the "participation of a rational creature in the eternal law."[50] "For St. Thomas eternal law is identical with God's being, his ideas, his providence and his government of the world."[51] In other words, all of creation participates in God's eternal wisdom, in the divine evangelical plan, and this participation is expressed in two ways. Irrational creatures participate in this "law" only in a metaphorical sense inasmuch as they are directed toward their end by their nature. Human beings, however, participate in the eternal law through their use of reason. "Natural reason is therefore directed toward what reason cannot ignore without denying itself."[52] For St. Thomas, then, natural law in this latter strict sense has priority over its metaphorical sense. He would not agree with those theologians who imply that humanity participates in the natural law on both rational and irrational levels.

By making rationality identical with human nature, we can seize it, and in this way it can give shape to a law that applies to all rational creatures in the same way. But by concentrating on rationality as such, we put it beyond the pale of every other created factor. For, as a rational being, man creates his own possibilities and realizes himself through these possibilities. He is for himself, "the being of endless tasks." He achieves himself in each of these tasks. Thus he is not only master of nature at large, but also master of *his* nature. . . . Natural law is itself the primary evidence that makes itself explicit constantly, and constantly demands to be translated into concrete human relationships. It is the motive force that drives us to give their full human value to all the relationships as they appear within the scope of man's concept of himself at any particular moment.[53]

This evolving and dynamic understanding of the "natural law" seen in the context of its historicity shows that it, indeed, participates in the *one* divine evangelical economy, which is geared toward reconciliation, peace and universal fellowship in the coming Kingdom of God. It is an inner dynamism both guiding humankind toward and preparing it for evangelization.

Viewed in the above sense, natural law is not really different from the law of Christ. The two-storey image of grace added to nature and of the divine positive law added onto the natural law is not valid in a gospel-worldview that admits of no purely natural order. "All men exist within the one order, subject to, modified by, reconciled by, and finally judged by, the divine self-giving in Christ."[54] The two are distinguished only on the basis that the natural law is revealed through humanity's shared experience and reflection by reason of creation, while the law of Christ is made known through God's direct intervention in the history of salvation. But the latter remains the completion and the judge of the former. As B. Häring states: "If a thesis of natural-law ethics contradicts the personalism revealed by Christ, it stands unmasked as error."[55]

2. *Commandments and Precepts*

The "manual" tradition conceived moral theology primarily as a legal exposition derived from an image of God as the Supreme Lawgiver. As E. McDonagh describes these manuals:

> They were for the most part composed of natural law, commands and prohibitions, plus divine positive laws based on revelation (with a generous measure of purely human canon law). The principle of unity was understood in an extrinsic fashion as the will of God, conceived as law.[56]

In this tradition positive law, whether divine or human, held primacy of place. Such a perspective, also, runs contrary to the teaching of St. Thomas who considered the "lex scripta" (the Gospel as a written code) as pertaining to the new law of grace only in a secondary way.[57] For him this written law served a two-fold purpose: (1) in the form of prohibitions it warns us of our sinfulness and our constant need for grace; and (2) it helps us to use grace correctly. Positive law is meant to give concrete, verbal expression to the inner law written on our hearts, but as St. Thomas also notes, the more detailed its applications are, the more likely it can err.[58] Positive law while necessary and helpful also bears an innate tendency to extrinsicism and absolutism, which it must always guard against. "Every positive law is by its very nature unsatisfactory; it has the tendency to place the value with which it is concerned in external actions, and it presents this particular way of acting as the best expression of that human value."[59]

In the Gospel Jesus rejects such legalism and such a hypocritical observance of the law. Rather, he sees all human reality as becoming an expression and reflecting the transcendent presence of which he himself was the personal and explicit realization—the Incarnation of "agape-kenosis," reconciling us to God and to one another. His moral teaching which we find formulated in Matthew's Sermon on the Mount is more illustrative of his demands and is not in any sense intended to be understood as a legal codification of them. He sets up *goal* values for the whole of our life.

> In a time like ours, when so many traditional laws and limiting norms are being desacralized and critically reviewed, it would be a disaster to deprive Christians of the clear orientations given by the goal commandments of the gospel. The catalogues of sin given in the Scriptures should not be considered as describing isolated acts but rather as criteria for discernment of what can and cannot be done in the name of redeemed and redeeming love.[60]

These "positive laws," then, serve primarily as guidelines in our personal process of on-going evangelization. Their application to given situations in our lives is left ultimately to the personal discernment of one's Christian conscience.

E. Conscience

Theological attempts to limit the study of conscience to the moral sphere fail to arrive at a full understanding of this uniquely personalizing reality. The Fathers of Vatican II provided a more comprehensive description when they stated:

> Conscience is the secret core and sanctuary of man. There he is alone with God, whose voice echoes in his depths. In a wonderful manner conscience reveals that law which is fulfilled by love of God and neighbor. (*GS* 16)

Only secondarily should conscience be viewed as one's capacity for making a practical judgment about the rightness or wrongness of a specific human action. It is primarily that most intimate, personal core of our being (our *heart*—2 Sam 24:10; Job 27:6; Jer 31:33; Eccl 11:9; Rom 2:12-16) where we hear the word of God (the gift-call) and with our whole self choose or refuse to respond to it. Conscience is the locus of our response-ability to God. It is where we either accept or reject being evangelized, that is, believing and living the Good News.

In the depths of his or her conscience a person encounters God, and there commences the divine-human dialogue that finds its concrete expression in genuine Christian living. There in the depths of one's most intimate self, one experiences an intrinsic dynamism to self-realization through a wholehearted search for the Truth. If this search is genuine and sincere, a human person gradually matures in his or her knowledge of Absolute Truth, who reveals himself as personal relationships of self-emptying love ("agape-kenosis"). This experience of Truth is, consequently, comprehended as a gift-call or "obligation" to do the Truth in love. B. Häring asserts:

> More and more, we see a growing conviction that a "faith that saves" is experienced above all in openness and a search for truth, in dedication to justice, peace, and brotherly love. These are the very signs of a sincere and deep faith. We have become allergic to sins of intolerance and to orthodoxy-without-orthopraxis. . . .[61]

This concern for expressing the truth in orthopraxis thus brings us to the consideration of conscience in its role of practical judgment.

1. *Decisions of Practical Judgment*

The decisions of conscience regarding orthopraxis enter the whole life of man. Classical theology distinguished two levels of conscience: (1) "synteresis," knowledge of the general principles of the natural law, and (2) "conscientia," the actual judgment of conscience applied to a particular situation. According to St. Thomas Aquinas, conscience pertains to the truth of practical reason rather than to the truth of speculative reasoning. For him human activity must be judged morally good or evil inasmuch as it is an "operatio" and not "operatum," for this latter, even if it be objectively wrong as such, can remain outside the intention of the agent. St. Thomas's understanding of conscience here differs considerably from the later "manual" tradition, which in its objectivistic and legalistic orientation merely assigns conscience the task of "applying the law to a concrete case." C. Curran in a return to the genuine Thomistic tradition describes "conscience" as

> . . . the concrete judgment of practical reason, made under
> the twofold influence of synteresis, about the moral goodness
> of a particular act. Conscience forms its judgment discursively
> from the objective principles of the moral order; but at the
> same time, there is also a direct connatural knowing process.
> The dictate of conscience is concrete, subjective, individual,
> and existential.[62]

In this sphere of practical judgment conscience is both antecedent (preceding the action) and consequent (following upon an action by either condemning or approving it).

In honest responsiveness the *person-in-Christ* guided by the Spirit's gift of wisdom seeks to determine the will of God for him or her in a given existential context by drawing upon one's life "in Christ" and the consciousness of value ("synteresis"). The believer seeks to incarnate the gospel mystery of kenotic love according to the measure of faith and grace at one's disposal in this here-and-now concrete situation. Guided further by the teachings of Christ and of the Church, the individual brings to bear not only his or her categorical understanding of reality, but also the whole personality in the important decisions of practical human activity. Through such orthopraxis, one continues to evangelize and to be evangelized as one's life itself "brings forth fruit in charity for the life of the world" (*OT* 16).

2. *The Formation of Conscience*

A person's capacity for making practical judgments is not something given ready-made. It is rather the result of a formation process. Its maturity depends on a continuing process of growth and evangelization, i.e., appropriating the gospel mystery in an integrated project of self-realization, which serves to make one ever more and more an "image of the Creator." On the most primitive or infantile level conscience is experienced primarily as an ambivalent feeling; it is an instinctive kind of warning that lacks clarity and insight. Through continuing activation of one's power of discrimination carried on within a healthy social and community environment, a person grows in self-understanding and in all that will promote authentic self-realization. Laws, then, no longer become taboos or prohibitions exerting pressure from without, but form a real part of one's own interior dynamism. L. Monden thus gives the following operative description of a mature Christian conscience:

> When he faces a decision of conscience, the adult Christian will not evade his responsibility by depending blindly on

the letter of the law. But he will *listen* with gratitude to what
the law can provide as a correction of his own views and as a
safeguard against the deforming influence of his drives and
prejudices. And more than any law he will take the *Person of
Christ* as his norm, adopt him as a model and as the test of authenticity.[63]

Christian maturity and conscientious living involve incarnating the gospel mystery of kenotic love in all the "big, little things" of daily life (cf.
Mk 9:41); they involve our sharing a symbiosis of life with Jesus Christ,
the incarnate Good News (cf. Gal 2:20).

3. *The Virtues of Prudence and Epekeia*

The application of this our life in and with Christ to concrete situations requires constant discernment, vigilance and prudence. For while
our subjective evangelization process (both as an individual *person-in-
Christ* and as a church community) is primarily under the influence of
the law of grace, it proceeds in the midst of a world that has not been
converted from its sinful ways. Within ourselves, too, the Word of God
finds varying degrees of reception. Beyond our personal limitations and
immaturities lie the lasting repercussions of being a child of Adam,
which, even after our baptism and fundamental response of faith, continue to sway us. Such *concupiscence* demands of us a constant vigilance
to discern the proper workings of the new Christ-life within us. Basic,
therefore, to the right development of conscience is the virtue of prudence, to which also the virtue of epekeia is closely connected.

> . . . on the one hand, prudence situates the trivialities of every
> day in the all-embracing dynamism of love, while, on the
> other, it helps when in doubt, to get beyond the rigid law and,
> as a genuine form of *epekeia* (the taking of a personal decision
> in one's own light), to find the concrete will of God in that
> source of law which is God himself, and therefore in love and
> goodness.[64]

For St. Thomas Aquinas prudence was the most important of all the
cardinal virtues, for to it belonged the task of coordinating and applying
the appropriate moral conduct to the concrete circumstances in life. To
this end St. Paul in his writings employed the Greek term "dokimazein"
("to test").

Closely related to prudence, then, is the virtue of epekeia,[65] which
denotes the exercise of the former with regard to the derived principles

and formulations of positive and natural law. The "manual" tradition in moral theology viewed epekeia as "the *interpretation* of a law in accordance with the *mind of the legislator*" when ready recourse to such could not be had. As B. Häring points out, the original Thomistic teaching on epekeia is quite different.

> Those who exhibit this virtue know well that it is wrong to cling to the letter of the law for security's sake when it is against the great law of love in responsibility. St. Thomas Aquinas finds that the adult Christian striving toward maturity is duty-bound to prefer a possible error by seeking the spirit of the law to the committing of a very probable error against the law of love by clinging to the letter of the law. If we rigidly abide by the letter of the law without attempting to search for its deeper spirit, we have not yet even reached the minimal level of maturity.[66]

Since one's conscience is the innermost personal sanctuary within which each one of us receives a *unique* gift-call to divine-human dialogue, our expected living out of this dialogue in orthopraxis requires a refined sense of listening discernment that is well attuned to the particular need(s) of a never-again-to-be-repeated situation.

"The root reason for human dignity lies in man's call to communion with God" (*GS* 19). It is in one's conscience, therefore, and in the prudent exercise thereof, that the *person-in-Christ* promotes his or her own process of self-realization by becoming ever more and more evangelized. Inserting oneself thus into the divine evangelical economy, the faithful follower of Christ continues the divinely initiated process of evangelization as he or she bears witness to the Gospel by the truth of one's own life, which in turn draws others to ask one "to give reason for the hope that is in him" (1 Pet 3:15). Our refusal and/or failure to respond to this gift-call and to enter ever more deeply into a divine-human dialogue is indeed the essence of sin.

F. Sin

When we go to the heart of the matter, sin is basically the refusal to love and to be loved; it is the rejection of the Truth, rejection, that is, of relationships with God and neighbor. Sin is a refusal to be evangelized, to believe and live the Good News of salvation. Sin is thus a power antithetical to grace. "As 'grace' symbolizes man in union with God, 'sin' symbolizes man alienated from God."[67] Sin is a relationship, a state of alienation from God, neighbor, world, and self, before it is an action.

1. *The Sin of the World*

Before being an individual, personal failure, sin is an objective de-personalizing and universal phenomenon; this latter situation is attributed traditionally to "original sin" and to what theologians today also refer to as "the sin of the world." As B. Häring writes:

> We are faced not only with the sum total of discrete sins but with that awful power of sinfulness that the Bible calls, in Greek, *hamartia*. It means that solidarity of corruption in which the world finds itself, surely because of all sins but particularly because of some very decisive sins throughout history.[68]

This solidarity of sin opposes itself to the "power of the Gospel" creating *one* "new man" in Christ Jesus. It opposes itself to God's *one* universal plan of salvation. It refuses to accept the divine gift-call of God the Father revealing-and-communicating-himself to us in Truth and Love. This power of sin pervades the entire human situation, which has not yet given itself over to God's redeeming love. This latter statement holds just as true for the Church as it does for the world.

Like the mystery of the person itself, the subtleties of evil are truly unfathomable. Perhaps this is why St. Paul portrays sin as a personal, demonical being (Rom 5:12, 21; 6:17; 7:14, 20), and why, also, ancient Christian tradition refers to the "wiles of Satan." Paul, too, frequently speaks of a spiritual battle (Eph 6:10-20) which is being waged in humankind's total environment, both within us and around us. It is within this context that B. Häring proposes the "main thesis" on the sin of the world:

> Wherever man transcends himself in unselfish love and invests in genuine liberating efforts with others, there Christ is present, even if those involved are not conscious of it. Whenever man refuses the solidarity in salvation he is, of necessity, opting for solidarity in corruption and implicitly rejects Christ. This is our main thesis; there is no third choice. Either we choose the one or we come under the other.[69]

Furthermore, our consideration of conscience in the immediately preceding section of this work could convey the idea that sin is solely a subjective reality, even though one's social, cultural and historical context, as well as one's relationship to Absolute Truth, are seen to play an important role in influencing one's human and moral activity. A human person, however, is a corporeal-spiritual reality, and his or her actions may be considered "materially evil" and contributing to the solidarity of sin even when there is no personal sinfulness involved. This is what moral theologians have traditionally referred to as "material" or "objective" sin. From such a materially sinful environment we have the obligation to defend ourselves. Thus, J. T. Burtchaell points out that

> . . . in Christ's parable on judgment the condemned are sent away for offences that were unwitting; by doing unloving things they had become unloving, to their surprise. . . . Situational variables may anaesthetize us to moral pain or mitigate the damage, but damage there is. We cannot long go through the motions of lovelessness without one day waking up to discover we have killed our love.[70]

Christ, however, was victorious over the "law of sin and death," over this sin of the world. It is by means of our growing communion and solidarity with him incarnated in lives of loving awareness and genuine Christian orthopraxis that the power of the Gospel and the process of evangelization move forward to ultimate victory over the power of sin and death.

2. Human Failure

Only within the context, then, of the solidarity of redemption in Christ and the solidarity of sin can we treat of sin as a human failure in given concrete situations. The "manual" tradition in moral theology considered sin, basically and extrinsically, as a transgression of the divine law.[71] Seen today from a more dynamic perspective, one may define "sin" as "a deformity in the expression of the transcendent dimension of human self-realization."[72] Here it is still related to the divine law interpreted primarily as the "new law" of grace. Sin is, thus, a failure to give oneself over to the divine gift-call, the divine-human dialogue. It is a failure to participate in our New Life of divine sonship, which would perforce make us into ever more perfect images of God. At its core sin is first an underlying basic attitude within us, which consequently expresses itself in human activity or the lack thereof.

> In the parable of the prodigal son Christ gives us the message that no specific action constitutes his sinfulness. The sinfulness of this young man consists in the self-seeking attitude in which he isolates himself from the community to which he belongs.[73]

It is only at this fundamental core level, where we can be fully accountable for our malice of heart that turns us away from our basic orientation to God, that we can speak of "mortal sin" or "sin unto death." Most of our activity is usually not expressive of our deepest selves. These lesser failures in realizing one's divine calling to growth and maturity in Christ, which can often be serious or even grave in themselves, have been traditionally classified as "venial sins." There is an essential difference between the two, but any attempt to rack one's brains to determine the precise quantitative difference between them runs contrary to the process of evangelization and the main task of moral theology, which is, namely, to call one to radical conversion and belief in the Good News.[74]

Sin is the human failure to respond to the persuasive love of God at work in our midst; it is the failure to respond to the demands of relationships and love which are made upon us in the situations of everyday living. "We spend our entire lives either not responding at all, or not responding enough or responding only indirectly. We are sinners all the time."[75] Yet, we are made in the image and likeness of God who gives and communicates himself to us in the divine evangelical economy through his activity "ad extra." This divine activity itself seeks incarnation in the orthopraxis of kenotic love. Our human activity, then, is meant to be a kind of incarnate "sacrament" of this divine working. Hence, sloth, indifference, the failure to care and to get involved can often be our most common sin. As C. van der Poel points out:

> Failure in human self-development doesn't result from a comparison between actual performance and an abstract ideal. There is failure when the performance doesn't measure up to the potential which the individual has and to the constructive realization of this potential.[76]

Such human failure is not limited to individuals alone. Particular groups and communities themselves are often the responsible subjects of much moral irresponsibility. The overly individualistic approach of moral theology during the long post-Tridentine era has tended to blind us to this reality. Although the group does not have the center of consciousness or decision-making which a person has, oftentimes individuals are particularly helpless to respond effectively in many morally demanding situations, such as is required by the needs of victims in natural disasters, apartheid, violence and injustice, or by those everywhere who are short of food, clothing, and of housing, education and employment opportunities. "It is only in organized groups, voluntary . . . or statutory and governmental, that any effective response can be made."[77] The failure to mobilize and cooperate when such group-effort is demanded contributes not a little to the continued propagation of sinful social structures and the solidarity of sin in our midst. The responsibility for such failure rests on the shoulders of the whole group and of each member in the group inasmuch as they have not done their part to overcome its blindness and inertia. This applies particularly to local church communities who are especially called to be images of the "new man" in the Spirit present and active in our midst. The Church in the world is characterized as a situation of grace confronting humankind with the true possibilities of its existence.

> The Christian community much like its God, cannot keep to itself. It is effusive, contagious, and seeks a dual role of service. It desires to serve God's redemptive vision for the world and also serve the world in its quest for fulfillment.[78]

The Church, then, is the world conscious of God's gift-call, and so conscious of its own sin and refusal to respond. Yet Christ by his Paschal Mystery has changed our sin into victory. In him, the Lord of history, the process of evangelization continues its triumph over sin and death as it brings about the reconciliation and recapitulation of all things in Christ Jesus, the Alpha and the Omega.

SUMMARY

The process of evangelization is carried on fundamentally through two moments: (1) God-revealing-and-communicating-himself to us in Truth and Love, and (2) our wholehearted personal and communal faith-response in love and hope. Theological reflection upon the *first moment* of this process since the time of Trent has been considered the true competency of dogmatic or doctrinal theology and its various tracts. Our personal response, or the *second moment,* was left in the hands of moral theologians, whose discipline after Trent became separated from dogma and tended to lean more and more heavily upon canon law. Indeed, the whole unity of theology in this period of the Church's history was almost totally obscure. It is really only with the renewed interest in biblical studies, liturgical reform, and ecclesiology which arose in the Church during the last half-century prior to Vatican II that a unitive view of theology once again began to take shape. The Second Vatican Council gathered together the fruits of the latest biblical and doctrinal insights, while requesting especially that a similar renewal be begun in moral theology to incorporate these insights there. Once wrenched from its nominalistic and legalistic foundations in the post-Tridentine "manual" tradition, moral theology soon rediscovered its close and intimate relationships with spiritual and pastoral theology, and the dependence of all three disciplines upon the doctrines and Christocentric focus of divine revelation. All of these theological disciplines thus became recentered in a gospel-worldview.

In this renewed Christocentric perspective, a human being is seen as a person called "in Christ" by the grace of the Holy Spirit to a newness of Life in divine sonship. In Christ and his Paschal Mystery the process of evangelization, which originated before time began in God's utterly free choice to give and communicate himself "ad extra," arrives at its revelatory summit, while at the same time God receives humankind's perfect response of obedience and love. In Christ's Paschal Mystery the *two moments* of evangelization become perfectly *one*; it is, indeed, seen as the "mystery of simplicity" in which we are restored to relationships of love with God and one another. Christ himself, the Good News Incarnate and the Lord of history, reveals and bestows on us New Life in the first moment of the evangelization process; in the *second moment* one responds in the Spirit as a person-in-Christ (a believer) living the Good News by incarnating the mystery of "agape-kenosis" in all the situations of quotidian life. This total faith-response in love and hope constitutes the core of our spiritual-moral life. The human person is here considered not just as a "moral subject," but as a subject of an entire evangelization process, who in turn evangelizes (bears witness to the gospel mystery) in the process of being evangelized.

A gospel-worldview sees a human being constituted as a *person-in-Christ* by reason of both creation and redemption. As an embodied spirit, one is called forth as a person-in-relationships, made in the "image and likeness of God" who is essentially "Relatio Subsistens." Created radically free, a person can accept or reject in a given historical, cultural and social context the gift-call to a divine-human dialogue of shared life. Historically humankind as a whole initially rejected the divine invitation and thus finds itself in a state of basic alienation from God, neighbor, world (cosmos) and one's own true self. Such sinfulness, however, has not radically changed God's original evangelical economy, for in Christ's Incarnation and Paschal Mystery the divine gift-call is manifested anew in human history. Jesus calls all of us to *conversion* and belief in the gospel mystery of God's extravagant mercy and self-emptying love. Jesus calls us to turn away from sin and our false "images" of God and to return home to our Father's house, there to accept the gentle suasion of his rule and Kingdom. Conversion is the divine gift-call to genuine orthodoxy, i.e., to a true categorical awareness of the gospel mystery and its concomitant implementation and incarnation in orthopraxis.

A person's positive *response of faith* to the gift-call of conversion lived out *in love and hope* bears witness to the Gospel and continues the process of evangelization by giving it an incarnate expression in human activity. Christian orthopraxis in a gospel-worldview finds its interpersonal, normative value primarily in the *law of Christ*, which is the interior grace of the Holy Spirit or God giving and communicating himself to us in an on-going process of evangelization; the positive formulations of law serve as the guidelines of this process. Their application to the concrete situations of life is left ultimately to the personal discernment of *conscience*, "the secret core and sanctuary of man," where one is alone with God (cf. *GS* 16). There, in honest responsiveness, the Christian believer guided by the Spirit's gift of wisdom seeks to determine the will of God for him or her in a given here-and-now situation (kairos) by drawing upon one's life "in Christ," consciousness of value, and knowledge of the teachings of Christ and the Church. Through this wise and prudent activation of one's conscience, the believer promotes his or her own process of self-realization and growth in the image of Christ by becoming ever more and more evangelized. Our refusal, however, to be evangelized, to believe and live the Good News of salvation, constitutes the essence of *sin*. Sin is a rejection of relationships of love with God and neighbor. It is primarily a power antithetical to grace, a state of alienation, before it becomes a particular human failure. The responsibility for this latter, however, can rest upon the shoulders of both an individual person and a given community. In Christ the community of believers has the power of victory over the law of sin and death, as sharing a symbiosis of life with its risen Lord it becomes more and more the "new man" renewed in his image. This, then, is the end and purpose of the entire process of evangelization—the reconciliation and recapitulation of all creation in Christ the Lord. And the study of our spiritual-moral life viewed and reflected upon from this perspective, rather than being strictly a "moral theology," becomes more truly a "theology of Christian living."

NOTES

1. P. Delhaye, "The Contribution of Vatican II to Moral Theology," *Concilium*, 75 (New York, 1972).

2. Delhaye, "The Contribution of Vatican II to Moral Theology," 75 *Concilium*, 61.

3. For a relatively complete bibliography on this question, see R. McCormick, "Notes on Moral Theology," *TS* 32 (1971), 71-78; and 34 (1973), 58-61.

4. J. Walters, "Christian Ethics: Distinctive and Specific?" in *AER* 169 (September 1975), 470-89.

5. Cf. E. McDonagh, *Gift and Call* (St. Meinrad, Ind., 1975) 2. J. Walter's choice of the phrase "Christian Ethics" in the title of the article cited in the previous footnote, however, does not advert to this its earlier distinctive association with the Reformed tradition.

6. Legrand, *GN&W*, 14.

7. Cf. F. Böckle, *Fundamental Concepts of Moral Theology* (New York, 1968), 9.

8. E. McDonagh, *Invitation and Response: Essays in Christian Moral Theology* (New York, 1972), 187.

9. M. Oraison, *Morality for Our Time* (Garden City, New York, 1968), 28.

10. Häring, *Morality Is for Persons* (New York, 1971), 41.

11. McDonagh, "Moral Theology: Need for Renewal," 17.

12. Häring, *Morality Is for Persons*, 90-91.

13. F. Böckle, *Fundamental Concepts of Moral Theology* (New York, 1968), 24.

14. *Ibid.*, 23-24.

15. *Ibid.*, 24.

16. C. van der Poel, *The Search for Human Values* (New York, 1971), 29.

17. B. Häring, *Medical Ethics* (Slough, England, 1972), 51.

18. Oraison, *Morality for Our Time* (Garden City, N.Y., 1968), 30.

19. Böckle, *Fundamental Concepts of Moral Theology*, 27.

20. R. Panikkar, "The Meaning of Christ's Name," *SAS* 252.

21. *Ibid.*, 251-52.

22. McDonagh, *Invitation and Response*, 47.

23. B. Häring, *The Law of Christ* (Cork, 1960-64), I, 89.

24. *Voltaire's Notebooks*, ed., T. Besterman (Toronto, 1952), I, 231.

25. J. T. Burtchaell, *Philemon's Problem* (Chicago, 1973), 16.

26. C. van der Poel, *The Search for Human Values* (Paramus, N.J., 1971), 15-20; and T. W. Guzie, *Jesus and the Eucharist* (Paramus, N.J., 1974), 128-44, respectively.

27. *Ibid.*, 139.

28. J. L. Segundo, *Our Idea of God* (Maryknoll, N.Y., 1974), 7-8.

29. Burtchaell, *Philemon's Problem*, 38-39.

30. C. E. Curran, *A New Look at Christian Morality* (Notre Dame, Indiana, 1968), 47.

31. Oraison, *Morality for Our Time*, 57.

32. McDonagh, *Invitation and Response*, 100-101.

33. *Ibid.*, 96.

34. McDonagh, *Gift and Call*, 33.

35. Curran, *A New Look at Christian Morality*, 49.

36. I. Hermann, *The Experience of Faith* (New York, 1966), 49.

37. B. Häring, *Faith and Morality in the Secular Age* (Garken City, N.Y., 1973), 163.

38. McDonagh, *Invitation and Response*, 88.

39. *Ibid.*, 72. See *Suma* II-II, q. 23, a. 8c.

40. McDonagh, *Invitation and Response*, 87.
41. B. Häring, *Hope Is the Remedy* (Garden City, N.Y., 1973), 41.
42. Böckle, *Fundamental Concepts of Moral Theology*, 29.
43. van der Poel, *The Search for Human Values*, 44.
44. *Ibid.*, 56.
45. *Summa* I-II, q. 106, a. 1.
46. J. Fuchs, *Human Values and Christian Morality* (Dublin, 1970), 82.
47. W. Kasper, "Law and Gospel," *SM*, III, 298.
48. Kasper, *SM*, III, 298.
49. McDonagh, *Invitation and Response*, 28.
50. *Summa* I-II, q. 91, a. 2.
51. J.T.C. Arntz, "Natural Law and Its History," *Concilium* 5 (New York, 1965), 43. See *Summa* I-II, q. 91, a. 2 ad 1.
52. *Ibid.*, 44.
53. *Ibid.*, 56.
54. McDonagh, *Invitation and Response*, 32.
55. Häring, *Morality Is for Persons*, 168.
56. McDonagh, *Invitation and Response*, 22.
57. See *Summa* I-II, q. 106-108.
58. *Summa* I-II, q. 94, a. 4, c.
59. van der Poel, *The Search for Human Values*, 91.
60. B. Häring, *Sin and the Secular Age* (Garden City, New York, 1974), 27.
61. *Ibid.*, 34.
62. C.E. Curran, *Christian Morality Today* (Notre Dame, Ind., 1966), 17.
63. L. Monden, *Sin, Liberty and Law* (New York, 1965), 104. Emphasis in the original.
64. F. Furger, "Prudence and Moral Change," *Concilium* 35 (New York, 1968), 126.
65. Cf. *Summa* II-II, q. 120, a. 1.
66. Häring, *Hope Is the Remedy*, 124.
67. J. Shea, *What a Modern Catholic Believes About Sin* (Chicago, 1971), 15.
68. Häring, *Sin and the Secular Age*, 114.
69. *Ibid.*, 112.
70. Burtchaell, *Philemon's Problem*, 82.
71. Thus, Jone-Adelman in *Moral Theology*, 96, define the concept and add: "Every law is, in a sense, a derivation from the divine law; therefore, the transgression of any law is sinful."
72. van der Poel, *The Search for Human Values*, 160.
73. *Ibid.*, 168.
74. A person who is evangelized, i.e., living in friendship with God, should not be overly anxious about losing that friendship and communion of life. In the words of St. Thomas: "Although grace is lost by a single act of mortal sin, it is not, however, easily lost. For the person in grace does not find it easy to perform such an act (mortally sinful) because of a contrary inclination" (*De Ver.*, q. 97, a. 1., ad 9).
75. Oraison, *Morality for Our Time*, 110.
76. van der Poel, *The Search for Human Values*, 192.
77. McDonagh, *Gift and Call*, 21.
78. Shea, *What a Modern Catholic Believes About Sin*, 91.

Part III
Evangelization: The Catholic Church
in the
United States of America
Yesterday and Today

Since evangelization is fundamentally an incarnational process in which the divine economy of salvation is made known to humankind through the revelation of the missions of the Son and Holy Spirit, it is appropriate now to review this process in relation to a given historical and cultural milieu. The United States of America stands unique among the nations of the world. Colonized first as a haven of refuge for religious dissidents outlawed in their native lands, she was looked upon as a new Promised Land and as a new Jerusalem by these Christian sectarians. The form of government established by her Founding Fathers was viewed as a new experiment. They envisioned a republic based upon creedal formulations, which nevertheless provided for a clear separation of Church and State. Her federal constitution, embodying deistic principles of the Enlightenment, guaranteed freedom of religion for the various Christian denominations in her several states. Protestant and pluralistic from the beginning, the American "Establishment" for two hundred years remained basically anti-Catholic. Yet, in her expansion westward, this new "Protestant" nation would acquire territory first explored and evangelized centuries earlier by French and Spanish missionaries, who left a sparse yet distinctively Catholic heritage in their wake. At the same time wave upon wave of immigrants from predominantly Catholic areas of Europe, fleeing dire economic and political circumstances, arrived at her eastern door. From approximately 35,000 Catholics amongst a population of 3,929,214 registered in the first federal census of 1790, the number of Catholics increased to an estimated 47,000,000 in a total population of 215 million in 1975. Today Roman Catholicism constitutes the largest Christian denomination in America, and numerically comprises the fourth largest Catholic body in the world.[1]

The story of American Catholicism has been as unique as the

199

country which has shaped her. It is a story of adaptation and acculturation in a rapidly growing, fast moving, and often hostile environment. It
is the history of great men and profound ideas which in retrospect have
been rarely reflected upon. From the viewpoint of evangelization, as
analyzed and presented in this study, the young Catholic Church in the
United States effected great strides on the practical level in order to
preserve and maintain the faith of the ever-increasing number of Catholic immigrants. Churches were erected and dioceses established at an as-
tounding rate. To protect the faith of her children from the heavily Protestant and anti-Catholic bias of the tax-supported public school system,
the American Catholic Church soon started to build and support what
would become the largest system of private education in the world—
ranging from kindergarten to the university level. The Catholic Church,
too, was largely instrumental in acculturating these millions of immigrants by often looking after and providing for both their material
and spiritual needs; this included building an ever-growing network of
charitable institutions, such as hospitals, orphanages, and homes for the
elderly. Meanwhile, the sacraments were administered and the basic
doctrines of the faith were taught according to the style of the age. Missionaries were even sent to the native Americans.

In 1858 a convert from Protestantism, Father Isaac Hecker, founded the Paulist Fathers, the first native religious community of men, for
the purpose of relating to that which was best in the American culture
and, thereby, promoting the Catholic religion within it. Such missionary
zeal for "spreading the faith" and for making the Catholic Church accepted in this "Protestant" land continued unabated down through the
years. With the election of the first Catholic President of the United
States in 1960, American Catholicism finally felt it had "arrived," while
at the same time it found itself constituting the single largest Christian
denomination in the country. The Catholic Church's evangelizing spirit
even today continues to run deep as is evidenced among other things by
the recent "Exploratory Consultation on Evangelizing the 80,000,000
Unchurched Americans," held in Marriotsville, Maryland in November
1975 and sponsored by the United States Catholic Mission Council, the
Catholic University of America, and the Glenmary, the Josephite and
the Paulist Fathers.[2] Furthermore, the Catholic Church in America during the first half of the twentieth century alone sent forth thousands of
religious and lay missionaries to preach the Gospel in Asia, Africa,
Latin America, and the South Pacific.

The primary aim of this part of our study, however, is to examine
the historical, social and cultural settings that influence present-day
American Catholicism and to seek therein some helpful directions for
promoting her own on-going evangelization process as well as that of the

society and culture of which she forms a part. To this end we will keep in mind the two moments of the evangelizing mission and their elementary categories developed in Parts I and II of this paper.[3] In Chapter VI, entitled "Evangelization and American Catholicism: An Historical Overview," we will study the Church's efforts to proclaim and incarnate (live) the Gospel during three successive periods of her history in the present continental United States. From this historical survey we want to ascertain the various factors influencing the Catholic Church in America as well as the strong points and weaknesses in her previous efforts both to evangelize and to be evangelized, i.e., to live ever more fully the gospel in her own spiritual-moral life as an identifiable, concrete Christian community. This information, then, will aid us in analyzing her current mission in Chapter VII: "Evangelization and the Catholic Church in the United States Today: The Continuing Mission." In this final chapter we shall construct a composite profile of the contemporary American scene. And from the application of our already completed analysis of the two moments of the evangelization process and their categories, we want to determine the current directions and related questions that need to be explored in order that the Catholic Church in America may carry forward in a most faithful and conscientious manner this continuing mission. The task is enormous and our space limited. Realistically, therefore, we can only make general observations with regard to a thoroughly pluralistic and "catholic" situation. Yet these observations we expect will be sufficiently concrete in their overall compass to aid in future research—whether by this author or others—into the more specific and regional exigencies of this evangelizing apostolate of the Catholic Church in the United States of America.

NOTES

1. Cf. Secretaria Status Rationarium Generale Ecclesiae, *Annuarium Statisticum Ecclesiae—1974* (Vatican Polyglot Press, 1975), 37-44, where "baptized Catholics" are listed by the 100,000's according to their country; the four largest Catholic bodies include Brazil, 94.754; Italy, 54.250; Mexico, 54.050; and U.S.A., 46.608.

2. The Glenmary Research Center, Washington, D.C., under the direction of Rev. Bernard Quinn, has just initiated a ten-year research project based on this theme.

3. That is to say, the *first moment* of Proclaiming the Good News in its three principal forms: kerygmatic, catechetical, and theological; and the *second moment* of Living the Good News with its six fundamental categories: person-in-Christ, conversion, faith-response in love and hope, law of Christ, conscience and sin.

VI
Evangelization and American Catholicism: An Historical Overview

"The higher man rides on the shoulders of the past, the more likelihood that his perspective of the present will be clear."[1] These words of the late Archbishop of Atlanta, Paul J. Hallinan, best explain the purpose of this present chapter. Herein we will survey the historical setting of Catholicism in America with regard to its efforts at evangelization in order to be able to comprehend more fully the needs of the present hour. On the theoretical level, the American church's historical understanding of evangelization, like that of the universal Church, has been limited to the concept of missionary outreach to unbaptized natives and on occasion to convert instructions for Protestants. On the more practical level, the Catholic Church has put forth near-heroic efforts in keeping alive and supporting the faith of million upon million of immigrants, who came to this country between 1820 and 1920, in caring for both their spiritual and material needs. She welcomed in one fold people of various nationalities and ethnic backgrounds. She continually sought to adapt herself to all the good that America had to offer, while at the same time contributing the best that she in good conscience felt she must and could give to this new nation. For example, the American church, unlike her sister churches in Europe, proved herself to be the champion of labor and the defender of the workingman during the great conflicts brought on by industrialization toward the end of the last century. Further, she continued to remain in the forefront of social action during the first half of the twentieth century. These and other incidences paint a historical scenario of living witness to the Gospel through genuine orthopraxis.

To facilitate our historical overview of this evangelization process in the United States, we shall divide this chapter into three successive periods. First we shall look at the Catholic Church and Colonial America (1492-1790). Secondly, we turn to the young Catholic Church in the United States (1790-1908) beginning with the appointment of the first American bishop, John Carroll of Baltimore, and ending with the American church's removal from the jurisdiction of the Congregation de Propaganda Fide. Finally, we shall look at American Catholicism in the twentieth century starting from 1908 and concluding with the election in 1960 of John F. Kennedy, the first Catholic President of the United States. The last fifteen years, then, from 1960 to 1975, will provide the backdrop for our analysis of the contemporary situation in the next and final chapter of this work.

A. THE CATHOLIC CHURCH AND COLONIAL AMERICA
(1492-1790)

Evangelization appears as one of the primary motives for Christopher Columbus's celebrated journey in 1492. In the first entry of his famous journal, he writes of his hope to contact the native peoples in order to discern "the manner in which may be undertaken their conversion to our Holy Faith."[2] With his discovery of the New World begins the history of Spanish influence in the Americas, as well as the history of the Catholic Church's evangelizing mission on those same continents.

1. The Spanish Missions

The close alliance between Church and State greatly affected the colonization and evangelization of New Spain. By reason of the "real patronato," a series of papal concessions to the Spanish monarchs, the Church in Spain came under virtually complete royal control. No Spanish expedition was complete if it was not accompanied by at least one or two missionary priests. Spanish explorations and missionary endeavors proceeded hand in hand. Thus, in the "cedula" authorizing the ill-fated colonial enterprise of Vasquez de Ayllòn on the North American coast in 1523, Charles V voiced his religious interests stating:

> Our principal intent in the discovery of new lands is that the inhabitants and natives thereof who are without the light of the knowledge of faith may be brought to understand the truths of our holy Catholic faith, and that they may come to the knowledge thereof and become Christians and be saved, and this is the chief motive you are to bear and hold in this affair, and to this end it is proper that religious persons should accompany you.[3]

The particular geographical area of our concern here is the Spanish borderlands, which later became the states of New Mexico, Arizona, Texas and California. Peculiar to the early government of these territories were the "presidio," and the mission, the former being the military outpost and the latter representing the civilizing forces of religion and education on these remote frontiers.

The "presidio" and the mission were often found in frequent conflict regarding the appropriate manner of treating the natives. From the legal standpoint, the Indian was a subject of the crown and valued solely as a source of labor. It is a credit, then, to the deep faith and Christlike charity of the missionaries that they organized a campaign to prevent the rise of Indian slavery. Bishop Bartholomé de las Casas, one of the missionary friars, was most instrumental in alerting Europe to the atrocities of Indian enslavement so avidly promoted and sanctioned by the Spanish "Conquistadores." At his instigation, Pope Paul III in 1537 issued the bull *Sublimis Deus* deploring and prohibiting Indian servitude. It was a most ironical twist of fate, however, that Bishop de las Casas's genuine humanitarian and charitable concern for these natives would in turn give rise to an even greater ignominy, the introduction of Negro slavery in America. While attempting to spare the Indians the deadly curse of slave labor, he recommended introducing Africans whom he considered to be of a stronger and hardier stock. Yet, as R. Lambert has observed: "In defense of the bishop, we may say that he certainly did not foresee the future inhuman development of Negro slavery, and when its evils became apparent to him, he strenuously protested against them."[4]

The dedication and compassion of these Spanish missionaries (mostly Jesuits and Franciscans) for the natives among whom they lived and served for three centuries writes well one of the most noble and inspiring chapters in the history of American Catholicism. Hundreds of men who were highly gifted and well educated, such as the renowned Franciscan Junipero Serra, left behind their cultivated surroundings and gave themselves totally to the spiritual and material advancement of these all-but-savage peoples. As S. Ahlstrom, a Protestant historian, points out: "It was the friars . . . traveling on foot, living amid the Indians without wealth or display and learning their languages, who came to understand the Indian."[5] They evangelized these native peoples by both preaching and living the Gospel in their midst. They showed a willingness to adapt to the religious tendencies of the natives, utilizing certain characteristics of the indigenous culture and its religions. In the Florida missions they translated catechisms and even attempted some elementary schooling. The missionaries in these borderlands also taught the Indians stockbreeding, horticulture, architecture and other useful labors. They introduced, too, Spanish culture and a way of life whose influence still remains forming a rich religious and cultural heritage. The presence of these Spanish missions, despite some obvious abuses, represents a genuine concern for Christian evangelization, as well as a humane regard for primitive peoples. In their defense of the human dignity of these natives these Spanish friars stand in marked contrast to the attitude of the later English colonists.[6] And because of these highly successful evangelizing efforts in the Spanish borderlands which later became part of the federal union, S. Ahlstrom concludes that "many Americans can draw sustenance from the fact that the country's oldest heritage is not Puritan but Catholic."[7]

2. French Missions in America

In the seventeenth century French missionaries engaged in similar efforts to evangelize the Indians in the territory of New France. The setup was basically the same with the close connection of Church and State. Thus, the historian G. Bancroft asserted: "The history of missionary labors is connected with the origin of every celebrated town in the annals of French Canada; not a cape was turned nor a river entered but a Jesuit led the way."[8] These French Jesuits were explorers and missionaries. Like their Spanish counterparts to the South, they, too, were men of superior education who had forsaken a great civilization to expend their lives in the service of a barbarous people. "Father Jean de Brébeuf, for example, lived nearly three years among the Hurons for the sole purpose of learning their language and gaining a knowledge of their customs."[9] Brébeuf then wrote a set of instructions for his confréres who were to evangelize the tribe. The success of their wide-ranging efforts in the present confines of the continental United States is born witness to by the fact of the numerous towns and cities of the Great Lakes region, the Midwest and along the Mississippi River which still bear French names—Marquette, Joliet, Louisville, New Orleans, to name but a few. Though less successful in making converts among the Indians than the Spanish, the Blackrobes' total dedication and Christian concern for these native peoples did not fail in comparison. Undaunted by what the world reckons as failure, they preached and lived the Gospel to its core, as the martyrdoms of Brébeuf, Isaac Jogues, and their companions bear proof. After the suppression of the Jesuits, French Recollects, Capuchins and diocesan priests remained to carry on the mission of evangelization in these territories. Ellis writes that

> In both Vincennes and Bardstown, a cathedral and a college were staffed by bishops and priests from France before the advancing frontier had passed their doors. Here, then, was a significant stabilizing factor in the maturing process of the new-

born states, an ancient and fixed tradition to mellow the rough and raw elements of the West.[10]

Later French Catholicism exerted still further influence on the United States as large numbers of French Canadians moved into the New England Commonwealths.

3. *Evangelization in the English Colonies*

An unquestionably Protestant and Puritan cast marked the evangelizing mission in the English colonies of North America. From these several colonies came the values, traditions and form of government which would decidedly shape the yet-to-be-born United States of America, its future citizens and the Catholic Church in that new nation. English colonization efforts in America were unable to make a successful start until after the beginning of the seventeenth century. The famed "Pilgrim Fathers" settled in New England as Puritan prospects were darkening in England in the 1620s. Congregationally inclined, these adherents of the Reformed tradition sought to establish a covenanted "theocracy" of an Old Testament flavor in this new Promised Land. Their coming they viewed as a new Exodus, an "errand into the wilderness."

At first the Puritans sought to evangelize the Indians and met with some success. The Bay Colony's charter contained a clear pledge to "wynn and incite the Natives of the Country to the knowledge and obedience of the onlie true God and Savior of Mankinde, and the Christian fayth." But their efforts to this effect soon waned. S. Ahlstrom interprets this situation thus: "Their conviction that England was an elect nation tended to minimize other peoples, and it may be that the theology of the covenant had a similar effect."[11] Indeed, it was this theology of the Reformed Calvinistic strain that would exert the most substantial influence in shaping, and we might even say "evangelizing," the future American way of life. It strongly encouraged rectitude, probity, industry, and individual responsibility in religious matters, this latter being made even more explicit by the Reformed doctrine of the priesthood of all believers. Furthermore, this tradition held the Mosaic Law in great esteem. It dwelt unremittingly on the value of Law as teacher and moral guide for the Christian. The Puritan thus "found much specific guidance in the Scriptures, very often in the Old Testament, for the ordering of personal life, the regulation of society, and the structuring of the Church."[12] The society that this tradition envisioned and attempted to establish as a holy commonwealth in the New World centered around the doctrines of divine sovereignty, human depravity and God's revealed

Law. All these found a lived expression in the practice of an austere "this-worldly asceticism."

In the view of S. Ahlstrom, however, "the New England Zion was never an untroubled utopia."[13] Indian wars, internal religious tensions, questions of church order, and declining fervor all contributed to the unsettlement and subsequent development of Separatist tendencies. One of the first and most famous of these originated with Roger Williams who, unwelcomed in the Bay Colony, moved to and founded Rhode Island in 1636. There for the first time was established the historic solution of a legal separation of Church and State—a solution which in later years, in the new United States, would aid the Catholic Church's evangelizing mission and fantastic growth in this predominantly "Protestant" country. In the other English colonies, various Christian denominations legally controlled both Church and State. In Virginia the representative House of Burgess established in 1619 was also responsible for ecclesiastical legislation, while the fortunes of individual parishes in this Anglican colony were put in the hands of the vestry. Here, too, the rise of the tobacco culture and the dependence on African labor was sanctioned by the Church, a state of affairs truly opposed to the Puritan culture of New England. "Their church was part of a gentleman's way of life, but it did not intrude on business."[14] The middle colonies meanwhile were populated by a mixture of Puritans, Quakers, and other Dutch and German sects. Under the leadership of William Penn and his Society of Friends, Pennsylvania alone among all the colonies promoted full religious toleration for all Christian denominations.

First settled in 1633, Maryland was the only colony established as a refuge for persecuted Roman Catholics in England. Under the proprietorship of the Lords Baltimore, themselves loyal Catholics, freedom of religion was extended to all the inhabitants of the colony in the famous Act of Toleration of April 1649. Two Jesuit Fathers, Andrew White and John Altham, arrived with the first expedition to the colony. Joined later by other Jesuit priests, they ministered freely to the white settlers and evangelized the Indians. The freedom for Catholics in Maryland, however, was short-lived. Puritan unrest in this colony, where Catholics were only a minority, and political upheavals in England conspired to eventually outlaw the religion of its founders. "The period from 1692 to the American Revolution justifiably became known as the Penal Period during which the church subsisted on a private, almost clandestine basis, while individual Catholics constantly were threatened or visited with legal sanctions."[15] During this long period, Catholics never numbered more than several thousand at any one time, many of whom moved over the border to live in Pennsylvania where the first completely public

Catholic Church in the colonies was erected in Philadelphia in 1733. Some seventy Jesuits and at least seven Franciscans are known to have served these Catholics during this period, although there were never more than two or three priests on hand at any one time.

The evangelization efforts of Roman Catholicism in the English colonies were limited by anti-Catholic bias and by the meager numbers of the faithful. The few priests who came to the colonies ministered to Catholics and sought to evangelize the Indians. Father White even translated a catechism for this latter purpose. A couple of Catholic elementary and secondary schools were also founded. J. Tracy Ellis probably best sums up the status of the Catholic Church in these English colonies by centering its history around four main points:

> First, a universal anti-Catholic bias was brought to Jamestown in 1607 and vigilantly cultivated in all the thirteen colonies from Massachusetts to Georgia. Second, the small body of Catholics, mostly English and Irish who settled on the Atlantic seaboard after more than a century of active persecution and handicap clung to their religious faith. Third, The Catholic minority in their brief tenure of power in two colonies introduced the principle of religious toleration. Finally, the absence of domination by any one of the different Protestant churches fostered the principle of religious freedom for all, a principle to which the Catholics gave full assent.[16]

4. *Principles Behind the Founding of the American Nation*

Our attention here focuses not on the historical facts of the Revolution and the founding of the new nation, but rather on the religious and philosophical principles underlying the Declaration of Independence and the federal Constitution, which portray a certain religious mind-set. They contain the creedal formulations (e.g., "We hold these truths . . .) of what would become the American way of life, a new "civil religion" drawing to itself the adherents of every religious denomination. A combination of Puritan susceptibility to transmute its power into secular impulses and the then contemporary development of a distinct form of Enlightenment theology underpinned the composition of these two most significant public documents.

From Puritanism the new nation acquired its immense respect for law—divine, natural, moral, and statutory, which would remain prominent even with the advancement of secularizing tendencies. The good citizen was a law-abiding man. "[Puritanism] helped to create a nation of individualists who were also fervent 'moral athletes,' with a strong sense of transcendent values which must receive ordered and corporate expression in the commonwealth."[17] As a French observer of the American scene, G. Tavard, has noted:

> The hard climate of the Puritan colonies allied itself exceptionally well with primitive Calvinism to form the rough type of Yankee: fundamentally "Protestant" even when he no longer had any religion, willingly "moralizing" even when he had forgotten the dogmatic justification for morality, full of drive and initiative even when it was no longer in the service of the "true religion". . . . Catholics did not escape this influence. Every minority wants to affirm itself either by opposition or by conformity.[18]

Also from Puritanism came the congregational method of governing churches which "prepared men to regard the social compact as the proper basis of government."[19]

From the Enlightenment there developed a new rationalistic theology which understood the human relationship to God on increasingly impersonal terms. Reserved and law-centered, its chief advocacy was a philosophical analysis of morality. Optimistic and confident about human destiny on earth, it accented the idea of progress, which looked for the realization of the Kingdom of God in history. Among the Enlightenment's main advocates in the colonies were many of the Founding Fathers, including John Adams, Benjamin Franklin and Thomas Jefferson. As M. Marty explains:

> The semisecular national founding fathers were discontented with and opposed to much of the Calvinism or Trinitarianism theology in the churches. But they did not stop talking about God and providence, meaning and mission. They translated it to other terms. . . . They took the shell and outline of the old religious systems and supplied their own. Theirs remains a part of American public school religion, the faith of Boy Scouts and service clubs, of people who never enter churches. They make much of equality, justice and freedom as being somehow divinely assured and rich in new meanings.[20]

This Enlightenment tradition would exert its effect on American Catholicism. Indeed, American Catholics would receive what W. Ong has called a "double charge of 'reason,' one national and the other religious," making them exceedingly slow to register romantic emphasis.[21] The religious "charge" he sees as descending from the post-Tridentine seminary education and catechism, and the fact that in the United States there were no pre-Christian social customs and observances to filter these heavy rationalistic doses as was done in Catholic Europe and Latin America. As a result, then, of this double dose, Ong maintains that "the Church in America is more legalistic in performance and more formalistic in general intellectualistic outlook than anywhere else in the world."[22]

B. THE YOUNG CATHOLIC CHURCH IN THE UNITED STATES (1790-1908)

The period of time covered in this particular section commences with the appointment of the first bishop in America, John Carroll, to the See of Baltimore in 1790 and extends through the whole era during which the American church came under the jurisdiction of the Congregation de Propaganda Fide. The newly formed church was from its beginnings much influenced by the mentality, traditions and customs of the new American experience which arose from the former English colonies. Its own growth, development and evangelizing efforts would be shaped by and adapted to an American heritage based on the principles of religious freedom, separation of Church and State, denominationalism or religious pluralism, voluntaryism, and patriotism. The Catholic Church in the first quarter century, under the leadership of Bishop Carroll, had to come to terms with each of these currents, embracing some and modifying others, while at the same time coping with an insidious and widespread anti-Catholic bias. Only later with westward expansion did the new church come in contact with the remaining effects and rich heritage left behind in this wilderness by the earlier Spanish and French missionaries. Throughout her history, however, the mentality and the traditions of the new American nation would principally predominate the Catholic Church's choice of direction.

1. *The Age of Bishop Carroll*

J. Tracy Ellis describes the situation within American Catholicism in 1790 when John Carroll assumed the reins of leadership:

> Some 156 years passed between the coming of the first missionaries to Maryland and the appointment in 1790 of a bishop for the American Catholics. This long period of abnormal rule not only deprived them of the sacraments of confirmation and holy orders but likewise left them with little or no knowledge

of the traditional form of church government, an ignorance that caused some very strange notions among both priests and laity concerning the episcopal office and its functions. . . . [Furthermore], most of Bishop Carroll's charges were poor and humble folk tilling their Maryland and Pennsylvania farms or keeping shop and laboring in the large seaboard towns.[23]

Infused with the spirit of the new nation, John Carroll, as vicar apostolic since 1784, insisted to Rome that, given American tenets and culture, the first bishop of the country should be elected by the American clergy and confirmed then by Rome. Approval was obtained on the basis that this was a one-time-only arrangement, and John Carroll was elected. Out of a deep concern to make the faith more thoroughly understood, Bishop Carroll unsuccessfully championed a vernacular liturgy in order to overcome obstacles to Christian unity and to promote "a much more general diffusion of our religion particularly in N. America," where books were scarce and the people often incapable of reading.

More successful were the first bishop's attempts to set up colleges and parochial schools to educate and support the people in their faith. In 1789 Georgetown College was founded, and in 1791 with the help of the French Sulpicians he founded St. Mary's Seminary in Baltimore to train future priests for the American church. Numerous parochial schools and other Catholic institutions were built in his day. His concern for Christian education is the first topic treated in his pastoral letter issued upon the occasion of the first National Synod of Baltimore (1791).

Totally American to the core, Bishop Carroll displayed his patriotism proudly. A century later Cardinal Gibbons would write of him:

His aim was that the clergy and people shall be . . . identified with the land. . . . From this mutual accord of Church and State there could but follow beneficient effects for both.[24]

Indeed, his calling of the National Synod showed him desirous of governing by consensus in keeping with the political and social culture of the country and with the practical necessities of his vast missionary territory. As permitted by canon law, a form of parochial trusteeism was introduced in America because the legal system in the United States did not at first allow ecclesiastical institutions to hold property. Nevertheless, this setup soon led to a number of open conflicts between bishops and laity from which schisms developed, as trustees, for want of knowledge about church government and/or on account of ethnic tensions, sought to maintain control over the appointment and dismissal of pastors, among other strictly episcopal prerogatives. These tensions continued sporadically to plague John Carroll and the other members of the American hierarchy for well over a century.

In 1808 Baltimore was made an archdiocese with four suffragan sees at Boston, New York, Philadelphia, and Bardstown. John Carroll became the first archbishop. During the twenty-five years that he shepherded the see of Baltimore, immigration, mostly from Ireland, quadrupled the number of Catholics in the country to well over 100,000. However, the majority of the clergy were French-born, which brought certain ethnic tensions to the surface. The French Sulpicians whom Bishop Carroll brought to America to establish St. Mary's seminary had a profound impact on the development of the young church, and yet figured in some of its problems. S. Ahlstrom assesses this situation:

> The nature of the theological and spiritual influence of the Sulpicians on the Roman Catholic Church in America is difficult to estimate. But the society was always known for its strict conception of orthodoxy rather than for its venturesomeness, and it is perhaps just to say that it propagated a similar spirit in America, where in any event the intensely practical necessities of an expanding church hindered the growth of theological profundity, a great tradition of learning, or even the ardent piety associated with Jean-Jacques Olier, the society's great founder. Here again a step taken by Bishop Carroll had a decisive impact on the church—in the immediate sense providing a source of priests and bishops when they were badly needed, but in the long run creating a very serious source of ethnic tension and jealousies that often sharpened trusteeship conflicts.[25]

Evangelization, during the era of Bishop Carroll, thus meant laying foundations and building a church on a nationwide level. It meant meeting the practical exigencies of the American scene—arranging and providing for the religious instruction of the young, erecting churches, schools, hospitals and other charitable institutions, acculturating the immigrants, securing the necessary priests, celebrating Mass and administering the sacraments, representing and explaining the faith to an American people who held a myriad of misconceptions about and prejudices against Catholicism. Amidst all this, Bishop Carroll had to contend with the abuses of trusteeism, schisms, malcontent clerics, meddling prelates abroad, and the evident lack of comprehension of the new American sit-

uation by the authorities in Rome. Yet, under his able direction, the
foundations for the evangelizing mission of the American church on the
levels of both proclamation and praxis were firmly laid. As we analyze
the rest of this period to 1908, we shall shift to a topical treatment of it
in order better to view the confluence and interdependence—or the concrete lack thereof—of the *two moments* of the evangelization process as
presented in the earlier parts of this study.

2. The Catholic Clergy and Their Formation

While an endless flow of immigrants from Catholic Europe kept
arriving at America's eastern doors, and the young nation kept rapidly
expanding westward, these happenings with their immediate needs demanded concrete and practical solutions to this here-and-now situation.
The Church's meeting these needs required an almost total involvement
on the level of praxis, for which the hierarchy and clergy provided initiative and leadership. The major thrust of the American Catholic church's
efforts at evangelization during this century and beyond thus centered
around the *moment* of practical Christian living. And, since the success
of these efforts for the most part depended upon the calibre and leadership role of the church's ministers, our attention now focuses on them
and their spiritual and theological formation.

The self-sacrificing dedication of the American Catholic clergy at
this time won the admiration of one Protestant observer from Great
Britain who in 1833 wrote:

> I am not a Catholic, but I cannot suffer prejudice of any
> sort to prevent my doing justice to a body of Christian minis-
> ters, whose zeal can be animated by no hope of worldly re-
> ward, and whose humble lives are passed in diffusing the influ-
> ence of divine truth, and communicating to the meanest and
> most despised of mankind the blessed comforts of religion.[26]

The intellectual training of the clergy, whether attained at home or
abroad, left much to be desired. "For the paranoia, if that not be too
strong a word, that took possession of the papacy and the Roman Curia
in the period known as the Restoration, gave birth to a siege mentality
that ultimately penetrated the whole Catholic community."[27] Contemporary discoveries and currents of thought were mistrusted and looked
down upon as threatening "eternal truths." Future priests for the American church trained at St. Patrick's College in Maynooth received their
instructions in moral theology from the textbooks (supplied by the Propaganda in Rome) of Paul Gariel Antoine, S.J. (d. 1743), a rigid moral-

ist of the French school. Such teaching only served to strengthen the Jansenistic strain of these Irish clerics in regard to moral issues, especially with regard to sexual problems, that continued to color the American Catholic psyche for well more than a century. In France the major emphasis was on forming devout priests rather than men of learning. Americans sent to study for the priesthood at Louvain and Rome hardly fared any better during these years, when philosophy was enforced not by reason but by authority and learnt by rote and by sheer memory. Only at the Catholic university circles of Tübingen and Munich was there any semblance of genuine intellectual and theological vitality, the spirit of which found its way to some of the German communities in the United States. What little intellectual output the American priest had time for necessarily tended to be defensive and apologetical by nature, given the prevailing anti-Catholic bias of many of his fellow citizens.

Archbishop Maréchal wrote one of his students in Paris, and his eventual successor, Samuel Eccleston, that if he were to prepare himself carefully in homiletics, he would

> . . . render to the Church in America an infinitely more important service than if he taught them the learned works of our most celebrated theologians or the lessons of Canon Law. . . .[28]

The Archbishop noted that the way most newly ordained in the country read and preached the Gospel was abominable and a source of derision for Protestants and of embarrassment for Catholics. Putting such criticism aside for the moment, M. V. Gannon observes that

> . . . the priest of the immigrants was to his own people nothing short of an intellectual giant, skilled in theology but, because of his educational advantages, competent also to give advice on politics, law, education, mechanics, pharmacy, banking, and social reform. The immigrant's view of him was part of the European heritage which they transplanted in the United States; it was likewise born of many fruitful experiences in this country where the American priest rather remarkably lived up to the expectations his people had of him.[29]

The spiritual formation provided in the seminary centered around a rigid schedule of Mass, prayer, meditation and other devotional practices with a primary emphasis placed on the "priestly virtues" of humility, obedience and the respect owed to superiors. Yet, despite the limitations of formation and training—at St. Mary's in Baltimore, for example, the first seminarians often found themselves necessarily spending more time teaching in schools and working in other apostolates than they did studying theology—the American clergy on the whole in the nineteenth century found themselves sufficiently equipped to advance the mission of evangelization required for their time. Oftentimes their best training came from frequent contact with many self-sacrificing pioneer bishops and priests. This is not to claim, however, that the bishops and priests were all saintly missionaries; their human limitations, lack of charity and self-seeking ambitions are also well documented.[30] Nevertheless, their overall dedication and practical wisdom served well in implanting a knowledge of salvation and a love of the Lord and his Church in the hearts of the faithful.

3. *Immigration and Acculturation*

While the intellectual and spiritual formation of the clergy exhibited basically a foreign and rigidly defensive cast, the concrete exigencies of the Church in the United States required a pragmatic prudence, implying a familiarity with and a certain adaptability to the ways and customs of this new secular and democratic society. "Americanizing" tendencies, therefore, were not lacking, and often were wholeheartedly supported and espoused by a goodly number of the hierarchy and clergy. J. T. Ellis succinctly describes this situation and its accompanying problematic:

> Willy-nilly the American Church had become catholic in the broadest sense, and the problem of how best to mold the congeries of nationalities that composed its faithful into a stable element of the American population became its most pressing occupation.[31]

Xenophobia quickly spread across the nation compounding the problem as horde upon horde of immigrants came ashore, most of them Catholic —one and a half million out of some 2.8 million immigrants from 1790 to 1870, with another 6.6 million Catholics arriving in the succeeding half-century.[32] American Protestants began to organize in the nativist movement to protect themselves, their jobs, and "the Kingdom of God in America" from this foreign "papist rabble" who refused religious assimilation and owed subservience to a foreign potentate. In 1830, an anti-Catholic weekly, the *Protestant*, was launched; in 1834 a nativist mob burned the Ursuline Convent in Charlestown, Massachusetts; in 1844 two Catholic churches were destroyed and thirteen people were killed by rioters in Philadelphia; and in 1853 Know-Nothing demonstrations protested the visit of the papal nuncio Archbishop Gaetano Bedini. Later on, the American Protective Association (APA) and the Ku Klux Klan would continue to promote anti-Catholic bigotry well into the twentieth century.

The immediate response of American Catholicism to this seemingly endless flowing tide from abroad was to give first priority to the preservation of the immigrant's faith. To this end churches, schools, and all types of charitable institutions were erected and the construction of a strong and vigorous Catholic subculture became a major preoccupation. Parishes for the various nationalities were also established. After 1850 the makeup of the American Catholic hierarchy had changed from Anglo-American and French background to become predominantly Irish and German corresponding to the two largest immigrant groups. In the process of acculturating and caring for these new charges, "the American Church came to be noted for cultural isolation, hierarchical centralization and institutional proliferation."[33] Yet she had become truly American: pragmatic, practical, adaptive, flexible. From its inception, the American Catholic hierarchy, adapting to the needs and customs of the culture, has been a forerunner in collegiality, having met in seven Provincial Councils between 1829 and 1849, and three Plenary Councils of Baltimore in 1852, 1866, and 1884. From 1890 onwards the bishops met annually with non-canonical status until the formation of the National Catholic Welfare Conference (NCWC) whose statutes were approved by the Holy See in 1922.

At these national meetings, the actual situation and pressing needs of the American church were reviewed, and pastoral letters were issued for the instruction and education of the clergy and laity alike. In the height of the nativist crisis, "the Council of Baltimore in 1843 showed wisdom when it recommended to the faithful that they tie their social bonds tighter with their non-Catholic neighbors. For the hierarchy, this was a serene way of expressing its desire to forget the recent outrages."[34] The clergy were constantly exhorted to a more fervent spirit of prayer, meditation, the reading and study of the Scriptures, etc.; the laity were urged to more fervent devotion, attendance at Mass, frequent communion, while also being requested to support the Church, Catholic education, the clergy, and the missions.

> You are to co-operate with us in preaching the Gospel of Christ by the care of your households and by the good example you give to all who come within your sphere of influence.[35]

In addition, all were asked to show patience in tribulation, especially in the midst of strong anti-Catholic prejudice, as well as being warned of the dangers of riches and intemperance. In their pastoral letter of 1884 the bishops took the opportunity to answer the accusation of double allegiance by firmly stating:

> We repudiate . . . the assertion that we need to lay aside any of our devotedness to our Church, to be true Americans; the insinuation that we need to abate any of our love for our country's principles and institutions, to be faithful Catholics. . . . The spirit of American freedom is not one of anarchy or license. It essentially involves love of order, respect for rightful authority, and obedience to just laws. There is nothing in the character of the most liberty-loving American which could hinder his reverential submission to the Divine authority of Our Lord, or to the like authority delegated by Him to His Apostles and His Church.[36]

The nativist accusations and bigotry in the end had the tendency to force Catholics to prove that they could be just as patriotic and loyal as any other American; they also served to strengthen the Catholic Church in the United States by providing one more good reason for displaying a unified presence. But basically, as A. Greeley observes:

> The patriotism of the Church leaders of the nineteenth century was part of their conviction that the freedom and democracy of the American republic constituted not only the most impressive polity that man had ever put together but also provided an atmosphere for the Church more favorable than any it had ever known.[37]

The American Catholic church thus sought on the practical level to incarnate the faith in a given historical, social, and cultural milieu the likes of which knew no prior existence. The call of this situation was unique, demanding an immediate response. With little self-conscious reflection but with living faith, Christlike charity, and undaunted hope, American Catholicism set its hands to the plow and did not hesitate until accused of a "phantom heresy" by Rome.

A convert from transcendentalism and the Utopian community of Brook Farm, Isaac Hecker, in 1858 founded the Paulist Fathers, the first religious community of men in the United States, for the purpose of better relating Catholicism to the American culture. The Paulists gave retreats, preached missions, and administered parishes. Truly American and truly Christian, Hecker insisted on the need to respect the dignity and the uniqueness of individual members of the community. At Rome, he openly expressed his conviction that "the longing after a more spiritual life is one of the characteristics of the American people."[38] Also, totally loyal to the voluntaryism of the American democratic spirit, he championed the close involvement of the laity with Church activity: "The blood must circulate through the limbs otherwise we shall die of apoplexy and the laity of paralysis."[39]

Other leading elements of the Church, too, responded well to the unique American opportunities for evangelization, such as in 1893 when Cardinal Gibbons lead twenty Catholic lecturers to the "Parliament of Religions" in Chicago, only to have Pope Leo XIII two years later forbid any such future Catholic participation in interfaith assemblies. Rome continued to grow leery and suspicious of the American experience, and in January 1899 Leo XIII issued his apostolic letter *Testem benevolentia* condemning the heresy of "Americanism," itself concocted from a hurried French translation of Father Hecker's biography. Among other things,

> . . . the pope condemned the proposition that "in order more easily to bring over to Catholic doctrine those who dissent from it the church should adapt itself somewhat to our advanced civilization and relaxing her ancient vigor, show some indulgence to modern popular theories and methods" . . . [that] the church should imitate in its internal life the liberty of civil society. Finally, Leo condemned the theories which were attributed to Hecker: the rejection of external religious guidance, the depreciation of passive in favor of active virtues and the dislike of religious vows.[40]

This ambiguous assignment of heresy thus tended to deaden the Americanizing impulse promoted by certain segments of the American hierarchy. But the translation of a living faith to the exigencies and circumstances of the American culture continued. And no single medium played a greater role in this translation than the vast and growing network of Catholic education.

4. *Catholic Education and Instruction in the Faith*

The task of evangelization by proclamation, or the exposition of orthodox instruction in the faith, assumed different forms, the most common being the sermon preached during Sunday Mass and at other religious devotions. The quality of such instruction and its kerygmatic character at this time is somewhat questionable, for the American bishops at the First Provincial Council of Baltimore in their pastoral letter to the clergy found it necessary to say:

> Brethren, we entreat you, not to be taken in the delusive snare which has entangled several, who, leaving the law and the gospel, have wasted their time and destroyed their usefulness by indulging in the study of vain and frivolous ephemeral productions, under the pretext of acquiring a pleasing style. The truths of religion should be delivered in becoming language, but it is a sad mistake to leave the substance in order to acquire the appearance.[41]

Another popular form of religious instruction was the parochial mission introduced from Europe with the arrival of such religious orders of men as the Vincentians (1817), the Redemptorists (1832), the Oblates of Mary Immaculate (1847) and the Passionists (1852). Over a period of one, two, or even four weeks, morning and evening sermons were preached on basic topics: salvation, the Four Last Things, confession, Holy Communion, Mass. Special sessions were also held to which non-Catholics were invited to hear an explanation of the Catholic faith. The custom of Forty Hours adoration was introduced to the United States early in this period and soon became widespread, providing further opportunity for teaching about Mass and the Eucharist. These, as well as other popular religious devotions and customs, kept the faith alive in the hearts of the poor, and most often uneducated, immigrant.

The children of the immigrants received their education in the faith from an ever-increasing number of parochial schools. It was this private educational system that also helped acculturate them to their new homeland. As J. T. Ellis points out:

> Through the medium of Catholic parochial schools, which by 1840 numbered at least 200 . . . the children of the immigrants were mingled with the children of the native-born Catholics. . . . The curriculum of these schools was in large measure that of the standard curriculum of the private Protestant and early public schools, with the exception that they taught classes in the Catholic religion rather than classes in the Bible and Protestant beliefs. Many teachers were native born Americans who used English exclusively in the classrooms, and

even in those parochial schools serving non-English speaking immigrants, notably Germans, some English was used in the instruction.[42]

By no means did this educational system reach a majority of Catholic children, but it did embrace an ever-increasing number so that by 1900 there were some four thousand of these schools in the country. Continuing to be disaffected with the public school system, the American bishops at the Third Plenary Council of Baltimore (1884) mandated parochial schools for every parish. But, beyond this level of elementary teaching, there was very little Catholic leadership in education. Bishop Spalding of Peoria received little encouragement from his confrères over the years in his long drawn-out attempt to establish an American Catholic university for graduate study in theology and other disciplines. Another lone voice in this regard was Archbishop Ireland who in his sermon marking the centennial of the American hierarchy proclaimed:

> This is an intellectual age. . . . Catholics must excel in religious knowledge. . . . They must be in the foreground of intellectual movements of all kinds. The age will not take kindly to religious knowledge separated from secular knowledge.[43]

History, unfortunately, would prove that hardly anyone was listening.

It was the same Third Plenary Council of Baltimore that proposed and ordered the publishing of the famed "Baltimore Catechism." Previous to this time a variety of foreign catechisms were in use in the United States, such as Tuberville's *An Abridgement of the Christian Doctrine: with Proofs of Scripture on Points Converted, Catechistically explained by Way of Question and Answer* (printed ca. 1649). In the words of G. Sloyan, "Tuberville's catechism is for adults, for late medievals under siege of heresy, for those who savor phrases like, 'fidelity, which makes us punctual observers of our covenant and promises.' "[44] At the Council's request, Monsignor Januarius de Concilio is said to have provided the text of a catechism in a week, which then went to Bishop Spalding for further revisions. "It never went out to teachers."[45] The catechism was approved only by Cardinal Gibbons and not by the conference of archbishops as recommended by the Council, "for once the Council was dissolved the archbishops of the country never attended to it further except to hear a chorus of complaint against it in their annual meeting of 1895."[46] Its format, geared toward memorization, had little contact with or resemblance to the Good News, yet it continued to be the basic, and, oftentimes, only source of religious knowledge for generations of American Catholics. Such forms of religious instruction almost begged the criticism levelled against them by Protestant observers, such as R. Baird who in 1842 wrote *Religion in America* wherein he accused Roman Catholicism of being unevangelical and consequently was opposed to public funds for "sectarian schools in which neither the Sacred Scriptures, nor any part of them are read."[47] In all fairness it must be said that Catholic education in America at this time was hampered by the prevailing counter-Reformation attitudes coming out of Rome and affecting the Church universal.

Another important instrument of religious instruction and acculturation was the Catholic press. In 1822 John England, the first Bishop of Charleston, founded the first American Catholic weekly, the *United States Catholic Miscellany*, which sought to enlighten Catholics as well as answer nativist misrepresentations and accusations against Catholicism. "During the next two decades Catholic newspapers were established elsewhere in the country at the rate of about one a year."[48] Thus, despite her obvious poverty in preaching and teaching doctrine, the American Catholic church utilized well the resources of her parochial schools and her diocesan press to evangelize and acculturate the faithful with regard to the practical exigencies and expectations of being both a Catholic and an American. They fostered one's becoming a living witness to the life of faith as encouraged by the American hierarchy in 1843:

> Your strict integrity in the daily concerns of life, your fidelity in the fulfillment of all your engagements, your peaceful demeanor, your obedience to the laws, your respect for public functionaries, your unaffected exercise of charity in the many occasions which the miseries and sufferings of our fellowmen present; in fine, your sincere virtue will confound those vain men whose ingenuity and industry are exerted to cast suspicion on our principles, and evoke against us all the worst passions of human nature.[49]

5. *Social Issues and the Catholic Church in America*

On the level of practical implementation and incarnation of the Gospel in the historical, social and cultural milieu of nineteenth-century America, two important issues stand out as worthy of investigation here: Negro slavery and labor unions.

Many Catholic plantation owners—including the Jesuits and the Carrolls themselves—held Negro slaves since they were first introduced to colonial Maryland.

Official Catholic doctrine held that slavery was not a necessary evil; it taught that slavery, thought of theoretically and apart from specific abuses to human dignity, was not opposed to the divine or natural law. Manumission was encouraged wherever circumstances would permit the slave to better his condition, and strong emphasis was always placed on the moral obligation of slaveholders to treat their subjects with justice and charity and to see that they received religious instruction.[50]

These in short were the views espoused as the Church's teaching by Bishop Francis P. Kenrick in his *Theologia Moralis* (3 vols., 1840-43). S. Ahlstrom comments:

But his teaching shows a persistent failure to clarify the differences between the actual American form of slavery and that which the church had condoned. He has been justly accused of equivocation.[51]

As a result, American Catholics expressed a full range of opinion on the slavery issue, but the pastoral letters of the American hierarchy between 1840 and 1852 continued to remain silent. As H. J. Nolan evaluates the situation: "Even if the council had promulgated a statement or decree concerning the institution of slavery, it probably would have served to keep alive a subject of controversy which moderate men at the moment hoped to stifle by silence."[52]

The Church, however, was not negligent toward the Negroes. In 1835 Bishop John England founded a school for free Negro children in Charleston, and nine years later Peter R. Kenrick, Bishop of St. Louis, did the same for free and slave children in his see city only to have the local civil authorities step in and recommend its closing. With emancipation, some 100,000 Catholic Negroes were set free. During the Civil War, Catholics fought for and defended the cause of both sides. Furthermore, American Catholicism because of its union with Rome and the prudent silence of its hierarchy preserved its corporate unity more than any other religious body throughout the crisis, as the Second Plenary Council of Baltimore in 1866 gave striking proof when forty-five bishops from all over the country met to carry on their common tasks. In their pastoral letter issued at this council, the bishops stated:

A new and most extensive field of charity and devotedness has been opened to us, by the emancipation of the immense slave population.[53]

No organized follow-up, however, emerged from the Council; and a "once-in-centuries opportunity" was lost according to Nolan. J. T. Ellis further elaborates:

> Thus through a combination of racial prejudice, timidity, and a scarcity of manpower and resources, the chance for large-scale conversion of the Negroes to Catholicism after the Civil War gradually slipped away.[54]

The years following the Civil War saw increasing industrialization and urbanization with large numbers of Catholic immigrants settling in the nation's big industrial centers. Here the Catholic Church continued to show her solicitude for the immigrants. The various national parishes provided the community atmosphere and security that the immigrants had known in the villages and small towns of Europe. As M. Marty points out, "people who had been less religious in traditional European Catholicism found that it paid to work at the faith and be supportive in America. They found themselves by building community."[55] In these cities Catholicism soon became the church of the workingman.

Unlike her sister churches in Europe, the American Catholic church identified with the laborer and his plight rather than with the "Establishment." Certain influential members among the American hierarchy championed the workingman's cause and successfully intercepted Rome's would-be fatal condemnation of the Knights of Labor, the first major American labor organization. As a highly secret society, it won the suspicion of a number of bishops who, indeed, wished to have it condemned. With wisdom and foresight, Cardinal Gibbons wrote the Congregation de Propaganda Fide in 1887, stating:

> To lose the heart of the people would be a misfortune for which the friendship of the few rich and powerful would be no compensation.[56]

He maintained that only their united strength could win a hearing of their just grievances from capitalists whose power and wealth subjected them to abuse. At the same time heavy Catholic membership in the Knights strongly helped balk socialist control of the American labor movement. In the words of J. Hennessy: "Catholic workingmen shared the general self-image of their peers. They were incipient capitalists, not members of the proletariat."[57]

Once again the practical foresight and wisdom of the Catholic Church in America advanced the process of evangelization by remaining in close contact with its people and their needs, by providing community and by defending the cause of the poor. Granted that throughout the nineteenth century there were many human failures, much sinfulness, and lost opportunities (such as the situation of the freed Negroes after the Civil War, and the loss of 250,000 Eastern Rite Catholics who joined Russian Orthodoxy after 1890); yet on the whole the American church was truly active and dedicated to the mission of making present in a concrete community and situation Christ's love and concern for his people. At the same time, however, overdependence of the immigrant on the Church would give rise to future problems. As Hennessy depicts the situation:

> The church also became part of the immigrants' defensive armor. Obedience to the parish priest rather than thinking for oneself solved petty but vexing problems. Defensive groups find strength in blind obedience. Concentration on personal discipline removed the need for concern with broader issues.[58]

Such an attitude, indeed, became very problematic when it was carried over to a later day.

C. American Catholicism in the Twentieth Century (1908-1960)

The major areas of concern already treated in the previous section were to prevail into the twentieth century. Catholic immigration continued unabated into the 1920s when it became greatly restricted by law. In the age of American imperialism Catholics followed the prevailing view despite the "Americanist" crisis. The independent Catholic school system was growing and strengthening. But the dual crisis of "Americanism" and "Modernism" stifled whatever initiative might have appeared on the levels of intellectual and theological inquiry. As S. Ahlstrom observed:

> In matters of theology and philosophy . . . seminaries and institutions of higher learning were providing only the minimum essentials for the priesthood and laity despite the great social and intellectual transformations which were in progress. Handbooks and compendia sufficed. The "Sulpician tradition" of the nineteenth century perpetuated itself uncreatively. The Thomistic revival promoted by Pope Leo XIII made slow advances. The vast problems of history, culture, science, and the social order—realms in which nineteenth-cen-

tury thinking had left a revolutionary legacy—were left not only unresolved but unapproached. Even among the leaders of Americanism few went beyond a call for accommodating the church to American ways, and those who did were warned against dangerous innovations in Pope Leo's encyclical. Hecker and Brownson won few disciples; and Father John A. Zahm of Notre Dame University, whose *Evolution and Dogma* (1896) attempted rapprochement with Darwinism was silenced. Though founded in a moment of educational idealism, the Catholic University of America lacked the resources to become the great center of learning which its founders dreamed.[59]

Throughout the nineteenth century there had been a certain "leakage" to Protestant churches of Catholics who in the rural South and West were often left without priests and churches. To tend to this problem, the National Catholic Rural Life Conference was organized in 1922. A number of such initiatives and continued hard work on the part of the clergy and religious again provided for the spiritual and material well-being of the faithful and the acculturation of the Catholic immigrant. Given the wide variety of racial and national strains, only one sizable and enduring schism developed—the establishment of the Polish National Catholic Church in 1907, which today, headquartered in Scranton, Pennsylvania, numbers around a quarter million communicants. The American church's efforts at evangelization begun in the nineteenth century continued into the twentieth basically unaltered. The new initiatives undertaken in this area prior to the opening of the Second Vatican Council can be considered under two headings: the National Catholic Welfare Conference (NCWC) and Social Action, and the New Catholicism.

1. *The NCWC and Social Action*

The National Catholic War Council was founded in 1917 to aid and coordinate Catholic participation in the war effort, from providing material assistance to chaplains to acting as an official agency promoting war-loan drives. Impressed by its success, members of the episcopal committee sought to convert it into a peacetime coordinating agency for Catholic affairs after the war's end. Its name was then changed to the National Catholic Welfare Council (soon altered to "Conference" with Roman approval in order to allay the fears of those members of the American hierarchy who saw it as a possible threat to their jurisdiction of their own dioceses). The original five departments of the Conference included Education, Lay Activities, Press, Social Action and Missions.

Speaking on behalf of the American hierarchy, its Administrative Board issued official policy pronouncements in these various areas of concern. One of the most important of its early statements was a pamphlet which appeared on February 12, 1919, entitled *Social Reconstruction: A General Review of the Problems and Survey of Remedies.* Authored by the director of the Social Action Department, Monsignor John A. Ryan, it "embodied a detailed set of principles and suggestions on such subjects as the need for minimum wage legislation, unemployment, health, and old-age insurance for workers, age limit for child labor, legal enforcement of the right of labor to organize, and need for a public housing program and for a national employment service."[60] The pamphlet was immediately accused of being "socialistic propaganda" by the president of the National Association of Manufacturers. During the 1930s eleven out of the twelve major proposals in this so-called "Bishops' Program of Social Reconstruction" became law, attesting to the progressive character of Catholic leadership in this particular field.

In the 1920s modern technocratic America came of age and urbanization characterized its prevalent mood. "On the popular level a dominant theme of American religion," writes S. Ahlstrom, "was exhibited by a new wave of best sellers, often conservative and non-committal on social issues but preoccupied with practical personal problems of health, harmony and successful living."[61] In 1925 an advertising executive, Bruce Barton, wrote a work on Jesus entitled *The Man Nobody Knows*, which won widespread popularity for its portrayal of the Man from Nazareth as one of the world's top-ranking business organizers. "The sanest religion is business" wrote Edward Purinton in the *Independent* in 1921. Against such a background then it can be seen why "Catholic employers . . . did not take kindly to the three 'Programmes'— *Rerum novarum*, the Bishops' Program of Social Reconstruction and the Bishops' Pastoral of the same year. These Catholics did not believe the Holy Father could possibly know anything about digging subways or getting honest work from 'Wops' and 'Hunkies.' "[62] Indeed, the efforts of Ryan and others promoting Catholic social reform "attracted relatively little grass-roots support, made only small impact on Catholic education, and at no time could command wide universal enthusiasm in the Catholic press."[63]

In the 1930s the Great Depression brought bishops, priests, and laymen alike to come to terms with the dire economic situation. Their confidence in the American way of life was severely shaken, "so that they began to take seriously those sections of the papal encyclicals that condemned unrestrained liberal capitalism."[64] In the wake of Pope Pius

XI's encyclical *Quadragesimo Anno* (1931), the NCWC's Department of Social Action issued another programmatic pamphlet, *Organized Social Justice—An Economic Program for the United States Applying Pius XI's Great Encyclical on Social Life* (1935), which was signed by 131 prominent Catholic social thinkers. During these years the Catholic Worker Movement was founded by Peter Maurin and Dorothy Day. The latter is a former Socialist who became a Catholic and started *The Catholic Worker*, a monthly paper which soon reached a circulation of more than 100,000. She also established houses of hospitality from coast to coast "to personalize Catholic sympathy for the harassed victims of depression, especially the homeless and unemployed worker."[65] In 1937 the Association of Catholic Trade Unionists (ACTU) was formed to help Catholics work effectively in their union organization drives and to instruct them in regard to the Church's teaching on labor and industrial relations.

Another prominent voice of social reform heard during these years was that of the "radio priest," Charles E. Coughlin, who by 1936 had an estimated ten million weekly listeners. He, at first, expounded upon the papal social encyclicals of 1891 and 1931 emphasizing their criticism of unchecked free enterprise. Disillusioned with the New Deal and President Roosevelt, he founded the Union Party to challenge FDR in the 1936 election. Manipulating the rhetoric of hate and fear, he soon espoused anti-Semitism as well as anti-Communism, and rallied to his side the religio-political Right. The resounding defeat of the Union Party, however, soon silenced his rhetoric. In 1936 Paul Hanley Furfey of Catholic University published his *Fire on the Earth* setting forth his basic theory of radical Catholicism. Influenced by the Catholic Worker Movement and convinced of the inadequacy of the social sciences to effect real reform, he maintained that "the only thing that would change society was the gospel, if people would truly live by it."[66] His prophetic message and denunciations of materialism, individualism, violence, racism, and inequality in American society received only a small hearing.

Despite these attempts and efforts to awaken the Christian consciences of Catholics and to bring the gospel message to bear on the burning social issues of the day, most members of the Church seemed to have other things more important to attend to. One diocesan paper in 1932 stated in an editorial:

Catholics should not be hewers of wood and the drawers of water. They should lead upright lives, but they should also, if possible, make a big success in life.[67]

Thus, D. O'Brien asserts that:

> It was one of the conditions of the church's success in holding
> the masses in the faith that it was willing to assist this yearning
> for mobility and status while tolerating many American prac-
> tices inimical to its teachings, which sometimes meant passive
> acceptance of racial discrimination, silence in the face of urban
> political corruption and explicit support for the dominant so-
> cial and economic values.[68]

Indeed, the Americanization of the immigrant Catholic has largely been
a regional adaptation process, going back historically to the slavery
question when local values and mores determined one's stance on the
issue. Taking a backward glance at predominant American attitudes, J.
Fichter wrote in 1960:

> Catholics share in the anti-Semitism of the Northeast, in the
> isolationism of the Midwest, in the prejudices against Mex-
> icans in the Southwest. Catholics acted like Californians when
> Japanese-Americans were dispossessed and sent to relocation
> camps, like Texans when off-shore oil disputes were discussed,
> and like Ciceronians when Negro families moved into the
> white neighborhoods in Illinois. On this level we are dealing
> with the moral and social problems on which the American
> people are confused, and on which Catholics demonstrate their
> achieved Americanization by sharing in the confusion.[69]

2. *The New Catholicism and Countervailing Influences*

This designation, "the New Catholicism," has been applied by S.
Ahlstrom to describe a new consciousness that appeared among some
American Catholics during the post-Depression years. It was inspired by
and paralleled the pastoral and theological ferment in Europe which at
the time was seeking to rediscover the true nature and scope of Church
and mission. This revitalization was evidenced in both a liturgical and a
biblical renewal, and eventually gave rise to a new historical consciousness within the Church. Headlining this new spirit in American Catholicism in the area of social reform were Dorothy Day and Peter Maurin.
"The lay apostolate which the Catholic Worker Movement inspired was
. . . marked by intense sacramental piety, self-abnegation, and
prayer."[70] Their influence continued as a strong but subdued force into
the 1960s. The "radio priest," Father Coughlin, gave way to Monsignor

Fulton J. Sheen, the reigning celebrity of "The Catholic Hour" in the 1940s and of the extremely popular television series "Life Is Worth Living" in the 1950s. Through his numerous publications and media programs, he espoused a total Catholic worldview from the Thomistic viewpoint, and succeeded in making numerous converts including Henry Ford II and Claire Booth Luce.

The weekly magazine *Commonweal* was founded by a Catholic layman, Michael Williams, in 1924. It soon became the guiding and intellectual force behind "liberal Catholicism," keeping the American church somewhat aware of the inadequacies of the nation's social system. The founding of other top-quality Catholic periodicals during this period also mirrored a certain intellectual and theological renaissance. *The Catholic Biblical Quarterly* appeared in 1939, and the Jesuit-edited *Theological Studies* began publication in 1940. It was in this latter periodical that the Jesuits Gustave Weigel and John Courtney Murray did much of their groundbreaking work, "Weigel in ecclesiology and ecumenical studies, Murray in the area of Church-State relations, religious freedom, natural law in public life, and morality of warfare."[71] Both had wide influence in the intellectual community outside the faith, as well as exercising leadership within the Church. Murray's thoughts are strikingly evident in Vatican II's Declaration on Religious Liberty.

Saint John's Abbey in Minnesota at this time became the center for liturgical renewal in America. Father Virgil Michael founded *Orate Fratres* (later renamed *Worship*) as the pioneer English mouthpiece of this apostolate. In Michael's understanding of the liturgy,

> It is not too much to say that the survival of true social human life will be achieved only under the inspiration of the liturgical life, since the specific divine purpose of the latter is to transform human nature after the mind of Christ and inspire it into a life replete like His love of God and man.[72]

This conception of the liturgy, nevertheless, was obviously foreign to most American Catholics of that time who lacked proper training and the necessary aids for following and participating in the Latin prayers.

More popular programs influencing the laity were the Cana Conference and the Christian Family Movement developed in Chicago during the 1940s. The Cana Conference "fit in perfectly with the great emphasis on family life in the postwar world, and was also easily legitimated by ecclesiastical authorities as being a response to the soaring divorce rate in the late 1940s."[73] The end of the Second World War also saw a great influx of hundreds of young Americans fresh from the military entering contemplative monasteries. Thomas Merton's autobiography, *The Seven Storey Mountain*, became a national best-seller giving "many reading Americans of all creeds their first glimpse of the mysteries of a contemplative monastery."[74]

Despite all this vitality and fervor in attempting to understand, live and proclaim the Gospel in modern twentieth-century America, such evangelizing efforts for the vast majority of American Catholics would come to nought. The "average" American Catholic was basically being driven by stronger undercurrents of another so-called "civil religion," i.e., the American Way of Life. W. Herberg spoke of this latter as "the characteristic American religion, undergirding life and overarching American society despite indubitable differences of religion, section, culture, and class."[75] A religious revival of sorts swept the United States after World War II. Being a church member during this Cold War era was being a true American, since the USSR and its Communist allies were committed to atheism. In the 1950s President Eisenhower himself symbolized this generalized religiosity and self-satisfied patriotic moralism, having once stated: "Our government makes no sense unless it is founded on a deeply felt religious faith—and I don't care what it is."[76]

In this post-war period the American Catholic finally came of age in American society.

> The G.I. Bill of Rights opened college education to millions of Catholics, promoting their ascendence from the ghetto to middle class suburbs. The C.I.O. unions brought improvements in income, living conditions and status to many Catholics who remained in the factories. Changes in national and international life reduced tensions between Catholics and others, gradually overcoming the minority consciousness prominent in the Church in earlier years.[77]

Proof of the Catholic's "arrival" in American society came with the election in 1960 of John F. Kennedy as the first Catholic President of the United States. But Americanization and acceptance of Catholics in a pluralistic and secularistic "post-Puritan" or "post-Protestant" America was indicative of another inadvertent, yet potently underlying and much less encouraging factor. W. Herberg explicated it by asking and answering the question:

> How can Americans be so religious and so secularistic at the same time? The answer is that for increasing numbers of

Americans religion serves a function largely unrelated to the content of faith, the function of defining their identity and providing them with a context of belonging in the great wilderness of a mobile American society. Indeed, for such a purpose, the authentic content of faith may even prove a serious handicap, for if it is Jewish or Christian faith it carries a prophetic impact which serves rather to unadjust than to adjust, to emphasize the ambiguity of every earthly form of belonging rather than to let the individual rest secure in his "sociability." For this reason the typical American has developed a remarkable capacity for being serious about religion without taking religion seriously. . . . His ideas, values, and standards he takes from what is so often really his ultimate commitment, the American Way of Life. He combines the two—his religion and his culture—by making the former the expression of the latter, his religion an expression of the "moral and spiritual values of democracy."[78]

From the empirical level, having gathered all the statistical and factual evidence, on the eve of the Second Vatican Council, the evangelization, acculturation, and growth of the Catholic Church in the United States of America appeared to be a huge success. A few short years would show, however, that the evangelizing apostolate of the American church had hardly begun.

CONCLUSIONS

This chapter itself has already been a historical summarization of the evangelizing process in the American church. Therefore, instead of presenting a further summary at this point, we will now draw some general conclusions as to what has been successfully undertaken and accomplished thus far regarding this mission, while at the same time looking for indications of developments and situations that are in need of further positive considerations. The overall understanding of the evangelizing mission in the American Catholic church during this entire period, were it to have been subjected to systematic reflection, would have been conceived primarily in terms of missionary outreach, implantation of the Church, and convert-making—general categories encompassing the universal Church's comprehension of this mission in the heydays of Christendom. From this viewpoint, America was considered missionary territory under the jurisdiction of the Congregation de Propaganda Fide. But beyond limited contact with the natives, most of the Catholic Church's time and efforts were devoted to maintaining and supporting the faith of

the already baptized, who emigrated here from their European home-
lands. To this extent and purpose the American missionary endeavor
can be considered eminently successful. Looked upon, nevertheless,
from our wider interpretation of evangelization, one may still apply this
same judgment with certain qualifications.

The Spanish and French missions on the North American continent
for well nigh three centuries embodied the best of the medieval tradition
of bringing the faith of Christendom to the unbaptized "pagans." This
interpretation of the evangelizing mission with much subsequent refine-
ment dates back to the times of St. Boniface and his work among the
Germans. The self-sacrificing and heroic efforts of these Spanish friars
and French Blackrobes brought the Christian faith and cultural advancement to the Indian peoples among whom they lived and served with
such total dedication and admirable respect for human dignity. The enduring fruits of their labors later contributed a certain cultural enrich-
ment and stability to the young American Catholic church spreading
westward and keeping pace with the new nation's expanding frontiers—a
contribution which still remains very much in evidence in some parts of
the country.

Founded upon the philosophical principles of the Enlightenment and
the religious tenets of Puritanism and other Protestant sectarians, the
United States of America from its earliest days nurtured the growth of a
genuinely pluralistic and secular society. Legally sanctioning the separation of Church and State and granting freedom of religion, the federal
Constitution embarked upon a totally new experience in the government
of nations. This state of affairs thus both fostered and shaped the growth
of the young Catholic Church in this predominantly "Protestant" nation. Throughout the whole period of time covered in this chapter, Catholicism in America has been considered a minority religion and a
foreign element. The Church in America had to confront, cope with and
adapt to situations previously unheard of and unimagined by Rome;
she had little time for theory and self-reflection. All her available talents
and resources had to be concentrated upon the more immediate practical tasks at hand, namely, caring for and acculturating the Catholic
immigrant, while supporting and strengthening the faith of all her
members. This involved a genuine effort to build Christian community.
As D. O'Brien has observed:

> This fantastic expenditure of men and resources to meet social
> as well as religious needs derived in the first instance not from
> a theory of the priest's role or from papal statements on social
> justice but from the deep commitment of bishops and priests to

the care of the people. "The energies of the ordinary clergy were almost totally consumed in pastoral work," Thomas T. McAvoy has written, and this pastoral work was defined in the broadest terms of charity and service.[79]

This undertaking of the Catholic Church in America to adapt, incarnate and live the Gospel in this unique historical, cultural and social circumstance can only be judged as a genuine objective example of Christian orthopraxis. Here, living faith was applied to a concrete existential experience with little if any prior reflection. Indeed, the formal teaching, proclamation and presentation of the "orthodox" content of faith during this period seemed to offer, at least on the pedagogical level, little that was relevant and applicable to the contemporary situation.

Catholics were instructed on "what" they must believe and assent to, and on a certain intellectual level they tenaciously, though simply and often uncomprehendingly, held to and defended this doctrinal belief system. They unquestioningly accepted doctrinal and moral formulas taught by the Church even if they did not understand their immediate applicability to the present time. Membership in the Church offered them the experience of community, identity, and a sense of belonging amidst the prejudices, fears, and other dizzying experiences of this rapidly moving world. The Church was solicitous of their needs, looking after their spiritual and material well-being while acculturating them to American society. In their poverty, suffering and disparagement, they needed the Church, and the Church was there at their side. Yet the Church itself could not remain unaffected, nor fully insulate her members from the culture and ways of American society and its countervailing influences. The inheritance of Puritanism and the Enlightenment as well as the alluring promises of vast wealth and illimitable land filtered into the bloodstream of all Americans: an Anglo-Saxon respect for law and order, individualism, rationalism, and a "this-worldly asceticism" which eventually gave way to secularism and utilitarianism. Anti-Catholic bias and prejudice, too, tended to foster an avid and almost blind patriotism on the part of American Catholics, clergy and laity alike, who were most zealous to prove their oft-questioned loyalty to their new homeland.

The Americanization of the Catholic immigrant eventually succeeded to the point where the Church was considered no longer quite so necessary. One's religious preference began to serve mainly as a fixed focus and label of identity in an increasingly mobile and pluralistic society. Nodding assent to the "unchangeable" contents of faith and Church law, the American Catholic as the twentieth century was well under way tended to relegate religion more and more to Sunday observance, while during the rest of the week being inspired, motivated and guided by the principles of the "American Way of Life." The Church's teaching, especially on social action, no longer seemed to gain and hold the attention as long as it did not pertain somehow to one's own benefit and betterment. American Catholicism in many areas of the country quickly became a middle-class religion and moved to the suburbs. Becoming better educated and more sophisticated, a few American Catholics began to see the Church's formulations of doctrine and morals as antiquated and unrealistic in the midst of the modern world; for others, this proved to be a most comfortable arrangement because one's "faith" could not get in the way of leading and living one's life as one chose.

On the eve of the Second Vatican Council, the gap between proclaiming and living the Gospel in modern times had reached truly problematic proportions. In the United States the allurements of materialism, secularism (against which the pastoral letters of the American hierarchy often inveighed during the post-World War II era), and individualism seemed to be winning the day. The last vestiges of Christendom, whether Protestant or Catholic, had come to an end in America, just as they were in various stages of disappearing throughout the Western world. Yet, the American bishops brought to Vatican II in their sponsorship of the Declaration on Religious Liberty a small portion of a vast and still rarely reflected upon experience in Christian orthopraxis. Indeed, the American church by its living faith for well over a century (despite many setbacks and failures) aptly attempted to live and incarnate the Gospel in a given concrete historical context. From the declarations and decrees of the Council would fortunately come the necessary ecclesiastical impetus for a theological renewal that could once again integrate faith and life ("theory" and "praxis") in the modern world. This new momentum would promote a more comprehensive understanding of the Church's evangelizing mission in a modern pluralistic and secular world, of which the United States had become the evident leader and prime exemplar.

In sum, regarding evangelization and the Catholic Church in America by 1960, three points become evident:

1. The Gospel had been transmitted and incarnated in a goodly number of concrete instances by integrating the experiences of faith and life in genuine examples of Christian orthopraxis.

2. The proclamation of the content of faith, whether in sermons, catechesis, or theological reflection generally, tended to be formalistic, static, objectivistic and basically out of touch with real-life situations.

3. The American experience itself had given rise to countervailing influences that were undermining the faith-life of American Catholicism.

NOTES

1. "The American Bishops and the Vatican Councils," *Catholic Historical Review*, LI (October, 1965), 380.

2. S.E. Morison, *Admiral of the Ocean Sea: A Life of Christopher Columbus* (Boston, 1942), I, 204.

3. Quoted in J.G. Shea, *The Catholic Church in Colonial Days* (New York, 1886), I, 104-107.

4. R.E. Lambert, "The Negro and the Catholic Church," in *Roman Catholicism and the American Way of Life* (Notre Dame, Indiana, 1960), T. McAvoy, ed., 157.

5. S.E. Ahlstrom, *A Religious History of the American People*, 2 vols. (Garden City, New York, 1975), I, 86.

6. Cf. M.E. Marty, *The Righteous Empire: The Protestant Experience in America* (New York, 1970), whose first chapter is entitled "Clearing Space: The Removal of the Native American." Therein he quotes a statement of the Harvard-bred Boston cleric, Cotton Mather, written in 1702: "We may guess that the *Devil* decoyed these miserable savages hither, in hopes that the gospel of the Lord Jesus Christ would never come here to destroy or disturb his absolute empire over them" (p. 6).

7. Ahlstrom, *Religious History*, I, 84.

8. G. Bancroft, *History of the United States*, 6 vols., 2nd ed., rev. (Boston, 1876), II, 300.

9. J.T. Ellis, *American Catholicism* (Chicago, 1969), 11.

10. *Ibid.*, 18.

11. Ahlstrom, *Religious History*, I, 206.

12. *Ibid.*, I, 174-75.

13. *Ibid.*, I, 201.

14. M.E. Marty, *The Pro & Con Book of Religious America* (Waco, Texas, 1975), con 19.

15. Ahlstrom, *Religious History*, I, 413.

16. Ellis, *American Catholicism*, 19.

17. Ahlstrom, *Religious History*, I, 424.

18. G. Tavard, *Catholicism U.S.A.* (New York, 1969), 14.

19. Ahlstrom, *Religious History*, I, 424.

20. M.E. Marty, *The Pro & Con Book* (Waco, Texas, 1975), con 116.

21. W. Ong, *Frontiers in American Catholicism: Essays on Ideology and Culture* (New York, 1957), 116.

22. *Ibid.*, 116-17.

23. Ellis, *American Catholicism*, 32-33 and 43.

24. Printed in P. Guilday, *The Life and Times of John Carroll* (New York, 1922), 223-27.

25. Ahlstrom, *Religious History*, I, 641.

26. [T. Hamilton], *Men and Manners in America* (Philadelphia, 1833), II, 108-9.

27. J.T. Ellis, "The Formation of the American Priest: An Historical Perspective," in *The Catholic Priest in the United States: Historical Investigations*, idem, ed. (Collegeville, Minnesota, 1971), 23.

28. Quoted in *ibid.*, 19.

29. M.V. Gannon, "Before and After Modernism: The Intellectual Isolation of the American Priest," in *The Catholic Priest in the United States*, Ellis, ed., 306-7.

30. Cf. R. Trisco, "Bishops and Their Priests in the United States," in *The Catholic Priest in the United States*, Ellis, ed., especially the conclusions, 270-73.

31. Ellis, *American Catholicism*, 51.

32. For the statistics, see G. Shaughnessy, *Has the Immigrant Kept His Faith?* (New York, 1925).

33. D. O'Brien, *The Renewal of American Catholicism* (New York, 1971), 85.

34. Tavard, *Catholicism U.S.A.*, 36.

35. H.J. Nolan, ed., *Pastoral Letters of the American Hierarchy*, First Plenary Council of Baltimore (1852) (Huntington, Ind., 1971), 141.

36. *Ibid.*, Third Plenary Council of Baltimore (1884), 167.

37. A. Greeley, *The Catholic Experience* (Garden City, N.Y., 1969), 25, footnote no. 2.

38. Quoted in V. Holden, *The Yankee Paul: Isaac Thomas Hecker* (Milwaukee, 1958), 302.

39. V. Holden, "Father Hecker's Vision Vindicated," *Historical Records and Studies*, 50 (1964) 49, citing a letter from Hecker to Archbishop Martin J. Spalding, July 10, 1866.

40. O'Brien, *Renewal of American Catholicism*, 106-7.

41. Nolan, ed., *Pastoral Letters*, 38.

42. Ellis, *American Catholicism*, 56.

43. Quoted in *ibid.*, 119.

44. G. Sloyan, "The Relation of the Catechism to the Work of Religious Formation," in *Modern Catechetics*, idem, ed. (New York and London, 1963), 79-80.

45. J.K. Sharp, "How the Baltimore Catechism Originated," in *Ecclesiastical Review*, 81 (December 1929) 579.

46. Sloyan, "The Relation of the Catechism to the Work of Religious Formation," 85.

47. Quoted in J. Hennessey, "Square Peg in a Round Hole: On Being Roman Catholic in America," in *Records of the American Catholic Historical Society of Philadelphia*, 83 (December 1973), 177.

48. Ellis, *American Catholicism*, 59.

49. Nolan, ed., *Pastoral Letters*, Fifth Provincial Council of Baltimore (1843), 110.

50. Ellis, *American Catholicism*, 89.

51. Ahlstrom, *Religious History*, II, 114.

52. Nolan, ed., "Introduction," in *Pastoral Letters*, 120.

53. *Ibid.*, 157.

54. Ellis, *American Catholicism*, 102.

55. Marty, *The Pro & Con Book*, pro 44.

56. Gibbons to Simeoni, Rome, February 20, 1887, H.J. Browne, *The Catholic Church and the Knights of Labor* (Washington, 1949), 372.

57. Hennessey, "Square Peg in a Round Hole," 178.

58. *Ibid.*

59. Ahlstrom, *Religious History*, II, 510-11.

60. Ellis, *American Catholicism*, 144.

61. Ahlstrom, *Religious History*, II, 391.

62. P.H. Callahan, "The Catholic Industrial Conference," *Fortnightly Review* XXXII (August 15, 1925), 333-35.

63. Greeley, *The Catholic Experience*, 219.

64. D. O'Brien, "The American Priest and Social Action," in *The Catholic Priest in the United States*, Ellis, ed., 443.

65. Abell, "The Catholic Factor in the Social Justice Movement," 84-85.

66. C.E. Curran, *New Perspectives in Moral Theology* (Notre Dame, Indiana, 1974), 90.

67. *Tablet*, July 30, 1932.

68. O'Brien, *Renewal of American Catholicism*, 111.

69. J.H. Fichter, "The Americanization of Catholicism," in *Roman Catholicism*, McAvoy, ed., 124.

70. Ahlstrom, *Religious History*, II, 518.

71. Gannon, "Before and After Modernism," 362.

72. V. Michael, "Social Aspects of the Liturgy," *Catholic Action* XVI (May 1934), 11.

73. Greeley, *The Catholic Experience*, 255.

74. Ellis, *American Catholicism*, 135.

75. W. Herberg, *Protestant, Jew, Catholic: An Essay in American Religious Sociology* (Garden City, New York, 1955), 77.

76. *Christian Century* 71 (1954) quoted in *Christianity Today*, May 8, 1961.

77. O'Brien, "The American Priest and Social Action," 453.

78. W. Herberg, "Religion and Culture in Present-Day America," in *Roman Catholicism*, McAvoy, ed., 14.

79. O'Brien, "The American Priest and Social Action," 433.

VII

Evangelization and the Catholic Church in the United States Today: The Continuing Mission

The sixties began as a decade of great promise and high expectations for both the United States and the Catholic Church in America. The new young president, the first Catholic ever to hold the nation's highest office, inspired America and the world with dreams of "Camelot" and the challenge of a "New Frontier." In Rome at the same time a short-statured, rotund and jovial old man, affectionately referred to as "Good Pope John," who had already captured the hearts of men of all faiths and even some of no professed faith, announced his intention to initiate an *aggiornamento* of the entire Roman Catholic Church by convoking a new ecumenical council. America and the Church appeared to come alive with new purpose and vision. The dreams of both were short-lived. In the United States international crises, assassinations, the Vietnam conflict, as well as student and racial unrest filled in the days and months of the passing decade. The close of the Second Vatican Council, with all its changes in doctrinal emphasis, ecclesial discipline, and institutional structure, was soon accompanied by an open and bitter controversy over birth control leaving American Catholicism confused and bewildered by the end of the decade.

The seventies ushered in an increasing polarization within both spheres once again. The nation was divided over an undeclared war, the longest armed conflict in her history, and the Church was polarized into "liberal" and "conservative" factions regarding a contemporary approach to doctrinal, moral and liturgical matters. The National Conference of Catholic Bishops in 1974 found the word "malaise" to be appropriately descriptive of the current state of American society in general and organized religion in particular. By this time, too, American troops had withdrawn victoryless from Southeast Asia, and the political scandals of Watergate were rocking the nation. Thus, "A Review of the Principal Trends in the Life of the Catholic Church in the United States" issued by the NCCB further delineated the *status quaestionis:*

Many observers find in both the secular and religious spheres a disturbing degree of polarization, confusion, self-doubt and uncertainty about fundamental values and purposes. The more optimistic view this as a necessary prelude to a new era of committed purposefulness, or, as they might say, the birth pangs of a "new consciousness." The more pessimistic hold that the current situation reflects decadence and portends collapse.[1]

The question that remains, then, is which observation will the last quarter of the twentieth century prove to be the more correct? The importance of a positive and hope-filled resolution to the current situation and the dangers threatening just such a response were outlined by a French observer of the Catholic Church in the United States less than a decade ago. G. Tavard at that time wrote:

> American Catholicism is carving a path at one of the most frequented crossroads of the dramas of our times. Because the United States is in the lead of technical progress, American Catholics are at one of the extreme points where Christians must work together to assure a communication of Christ's message. But their philosophy of life on the whole still lacks theological and spiritual depth. Instead of dominating technology and the policies that it inspires from the heights of Catholic tradition, it is in danger of slumbering to the song of factory whistles and to the soothing rhythm of comfort.[2]

Our method of procedure in this chapter, therefore, will start with an overview of the current American scene, analyzing especially the implications of a pluralistic and secular age for the Church in America. Secondly, we shall take the *first moment* of proclaiming the Good News (which our historical study in the previous chapter has shown to have been basically formalistic and unrelated to real life situations), and with a view toward the integration of the entire evangelization process have it address the six fundamental categories of Christian living. This address to the *second moment* will be undertaken in light of present-day values and exigencies. Finally, we shall direct our attention to this *second moment* of living the Good News to determine what it demands of the American church both now and in the future to insure the continued effectiveness of her evangelizing mission.

A. AMERICAN CATHOLICISM TODAY IN A PLURALISTIC AND SECULAR AGE

"*E pluribus unum*" is the motto of the United States of America. Indeed, the United States is the most ethnically, racially, culturally, and religiously pluralistic nation on earth. From the very beginnings of her history, the English colonies in America provided a haven for a diversity of beliefs and religious philosophies. Later territorial expansion and immigration greatly multiplied this basic pluralism in every direction. Some historians and social philosophers first saw America as the great "melting pot," which, in truth, they now admit she never really became. The rich mosaic of her inhabitants with their own very distinct customs and traditions has been for the most part continually maintained despite all Anglo-Americanizing efforts and tendencies to the contrary. The young nation's own roots in the tenets of Puritanism and the principles of the Enlightenment genuinely, though not necessarily intentionally, fostered and promoted the birth of a thoroughly secular society. The unbridled extension and evolution of this secularization process was later observed in an unfavorable light by many critical analysts. Thus, G. Tavard views American society as "on the way to becoming an officially secular society (neutral between atheism and religion) instead of being, as it formally was, a pluralistic religious society (neutral in respect to the different religions)."[3] Far from bemoaning this aprioristically given context of American society, we will endeavor in this particular section to weigh the pros and cons, the advantages as well as the disadvantages which a thoroughly pluralistic and secular culture present to the mission of evangelization.

1. *The Factor of Pluralism*

Within any society or homogeneous grouping of people, pluralism is eyed more suspiciously as a potential threat rather than accepted as a real gift and guarantee of freedom. People basically tend to fear others who are markedly different in physiognomy, skin-color, language, customs, traditions, style of dress, religious beliefs, etc. Since the beginning of time, people have always clung together in homogeneous groupings determined by culture, life-style, mentality and religion. And the person who begged to be different was indubitably treated as an outcast, a foreigner, or a heretic (its root "haeresis" literally means "choice"). In such homogeneous societies conformity and unquestioned obedience to civil and religious authority, law and custom are esteemed as virtue; personal initiative arising from a genuine sense of responsibility is ardently suppressed as unorthodox behavior, detrimental to both the common good and the rightful ordering of society.

Only with the secularization of Western culture and the increased mobility and communications of modern times have people been presented with the opportunity to choose between a number of viable options in philosophy, life-style and belief systems. The Enlightenment, with its emphasis on individual freedom, rational choice and equal rights, gave rise to the revolutions and the new democracies in America and Europe. Yet, even here, toleration and respect for such freedom has been slow in coming as racial, ethnic and other prejudices against any sizable minority within American society itself have born witness.

Congressman Drinan once stated that "America has always exercised a massive thrust toward homogeneity."[4] The "WASP Establishment," he maintains, only recognizes and awards the conformist, the orthodox and the conservative. It expects one to jump into the melting pot forsaking all that is "un-American" in language, culture and creed. Differences in people and ideas along with rapid change of all types rattle our underlying insecurities and fears, and lay bare our basic fear to trust in God and one another. Pluralism in all forms threatens us because it menaces our cherished values of order and control. "Law and order" originated as the Southern slogan for keeping the Blacks down; in the prejudicial value system of many middle-class American Whites, Blacks are looked upon as good, simple folk, yet shiftless, irresponsible, and incapable of being good citizens. Much the same is usually held of native Americans, Chicanos, Puerto Ricans and other Hispanics, Italians, etc. Those with Latin and Eastern European blood have always been ranked "inferior" by the predominantly "WASP Establishment."

Regarding the Christian church, pluralism itself is to be considered of the essence of catholicity. Pope Paul VI has affirmed this.

> In the ecclesial field . . . the complexity of its doctrinal, hierarchical, ritual and moral components cannot be expressed in any other way than through pluralistic words and pluralistic forms. . . . We are pluralists precisely because we are Catholics, which means universal.[5]

The *General Catechetical Directory of the Sacred Congregation for the Clergy* explains the change and implications brought about by pluralism in our day:

> In Christianity of old, religion was regarded as the chief principle of unity among peoples. Things are otherwise now. The cohesion of peoples which stems from the phenomenon of democratization promotes harmony among various spiritual

families. "Pluralism," as it is called, is no longer viewed as an evil to be eliminated, but rather as a fact which must be taken into account; anyone can make his own decisions known without becoming or being regarded as alien to society.[6]

Theological justification for such pluralism may be found in the scholastic theology of the Trinity and in contemporary ecclesiological studies. The divine nature of the Trinity, according to the scholastics, is constituted by "relations of opposition" whereby the Persons are mutually acceptable to each other precisely in their distinction from each other. There is a plurality of persons in one God. Research in ecclesiology bears proof of the fact that, in New Testament times, an ecclesial or institutional pluralism flourished among the various local churches, such as at Jerusalem, Antioch, Corinth, etc. But each local community was considered the genuine embodiment and actualization of Church. Likewise, a widely extended pluralism existed for many centuries before the East-West schism without the differences involved preventing full communion at that time. During the Patristic era there also existed the very independent Latino-African churches. Indeed, a certain authentic pluralism from the viewpoint of the Christian tradition is to be looked upon as a genuine gift of the Spirit (cf. 1 Cor 12:4). Only the mosaic of various peoples, cultures, talents, traditions and values can hope to give sufficient inkling of the ineffable richness and goodness of the Triune Godhead's creative and life-giving presence.

The acceptance of pluralism, furthermore, constitutes a guarantee for continuing political, social, religious and personal freedom. Today, sociological data allows us to see that only a pluralistic society rightly provides the necessary opposition and external criticism which all public institutions, including the Church, require to remain faithful to their original purpose and/or calling. Pluralism *among* and *within* cultures and groups keeps people alert and alive to a rich array of legitimate options and possibilities. It serves both a clarifying and a prophetic function. As one observer has remarked, "the tragedy of western theology is precisely its development in an essentially homogeneous society."[7] Rather than exerting a negative influence on a community, differences deriving from pluralism "may contribute to the maintenance of community, in that conflict and cooperation are not separable states but rather distinct phases of one and the same process."[8]

The negative extremes of pluralism, nevertheless, must not be overlooked. In a free society pluralism can arrive at the point where the needed consensus for public harmony and governability cannot be obtained. Within the Church pluralism can surpass the limits of orthodoxy and lead to theological syncretism. And it hardly has to be mentioned that the pluralism of divisions among Christian denominations and sects constitutes the scandal of Christianity. To establish and maintain a well-ordered society in the midst of cultural, racial, ideological and ritual differences without resorting to force or violence, a certain moral consensus of the people is required. Indeed, a great majority of the people must affirm "There are truths and we hold them." Such a consensus has been noted as on the wane in contemporary America.

Increasing pluralism and secularization supported by an exaggerated individualism with its heavy accent on subjective autonomy and private rights has forced the United States today to lean ever more appreciably upon its constitutional structure and its inherited code of law to insure governability. Such a state of affairs can lead to majoritarian legalism in a culture already manifestly shaped by Puritan and Anglo-Saxon attitudes toward law. Congressman Drinan, thus, views it as an important part of the evangelizing mission of the churches in America to promote the reestablishment of a genuine moral consensus. With 68 percent of the American people, according to a recent Gallup survey,[9] placing a "great deal" to "quite a lot" of confidence in organized religion, religious institutions would appear to be the most likely and effective instruments for reawakening this consensus.

Furthermore, the extent and limits of pluralism become particularly problematic within a church that sees itself divinely established as the guardian of Truth. Yet, as we have seen from the statement of Paul VI above, the Church recognizes the legitimacy of pluralism. Indeed, it provides the context for the evangelizing mission. And according to the Second Vatican Council the preaching of the Word must accommodate itself to the culture it addresses (cf. *GS* 44). As Pope Paul VI has also stated:

> We consider necessary a word on the need of finding a better expression of faith to correspond to the racial, social and cultural milieux. This is indeed a necessary requirement of authenticity and effectiveness of evangelization; it would, nevertheless, be dangerous to speak of diversified theologies according to continents and cultures.[10]

The Pope is anxious that such accommodation of the Gospel to a plurality of cultures avoid being confused with theological syncretism, which terminates in propounding new doctrines by integrating elements of the culture it seeks to evangelize.

Evangelization in a pluralistic society may indeed be genuinely promoted by the extent of personal freedom fostered therein. The choice of faith is an altogether free decision. One is no longer coerced by cultural heritage or social pressure. Pluralism in providing such freedom can promote personal responsibility and authentic moral and spiritual growth. On the other hand, the abundance of options and choices presented by such a culture may produce a moral inertia arising out of a fear of making a wrong decision. Or one may opt for a competing and seemingly equally attractive alternative. Again on the positive side, a pluralistic setting may further advance the process of evangelization with the greater opportunities it affords for the practice of Christlike charity and humble service to all our brothers and sisters, and for the appreciation of the rich variety of gifts, talents, traditions and customs which can more easily reflect the grandeur of God's graciousness to humankind. And, yet again, these same opportunities and differences may also harden one's heart to the gospel message because they pose as threatening our false sense of security. In sum, when all the pros and cons have been weighed, the evangelizing mission as developed in the first two parts of this study seems to be more aided than impeded in a pluralistic context.

2. *The Secularization Process*

In contemporary society the autonomy of science, art and culture in their own fields of competence is taken for granted (cf. *GS* 36). Our secular culture today, nevertheless, results from a long historical process. Its beginnings can be traced back to a developing pluralism in the intellectual sphere of human understanding which originated in the Middle Ages. Secularization, in fact, is a demythologization process that is generally Christian in origin. J. B. Metz even views the advent of the secular age as a genuine Christianization of the world; he thus maintains that "Christianity as it is understood more and more from its own origins, had to appear not as a growing divinization, but precisely as an increasing de-divinization and, in this sense, profanization of the world dispelling magic and myth!"[11] On one hand, then, secularity may rightfully be considered an authentic Christian development, and yet, on the other hand, secularization has in many instances devolved into "secularism," an ideological phenomenon that attempts to comprehend all of reality, including religion and transcendence, in its own horizontal framework. It is this latter secularism and all the subsequent ideologies spawned in its wake that constitutes probably the greatest obstacle and challenge to the contemporary mission of evangelization. So successful and vast have been its inroads into Christian cultures that many today speak of the need of the "second evangelization" or "re-evangelization" of these traditionally Christian societies. However, since our study shows evangelization to be a continuing mission, we deem it inappropriate to speak in such terms. What is presently required, in our viewpoint, is an updated reconceptualization and revitalization of this on-going task.

To carry forward this mission of evangelization in the United States today, the Church must first identify and unmask these ideologies that have sprung up with secularization and that are so alien to the Good News and the Life we share "in Christ." The ideological roots of modern industrial America can be traced to the Enlightenment with its emphasis on rationalistic positivism and exaggerated individualism, two fundamental assumptions which with some modifications were quite easily complemented by certain religious tendencies within Puritanism. Rationalistic positivism first gave a new meaning to the word "real." From its point of view there is no inner reality or center of history. Reality consists only of empirically verifiable phenomena. Such empiricism has made idols of science, technology and progress. It breathes forth the spirits of pragmatism, utilitarianism and materialism which in America find their ultimate incarnate expression in a highly organized, mobile and consumer-oriented society. By such ideologies the human person is reduced to a means, to a simple cog in the wheels of industry and commerce. This rationalistic positivism, or scientific thinking, is itself complemented by rugged individualism that places the accent on competition and privatization, fundamental requirements of an extremely efficient and competitive society.

Taken together these various ideologies constitute the integral components of a "secular faith" which *relativizes* everything while concentrating our attention upon the practical world of everyday experience. It is this "secular faith," or what the American philosopher James Dewey referred to as the "common faith," that has inspired the "American dream" and the "American Way of Life." In some or in all of its varying components, this "faith" has proved a most alluring and attractive alternative to the Christian way of living, and thus has become a formidable obstacle and challenge to our evangelizing mission in both American society and the American church. We shall see how the two moments of the evangelization process can address its tenets in the immediately succeeding sections of this chapter.

In sum, pluralism and secularization are integrally related phenomena. They are respectively the cause and effect of the demise of "Christendom" or Christian culture in recent centuries. They provide both the context and backdrop for the mission of evangelization in the United States today. Their progress and presence within our society should not, however, be received as a regression. In the words of K. Rahner:

> The homogeneous Christian character of our Western civilization throughout a thousand years was not the effect of a miracle of God's grace, external and additional to the intramundane causes and elements of a secular-homogeneous culture and society, nor was it really constituted by the free decision of faith on the part of all individuals, which was directed to the same end but could then be understood only as miraculous; the homogeneous . Christian character of that former culture and society was simply of one piece with the homogeneousness of secular culture and society.[12]

The Church today in her evangelizing mission, rather than fearing and condemning this new context, must meet the challenges and tasks it now presents.

In the American setting the evangelizing efforts of the Church must recognize, accept, and encourage the rightful and rich variety of gifts, talents, traditions and customs our society embodies. At the same time the Church with prophetic boldness must defend and promote the rights, freedom and expression of the various minority groupings from open and subtle coercion and manipulation. The evangelizing apostolate must further address and challenge the insecurities and fears that are masked by bigotry and prejudice. It must unveil the underlying unity that supports and finds expression in all legitimate diversity. In a pluralistic society and culture offering a number of positive and attractive views of humanity, the witness of a genuine Christian orthopraxis often contributes more to evangelization than any number of inspired verbalizations.

Within the Church, too, this apostolate remains essentially the same, but assumes the additional task of conserving the Gospel from theological syncretism and of reconciling the polarized ideologies of conservatism and liberalism which have increasingly divided American Catholicism in the decade since Vatican II. Regarding the process of secularization, the Church in its efforts to proclaim the Gospel is again called upon to recognize, accept and promote the rightful autonomy of science, art and culture in their own areas of competence, while at the same time seeking to enter into open and fruitful dialogue with these disciplines in order to truly learn from them. She may never forget, however, her entrusted role of prophetic criticism as she confronts and takes to task the ideological extremes expressed in any number of "isms" which objectify, manipulate and dehumanize a person.

B. THE FIRST MOMENT: PROCLAIMING THE GOOD NEWS

Our historical investigations of evangelization in the United States have shown that the Church's efforts to proclaim the content of faith have been generally couched in antequated formulas while being both formalistic and often removed from real-life situations. The aim of this particular section is not to delve into the specific theories and methodologies that pertain to each of the three forms of proclaiming the Word: *kerygmatic*, *catechetical*, and *theological*. This is continually being done by those involved with each of these specializations. Here, first, we wish to discuss *how* each is related to carrying out the *first moment* of the evangelization process and *what* are the questions and directions they together must pursue in order better to reach and accomplish their common goal in the United States today. Secondly, the major thrust of this section will be to foster the reintegration of "theory" and "practice" by demonstrating how the *first moment* with its gospel message can best address the *second moment* and thereby arrive at the goal of the entire evangelization process, namely, our integration and sharing in the divine evangelical economy—an authentic and living relationship (koinonia) with the Father, Son, and Spirit. To this end the *first moment* will address the fundamental categories of the *second* as they appear in their contemporary American context.

We have already elaborated upon the necessity of proclaiming the Good News in both *word* and *deed*. The importance of *words* for such a task has been further explicated by the American Catholic hierarchy in their pastoral letter, "The Church in Our Day," when they stated:

> Words are not solutions in themselves, but words convey saving ideas indispensable to order here and salvation hereafter. Words are not only a means of instruction; they are, in their own way, sacramental, even redemptive. Through words, we come to understand one another and we are often healed by this understanding. It is through words, above all through the Incarnate Word, that we come to know something of the destiny of man as faith perceives that destiny.[13]

But people can and do put too much stock in words, formulas and pat answers, endowing them with salvific value that appears automatic and magical in nature. Such is the case when they demand to know, once and for all, *what* they must believe. It is with this latter attitude in view that we can aptly benefit in our task of evangelization from the observation put forward recently by J. Tracy Ellis in his *Commonweal* article,

"American Catholicism in 'an uncertain and anxious time.' " There Ellis stated:

> While the genuinely informed Catholic teacher never explicitly taught that the Church had an answer to every question, often the atmosphere that pervaded in Catholic schools from kindergarten to university was conducive to that assumption on the part of most students. Thus up to a decade ago the latter partook pretty generally to the natural human tendency to accept authority's explanation for the abstruse concepts with which religion necessarily deals. Consequently lacking an emphasis on the mystery that is involved in much that pertains to religious beliefs, students and mature Catholics alike were prone to rest content with the teacher's or the catechism's ready answers to quick and comfortable solutions to their religious problems.[14]

Words, concepts and theories, however, are servants of the Mystery and not Reality itself. M. Novak further defends and explains their necessarily important role in the overall context of life:

> . . . theory only *seems* to be irrelevant to life. In fact, the way we experience things—even our own bodies—is mediated by insights we have had and networks of theories which have been, since birth, constituting our language and directing our attention. Theory serves life. Conceptualization serves insight. But notice which is master, which the slave.[15]

Up-to-date, relevant and correct formulations, concepts and narratives are, indeed, indispensable for proclaiming the Good News in all its forms. Most useful to our contemporary apostolate would be detailed research into the actual impact of the religious language we employ in proclaiming the Word. What images and concepts does our religious language—biblical, doctrinal and liturgical—evoke in the minds of our hearers? What do terms such as "Paschal Mystery," "covenant," "love," "faith," "salvation," "eternal life," "heaven," etc., actually mean to the average American Catholic? To what real-life experiences does he relate them? In this regard M. Novak maintains that "the discerning of a faulty imaginative expectation and the construction of a good one enormously raise the probabilities of insight."[16] Little empirical research seems to have been undertaken in this most important area. Furthermore, primitive kerygma and doctrinal definitions are socially and culturally conditioned, and if they are not continually reinterpreted to meet present pastoral needs, their original formulation may easily convey an unorthodox meaning in a given contemporary context. There is hence an obvious need and duty for the Church to present the content of faith in terms of the contemporary experience of her hearers. What that contemporary experience is and what the terms are that can best help integrate faith and life today may be ascertained only through careful listening and open dialogue with one another and the secular world, especially with its social or life sciences and philosophies.

1. *Reflections on the Forms of Proclamation*

Each of the three forms of proclaiming the Good News has as its goal the unveiling and presentation of the divine evangelical economy, i.e., God-revealing-and-communicating-himself to us in Truth and Love. The first prerequisite in employing any of the forms is to start with the people where they are, "not where they should be, not where we think they ought to be, but where, in fact, we find them."[17] Pastoral sensitivity to the existential situation of one's flock is paramount in importance here, and training in this area can be of much help. The evangelizing mission of the Church in the United States could be considerably facilitated, if, to this end, a professional and nationally coordinated program of pastoral research were inaugurated and sponsored in order to determine patterns of religious attitudes and orientations in all the dioceses and regions of the country. Although every person is uniquely different and has his own religious existence, overall patterns of similarity are discernible and, according to A. Greeley, "can be extraordinarily useful to one engaged in pastoral work if only because such patterns will give him some idea both of the religious antecedents and of the religious problems of the people with whom he is working."[18] Such a nationally coordinated program could facilitate its funding in poorer regions and dioceses, prevent reduplication of effort, and serve the planning efforts of the NCCB, the USCC and other religious institutions and bodies with nationwide and/or regional interests.

Turning our attention now briefly to each of the three forms of proclaiming the Good News, we have already pointed out that preaching or *kerygma* has as its principal task the opening of its hearers to a personal encounter with the risen Lord. More than just providing information and edification, kerygma unveils the presence of God here and now giving himself to us in the Word of Truth and the Spirit of Love. The proclaimer of the Word must first know him and have experienced him in reflection and prayer; he or she must strive to discern his Spirit abroad in our day in the signs of the times, in our contemporary human experience. The evangelizer must be able to distinguish his Spirit from the spirit of this passing age, and point him out as calling us in our particular situation—in the American scene—to continuing conversion and

to communion of life with him. *Kerygma*, then, is essentially the proclamation of the God-event in our everyday, real-life situations. Along
these lines, P. Berger speaks of "signals of transcendence" by which he
means "phenomena that are to be found within the domain of our 'natural reality' but that appear to point beyond that reality."[19] These signals, he suggests, are constituted of prototypical human gestures, such
as hope, play, order, damnation, humor, etc. Thus, relating to everyday
human experiences, kerygma unveils God's gracious plan and loving
presence ("agape-kenosis") in our life, while at the same time it invites
and challenges us to integrate our lives with this divine evangelical economy.

Catechesis, too, while providing doctrinal and moral instruction
("fides quae"), cannot forget that its first and primary task is to prepare
and to open the heart for a loving dialogue, for a living and dynamic
faith-response in hope and love ("fides qua"). Its emphasis must bring
one into contact with the Mystery involved, and not seek to provide
ready answers to religious and moral problems. Catechesis must first
place its accent on the Good News rather than on sin, duty, law, precepts and commandments if it truly strives "To Teach as Jesus Did." In
their pastoral letter bearing this title, the American Catholic hierarchy
elaborated upon three essential elements of religious education:

> The educational mission of the Church is an integrated
> ministry embracing three interlocking dimensions: the message
> revealed by God (*didache*) which the Church proclaims; fellow-
> ship in the life of the Holy Spirit (*koinonia*); service to the
> Christian community and the entire human community (*dia-
> konia*). While these three essential elements can be separated
> for the sake of analysis, they are joined in one educational
> ministry.[20]

Also, to teach in the manner of Jesus, it seems more emphasis is to be
placed on appealing narratives, parables and stories, rather than on
questions and answers, definitions and doctrinal formulas. H. Weinrich
maintains:

> Jesus of Nazareth is presented to us primarily as a person
> about whom stories are told, and frequently also as a person
> about whose storytelling stories are told, and the disciples ap-
> pear as listeners to stories, who then spread and retell, orally
> or in writing the stories they have heard. This is how the
> stories have come down to us, and when we retell the biblical

stories to our children—if we are wise, we don't repeat them word for word—we too become part of an unbroken tradition of storytelling.[21]

For this purpose today one can fruitfully employ many easily available audiovisual aids. Finally, the revised catechumate, where properly implemented, can serve to integrate all the essential elements of religious education outlined above by the American bishops. The *General Catechetical Directory*, in fact, affirms that the adult catechumate and catechesis for adults "must be considered the chief form of catechesis," since it deals with persons who are fully capable of responsible adherence.

A few words need to be said concerning the *theological* form. Evangelization is both the context and the end of all theological research and reflection. B. Lonergan, thus, lists *communications* as the eighth and final functional specialty in his *Method in Theology*. Therein he states:

It is the major concern, for it is in the final stage that theological reflection bears fruit. Without the first seven stages, of course, there is no fruit to be born. But without the last the first seven are in vain, for they fail to mature.[22]

Theology's ultimate objective is to facilitate our encounter with and understanding of ineffable Mystery revealing and communicating himself to us in human history through the Christ-event. M. Novak, thus, aptly describes theology as "a systematic articulation of a sense of reality, stories, symbols. In its highest and most vital moments, theology is a silent and nonverbal reflection, it is an act of recognition, of affirmation, of denial."[23] Regarding its evangelizing mission, however, Monika Hellwig has criticized theology for spending too much time on the young, the healthy, the married, the activist and the laity. More attention, she maintains, should be given to such perennial problems as old age, ill health, widowhood and death.[24] In all these areas, the Church must continue to relate theology to life and teach both young and old to think theologically.

Finally, serving all these forms is the Catholic press with its diocesan newspapers, periodicals, and other publications, such as those published by the United States Catholic Conference in Washington, D.C. The Pastoral Letters of the American Hierarchy have sought to integrate the life of faith and Catholic teaching down through the years, but their publication has only on rare occasion received widespread distribution and coverage. It appears that with better-coordinated efforts the Catholic Church in America could make much more effective use of the modern communications media as suggested by Archbishop Bernardin at the 1974 Roman Synod of Bishops. There, in a written intervention, he stated:

> Opportunities for use of media as direct instruments of evangelization obviously vary greatly from place to place. However, the church should everywhere make maximum use of whatever opportunities do in fact exist. It should be prepared to devote resources of money and personnel to this work in proportion to the opportunities. This is true of both Catholic and secular media, insofar as the latter may be accessible to the church for direct evangelization.[25]

2. *Addressing the Fundamental Evangelical Categories of the Second Moment*

The proclamation of the Good News in order to be effective and to bear fruit must address itself to the contemporary concrete human situation. The gospel-worldview presents us with basic factors or fundamental categories that perennially come into play in the divine-human dialogue. In Chapter Five we determined from Scripture and the traditional teaching of the Church that these constant factors involved in the Christian's relationship to God are basically six: *person-in-Christ, conversion, faith-response in love and hope, the law of Christ, conscience, and sin.* These fundamental categories, while remaining constant, are nevertheless colored by historical and cultural circumstances. In this particular section, therefore, we want to unveil the various positive and negative influences enveloping these categories in contemporary American culture and society. We are hereby seeking to facilitate the Church's effective proclamation of the Good News in the United States today.

(a) *Person-in-Christ.* In his presidential address to the American Historical Association during World War II, entitled "What Then Is the American, This New Man," Arthur Schlesinger drew a composite portrait of the American as pictured by foreigners:

> The attributes most often noted are a belief in the universal obligation to work; the urge to move about; a high standard of comfort for the average man; faith in progress; the eternal pursuit of material gain; an absence of permanent class barriers; the neglect of abstract thinking and of the aesthetic side of life; boastfulness; a deference for women; the blight of spoiled children; the general restlessness and hurry of life, always illustrated by the practice of fast eating; and certain miscellaneous

traits: such as over-heated houses, the habit of spitting, and the passion for rocking chairs and ice water.[26]

Although depicted more than three decades ago, these many qualities persist in the national character today because they are rooted in the history and culture of the American nation. Thus, M. Novak has more recently maintained that

> Central, unforgettable experiences of American history have given rise to basic metaphors in our national consciousness: virgin newness; the birth of a nation; lawlessness; the restless pull of frontiers; oppression in field and factory; the Civil War; foreignness; action and violence and will; empire; hard work; con men and hucksters; the deeply nourished desire of many to be "good." Unless foreign observers know of these experiences, they can scarcely understand some of our discourse or the images of our advertising or our activities.[27]

The typical, average, middle-class, white American may rightly be said to have been in-formed by these and other common attributes and experiences. Yet, it may not be forgotten that the United States is a highly pluralistic country; besides regional differences there are the vastly different experiences and value systems of the nation's minorities: the Blacks, Hispanics, Orientals, and native Americans. It is next to impossible to speak for all these in this brief presentation. We will necessarily limit our observations and comments here to the mainstream of American life and its Americanizing tendencies.

A 1974 "Report of the Ad Hoc Committee on Moral Values in Society" sponsored by the NCCB has pointed out that "the vast majority of Americans take their values more or less uncritically from the society around them. This is not said as a criticism or condescension, for society exercises its influence upon all of us in ways that are both pervasive and subtle."[28] Typical qualities, then, to be tapped and/or challenged within American society include: a basic religiosity; a love for life, freedom, and justice; a pervasive optimism; mobility; pragmatism; a desire for moral probity; a belief in progress; voluntaryism and humanitarian impulses; neo-romanticism and the counterculture. At the same time other attitudes and attributes call for prophetic criticism and confrontation: secularism; rationalism or scientific positivism; individualism; racism, prejudice and bigotry; consumerism; legalism; libertarianism; utilitarianism; conservatism and liberalism, and other ideologies. All these and others varying according to place and cultural groupings must be taken into account and studied by whoever undertakes the proclamation of the Good News in the present-day United States.

To the "average" American mind, a human person conceived as "made in the image and likeness of God" is primarily associated with being a "rational animal." Puritanism emphasized the transcendence of God and one's individual accountability before one's Creator, Law-giver, and Judge. Deism and the Enlightenment paid tribute to an invisible and impersonal Transcendence who orders all things rationally. The blend of the two conjures up images of an absolute and transcendent monarch, a lonely individual, quite removed from the human world, who is the creator and orderer of all things made, the heavenly law-giver, policeman and judge, who can be begged to act paternally and mercifully toward us poor, sinful creatures. Such an image of God leaves the world here below to the rational designs, whims and powers of humankind. This image has received additional popular reinforcement in Catholicism through the influences of post-Tridentine scholasticism. Applied to the concrete human situation, it fostered the development of our technological, industrial society.

> For those Americans whose normal thought-world is more or less contemporary, the two chief models for understanding "Reason" are science and its application. Prediction and control are the dominant interests. To be reasonable is to be analytical, clear, detached, and—it appears—manipulative. Treat the world as a giant mechanism, and take parts of it apart to discover what makes them tick and to subordinate them to one's own desires.[29]

This vision of Reality gives birth to the totally practical "person" who is fundamentally an instrumentalist. Progress is the most important product with effectiveness and efficiency serving as cardinal virtues. Persons are "thing-ified" as producing supplants loving, and doing supplants being. Such a worldview has opened the door to consumerism, for as G. Weigel points out: "The strong accent is to sell more in order to produce more and on this ascending spiral national well-being is said to depend. We do not produce what we need but we produce and then persuade men they need the product."[30] Creation becomes a mere pawn in the hands of technological men and women bent toward sheer utilitarianism, and leading necessarily toward an ecological crisis.[31]

Confronted with such a horizon, the Christian evangelizer (preacher, catechist, theologian) must proclaim the gospel-worldview of the human person as a social or relational being, made in the image and likeness of the Triune God and called to a communion of life and love with him. Herein lies our dignity as persons, whose rationality and technical knowledge have been given us that we might first know and respond to God in love. Through science and technology, we unravel the mysteries of the universe drawing people closer to one another and making them more and more dependent upon one another as our considerably vast planet becomes a global community, "spaceship earth." Progress is to be defended as good when through the use of our talents and technical skills we facilitate relationships and the humanizing activities of leisure, reflection, play and the arts. In this manner we ourselves become more and more the sacrament and glory of God. The *person-in-Christ*, more than a "rational animal," is a relational and symbolic being. And the content of faith reveals and proclaims the almost unbelievable Good News that God is an all-gracious and merciful Father "from whom all fatherhood in heaven and on earth receives its name" and that he is intimately involved with our lives, even with the very smallest of our daily concerns.

The Church, too, in remaining true to Scripture can only promote a vision of a man or a woman as an undivided and personal whole, an embodied spirit, in other words. Dispelled must be the popular myth which dualistically divides one into "a body" and "a soul," thus fueling a false asceticism and a Jansenistic attitude toward human sexuality. Contemporary viewpoints either denying or questioning the existence of the "soul" treat the body simply as a complicated biological machine with sexuality and physical pleasure being considered as part and parcel in a consumer society. Still, we can no longer rightfully speak of "saving souls," if by that phrase we are operating out of a dualistic and individualistic framework. The Good News proclaims Christ risen in the body. Rather than just possessing them, we are our bodies and our sex in a very real sense. The human body both expresses and makes possible our personhood through which we as humans enjoy our dignity as relational beings, as children of God and images of Christ. The evangelizer, then, must work for and proclaim the salvation and liberation of the entire human person.

Taking into consideration the concept of personal freedom, we are quite cognizant, on the one hand, that individual liberty has been cherished as an "inalienable right" in American tradition. But this notion, too, has been heavily tinged with individualism. Indeed, it is integrally tied to other individualistic notions of equality, mobility, pragmatism, independence, opportunity, private property, and the like. Derived from Enlightenment principles,

Freedom is the tiny light of the individual emerging out of social darkness. The image glorifies originality as opposed to conformity, individuality as opposed to community, self-direction as opposed to communal harmony. The free person is solitary, and stands *over against* community.[32]

On the other hand, more recent trends developing from scientific positivism, such as psychological behaviorism, deny that a person is free. Considering the human being to be basically a technical animal, some maintain that all decisions and actions are conditioned and determined by society, environment and upbringing. People are considered incapable of sinning. The preacher of the Gospel, nevertheless, may appeal to the "average" American's basic love of freedom while affirming the divine gift-call to a radical, personal freedom. This freedom, however, does not have as its goal individual self-fulfillment and self-aggrandizement, but rather growth in personal relationships. It is freedom to enter into a communion of life with the Triune God and with one another. Individualism is its abuse; it is of the essence of sin. The evangelizer must, therefore, proclaim the Good News that "in Christ" we have been set free *from* selfishness, *from* the law of sin and death; and have been freed *for* growth in love and communion, the highest wisdom and the essence of eternal life.

Probably the greatest challenge within our American context is conveying the gospel view that a *person-in-Christ* is essentially a person-in-community. According to G. Gallup, "we have one of the highest church attendance records in the world."[33] America, on the surface at least, is impressively "religious." But religion for the "average" American is basically a "privatized" affair. We seem to have very little notion and feeling of what it really means to be church, a believing *community*, so deeply has individualism penetrated our deepest consciousness.

American literature celebrates the hero who is not married and for whom marriage is not a prime relationship. . . . Americans are shy on emotion. They talk of projects and plans, of goals and successes rather than of the meaning people have for them. . . . Indeed, even today the fear of excess in personal relationships worries Catholics more than excess in management or structuring.[34]

Yet dissatisfaction with this state of affairs within American society has become evident in recent years.

. . . men found that loneliness and the isolation of the impersonal mass society was intolerable. They turned to radical political movements, psychological encounter groups, new religious forms (such as astrology and the Jesus people), and
counter-culture communes in order to recapture the intimacy
that had been lost on the pilgrimage from *Gemeinschaft* to
Gesellschaft.[35]

Still, individualism prevails as witnessed by the steady growth in membership of evangelical groups and fundamentalistic sects in the United
States. Their style of Christianity appeals to the "private sphere,"
avoiding political and social issues while making demands only in the
realm of individual and family morality. "They offer the intensity, direct
experience, and enthusiasm traditional to sects. . . . They comfort."[36]

With individualism so heavily ingrained in the American fabric of
life, the Church's evangelizing apostolate of preaching and building
community (koinonia) becomes as important as it is difficult. With un-
remitting effort and patience, the communal aspect of the Christian
faith and our fellowship with the Father, Son, and Holy Spirit must be
proclaimed. The evangelizer can do well to take his theme from *Lumen
Gentium:*

God does not make men holy and save them merely as individuals without bond or link between one another. Rather has it
pleased Him to bring men together as one people. . . . (*LG 9*)

All the time, too, the proclaimer of the Word must be pastorally attuned and sensitive to the historical, cultural and social background of
his hearers. In such a highly pluralistic society as America there exist
significant regional differences and value systems. Nor can one overlook
the tremendous cultural impact of the media, especially television. It is
estimated that on the average American children watch TV six hours a
day. There is no escaping the initial formational role played by the value
symbols, life-style and emotional patterns displayed on the screen.

Switch the channel and you switch realities. Turn on the tube
and you engage in a set of values quite different from your
own. Listen to the endless calm, controlled, superficial talk and
your sense of what a good argument is withers. Watch important matters interrupted for silly, singing commercials and
your confidence in intelligence weakens.[37]

The media is the foremost mouthpiece of the completely secular and technological world. Value questions seldom arise. It maintains a pretense of rationality and objectivity via its inoffensive talk.

(b.) *Conversion.* Americans consider themselves to be a basically religious people. Recent surveys show that only one out of twenty admits to having no religious preference. Religion, too, has traditionally been defended as the source of the nation's strength. Seven out of ten interviewed in a recent Gallup survey claim to be a member of a church (or synagogue). M. Marty points out that forty percent of all Americans attend religious services every week and maintains that this is ten to twenty times higher than most European nations from which the majority of our ancestôrs came.[38] Yet, despite this impressive religiosity,

> . . . survey evidence indicates that we are, as someone has put it, "spiritually illiterates." We reveal, for example, a shocking lack of knowledge regarding the Bible.
>
> And there is a profound gap between religious belief and practice. Roughly three out of four among the public, for example, do not consciously connect religion with their judgments of right and wrong. Thus God in His highest ethical dimension is denied. It would accordingly be at once possible for almost all American people to "believe in God" and yet for society to be essentially materialistic.[39]

Americans are religious for many reasons. Pragmatism comes to the fore even here, as religion is sometimes viewed as "a means of getting the most out of life. Religion is expected to bring about peace of mind, happiness, and secular success."[40] Religion, too, is considered mainly important for the proper moral upbringing and discipline of children. It also serves many other useful purposes: reinforcing the cultural status quo; providing a sense of identity and belonging; serving aesthetic impulses; quelling anxiety with dogmatic certainties; functioning as an emotional crutch and cover-up for pain, suffering, absurdity and madness. Religion can and has served all these purposes.

Besides being pragmatic, Americans are also basically an insecure people. Perfectionistic, we feel responsible and blame ourselves when our ideals continue to outdistance reality.

> The Puritans believed they could create a church in America without spot or wrinkle. Nathaniel Hawthorne notes their disillusionment when they are compelled to build prisons and

cemeteries . . . failure and sin are somehow always unexpected and resented.[41]

In this sort of setting, revivalism and conversion have always played an important role. The conversion experience promoted by American revivalism and evangelical groups, however, has itself been radically individualistic. "Concentration upon the individual sinner led inexorably to a preoccupation with exceedingly personal sins."[42] Even within American Catholicism, which is not prone to such revivalism, an individualistic approach to sin and conversion still prevails.

The Church in America today must issue the Gospel's call to conversion, to return to the one true God revealed through Jesus Christ and the power of his Spirit. In other words, the evangelizer must unmask the deformed and confused images of God propagated in our culture. Appealing to the spirit of the frontiersman in us, to our belief in the "New Man" and our inherent desire for new innocence, the evangelizer must lay bare all our pragmatic motives for belief, our arrogance and our false securities, so that in true humility and poverty of spirit we may open ourselves to the divine gift-call. Conversion, then, must be presented as the call of the Triune God issued in and by the ecclesial community, through which he gives himself to us in Word and Spirit. It is the call to overcome our rationalistic and individualistic tendencies and to believe the orthodoxy of the Gospel, to see God as a Trinity of personal relationships: the Father as the source of all perfection, compassionate and forgiving; the Son who emptied himself to become man, as revealer, healer, and reconciler; the Spirit sent by the Father and the Son, as creative power, giver of life, and unifier. Conversion implies the challenge to see reality from the standpoint of the Good News, and to focus one's way of life in view of it.

To call people to conversion is to challenge them to accept God's rule and Kingdom in their lives, to place all their trust and confidence in God who reveals himself in the Good News of Jesus Christ. Thus, the Church here must appeal to the "average" American's basic belief in God. It must invite us to forsake our false securities and dreams, to grow in our orientation to God and to see him revealing-and-communicating himself to us. The Church must then demonstrate that God primarily does this through the Christian community and its sacramental life, which is meant to nourish, support and purify our faith in the gospel mystery. The prophetic voice of the Church must furthermore call us away from our pursuit of and reliance upon the securities and comforts promised by the spirit of this passing age—money, power, prestige, success, self-fulfillment, the good life, and the "American dream." It must call us to trust in God alone, to recognize and accept our status as pilgrims who paradoxically only find security in losing ourselves.

Finally, the evangelizer has the task to point out that conversion and belief imply "doing the truth in love." A return to the true God means living our lives in conformance with his Will. According to the Gallup poll cited above this constitutes a major, if not *the* major, misconception among professed Christians in the United States today. This misconception is also in evidence among American Catholics, as "A Report of the Ad Hoc Committee on Moral Values in Society" observed when discussing the topic of "metanoia":

> Perhaps the greatest scandal in the Church today is the number of unconverted, half-hearted, indifferent Catholics . . . by whom the message and example of Jesus are unheeded or considered matters of indifference. . . .

(c.) *Faith-Response in Love and Hope.* "The American is profoundly interested in morality, the scheme of correct behavior. The past has imposed upon him a high regard for truthfulness, neighborliness, personal dignity and self-reliance."[43] In appealing to Americans to activate their basic belief in God, the evangelizer can build upon these virtues, as well as upon their inherent desire "to do the right thing." He or she can further prevail upon our pervasive optimism and deep-seated generosity. At the same time the preacher of the Good News must unmask a fundamental religious extrinsicism which shuns personal responsibility and commitment through dogmatism in faith and legalism in morals. Agnes Cunningham thus notes:

> Influences which have formed and nourished the spiritual life of American laymen have, on the whole, tended to overlook the action of the Holy Spirit. Heir to a strong tradition of Jansenism (from France *via* Ireland), American Catholicism has long been marked by a juridical approach to religious practices, a legalistic interpretation of the commandments and church law, a tendency to minimize the Fatherhood of God. Contact with early Puritanism served only to emphasize these traits. America is known throughout the world for its sacralization of the letter of the law. Equally as dominant is the emphasis on the need for strong "will power" to overcome the

sinful weakness of human nature, often accompanied by stress
on the binding force and intrinsic value of duty. . . .[44]

Within this context many people demand to "know once and for all exactly *what* I must believe" and further want to be "told precisely *what* I
may and may not do." Their approach to "faith" often tends to be
strictly impersonal and automatic, a matter of intellectual assent, moral
obligations, and outward gestures. Thus by fulfilling their *duty* and
keeping the letter of the law, they hope to avoid the wrath of God and
"save their souls." Bringing Americans to understand that Christian living and the "obedience of faith" involves a deep personal relationship
with the Triune God lived out in the Spirit's gift of faith-hope-love constitutes a major task for the Church today.

The Church must further maintain the primacy of love in this faith-
response, that Christian living means sharing in the gospel mystery of
kenotic love. In proclaiming the primacy of love, the evangelizer can appeal to the basic generosity of the American people evidenced in the outpouring of charitable aid to those less fortunate or to those afflicted by
natural disasters and the ravages of war. G. Tavard has described it as
"nothing more than the pure gesture of charity performed by the man
who suffers less for the man who suffers more."[45] The Puritan heritage,
in the long run, seems to have affected American Catholicism's overall
understanding of love. In his article "The American Catholics as a Minority," R. L. Bruckberger maintains that traditionally Catholic societies are more given to associate tolerance and love.

> To put up with many things of which one does not approve is
> sometimes the greatest charity—and that is what Puritans do
> not understand, because they do not understand love. This tol-
> erance does not stand in the way of saintliness . . . if Rome
> has had so many saints, it is because she has never made saint-
> liness a matter of law. Law never makes saints, only God's
> love can do that.[46]

Today's American seems to be searching for a genuine experience
of love and community. He or she often feels alienated by the total
complexity and depersonalization of society. To the government and
one's employer one seems to be little more than a number on a com-
puter card that reads: "Please don't staple, fold or mutilate." With urbanization and changing family structures in a highly mobile society, the
"average" American feels less secure and more anonymous. With more

leisure time on our hands and with modern advances in psychology, our expectations for psychological satisfaction from human relationships have increased more rapidly than their actual quality. Thus we have recently witnessed new experiments in commune living and the popularity of T-groups, sensitivity sessions, nude marathons, etc., which have tried to program instant intimacy. Thus, there appears to be sufficient fertile ground for the evangelizer to till in proclaiming the primacy of Christ's two great commandments in Christian living. Americans, however, have many romantic conceptions of love, which must be corrected by the gospel view of *"agape-kenosis."* Kenotic love itself is intimately connected with the virtues of fidelity and justice. The evangelizer must bring his or her hearers to see that

> The range of love is as wide as humanity. Whoever the man is whom I confront, I am to love him. Samaritan, Jew and Gentile are alike: humanity is the limit. And *com-passion* rather than possession is the motivation. We enter into the other's being, feel, think and act with him and in his best interests. We allow him to enter into our world as well. This is true *com-passion*, true Kindness, true intersubjectivity. It is not simply dialogue and communication, but rather communion, or *koinonia*. . . . It can hardly be built into structures of social justice, though these structures are necessary for its expression. A truly pluralistic community is one where love exists. A just society does not guarantee love. Love can exist even where there is social injustice. But without love even the just society perishes.[47]

Love inspired by hope constitutes the essence of fidelity. Americans are by nature optimistic, which may tend to make them receptive to the gospel message of hope in God's promises. The immigrants who landed on our eastern shores were an adventurous folk, and a whole land laid open before them—the "illimitable land," a land of opportunity, a land full of promise. This state of affairs gave birth to the frontiersman in all of us—that rugged individual constantly on the move in search of new adventure and new fortunes. For the contemporary American, however, the frontier has become temporalized. We have become a future-oriented society which has made futurology a science. For the American living today in a "post-industrialized" society, the spirit of the frontiersman continues to bring forth an eagerness for change and novelty, a restless mobility, and a general lack of permanency. America, in fact, has been designated a "throw-away" society. Coupled with Puritan idealism and human failure, these latter qualities evoke a sense of uncertainty and despair that tends to hold God or others responsible—another Puritan carry-over tied in with the doctrine of predeterminism. This basic insecurity seeks to apologize for failure and to eliminate it. Americans, thus, assess

> . . . the system or the culture, devious leaders or bad economics, sinister education or the perverse media for their plight. In the life of the American church there is a strong tendency to indict the Council or the hierarchy, religious educators or theologians, the Catholic Press or the Pope for the failure of this or that scheme.[48]

The evangelizer must therefore hold up the Christian community's hope in God's fidelity to his promises which the Gospel proclaims. God is faithful even though we are not. Needed in American society today are, first, a recognition and acceptance of human limitation and failure, and, then, a spirit of poverty with regard to knowledge and novelty (a person doesn't have to know or experience all things) and a singleness of purpose (fidelity to one's personal vocation, commitments, and relationships), both of which Christ called for in the Beatitudes. Such attitudes can readily convert fleeting optimism into genuine Christian hope.

Finally, the proclaimer of the Word must convey the necessity of bringing this Christian faith-hope-love to bear on our everyday activities. With gratitude and praise the Christian is called to do the truth by living in accordance with his or her new life and with the measure of the Spirit's gifts that one has been given. A Christian must be brought to understand that to act morally is more a matter of personal relationship than of keeping a law or realizing an abstract ideal. Here the preacher can appeal to the Americans' pragmatic spirit, our ritual need to do something effective, while endeavoring to correct a predominant tendency toward activism. Thus, Americans must also be brought to develop an appreciation for *immanent* activity: solitude, prayer, silence and reflection. Furthermore, the sacramental value and evangelizing effect of Christian orthopraxis must be accented, as well as the Christian's joyful task to bear such witness to the Good News by our fulfilling the law of Christ.

(d.) *The Law of Christ.* "It is instructive, encouraging, and intriguing to observe the reverence which Americans have for law-abidingness and the scorn they have for lawlessness."[49] For the "average" American, obedience to the law is seen as the first moral imperative. Such respect appears to flow less from a pragmatic notion that holds law to be a necessary evil than it does from a Puritan emphasis on positive law arising out of the Judaeo-Christian tradition. An often exaggerated concern for "law and order" places a major obstacle in the way of an American's understanding of the "law of Christ." It is quite difficult for him or her to comprehend law as primarily grace, the revelation of God sharing with us his own Trinitarian Life and directing us toward himself by the power of his self-emptying love. In this "law of Christ," Christian orthopraxis and morality receive their interpersonal and normative value.

Conveying this primacy of grace and its interpersonal quality is a most important but difficult task for the American church, since the already mentioned Puritan idealism and attitudes toward law have fostered both moralism and moralizing. Morality, as opposed to moralizing, pertains to a way of life that embodies one's understanding and sense of reality; moralizing is given to the mouthing of pious platitudes. Variant popular forms of moralism came to the fore during the recent Vietnam conflict with Richard Nixon and George McGovern representing two opposite poles. Moralism is furthermore inherently connected with "civil religion." M. Novak distinguishes five major Protestant approaches to "civil religion" in America that exert influence on both politics and public morality: (1) the "high church" tradition of New England with its respect for institutions, law, civil liberties, tolerance and compromise; (2) the populist tradition of the Southern Bible Belt with its emphasis on decency, order, kindliness, and its suspicion of formal authority, its xenophobia, and its ideology of individualism; (3) the moralism of the middle-class heartland churches which is Reformist and yet practical, determined to produce good citizens, while relying on enthusiasm, experience, and energy of the individual; (4) the Awakening type, more cyclical than permanent, that surfaces when there is a need for a major political and moral realignment; (5) Black Protestant experience, more interpersonal, emotional, depending on raw experience and given to vibrant and communal networks while sharing in the above traditions common to White Protestantism.[50]

Given, then, the pluralism of traditions running through contemporary society and the American penchant for "law and order," the evangelizer must foster an awareness of the differences that exist between public morality and the Roman Catholic tradition, and point out the fact that just because something is permitted by civil authority (such as abortion) does not mean that it is necessarily morally justifiable. Nor is the juridical positivism with which civil laws are often enforced truly just. In fact law enforcement is often selective and given to violence. Wm. Emerson, Jr., has observed that

Derelicts, scruffy-looking kids, long-haired rock-concert goers, blacks had all better be especially orderly, or they will get punched and clubbed and then arrested for disorderly conduct. To be *orderly* is to do and look the way I tell you, and that may be *not to be yourself.*[51]

More generally poverty is associated with crime and success with respectability. "A thousand indicators suggest, however, that the poor and uneducated are disproportionately represented among those persons indicted, convicted, and sent to jail."[52]

The proclaimer of the Word must first, then, raise the consciousness of the Christian community to realize the primacy of the "law of Christ" (i.e., Christ's life and love within us), empowering us to assume his attitudes and making them our own through our appropriation of the gospel mystery of his kenotic love. Secondly, the evangelizer must point out that all positive laws, precepts and commandments are meant to be only guidelines geared to this one purpose while themselves remaining truly incapable of formulating and objectifying it. The "law of Christ," while in-forming positive law, transcends it as the ultimate norm, at the same time that it calls us to ever greater personal growth and maturity "in Christ" through his Spirit. The ability to discern then the just demands of positive law in view of the "law of Christ" depends on the correct formation of conscience.

(e.) *Conscience.* If one had to choose the *one* area in the spiritual-moral life of the American church requiring the evangelizer's most immediate and concentrated attention, formation of conscience would have to receive first mention. Legalism and positivism derived from Puritanism and reinforced by the post-Tridentine "act-centered" approach to morality, have reduced the American Catholic's understanding of conscience to the almost mechanical application of the law to a proposed action beforehand, and to the role of acquitter or guilt-sayer after the fact. An understanding of conscience as *the* personalizing reality in a person, the *locus* of a person's encounter with and response-ability to God is all but completely foreign to the American mind. Furthermore, Americans are jealous of their personal freedom and remain distrustful of authority. Padovano notes that

An effort was made to dilute the concentration of authority in the political order by checks and balances, in the ecclesiastical order by lay supervision of the churches, in the legal order by a jury of peers and by the principle of due process.[53]

The evangelizer consequently, in attempting to form consciences, can profitably tap this love of freedom while straining it of its ingrained individualism.

On the whole, Americans have used their freedom responsibly. Comparing the American Revolution to the French and the Russian, Padovano maintains that

> Americans create order and more freedom out of freedom rather than chaos and anarchy. . . . The American Revolution worked. It is the only revolution in history which kept more promises than it broke. The Bill of Rights derives from a creative use of the notion of personal freedom. It is in fact, a remarkable codification of major themes of the Gospel concerning human dignity.[54]

The Church in forming consciences may build on this creative use and love of freedom by devising and encouraging a pluralism of legitimate options. At the same time the Church must also educate the faithful not to avoid responsibility by depending blindly on the letter of the law, but rather to seek the will of God in any given existential context by drawing upon their life in Christ, their consciousness of value, and the teaching of the Church. Indispensable to the whole process is the conveying of a correct notion of the virtues of prudence and epekeia. The goal of such education, then, is to develop a genuine religious conscience.

> The religious man struggles to discern, from the signals of daily life, what is intended for him in each event. He responds to life as if it were a conversation. Life is not, for him, "one damned thing after another." It is a voyage along which he is being led. The signals he receives are neither magical or mystical, and contain no more than life contains for anybody else. But in those events which promote (or hinder) honesty, courage, freedom, compassion, community, and other values nourished in his religious community, he discerns the working out (or the obstruction) of God's creative will. To have a religious conscience is to cherish concrete other persons (neighbors, not "mankind") and concrete, ordinary reality—to love this world and to respond to its need creatively—not out of self-indulgence, and not out of missionary zeal, but because to create is to be like life itself. To have a religious conscience is to wish to imitate whatever one can best discern as being most like God.[55]

In the end, conscience itself must be presented as being the ultimate authority governing personal moral activity, whether or not such activity may be commonly considered objectively or materially sinful.

(f.) *Sin*. The evangelizer in proclaiming the Good News of our redemption and our solidarity "in Christ" must also, in view of it, unmask the power of sin which is at enmity with the divine evangelical plan. Christ has indeed conquered "the law of sin and death," but in the present state of the human condition its power has not been routed. In America today the reality of sin is either denied or else is still viewed as a "privatized" transgression of some commandment or law. The denial of sin, once again, can be attributed to the influence of the Enlightenment and its rationalistic affirmation of human autonomy. P. Keran in *Sinful Social Structures* states:

> I would however suggest that there is a tendency in our culture to think that what has gone wrong is only a matter of limits—especially limits of knowledge, limits of policy—as essentially technical problems to be corrected. This, I would suggest, has happened because our success through science and technology has occurred precisely because we became practical, and bracketed (i.e., systematically overlooked) the rift in our being. . . .
>
> There is then an unspoken assumption behind the adoption of the scientific method as the core of our culture . . . that all things ultimately are capable of rational ordering, that all things will eventually cohere. This view leaves out of account malice, persistent bad faith and bad will. It leaves out of account the necessity and possibility of conversion and forgiveness.

This same scientific positivism, where it has infiltrated the life sciences, accounts also for the denial of sin in these anthropological disciplines. The individualistic approach to sin in American Catholicism can be traced to the post-Tridentine "manual" approach to morality, strengthened further in the American context by the Puritan tradition's emphasis on the individual's responsibility to God alone.

The evangelizer, after having proclaimed the Good News of salvation, must advert to our rejection (both collective and personal) of the gospel mystery, i.e., our choice to remain in a state of alienation from God, neighbor, world, and self. It belongs to the Church's prophetic role to unveil and to identify the concrete forms assumed by the sin of the world in a given social and cultural context. The Church must further bring us to an awareness of our collective and personal responsibility for this latter sinful condition.[56] Trusting in God's promise of forgiveness, we must then admit our guilt—a traditionally difficult matter for Americans—and thereby become truly liberated to grow in solidarity and communion with Christ the New Adam. Thus freed by God's forgiveness and love for sinners, we may again strive to incarnate the power of the Gospel in lives of loving awareness and genuine Christian orthopraxis. Although redeemed in Christ, it must be remembered that we remain sinful and are constantly in need of on-going conversion and forgiveness. Realistically, too, we cannot expect public institutions and governments to arrive at the same level of morality as families and persons. As M. Novak observes,

> Under modern conditions, the family has difficulty fulfilling its own ideals. That many would have the government provide intimate caring, which even families can scarcely manage, is sublime naiveté.[57]

Yet, in the "law of Christ" to rest content with the "status quo" is to fail to grow, which is to sin.

On the level of personal sin the evangelizer must bring American Catholics to an understanding of the essentially dynamic and interpersonal nature of sin. Before it is a particular act, sin is an underlying fundamental attitude that refuses to respond to the persuasive love of God at work in our midst (i.e., grace). Sin must be presented then, as the failure to respond to the demands of relationships and love that are made upon us in situations of daily living. Within this context the distinction between mortal and venial sin must be explained, thereby correcting the act-centered, legalistic and ritualistic concept of sin that rests in the minds of most American Catholics. This latter concept, on the one hand, often multiplies "mortal sins" and "guilt complexes" without legitimate reason, while on the other hand, more serious, underlying, fundamental attitudes and value systems receive little or no attention.

The evangelizer must also point out our responsibility to counteract the evil effects of our "material" sins, for which we may not in the beginning have been morally and objectively accountable. Such moral responsibility and accountability pertains to groups and local communities as well as to individuals. It should also be brought to the attention of American Catholics that our most common sin is often the failure to care and to get involved. In the end, however, the evangelizer cannot emphasize enough the fact that sin is only truly comprehensible within the context of the Good News proclaiming the solidarity of our redemption in Christ.

C. The Second Moment: Living the Good News

Communication through deed is the essence of Christian presence. The word is commentary on the deed, not the other way around.   —Robert McAfee Brown[58]

The primary importance of orthopraxis or genuine Christian witness for the evangelizing mission in today's pluralistic, secular society has already been demonstrated in this work. In his intervention at the 1974 Rome Synod, Cardinal Dearden, speaking on "Evangelization and Secularization," concurred with this viewpoint, stating: "In a secular culture the church's claim to stand and speak for Christ must be proven by word and deed; the identification of the Church and Christ cannot be assumed."[59]

Such Christian witness, moreover, is not lacking within American Catholicism today. Archbishop Jean Jadot, the present Apostolic Delegate to the United States, recently ennumerated *four* "signs of hope" he sees as becoming evident in the American church:[60]

First of all, *a renewal of Christian responsibility* is apparent in the emergence of the laity, in collegiality, in the growth of diocesan and parish councils, in more mature concepts of obedience and authority, in the renewed dedication of priest and religious after a time of numerous defections, and in the rising concern over moral decay that threatens human dignity and the respect for human life.

Secondly, *an increased sense of community and fellowship* is evident in rapidly evolving parish communities, in the appearance of charismatic prayer groups and the marriage encounter movement. There is also strong evidence of a growing awareness among Catholics of the social dimensions of the Church's mission, and of a growing concern for social justice and international peace.

Thirdly, *expanded information and education leading to a broader view of reality* can be witnessed in the healthy concern for the future of religious education, in growing comprehension of a sensitivity toward international concerns and in programs of continuing education for the clergy and religious.

Lastly, *a growing movement toward interiorization* finds expression in the renewed emphasis given, in the Apostolic Delegate's words, "toward the development of what one is rather than the accumulation of what one has." Thus we discover attempts at profound spiritual renewal, and increasing interest in prayer and spirituality, and the active participation of young people in charismatic prayer groups and in the liturgical life of the Church.[61]

1. *Critiquing the Proclamation of the Word*

Incarnating the gospel mystery in daily Christian living remains the American church's foremost evangelizing task. In the last part of the previous section we had the *first moment* of the evangelization process address the *second*. We now turn the tables briefly and evaluate the effectiveness of the American church's proclamation. Recent surveys on the matter provide some sobering thoughts for those involved in proclaiming the Good News in its various forms.

> Whatever general approval American Catholics feel toward the work of their clergy does not extend to the quality of their sermons. In 1957, in the Ben Gaffin *Catholic Digest* study, 43 per cent described the Sunday sermon as "excellent." In a replication of this study done by Gallup in 1965, the percentage had fallen to 30; and in our project of 1974, the percentage had fallen still further to 22. Thus in a little over two decades, satisfaction with the professional quality of sermons has diminished by half.[62]

Among adolescents only 16 percent rated the sermons they heard as "excellent"; at the same time their religious devotion was substantially higher than that of their parents.

Regarding the Church's teaching authority, there appears to be a substantial decline in the number of American Catholics who accept its legitimacy. Within a period of ten years there has been a drop from 70 to 42 percent in the number who consider it "certainly true" that Jesus handed over the leadership of his Church to Peter and his successors. "Only 32 percent think that it is 'certainly true' that the pope is infallible when he speaks on matters of faith and morals." Also, in ten years the number of Catholics who read a spiritual book is down from 58 to 33 percent; likewise, those who read a Catholic magazine or newspaper declined from 61 to 56 percent. Unchanged, however, is the support for parochial schools. "Eighty-nine percent reject the idea that the Catholic school system is no longer needed in modern-day life." Some 35 percent of Catholic parents with school-age children have them enrolled in parochial schools (down 4 or 5 percentage points in ten years). Of those whose children don't attend Catholic schools, the first most-mentioned reason, by 38 percent, is their unavailability; the first reason for another 24 percent of the parents is the expense involved. Yet, there are those— eight percent—who are willing to contribute substantially more than they now do in order to keep their parish schools operating.

The popularity of the leadership provided by the Church remains significantly higher than those who approve of the way politicians handle their jobs—percent of approval: parish priest, 82; the pope, 71; bishops, 62. Yet, those who find their clergy "very understanding" of parishioners' problems is down from 72 percent in 1952 to 48 percent in 1974. Within ten years the number of Catholics who would be very pleased to have their son become a priest has, also, declined from 66 to 50 percent. Of the young people questioned, only 30 percent found their priests very understanding, and only 15 percent reported very much admiring the life that priests and nuns lead. In his intervention at the 1974 Rome Synod, Archbishop Quinn proffers an explanation for the youths' disenchantment with the church:

> The only time young people see a priest or bishop is at the liturgy. If they do not perceive in him on those occasions the qualities described above [joy, love and kindness, patience and tolerance, an open mind and a willingness to listen, a spirit of compassion and concern, a sincere and honest simplicity and directness] and especially joy and a spirit of faith, they do not believe in the church. They frequently find that the liturgy is celebrated in an impersonal manner without joy and without any really obvious faith on the part of the celebrant. This does not seem to them to reflect the gospel as they understand it. They recognize the paradox of the joyless herald of the good news and are repelled by it.[63]

From the brief and scattered observations presented here so far, there is indicated an obvious need for greater effort at genuine orthopraxis on behalf of those who bear the primary responsibility for the *first moment* of the evangelization process in the American church.

2. *Witnessing to the Gospel through Christian Orthopraxis*

The greatest hope for evangelizing American society and culture today lies in the gospel witness provided by genuine Christian living. As the NCCB's "Report of the Ad Hoc Committee on Moral Values in Society" has stated:

> Counter-values presented by the example of a good life are much more convincing and attractive than critiques of existing values, however, scholarly and logical or, for that mat-

ter, impassioned. There is good reason for this. One cannot
respond very positively to what is simply negative: affirmations
exert more appeal, to both the mind and heart. Most important, example wins more hearers than words. The proclamation of Christian moral values must be a lived sermon, not just
an exercise in argumentation, even though it is important that
we be able to support the moral values we propose with sound
moral reasoning.

Throughout her early history the Catholic Church in America has given
such witness, especially in her practical concern and care for the spiritual and material well-being of millions of Catholic immigrants who
swarmed ashore for well over a century beginning in the 1820s. The
Church sought to make them at home in this new land. She provided
them with the experience of community amid prejudice and hostility.
With Americanization the descendants of the immigrants had less time
and need for the Church. Advancement on the educational and social
ladders gradually brought them to question the relevancy of her teaching
in the present day. But having "arrived," many today are beginning to
feel the emptiness and futility inherent in chasing "the American
dream." This contemporary experience verifies humankind's principal
and perennial need for meaning and for belonging. The Christian community in living the gospel mystery of Jesus Christ responds to both.

The Church in the United States today must become ever more
cognizant of its special task to listen, discern, and reflect on how it can
best incarnate the Good News of the Kingdom of God in our pluralistic
and secular society. An American Catholic ecclesiologist, R. McBrien,
writes:

> Indeed, the world is called to become the Kingdom of God, not
> to become the Church. In so far as the Church is already the
> embodiment of fellowship (*koinonia*), it serves as an anticipa-
> tory sign for the rest of the world of that final perfect commu-
> nity, which is the Kingdom.[64]

All the Church's efforts must, therefore, be directed toward this one real
goal. In order to remain faithful to this divinely entrusted, essential and
constitutive mission, the Church must strive to keep alive and to incarnate through word, sacrament, and Christian orthopraxis the New Life
(at once spiritual and moral) she shares in fellowship with the Father,
Son, and Spirit. This apostolate is primarily a ministry of service, which
places a high premium on reconciliation. In the words of R. McAfee

Brown: "A church that is not trying to dominate but to serve will be a vehicle through which those who do seek to dominate may be persuaded to be reconciled."[65] The Church's leadership in being faithful to its vocation must give first priority to this evangelizing mission, placing it far ahead of all merely administrative concerns. As the American hierarchy in its pastoral letter "The Church in Our Day" reflectively and perceptively observed:

> Within recent years the Church has maintained the high level of its official teaching in encyclicals, in Council, in Synod, in papal addresses. . . . She has addressed herself to social justice, world peace, the political order, the underdeveloped nations. By all this, many were moved to put their hopes in her. If Catholic performance does not match Catholic promise, then truly we shall have failed. If our deeds contradict our statements, then we shall have doubly sinned. We were warned once: "It is not your encyclicals which we despise; what we despise is the neglect with which you yourselves treat them!" (Rappoport as quoted by Richard in *Le Pape et le Communisme*.) This was said in indictment of the People of God in another nation and another generation, but there is no point in pretending that it cannot be applied with equal force in America in our decade.[66]

"Performance" should be an easy notion to convey to American Catholics already so infused with a pragmatic spirit. Yet, in 1974, the Catholic Bishops of the country deplored the assimilation by American Catholics of the values and attitudes dominant in the general society. They cite evidence indicating that "many Catholics are tolerant of abortion in at least some circumstances, reject official Church teaching on means of family limitation, have a divorce rate not markedly different from that of other Americans, and regard most social issues very much as their non-Catholic countrymen do."[67]

The church as an evangelizing community is both "ekklesia" and "koinonia." In fellowship it is gathered-sent in the Spirit to live, celebrate, and proclaim through word, deed, and sacrament the Good News and Mystery of New Life and kenotic love that we share "in Christ." This mission belongs to the whole Church, and not to the hierarchy and clergy alone.

> The church is a totality, a oneness, a community, in which the basic relationship is equality in the Spirit. The people of God is

not divided into "two species of Christian," cleric and lay. The laity are part of the one people united in the unity of the Trinity. (cf. *LG* 4)[68]

The American Catholic laity may justifiably deplore at times the lack of orthopractic consideration and collaboration they receive from the Church's pastors. In the Church's evangelizing apostolate, the whole Church must be actively involved. Ignorance and confusion concerning the necessary and rightful role of the laity can only lead to indifference on their part. As Cardinal Krol maintained at the 1974 Rome Synod:

> Bishops and other clergy must promote the dignity and responsibility of the laity, by respecting their proper freedom and recognizing their charisms. . . . The laity have certain rights that belong to their specific manner of participating in the priesthood of Christ; these must be protected. In brief, not domination but collaboration.
>
> . . . .
>
> Pastors of the flock must learn and teach the basic equality of all the baptized in Christ and the Spirit, must stress the *koinonia*, the single community of faith and love with an astounding diversity of charisms, all focused on *diakonia*, on service to the human person.
>
> Special attention, theological and pastoral, should be given to the role of women and ethnic minorities in the evangelizing apostolate of the church. Moreover, the concentrated effort of clergy and laity must aim at tapping the rich potential that Catholic youth have for evangelizing.[69]

Thus the whole Church gathered together in Christ's Spirit, in his reconciling, creative and redeeming love, becomes an anticipatory sign of the coming final and perfect community, which is the Kingdom. Through ever-deepening faith and on-going conversion, Christian living or orthopraxis again incarnates and makes present the gospel mystery of kenotic love here and now in our contemporary world. At the same time it proclaims to all peoples the Good News of "the hope that is in us"— Jesus Christ, the crucified and risen Lord, the Coming One whose rule and Kingdom is without end.

CONCLUSIONS

The overview of the contemporary American scene presented in this chapter has been perforce limited to general observations about various influential factors and tendencies found in the mainstream of our culture and society. Each of these influences, furthermore, continues to affect the Church's evangelizing mission in the United States today. Because America is so vastly pluralistic, our comments have hardly been able to do justice to the present situation. Detailed study, analysis and research are obviously needed. Our intention, indeed, has been only to scratch the surface, picking away at some of the stones in the road, as it were, while hoping that others will come along to grade in the holes and do the paving. The wide and rich mosaic of cultures and traditions that constitute present-day America call for respect and study in order to bring to light, renew and incarnate the gospel mystery in their midst. Neither diversity nor secularity should be viewed as an obstacle or a threat to evangelization. Indeed, as Cardinal Dearden pointed out at the 1974 Rome Synod, secularization must be seen as the purlieu which today conditions the church's ministry.

> . . . this means accepting secularity as the context for the call to conversion, then bearing witness to Christ by teaching and life in such a manner that people and societies are called beyond the secularity of their culture to the sanctity of the kingdom.[70]

Evangelization, like Lot's wife, can quickly become calcified if it nostalgically looks backwards, seeking only to regain a lost Christendom.

Bringing into focus the present situation of the Catholic Church in the United States, we find a number of various elements and factors requiring the concentrated attention and efforts of those entrusted with carrying forward the Church's evangelizing mission. In the article-summary of the recent NORC project referred to frequently throughout this chapter, the authors conclude by stating that

> No single discriptive conclusion of the present state of American Catholicism is possible.
>
> On the one hand the changes in the Church have proved popular (and the notion that the new liturgy has driven people away can safely be described as complete fiction). Fundamental loyalty to the Church continues, parochial schools are vigorously endorsed, and there are more financial resources available to support the schools than the church has yet been willing to use. There are no signs of vigorous antipathy to Church leadership or of anticlericalism. Church attendance is down among adults (though it remains high among teenagers), com-

munion reception is up. Some traditional forms of piety have declined, but other, newer, forms seem to have attracted surprisingly large numbers.

Catholics have accepted integration, and while the majority does not yet support the ordination of women (though some might think that the size of the minority supporting it is fairly large), they would vote for a qualified woman (or black or Jew) for the presidency.

On the other hand, the image of the priesthood has slipped badly with both adults and with young people. On two important measures of professional performance, sermons and sympathy in dealing with people, the decline of the priestly image in the last twenty years has been very great. Acceptance of the Catholic sexual ethic has declined dramatically despite *Humanae Vitae.* Catholics seem uncertain about some tenets of the faith that were once considered to be of critical importance, and they lack confidence in their capacity to hand on religious values to their children.

The picture is a mixed one. While there is not yet reason to despair over the future of Catholicism in the United States, neither is there reason for easy optimism.[71]

In each of the two *moments* of the evangelization process certain elements stand in need of preferential consideration. Those commissioned to proclaim the Word must evidently concentrate more on the quality and preparation of their presentations. While surveys demonstrate a growing dissatisfaction with the quality of the sermons heard today, it may be wondered if this substantial decline over the last twenty years is not in a large measure attributable to the growing educational sophistication and intellectual skepticism, as well as the heightened expectations of the American layperson. Yet, whatever the reasons, those who preach the Word today must expend more effort in this regard in better attuning themselves to the spiritual-moral needs of their flocks and bringing the gospel message to bear directly on these exigencies. Better education and training during the seminary years, and later, in this area could indeed prove advantageous.

Preaching and catechesis must pursue a more kerygmatic approach, both revealing and making possible a personal encounter with the risen Lord. An awareness of the Good News and the Mystery involved must be instilled and nurtured. To this end a true celebration of the Church's sacraments is of utmost importance here. Primary emphasis should be given to persons and relationships, rather than to rites, laws and isolated actions. The personal nature of faith, conscience, law and sin must be accented and explained. Nor is the prophetic role involved in proclaiming the Gospel to be shunned. The ideological appurtenances of positivism, rationalism, individualism, pragmatism, utilitarianism, etc., leading to alienation and depersonalization, must be pinpointed, unmasked and challenged. There comes to the fore here an obvious need to accent the essential unity between faith and life, and to convey the fact that genuine orthodoxy requires "doing the truth in love." As well as having explained and opened up to them the content of faith, Christians must be exhorted to lead lives worthy of their calling. Furthermore, the current confusion and uncertainty of American Catholics concerning the Church's doctrinal and moral teaching must be addressed within the context of the gospel mystery, rather than by generalized dogmatizing and moralizations.

The most fruitful area for evangelization today, as pointed out numerous times in this work, is that of genuine Christian living or orthopraxis. In a pluralistic and secular society, such as the United States, the witness of genuine Christian living can convey more than any number of words. Surveys indicate that today's youth, who are the hope for the Church of tomorrow, are even more religious than their parents, that they are genuinely searching for meaning and belonging. Yet the image of the Church and the priesthood in their eyes is much less attractive. Combined with the declining image and pastoral understanding afforded parishioner's problems on the whole, the implementation of Christian orthopraxis could well start with the Church's hierarchy and clergy in regard to their professional performance. Historically, in the American church, it has been the practical concern and selfless service of these men to their people that has proven to be one of the strong points in the Church's rapid growth. The complexity of modern society, however, demands greater sensitivity and awareness for making a comparable contribution today.

The laity, themselves, must be made cognizant of their rightful, unique, and necessary part in the Church's evangelizing apostolate. They must be brought to understand that they essentially *are* the Church, and not mere subjects or spectators. In this regard, G. Gallup draws "one final point" from his statistical analysis:

> Our surveys strongly suggest that the segment of the population who are "intrinsically" religious as opposed to those who are "extrinsically" religious are the real movers of the Church. Although small in numbers, undoubtedly, these people have a great deal of influence on society as a whole, and in ways

which in some respects are, I'm sure, unmeasurable. These are people—and I suspect they cut across socio-economic lines—who have a lively and joyful faith, who have a close personal relationship with God. They are thrilled by the life of Jesus. The forms and structure of the Church are not obstructions to them but channels through which they can share their love with other people.

While the Church must be concerned with numbers and getting more people to go to church and to become members, the ultimate goal would surely seem to be to bring people to a personal loving relationship with God. The really exciting news from our surveys is that "intrinsically" religious people—those who truly live their faith—reinvigorate society far more than those who are "extrinsically" religious, those who are religious for social reasons and who are drawn to the Church as an institution rather than to the Church as an expression of God's love for mankind.[72]

The United States and American Catholicism on the eve of the third centenary of national life appear ready for a new thrust of evangelization. The continuing mission in some ways is just beginning.

> . . . I tell you:
> Look around you, look at the fields;
> already they are white, ready for harvest!
> Already the reaper is being paid his wages,
> already he is bringing in the grain for eternal life,
> and thus the sower and reaper rejoice together.

(Jn 4:35-36)

NOTES

1. NCCB (Washington, D.C., 1974), 1.
2. G.H. Tavard, *Catholicism, U.S.A.* (New York, 1969), 104. This importance of what takes place in the United States for the rest of the world has been further confirmed by E. Schillebeeckx in "Future Shock in America," *Critic* xxxi (November-December, 1972), 12: "To spend four months in the United States is to get a foretaste of what is unmistakingly becoming Europe's life-atmosphere, although at a slower pace than is happening in America."
3. Tavard, *Catholicism, U.S.A.*, 111.
4. R.F. Drinan, *Democracy, Dissent, and Disorder* (New York, 1969), 45.

5. *TPS*, 14 (1969), 117 ("Abbiamo altre volte parlato," *L'OR* 15 May 1969).

6. Approved English translation of the *Directorium Catechisticum Generale*, USCC (Washington, D.C., 1971), 6, no. 3.

7. P. Verghese, "Secular Society or Pluralistic Community?" in *Contemporary Religion and Social Responsibility*, N. Brockman and N. Piediscalzi, eds. (New York, 1973), 80.

8. R. Modras, "The Elimination of Pluralism between Churches through Pluralism within Churches," *Concilium* 88 (New York, 1973), 77.

9. G. Gallup, Jr., "What We Know And What We Do Not Know: A Statistical Analysis of the Unchurched American," a report given at The Catholic University of America, Washington, D.C., November 11, 1975 and the Consultation at Glenmary Research Center, Maryland, November 12, 1975. Later published in *New Catholic World*, 219 (July/Aug. 1976) 148-154.

10. "Closing Address," *Synod of Bishops 1974* (USCC: Washington, D.C., 1975), 12.

11. J.B. Metz, *Theology of the World* (London, 1969), 34.

12. K. Rahner, *The Shape of the Church to Come* (New York, 1974), 22-23.

13. H.J. Nolan, ed., *Pastoral Letters of the American Hierarchy, 1792-1970* (Huntington, Ind., 1971), 627.

14. 98 (April 27, 1973), 180.

15. M. Novak, *Ascent of the Mountain, Flight of the Dove* (New York, 1971), 20.

16. *Ibid.*, 18.

17. A. Greeley, *The Crucible of Change: The Social Dynamics of Pastoral Practice* (New York, 1968), 33.

18. *Ibid.*

19. P. Berger, *A Rumor of Angels* (Garden City, New York, 1969), 53.

20. The NCCB's pastoral message on education, November 1972 (USCC: Washington, D.C., 1973), no. 14.

21. H. Weinrich, "Narrative Theology," *Concilium* 85 (New York, 1973), 48.

22. B. Lonergan, *Method in Theology* (New York, 1972), 355.

23. Novak, *Ascent of the Mountain*, 181.

24. M. Hellwig, in *Cross Currents*, xxii (Spring 1972), 210ff.

25. "The Church and the Media: Partners in Evangelization," *Synod of Bishops* 1974, 50.

26. Washington, December 30, 1942 in *American Historical Review*, xlviii (January 1943), 226.

27. M. Novak, *Choosing Our King* (New York, 1974), 16-17.

28. November 19, 1974 (USCC, Washington, D.C., 1975), 10-11.

29. Novak, *Ascent of the Mountain*, 84.

30. G. Weigel, *The Modern God: Faith in a Secular Culture* (New York, 1963), 144.

31. Novak in *Choosing Our King*, 167, asks: "Who among our experts, academics, planners, architects have given thought to *human* ecology—to living cultures, local ways, and family networks?"

32. Novak, *Ascent of the Mountain*, 125.

33. Gallup, "A Statistical Analysis of the Unchurched American."

34. A. Padovano, "The Serpent of Eden and the American Eagle," *Spiritual Life*, xxi (Winter 1975), 227-28.

35. A. Greeley, "The Persistence of Community," *Concilium* 81 (New York, 1973), 26.

36. Novak, *Ascent of the Mountain*, 175.

37. *Ibid.*

38. M.E. Marty, *Pro & Con Book of Religious America* (Waco, Texas, 1975), pro 16-17.

39. Gallup, "A Statistical Analysis of the Unchurched American."

40. A. Padovano, *American Culture and the Quest for Christ* (New York, 1970), 116. Idem., in "Serpent of Eden and American Eagle," 229, observes: "The American . . . tends to wonder about God not in terms of relationship but in terms of value to be derived from believing. The church is often judged as an institution where one fulfills a certain responsibility to God or affirms a particular ideal image of self as a believer rather than as a place where one goes to experience community and rejoice."

41. Padovano, "Serpent of Eden and American Eagle," 222.

42. S.E. Ahlstrom, *A Religious History of the American People* (Garden City, N.Y., 1975), II, 320.

43. Weigel, *The Modern God*, 34.

44. A. Cunningham, "Complexity and Challenge: The American Catholic Layman," *Concilium* 9 (New York, 1965), 122-23.

45. Tavard, *Catholicism, U.S.A.*, 56. Americans themselves appear to be more critical of such generosity. Weigel in *The Modern God*, 141, maintained that, "there is much generosity which is only extravagance."

46. In T. McAvoy, ed., *Roman Catholicism and the American Way of Life* (Notre Dame, Ind., 1960), 47.

47. Verghese, "Secular Society or Pluralistic Community?" 78-79.

48. Padovano, "Serpent of Eden and American Eagle," 223.

49. Drinan, *Democracy, Dissent, and Disorder*, 84.

50. Novak, *Choosing Our King*, 131-36.

51. Emerson, *Sin and the New American Conscience*, 19.

52. Drinan, *Democracy, Dissent and Disorder*, 127.

53. Padovano, "Serpent of Eden and American Eagle," 226.

54. *Ibid.*, 225.

55. Novak, *Ascent of the Mountain*, 83-84.

56. For a detailed and prophetic analysis of sinful social structures in contemporary American society, see the NCCB's "Review of the Principal Trends," (Washington, 1974), 2-3; and "This Land Is Home to Me: A Pastoral Letter on Powerlessness in Appalachia by the Catholic Bishops of the Region," in *Origins* 4 (February 13, 1975), 529, 531-43.

57. Novak, *Choosing Our King*, 280.

58. R.M. Brown, *Frontiers for the Church Today*, (New York, 1973), 117.

59. *Synod of Bishops* 1974, 30.

60. Address at the rededication of Chicago's Holy Name Cathedral published in *Origins* 4 (October 3, 1974), 228-32; also, see positive signs pointed out by the NCCB in "Review of the Principal Trends," 7, which are incorporated here.

61. Regarding the religious character of American youth, see Gallup, "A Statistical Analysis of the Unchurched American": "One-third of the youth in

the U.S. said they attend church in a typical week, a higher figure than recorded in nine other nations. In addition, far fewer young people in the U.S. than abroad say they have 'no interest' in religion."

62. Saldahna, *et al.*, "American Catholics—Ten Years Later," *Critic* xxxiii (January-February, 1975), 17. *Note:* All percentages in this section are taken from this report.

63. *Synod of Bishops 1974*, 58-59.

64. R.P. McBrien, *The Remarking of the Church* (New York, 1973), 140.

65. Brown, *Frontiers for the Church Today*, 107.

66. Nolan, ed., *Pastoral Letters*, 637, no. 62.

67. NCCB, "Review of Principal Trends," 6. *Note:* The juxtaposition here of "abortion" and "means of family limitation" deserves comment. Cf. J.B. Hehir, "The Church and the Population Year: Notes on a Strategy," *TS* 35 (March 1974) 71-82, wherein is emphasized the need "to distinguish the issues of abortion and contraception in the mind of Catholics and in the public mind" (p. 78).

68. John Cardinal Krol, "The Laity: Pastoral Considerations," written intervention in *Synod of Bishops 1974*, 34.

69. *Ibid.*, 36-37.

70. *Synod of Bishops 1974*, 30.

71. Saldahna, *et al.,* "American Catholics—Ten Years Later," 19-20.

72. Gallup, "A Statistical Analysis of the Unchurched American."

A SELECTED BIBLIOGRAPHY

PART I: GENERAL REFERENCE WORKS, DOCUMENTS, ADDRESSES, ETC.
(not listed under "Abbreviations" at the front of this work)

Jadot, J. "Signs of Hope in the American Church." Address given at the rededication of Chicago's Holy Name Cathedral. *Origins* 4 (October 3, 1974) 228-32.

Lorscheider, A. "Panorama: A General Look at the Life of the Church since the Last Synod of Bishops." *L'Osservatore Romano.* Eng. ed. 41 (October 10, 1974) 10.

National Conference of Catholic Bishops. *Liberty and Justice for All.* Discussion guide by the Committee for the Bicentennial. Washington, D.C., 1974.

———. "Report of the Ad Hoc Committee on Moral Values in Society." November 19, 1974. Washington, D.C.: USCC.

———. "A Review of Principal Trends in the Life of the Catholic Church in the United States." Washington, D.C.: USCC, 1974.

———. "To Teach as Jesus Did." A Pastoral Message on Catholic Education, Washington, D.C.: USCC, 1973.

Nolan, H.J., ed. *Pastoral Letters of the American Hierarchy, 1792-1970.* Huntington, Indiana: Our Sunday Visitor, 1971.

Paul VI. "Address at the Conclusion of the Synod of Bishops." *L'Osservatore Romano.* Eng. ed. 45 (November 7, 1974) 8-10.

———. *Evangelii Nuntiandi.* Eng. trans. Vatican Plyglot Press, 1975.

———. "Evangelization of the World: essential mission of the Church." *L'Osservatore Romano.* Eng. ed. 45 (November 7, 1974) 1.

———. "Message for World Mission Sunday." Dated June 5, 1970. *The Pope Speaks*, 15 (1970-71) 105-6.

Rome Synod Secretariat, "Evangelization in the Modern World"—Synod Working Paper. (Unofficial translation of the working text.) *Origins*, 4 (August 29, 1974) 147-53.

Runda, J. "Annotated Bibliography of Research on the Unchurched in Rural America." CARA project no. 135. Washington, D.C., 1971.

Sacred Congregation for the Clergy. *General Catechetical Directory.* Approved Eng. trans. Washington, D.C.: USCC, 1971.

"Synod of Bishops—Evangelization of the Modern World." Washington, D.C.: USCC, 1973.

Synod of Bishops, *Justice in the World.* Vatican Polyglot Press, 1971.

"This Land Is Home to Me: A Pastoral Letter on Powerlessness in Appalachia by the Catholic Bishops of the Region." *Origins*, 4 (February 13, 1975) 531-43.

PART II: BOOKS AND ARTICLES

Ahlstrom, S.E. *A Religious History of the American People.* 2 vols. Image

Books. Garden City, New York: Doubleday, 1975.

Arntz, J.T.C. "Natural Law and Its History." *Concilium* 5 (New York: Paulist Press, 1965) 43.

Audinet, J. "Catechesis." *Sacramentum Mundi.* Vol. I.

Baillaregon, A. "Missions, Parochial." *New Catholic Encyclopedia.* Vol. IX.

Baum, G. "The Survival of the Sacred." *Concilium* 81 (New York: Herder and Herder, 1973) 11-22.

Berger, P.L. *A Rumor of Angels.* Anchor Books. Garden City, New York: Doubleday, 1970.

Bier, W.C., ed. *Alienation: Plight of Modern Man?* New York: Fordham University Press, 1972.

Böckle, F. *Fundamental Concepts of Moral Theology.* New York: Paulist Press, 1968.

Bonhoeffer, D. *The Cost of Discipleship.* London: SCM Press, 1959.

Boorstin, D.J. *The Americans: The Democratic Experience.* Vintage Books. New York: Random House, 1974.

Bouyer, L. *The Spirituality of the New Testament and the Fathers.* New York: Desclee, 1963.

Brown, R.E. *The Gospel According to John.* 2 vols. Anchor Bible. Garden City, New York: Doubleday, 1966-70.

Brown, R. McAfee. *Frontiers for the Church Today.* New York: Oxford University Press, 1973.

Browne, H.J. *The Catholic Church and the Knights of Labor.* Washington, D.C.: Catholic University of America Press, 1949.

Byers, D.M. and Quinn, B. *Evangelists to the Poor.* Washington, D.C.: Glenmary Research Center, 1975.

Cambon, E. *L'ortoprassi.* Rome: Citta' Nuova, 1974.

Capone, D. *Introduzione alla teologia morale.* Bologna: EDB, 1972.

———. *L'uomo e' persona in Cristo.* Bologna: EDB, 1973.

Cayré, F. *Spiritual Writers of the Early Church.* New York: Hawthorn Books, 1958.

Commager, H.S. "America in the Age of No Confidence." *Saturday Review World* (August 10, 1974) 15-21.

Crotty, N. "Biblical Perspectives in Moral Theology." *Theological Studies,* 26 (December 1965) 574-95.

Cunningham, A. "Complexity and Challenge: The American Catholic Layman." *Concilium* 9 (New York: Paulist Press, 1965) 111-26.

Curran, C.E. *Christian Morality Today.* Notre Dame, Indiana: Fides, 1966.

———. *A New Look at Christian Morality.* Notre Dame, Indiana: Fides, 1968.

———. *New Perspectives in Moral Theology.* Notre Dame, Indiana: Fides, 1974.

Decker, R.G. "The Secularization of Anglo-American Law." *Thought* 49 (September, 1974) 280-98.

Delhaye, P. "The Contribution of Vatican II to Moral Theology." *Concilium* 75 (New York: Herder and Herder, 1972) 58-67.

Drinan, R.F. *Democracy, Dissent and Disorder: The Issues and the Law.* New York: Seabury Press, 1969.

Dunne, G.H. *The Right to Development.* New York: Paulist Press, 1974.

Duquoc, C. "Yes to Jesus—No to God and the Church." *Concilium* 93 (New York: Herder and Herder, 1974) 17-30.

Elizondo, V. "Biblical Pedagogy of Evangelization," *The American Ecclesiastical Review* 168 (October, 1974) 526-43.

Ellis, J.T. *American Catholicism.* 2nd ed. rev. Chicago: University of Chicago Press, 1969.

————. "American Catholicism in 'an uncertain, anxious time.'" *Commonweal* 98 (April 27, 1973) 177-84.

————, ed. *The Catholic Priest in the United States: Historical Investigations.* Collegeville, Minnesota: St. John's University Press, 1971.

Emerson, W.A., Jr. *Sin and the New American Conscience.* New York: Harper and Row, 1974.

Fransen, P. *The New Life of Grace.* London: G. Chapman, 1969.

Fuchs, J. *Human Values and Christian Morality.* Dublin: Gill and Macmillan, 1970.

Furger, F. "Prudence and Moral Change." *Concilium* 35 (New York: Paulist Press, 1968) 119-31.

Galilea, S. "Liberation as an Encounter with Politics and Contemplation." *Concilium* 96 (New York: Herder and Herder, 1974) 19-33.

Gallup, G., Jr. "What We Know And What We Do Not Know: A Statistical Analysis of the Unchurched American." Report given at the Catholic University of America, Washington, D.C., November 11, 1975 and the Consultation at the Glenmary Research Center, Maryland, November 12, 1975. [Later published in *New Catholic World* 219 (July-August, 1976) 148-54.]

Gill, J. "Religious Expression and the Language of Popular Culture." *Concilium* 85 (New York: Herder and Herder, 1973) 107-13.

Gleason, P., ed. *Contemporary Catholicism in the United States.* Notre Dame, Indiana: University of Notre Dame Press, 1969.

Grand'Maison, J. *Seconda evangelizzazione.* 3 vols. Bologna: EDB, 1975.

Grasso, D. *Proclaiming God's Message.* Notre Dame, Indiana: Notre Dame University Press, 1965.

Greeley, A. *The Catholic Experience.* Garden City, New York: Doubleday, 1969.

————. *The Crucible of Change: The Social Dynamics of Pastoral Practice.* New York: Sheed and Ward, 1968.

————. *A Future To Hope In.* Garden City, New York: Doubleday, 1969.

————. *The New Agenda: A Proposal for a New Approach to Fundamental Religious Issues in Contemporary Terms.* Garden City, New York: Doubleday, 1973.

————. "The New American Religion." *Concilium* 69 (New York: Herder and Herder, 1971) 111-23.

————. "The Persistence of Community." *Concilium* 81 (New York: Herder and Herder, 1973) 23-35.

Guilday, P. *The Life and Times of John Carroll.* New York: Ency. Press, 1922.

Gustafson, J. *Can Ethics Be Christian?* Chicago: University of Chicago Press, 1975.

Gutierrez, G. "Liberation Movements and Theology." *Concilium* 93 (New York: Herder and Herder, 1974) 135-46.

————. "Liberation Theology and Proclamation." *Concilium* 96 (New York: Herder and Herder, 1974) 57-77.

————. *A Theology of Liberation.* Maryknoll, New York: Orbis Books, 1973.

Guzie, T.W. *Jesus and the Eucharist.* New York: Paulist Press, 1974.

Hallinan, P.J. "The American Bishops and the Vatican Councils." *Catholic Historical Review* 51 (October 1965) 379-83.

Häring, B. *Evangelisation Today.* Slough, England: St. Paul Publications, 1974.

———. *Faith and Morality in the Secular Age.* Garden City, New York: Doubleday, 1973.

———. *Hope Is the Remedy.* Image Books. Garden City, New York: Doubleday, 1973.

———. *The Law of Christ.* 3 vols. Cork: Mercier Press, 1960-64.

———. "Moral Theology I." *Sacramentum Mundi.* Vol. IV.

———. *Morality Is for Persons.* New York: Farrar, Straus and Giroux, 1971.

———. *Prayer: The Integration of Faith and Life.* Slough, England: St. Paul Publications, 1975.

———. *The Sacraments and Your Everyday Life.* Liguori, Missouri: Liguori Publications, 1976.

———. *Sin and the Secular Age.* Garden City, New York: Doubleday, 1974.

Hennessey, J. "American History and the Theological Enterprise." *Proceedings CTSA* 26 (June 14-17, 1971) 91-115.

———. "Dimensions of American Catholic Experience." *Catholic Mind* 74 (May 1975) 18-26.

———. "Square Peg in a Round Hole: On Being Roman Catholic in America." *Records of the American Catholic Historical Society of Philadelphia* 83 (December 1973) 167-95.

Herberg, W. *Protestant, Catholic, Jew: An Essay in American Religious Sociology.* Garden City, New York: Doubleday, 1955.

Hermann, I. *The Experience of Faith.* New York: Kenedy, 1966.

Hervieu-Leger, D. "The Crisis in Doctrinal and Kerygmatic Language." *Concilium* 85 (New York: Herder and Herder, 1973) 19-30.

Hesburgh, T.M. *The Humane Imperative: A Challenge for the Year 2000.* New Haven and London: Yale University Press, 1974.

Hofmann, R. "Conscience." *Sacramentum Mundi.* Vol. I.

Holden, V. "Father Hecker's Vision Vindicated." *Historical Records and Studies* 50 (1964) 49.

———. *The Yankee Paul: Issac Thomas Hecker.* Milwaukee: Bruce, 1958.

Jegen, M.E. "Catechesis, II (Medieval and Modern)." *New Catholic Encyclopedia.* Vol. III.

Jeremias, J. *The Parables of Jesus.* New York: Scribner, 1963.

———. *The Sermon on the Mount.* Philadelphia: Fortress Press, 1963.

Jossua, J.-P. "Christian Experience and Communicating the Faith." *Concilium* 85 (New York: Herder and Herder, 1973) 57-69.

Jungmann, J. *Announcing the Word of God.* New York: Herder and Herder, 1967.

———. *The Early Liturgy: To the Time of Gregory the Great.* London: Darton, Longman & Todd, 1959.

———. *The Good News Yesterday and Today.* Translated and abridged by W.A. Huesman from *The Good News and Our Proclamation of the Faith.* New York: W.H. Sadlier, 1962.

———. "Theology and Kerygmatic Teaching." *Lumen Vitae* 5 (1950) 558-63.

Kasper, W. "Law and Gospel." *Sacramentum Mundi.* Vol. III.

Kennedy, E.C. *The People Are the Church.* Garden City, New York: Doubleday, 1969.

Kerame O. "Pluralism in the One Church: The Apostolic Churches of the East." *Concilium* 88 (New York: Herder and Herder, 1973) 59-72.

Kerans, P. *Sinful Social Structures.* New York: Paulist Press, 1974.

Kloppenburg, B. *The Ecclesiology of Vatican II.* Chicago: Franciscan Herald Press, 1974.

Latourelle, R. *Christ and the Church: Signs of Salvation.* New York: Alba House, 1972.

————. *Theology of Revelation.* New York: Alba House, 1966.

Legrand, L., Pathrapankal, J. and Vellanickal, M. *Good News and Witness: The New Testament Understanding of Evangelization.* Bangalore: Theological Publications of India, 1973.

Le Guillou, M.-J. "Mission as an Ecclesiological Theme." *Concilium* 13 (New York: Paulist Press, 1966) 81-130.

Lehmann, P.L. *Ethics in a Christian Context.* New York and Evanston: Harper and Row, 1963.

Lonergan, B. *Method in Theology.* New York: Herder and Herder, 1972.

Lyonnet, S. and de la Potterie, I. *The Christian Lives by the Spirit.* New York: Alba House, 1971.

McAvoy, T., ed. *Roman Catholicism and the American Way of Life.* Notre Dame, Indiana: University of Notre Dame Press, 1960.

McBrien, R.P. *The Remaking of the Church.* New York: Harper and Row, 1973.

McCready, Wm. and N. "Socialization and the Persistence of Religion." *Concilium* 81 (New York: Herder and Herder, 1973) 58-68.

McDonagh, E. *Gift and Call.* St. Meinrad, Indiana: Abbey Press, 1975.

————. *Invitation and Response: Essays in Christian Moral Theology.* New York: Sheed and Ward, 1972.

————, ed. *Moral Theology Renewed.* Dublin: Gill & Son, 1965.

McNally, R.E. *The Unreformed Church.* New York: Sheed and Ward, 1965.

Mally, E.H. *Sin: Biblical Perspectives.* Dayton, Ohio: Pflaum/Standard, 1973.

Marranzini, A. *Evangelizzazione e sacramenti.* Rome: Citta' Nuova, 1973.

Marty, M.E. *The Fire We Can Light.* Garden City, New York: Doubleday, 1973.

————. "A Nation of Behavers." *Worldview* 17 (May 1974) 9-13.

————. "The Persistence of the Mystical." *Concilium* 81 (New York: Herder and Herder, 1973) 36-45.

————. *The Pro & Con Book of Religious America.* Waco, Texas: Word Books, 1975.

————. *Protestantism.* Image Books. Garden City, New York: Doubleday, 1974.

————. *Righteous Empire: The Protestant Experience in America.* New York: Dial Press, 1970.

Merton, T. *Conjectures of a Guilty Bystander.* Image Books. Garden City, New York: Doubleday, 1968.

————. *Contemplative Prayer.* Image Books. Garden City, New York: Doubleday, 1971.

Metz, J.B. "A Short Apology of Narrative." *Concilium* 85 (New York: Herder and Herder, 1973) 84-96.

————. *Theology of the World.* London: Burns and Oates, 1969.

Miller, P. *Errand into the Wilderness.* Harper Torchbooks. New York: Harper and Row, 1956.

Mirgeler, A. *Mutations of Western Christianity.* New York: Herder and Herder, 1964.

Modras, R. "The Elimination of Pluralism between the Churches through Pluralism within the Churches." *Concilium* 88 (New York: Herder and Herder, 1973) 73-85.

Monden, L. *Sin, Liberty and Law.* New York: Sheed and Ward, 1965.

Mulherin, P.L. "Preaching, I, In the U.S." *New Catholic Encyclopedia.* Vol. XI.

Murphy, F.X. "Catechesis, I (Early Church)." *New Catholic Encyclopedia.* Vol. III.

———. "Kerygma." *New Catholic Encyclopedia.* Vol. VIII.

———. *Moral Teaching in the Primitive Church.* Ramsey, N.J., New York: Paulist Press, 1968.

Murray, J.C. *We Hold These Truths: Catholic Reflections on the American Proposition.* Image Books. Garden City, New York: Doubleday, 1964.

Nearon, J.R. "The Situation of American Blacks." *Proceedings CTSA* 30 (1975) 177-202.

Niebuhr, H.R. *Christ and Culture.* Harper Colophon Books. New York: Harper and Row, 1951.

———. *The Kingdom of God in America.* Harper Torchbooks. New York: Harper and Row, 1937.

Norgen, W.A., ed. *FORUM: Religious Faith Speaks to American Issues.* New York: Friendship Press, 1975.

Novak, M. *Ascent of the Mountain, Flight of the Dove.* New York: Harper and Row, 1971.

———. *Choosing Our King.* New York: Macmillan, 1974.

O'Brien, D.J. *The Renewal of American Catholicism.* New York: Paulist Press, 1972.

O'Connell, T. "The Point of Moral Theology." *Chicago Studies* 14 (Spring 1975) 61.

Ong, W. *Frontiers in American Catholicism: Essays on Ideology and Culture.* New York: Macmillan, 1957.

Oraison, M. *Morality for Our Time.* Garden City, New York: Doubleday, 1968.

Padovano, A.T. *American Culture and the Quest for Christ.* New York: Sheed and Ward, 1970.

———. "The Serpent of Eden and the American Eagle." *Spiritual Life* 21 (Winter 1975) 227.

Panikkar, R. *Worship and Secular Man.* Maryknoll, New York: Orbis Books, 1973.

Pathrapankal, J., ed. *Service and Salvation: Nagpur Theological Conference on Evangelization.* Bangalore: Theological Publications of India, 1973.

Powers, J. *Spirit and Sacrament: The Humanizing Experience.* New York: Seabury Press, 1973.

Rahner, H. *A Theology of Proclamation.* New York: Herder and Herder, 1968.

Rahner, K. *The Christian Commitment.* New York: Sheed and Ward, 1963.

———. *The Shape of the Church to Come.* New York: Seabury, 1974.

Ratzinger, J. *Dogma e predicazione.* Brescia: Querianna, 1974.

————. *Introduction to Christianity.* London: Burns & Oates, 1969.

Reisman, D., *et al. The Lonely Crowd.* New Haven, Conn: Yale University Press, 1969.

Saldahna, S., *et al.* "American Catholics—Ten Years Later." *Critic* 33 (January-February, 1975) 14-20.

Salm, L. *Readings in Biblical Morality.* Englewood Cliffs, New Jersey: Prentice Hall, 1966.

Schelke, K.H. *Theology of the New Testament.* Vol. 3. Collegeville, Minnesota: Liturgical Press, 1970.

Schillebeeckx, E. *God the Future of Man.* New York: Sheed and Ward, 1968.

————. *The Understanding of Faith: Interpretation and Criticism.* New York: Seabury Press, 1974.

Schlesinger, A.M. "What Then Is the American: This New Man?" President's Address before the American Historical Association, Washington, D.C.: December 30, 1942. *American Historical Review* 48 (January 1943) 225-44.

Schmaus, M. "Holy Spirit." *Sacramentum Mundi.* Vol. III.

Schnackenburg, R. *Christian Existence in the New Testament.* 2 vols. Notre Dame, Indiana: University of Notre Dame Press, 1968-69.

————. *The Moral Teaching of the New Testament.* New York: Herder and Herder, 1965.

Segundo, J.L. *The Community Called Church.* Maryknoll, New York: Orbis Books, 1973.

————. *Evolution and Guilt.* Maryknoll, New York: Orbis Books, 1974.

————. *Grace and the Human Condition.* Maryknoll, New York: Orbis Books, 1973.

————. *Our Idea of God.* Maryknoll, New York: Orbis Books, 1974.

————. *The Sacraments Today.* Maryknoll, New York: Orbis Books, 1974.

Shaughnessy, G. *Has the Immigrant Kept the Faith?* New York: Macmillan, 1925.

Shea, J. *What a Modern Catholic Believes About Sin.* Chicago: Thomas More Press, 1971.

Shea, J.G. *The Catholic Church in Colonial Days.* New York: J.G. Shea, 1886.

Simons, E. "Kerygma." *Sacramentum Mundi.* Vol. III.

Sittler, J. "An Aspect of American Religious Experience." *Proceedings CTSA* 26 (June 14-17, 1971) 1-17.

Slater, P. *The Pursuit of Loneliness.* Boston: Beacon Press, 1970.

Sloyan, G.S. *Shaping the Christian Message.* New York: Paulist Press, 1958.

————, ed. *Modern Catechetics.* London: Macmillan, 1963.

Spicq, C. *St. Paul and Christian Living.* Dublin and Sydney: Gill & Son, 1963.

Stanley, D. *The Apostolic Church in the New Testament.* Westminster, Maryland: Newman Press, 1967.

Stockmeier, P. "Early Church." *Sacramentum Mundi.* Vol. III.

Tavard, G.H. *Catholicism, U.S.A.* New York: Paulist/Newman Press, 1969.

Thils, G. "Pivotal Positions on 'Evangelization' and 'Salvation,' " *Lumen Vitae.* Eng. ed. 30 (March 1975) 75.

van der Poel. C. *The Search for Human Values: Moral Growth in an Evolving World.* Paramus, New Jersey: Newman Press, 1971.

Verghese, P. "Secular Society or Pluralistic Community?" in *Contemporary Religion and Social Responsibility.* Brockman N. and Piediscalzi, N., eds. New York: Alba House, 1973.

Walgrave, J.H. "Is Morality Static or Dynamic?" *Concilium* 5 (New York: Paulist Press, 1965) 22-38.

Walters, J. "Christian Ethics: Distinctive or Specific?" *American Ecclesiastical Review* 169 (September 1975) 470-89.

Weigel, G. *The Modern God: Faith in a Secular Culture.* New York: Macmillan, 1963.

Weinrich, H. "Narrative Theology." *Concilium* 85 (New York: Herder and Herder, 1973) 46-56.

Westow, T.L. *The Variety of Catholic Attitudes.* New York: Herder and Herder, 1963.

Wright, J.H. "The Meaning and Characteristics of an American Theology." *Proceedings CTSA* 26 (June 14-17, 1971) 18-32.